ELECTRICAL
SAFETY HANDBOOK

Other Books of Interest

Croft, Summers • AMERICAN ELECTRICIANS' HANDBOOK
Denno • ELECTRIC PROTECTIVE DEVICES
Johnson • ELECTRICAL CONTRACTING BUSINESS HANDBOOK
Johnson • SUCCESSFUL BUSINESS OPERATIONS FOR ELECTRICAL CONTRACTORS
Kolstad • RAPID ELECTRICAL ESTIMATING AND PRICING
Kusko • EMERGENCY/STANDBY POWER SYSTEMS
Linden • HANDBOOK OF BATTERIES AND FUEL CELLS
Lundquist • ON-LINE ELECTRICAL TROUBLESHOOTING
McPartland • McGRAW-HILL'S NATIONAL ELECTRICAL CODE® HANDBOOK
McPartland • McGRAW-HILL'S HANDBOOK OF ELECTRICAL CONSTRUCTION
   CALCULATIONS
McPartland • HANDBOOK OF PRACTICAL ELECTRICAL DESIGN
Pete • ELECTRIC POWER SYSTEMS MANUAL
Richter, Schwan • PRACTICAL ELECTRICAL WIRING
Seidman, Mahrous, Hicks • HANDBOOK OF ELECTRIC POWER CALCULATIONS
Smeaton • SWITCHGEAR AND CONTROL HANDBOOK
Traister • DESIGN AND APPLICATION OF SECURITY/FIRE ALARM SYSTEMS

ELECTRICAL SAFETY HANDBOOK

John Cadick, P.E.

Cadick Professional Services, Garland, Texas

McGRAW-HILL, INC.

New York   San Francisco   Washington, D.C.   Auckland   Bogotá
Caracas   Lisbon   London   Madrid   Mexico City   Milan
Montreal   New Delhi   San Juan   Singapore
Sydney   Tokyo   Toronto

Library of Congress Cataloging-in-Publication Data

Cadick, John.
    Electrical safety handbook / John Cadick.
       p.   cm.
    Includes index.
    ISBN 0-07-009514-0 (alk. paper)
    1. Electric engineering—Safety measures.   2. Industrial safety.
I. Title.
TK152.C22   1994
621.319'028'9—dc20   94-13347
                                                          CIP

    5 6 7 8 9 0   DOC/DOC   9 0 9 8

ISBN 0-07-009514-0

The sponsoring editor for this book was Harold B. Crawford, the editing supervisor was Paul R. Sobel, and the production supervisor was Pamela A. Pelton. It was set in Times Roman by North Market Street Graphics.

Printed and bound by R. R. Donnelley & Sons Company.

This book was printed on acid-free paper.

To my father, Ross M. Cadick, who taught me how to work and to pursue excellence; my mother, Melba K. Cadick, who taught me how to have fun; my wife, Sheryl Cadick, who taught me patience; my children, Ross, Anna, Jessica, and Julia, who have kept me young; and my friend, Thad Brown, who taught me how to do business and still be kind to people

CONTENTS

Chapter 9. Safety Training Methods and Systems   9.1

PREFACE

Each year hundreds of people are killed and hundreds more are injured by electrical energy. Many, if not most, of these deaths and injuries could be prevented by the use of appropriate electrical safety techniques and equipment.

The book was written as a reference for personnel working on or near electrical circuits of any voltage level. Safety personnel, electricians, line workers, engineers, and supervisors will find the book to be an invaluable aid to safe and efficient work with electrical energy systems. Management and safety training personnel will also find sections which aid them in the setup and implementation of organizational and training programs.

Chapter 1 provides an overview of an often overlooked aspect of electrical safety—the nature of the hazard. Many accidents could be prevented if personnel were simply made aware of how and why electricity is dangerous.

Chapters 2 and 3 present equipment and procedures that are used throughout the electrical industry. The information in these two chapters can be used in the development of electrical safety programs for utility, industrial, and commercial electrical workers.

Chapter 4 identifies both consensus and mandatory standards and standards organizations. Referral to this chapter will provide the reader with information about the codes and standards which regulate the way that electrical work is performed. Of course, the reader should always refer to the current versions of all of the standards which are described in Chapter 4. Standards covered include the National Electrical Safety Code, the National Electrical Code, American Society of Testing and Materials, and other key publications and organizations. Complete listings of some standards are included.

Chapter 5 focuses on what to do if an accident does happen. Starting with a detailed description of accident prevention concepts, this chapter then provides the reader with information on rescue, first aid, and accident investigation. The proper investigation of accidents is a science that should only be performed by qualified, experienced personnel. Chapter 5 describes what to do, and perhaps more importantly, what not to do during an accident investigation.

Low voltage circuits can be just as deadly as high voltage circuits. Chapters 6 and 7 define the key elements of electrical safety for low voltage and medium/high voltage circuits respectively. Readers will be surprised at how little difference exists between low and medium/high voltage safety.

Management often loses sight of its obligation in the provision of a safe work environment. A well structured, safe work place goes beyond simply obeying the law. Chapter 8 describes the elements of a well structured, efficient electrical safety program. Managers may refer to this chapter for direction during the setup and or modification of a company safety program.

Procedures, equipment, programs, and rules can never replace well trained, competent personnel. Chapter 9 presents information that will allow the setup, implementation, and evaluation of a successful electrical safety training program.

This Electrical Safety Handbook presents, for the first time, a comprehensive guide to electrical safety equipment, procedures, training, and standards.

ACKNOWLEDGMENTS

The author gratefully acknowledges the following: Kathy Hooper, ASTM; Robert L. Meltzer, ASTM; Laura Hannan, TEGAM, Incorporated; Raymond L. Erickson, Eaton Corporation, Cutler-Hammer Products; H.G. Brosz, Brosz and Associates Archives; P. Eng, Brosz and Associates Archives; Ellis Lyons, W.H. Salisbury and Co.; Tom Gerard, TIF Instruments, Inc., Miami, FL; LaNelle Morris, Direct Safety Company, Phoenix, Arizona; Tony Quick, Santronics Inc.; Ed DaCruz, Siebe North, Inc.; Benjamin L. Bird, CIP Insulated Products; E.T. Thonson, AVO Biddle Instruments, Blue Bell, PA; Terry Duchaine, Ideal Industries, Inc., Sycamore, IL; Mary Kay S. Kopf, DuPont Fibers; Stephen Gillette, Electrical Apparatus Division of Siemens Energy and Automation, Inc.; Mary Beth Stahl, Mine Safety Appliances Company; Debbie Prikryl, Encon Safety Products; Craig H. Seligman, NOMEX® III Work Clothing, Workrite Uniform Company, Oxnard, CA; Kareem M. Irfan, Square D Company, A.B. Chance Co., AVO Multi-Amp Institute; Alan Mark Franks; and Sandy Young.

John Cadick

CHAPTER 1

HAZARDS OF ELECTRICITY

INTRODUCTION

Understanding the steps and procedures employed in a good electrical safety program requires an understanding of the nature of electrical hazards. Although they may have trouble writing a concise definition, most people are familiar with electric shock. This often painful experience leaves its memory indelibly etched on the human mind. However, shock is only one of the electrical hazards. There are two others—arc and blast. This chapter describes each of the three hazards and explains how each affects the human body.

Understanding the nature of the hazards is useless unless protective strategies are developed to protect the worker. This chapter also includes a synopsis of the types of protective strategies that should be used to protect the worker.

HAZARD DESCRIPTIONS

Shock

Description. Electric shock is the physical stimulation that occurs when electric current passes through the body. The effect that electric shock has on the body depends on the magnitude of the current flow, the body parts through which the current flows, and the general physical condition of the person being shocked.

Current Magnitude. The magnitude of the current which flows through the body generally obeys Ohm's law, that is,

$$I = \frac{E}{R} \tag{1.1}$$

where I = current magnitude, amperes (A)
E = applied voltage, volts (V)
R = resistance of path through which current flows, ohms (Ω)

In Fig. 1.1 the worker has contacted a 120-V circuit when an electric drill short-circuits internally. The internal short circuit impresses 120 V across the body of the worker from the hand to the feet. This creates a current flow through the worker to the ground and back to the source. The total current flow in this case is given by the formula

1.1

Electric drill

Current path

Physical circuit
(a)

Drill case R_1

120   R_1 = Resistance of body R_2
             R_2 = Resistance of earth

Electrical equivalent
(b)

FIGURE 1.1   Electric shock current path.

$$I = \frac{E}{R_1 + R_2} \tag{1.2}$$

Variable R_2 is the resistance of the earth and for the purposes of this analysis may be ignored. Variable R_1 is the resistance of the worker's body and includes the skin resistance, the internal body resistance, and the resistance of the shoes where they contact the earth.

Typical values for the various components can be found in Tables 1.1 and 1.2. Assume, for example that a worker shown in Fig. 1.1 is wearing leather shoes and is standing in wet soil. This person is perspiring heavily and has an internal resistance of 200 Ω. From Tables 1.1 and 1.2 the total resistance can be calculated as

500 Ω (drill handle) + 200 Ω (internal) + 5000 Ω (wet shoes) = 5700 Ω

From this information the total current flow through the body for a 120-V circuit is calculated as

$$I = \frac{120}{5700} = 21.1 \text{ milliamperes (mA)} \tag{1.3}$$

TABLE 1.1 Nominal Resistance Values for Various Parts of the Human Body

Condition (area to suit)	Resistance	
	Dry	Wet
Finger touch	40 kΩ–1 MΩ	4–15 kΩ
Hand holding wire	10–50 kΩ	3–6 kΩ
Finger-thumb grasp*	10–30 kΩ	2–5 kΩ
Hand holding pliers	5–10 kΩ	1–3 kΩ
Palm touch	3–8 kΩ	1–2 kΩ
Hand around 1½-inch (in) pipe (or drill handle)	1–3 kΩ	0.5–1.5 kΩ
Two hands around 1½-in pipe	0.5–1.5 kΩ	250–750 Ω
Hand immersed	—	200–500 Ω
Foot immersed	—	100–300 Ω
Human body, internal, excluding skin	—	200–1000 Ω

* Data interpolated.
Source: This table was compiled from Kouwemnoven and Milner. Permission obtained from estate of Ralph Lee.

TABLE 1.2 Nominal Resistance Values for Various Materials

Material	Resistance*
Rubber gloves or soles	>20 MΩ
Dry concrete above grade	1–5 MΩ
Dry concrete on grade	0.2–1 MΩ
Leather sole, dry, including foot	0.1–0.5 MΩ
Leather sole, damp, including foot	5–20 kΩ
Wet concrete on grade	1–5 kΩ

* Resistances shown are for 130-cm² areas.
Source: Courtesy of Ralph Lee.

Table 1.3 lists the effects that various currents will have on a 68-kilogram (kg) human being. The current flow of 21.1 mA is sufficient to cause the worker to go into an "electrical hold." This is a condition wherein the muscles are contracted and held by the passage of the electric current—the worker cannot let go. Under these circumstances, the electric shock would continue until the current was interrupted or until someone intervened and freed the worker from the contact. Unless the worker is freed quickly, tissue and material heating will cause the resistances to drop, resulting in an increase in the current. Such cases are frequently fatal.

Parts of the Body. Current flow affects the various bodily organs in different manners. For example, the heart can be caused to fibrillate with only 75 mA. The diaphragm and the breathing system can be paralyzed, which possibly may be fatal, with less than 30 mA of current flow. The specific responses of the various body parts to current flow are covered in later sections.

TABLE 1.3   Nominal Human Response to Current Magnitudes*

Current (60 Hz)	Physiological phenomena	Feeling or lethal incidence
<1 mA	None	Imperceptible
1 mA	Perception threshold	Mild sensation
1–3 mA		Painful sensation
3–10 mA		
10 mA	Paralysis threshold of arms	Cannot release hand grip; if no grip, victim may be thrown clear (may progress to higher current and be fatal)
30 mA	Respiratory paralysis	Stoppage of breathing (frequently fatal)
75 mA	Fibrillation threshold 0.5%	Heart action discoordinated (probably fatal)
250 mA	Fibrillation threshold 99.5% (≥ 5-s exposure)	
4 A	Heart paralysis threshold (no fibrillation)	Heart stops for duration of current passage. For short shocks, may restart on interruption of current (usually not fatal from heart dysfunction)
≥5 A	Tissue burning	Not fatal unless vital organs are burned

* *Notes:* (1) This data is approximate and based on a 68-kg (150-lb) person. (2) Information for higher current levels is obtained from data derived from accident victims. (3) Responses are nominal and will vary widely by individual.
   Source: Courtesy of Ralph Lee.

General Physical Condition.   The physical condition of the individual greatly modifies the effects of current flow. A person in good physical condition will be affected much less severely than a person in poor health by the same amount of current flow. If the individual has any specific problems such as heart or lung ailments, these parts of the body will be severely affected by relatively low currents. For example, an individual who suffers from heart rhythm problems is more likely to develop fibrillation than one with a healthy heart.

Burns.   Electric current can cause severe tissue damage through burning. Burns caused by electric current are almost always third-degree because the burning occurs from the inside of the body. This means that the growth centers are destroyed. Electric-current burns can be severe when they involve vital internal organs.

Arc

Definition and Description.   Electric arcing occurs when a substantial amount of electric current flows through what previously had been air. Since air is not a conductor, the current flow is actually occurring through the vapor of the arc terminal material and the ionized particles of air. This mixture of materials, through which the arc current flows, is called a *plasma.*

Arcs can be started in several ways:

- When the voltage between two points exceeds the dielectric strength of the air. This can happen when overvoltages due to lightning strikes or switching surges occur.
- When the air becomes superheated with the passage of current through some conductor. For example, if a very fine wire is subjected to excessive current, the wire will melt, superheating the air and causing an arc to start.
- When two contacts part when they are carrying a very high current. In this case, the last point of contact is superheated and an arc is created because of the inductive flywheel effect.

Electric arcs are extremely hot. Temperatures at the terminal points of the arcs can reach as high as 50,000 kelvin (K). Temperatures away from the terminal points are somewhat cooler but can still reach 20,000 K. These high temperatures can cause fatal burns at distances of up to 8 feet (ft) or more. Even if the direct burns are not immediately fatal, clothing can be ignited which can cause fatal secondary burns.

The amount of energy, and therefore heat, in an arc is proportional to the maximum available short circuit volt-amperes in the system at the point of the arc. It has been shown that the maximum arc energy is equal to one-half of the available fault volt-amperes at any given point. Since the amount of arc energy determines that degree of heat and, therefore, the degree of injury, the system voltage level has only a minimal effect on the arc hazard. *Low-voltage systems have just as significant an arcing hazard as high-voltage systems.*

Four major factors determine the effect of an electric arc on the exposed person or object. Table 1.4 describes each of these factors. Figures 1.2 and 1.3 show the results of two experiments that were conducted with manikins exposed to electric arcs. As can be seen, both high and low voltages can create significant burns.

Arc Burns. Arc burns are thermal in nature and, therefore, fall into one of the three classical categories:

- *First-degree burns.* First-degree burning causes painful trauma to the outer layers of the skin. Little permanent damage results from a first-degree burn because all the growth areas survive. Healing is usually prompt and leaves no scarring.
- *Second-degree burns.* Second-degree burns result in relatively severe tissue damage and blistering. If the burn is to the skin, the entire outer layer will be destroyed. Healing occurs from the sweat glands and/or hair follicles.

TABLE 1.4 Factors which Effect Injuries Due to Electric Arc

Distance	The amount of damage done to the recipient diminishes as the square of the distance from the arc. Twice as far means one-fourth the damage
Absorption coefficient	Different materials will absorb different amounts of radiant heat
Temperature	The greater the temperature, the greater the injury potential
Time	The longer the exposure, the greater the damage. If protective systems operate quickly, the exposure and therefore the injury will be reduced

(a)

(b)

(c)

FIGURE 1.2 Electric arc damage caused by a medium voltage arc. (*Courtesy Brosz and Associates.*)

(a)

(b)

(c)

FIGURE 1.3 Electric arc damage caused by 240 volt arc. (*Courtesy Brosz and Associates.*)

1.7

- *Third-degree burns.* Third-degree burns to the skin result in complete destruction of the growth centers. If the burn is small, healing may occur from the edges of the damaged area; however, extensive third-degree burns require skin grafting.

Blast

When an electric arc occurs, it superheats the air instantaneously. This causes a rapid expansion of the air with a wavefront that can reach pressures of 100 to 200 pounds per square foot (lb/ft^2). Such pressure is sufficient to explode switchgear, turn sheet metal into shrapnel, turn hardware into bullets, push over concrete walls, and blow molten metal at extremely high velocities.

Blasts do not always occur. Sometimes an arc is not accompanied by a blast, but when it is, it can be lethal. Figure 1.4 shows physical evidence of the pressure exerted by an electric blast.

FIGURE 1.4 Ruptured pole transformer shows the power of electric blast. (*Courtesy Alan Mark Franks.*)

AFFECTED BODY PARTS

Skin

Definition and Description.   Skin is the outer layer which completely encloses and envelopes the body. Each person's skin weighs about 4 lb, protects against bacterial invasion and physical injury of underlying cells, and prevents water loss. It also provides the body with sensation, heat regulation, excretion (sweat), and absorbs a few substances. There are about 20 million bacteria per square inch on the skin's surface as well as a forest of hairs, 50 sweat glands, 20 blood vessels, and more than 1000 nerve endings. Figure 1.5 is a cross section of the upper layers of skin tissue.

The main regions of importance for electrical purposes are the horny layer, the sweat glands, and the blood vessels. The horny layer is composed primarily of a pro-

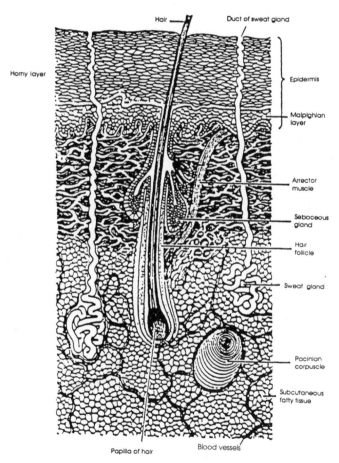

FIGURE 1.5   Typical skin cross sections.

tein material called keratin. Keratin exhibits the highest resistance of all the skin parts to the passage of electricity. The sweat glands and the blood vessels have relatively low resistances to the passage of electricity and provide a major means of access to the wet, fatty inner tissues. As you can see from Table 1.1, most of the electrical resistance exhibited by the human body is centered on the external skin layers—the horny layer.

Effects on Current Flow.   Since the body is a conductor of electricity, Ohm's law applies as it does to any other physical substance. The thicker the horny layer, the greater the skin's electrical resistance. Workers who have developed a thick horny layer have a much higher resistance to electricity than a child with an extremely thin layer. However, as Table 1.1 shows, even high skin resistance is not sufficient to protect workers from electric shock.

Skin resistance is also a function of how much skin area is in the circuit. Therefore, grasping a tool with the entire hand gives a much lower resistance than touching the tool with a finger. Also, any cut or abrasion penetrates the outside horny layer and significantly reduces the total resistance of the shock circuit. Moisture, especially sweat, greatly reduces the skin's resistance. A remarkable thing occurs to the skin insulation when voltages around 600 V are applied. At these voltages the horny layer is punctured like any film insulation, and only the low-resistance inner layers are left. This is an extremely important phenomenon to take into consideration in commercial and industrial power systems because of the high proliferation of 480-V distribution systems. Note that the horny layer may not puncture, but if it does, the current flow increases and shock injury is worse.

Burns.   Electrical skin burns can come from two different sources. Current flow through the skin can cause burns from the I^2R energy. Thermal or radiation burns are caused by the radiant energy of the electric arc as shown in Fig. 1.6.

The Nervous System

Definition and Description.   The nervous system is comprised of the electrical pathways that are used to communicate information from one part of the human body to another. To communicate, electric impulses are passed from one nerve to another. For example, the heart beats when an electric impulse is applied to the muscles which control it. If some other electric impulse is applied, the nervous system can become confused. If the current is high enough, the damage can be permanent.

Shock.   As far as the nervous system is concerned, at least three major effects can occur when current flows through the body:

- *Pain.*   Pain is the nervous system's method of signaling injury. When current flows through the nerves, the familiar painful, tingling sensation can result.
- *Loss of control.*   An externally applied current can literally "swamp" the normal nervous system electric impulses. This condition is similar to electrical noise covering an information signal in a telemetering or other communications system. When this happens, the brain loses its ability to control the various parts of the body. This condition is most obvious during the electrical paralysis, or electrical hold, that was described previously in this chapter.

FIGURE 1.6 Thermal burns caused by high-voltage electric arc. (*Courtesy Brosz and Associates.*)

- *Permanent damage.* If allowed to persist, electric current can damage the nervous system permanently. This damage takes the form of destroyed neurons and/or synapses. Since the nervous system is the communications pathway used to control the muscles, such damage can result in loss of sensation and/or function depending on the type of injury.

Muscular System

Definition and Description. The muscular system provides *motor* action for the human body. When the nervous system stimulates the muscles with electric impulses, the muscles contract to move the body and perform physical activity. The heart and pulmonary system are also muscle related. They will be covered in a later section.

Shock. Electrical shock can affect muscles in at least three significant ways:

- *Reflex action.* Muscular contractions are caused by electric impulses. Normally these impulses come from the nervous system. When an externally induced current flows through a muscle, it can cause the muscle to contract, perhaps violently. This contraction can cause workers to fall off of ladders or smash into steel doors or other structures.

- *Electrical paralysis.* Current magnitudes in excess of 10 mA are sufficient to block the nervous system signals to the muscular system. Thus, when such an external current is flowing through the body, the victim may be unable to control his or her muscles. This means that the victim cannot let go—he or she is caught in an electrical hold. As the current continues, the heating and burning action can lower the path resistance and cause an increase in the current. If the current is not cut off or if the victim is not freed from the circuit, death will occur.

- *Permanent damage.* If the current is high enough, the muscle tissue can be destroyed by burning. Currents of even less than 5 A will cause tissue destruction if they last long enough. Because such burning destroys the growth areas in tissue, the damage can be extremely slow to heal. Physical therapy and other extraordinary methods may be required to restore muscular function.

The Heart

Definition and Description. The heart is a fist-sized pump that beats more than 2.5 billion times in a 75-year lifetime. Even a few minutes of heart failure can cause death. Figure 1.7 shows the structural layout of the heart. High on the right arterial wall, a tiny bundle of nerve tissue called the *sinus node* ignites an impulse that races across the wall and down to the atrioventricular (AV) node, a cell cluster at the gateway to the ventricles. In the wake of this impulse, a contraction ripples the atrium, sending blood to the heart's lower chambers.

The AV node, in turn, flashes the spark through the conduction pathways into a nerve network that lines the ventricles. The spark leaps across the ventricle's muscle fibers at almost 7 feet per second (ft/s). The resulting contraction sends blood flowing from the heart.

A set of backup devices sustains the heart's electrical system in times of need. If the sinus node fails, the AV node initiates the heartbeat. There are even special muscle cells that can deliver an impulse if the AV node does not.

Shock. When the heart's electrical system is disturbed for any reason, such as an outside current from an electric power shock, the whole process can fail. In fact, electrical disruptions cause a large percentage of heart deaths.

The electric impulses in the heart must be coordinated to give a smooth, rhythmic beat. An outside current of as little as 75 mA can disturb the nerve impulses so that there is no longer a smooth, timed heartbeat. Instead the heart fibrillates—that is, it beats in a rapid, uncoordinated manner. When a heart is fibrillating, it flutters uselessly. If fibrillation is not ended quickly, death will follow.

Like any muscle, the heart will become paralyzed if the current flowing through it is of sufficient magnitude. Oddly, paralysis of the heart is not often fatal if the current is removed quickly enough. In fact, such paralysis is used to an advantage in defibrillators. A defibrillator intentionally applies heart-paralyzing current. When the current is removed, the heart is in a relaxed state ready for the next signal. Frequently the heart restarts.

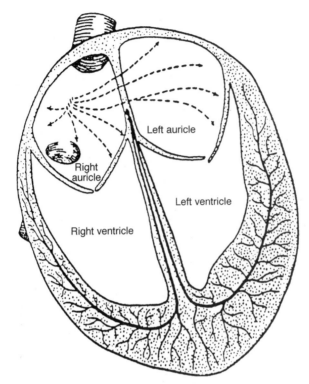

FIGURE 1.7 The heart.

Burns. Burnt heart muscle often can be fatal depending upon the amount of tissue burnt and which part of the heart is affected. Like all electric current burns, heart burns are frequently third-degree burns.

The Pulmonary System

Definition and Description. With the exception of the heart, the pulmonary system is the most critical to human life. If breathing stops, all other functions cease shortly thereafter. When the lower diaphragm moves down, it creates a vacuum on the chest chamber. This in turn draws air into the sacs in the lungs. The oxygen is then passed to the bloodstream through the tiny capillaries. At the same time, carbon dioxide is returned to the air in the lungs. When the lower diaphragm moves up, the air is forced out of the lungs, thus completing the breathing cycle.

Shock. Current flow through the midsection of the body can disrupt the nervous system impulses which regulate the breathing function. This disruption can take the form of irregular, sporadic breathing, or—if the current flow is sufficient—the pulmonary system may be paralyzed altogether. When such stoppage occurs, first aid is often required.

SUMMARY OF CAUSES—INJURY AND DEATH

Shock Effect

Table 1.3 summarizes the effects that electric shocks of varying amounts of current will have on a 68-kg (150-lb) person.

Causes of Injury

Injury from electrical hazard can come from both direct and indirect sources:

- The reflex action caused by the passage of current flow can cause falls resulting in cuts, abrasions, or broken limbs.
- Nerve damage from shock or burns can cause loss of motor function, tingling, and/or paralysis.
- Burns, both thermal- and current-induced, can cause extremely long duration and intensely painful suffering. Third-degree burns may require skin grafting to heal.
- Molten metal and/or burns to the eyes can cause blindness.
- The concussion of a blast can cause partial or complete loss of hearing.
- Current-induced burns to internal organs can cause organ dysfunction.

Causes of Death

If the electrical injury is severe enough, death can result.

- An electric shock–induced fall can cause fatal physical injuries.
- When the skin is severely burnt, large quantities of liquid are brought to the burnt areas to aid in the healing process. This creates a stress on the renal system and could result in kidney failure.
- Severe trauma from massive burns can cause a general systemic failure.
- Burnt internal organs can shut down—causing death. Thus, the more critical the organ that is burnt, the higher the possibility of death.
- If the victim inhales the superheated plasma and molten products from an electric arc, the lungs will no longer be able to perform correctly. Death may follow.
- Heart failure can result from fibrillation and/or paralysis.

PROTECTIVE STRATEGIES

The types of strategies that may be employed to protect from each of the three electrical hazards are remarkably similar. Table 1.5 summarizes the types of protective strategies that may be used. Note that the information given in Table 1.5 is general. Specific equipment and procedures are covered in Chaps. 2 and 3.

TABLE 1.5 Equipment and Procedural Strategies for Protection from the Three Electrical Hazards

Hazard	Equipment strategy	Procedural strategy for all three hazards
Shock	• Rubber insulating equipment including gloves with leather protectors, sleeves, mats, blankets, line hose, and covers • Insulated tools when working near energized conductors	• De-energize all circuits and conductors in the immediate work area • Develop and follow a lockout/tagout procedure • Maintain a safe working distance from all energized equipment and conductors
Arc	• NOMEX or other approved flash/flame-resistant work clothing • NOMEX or other approved flash suits when performing work with a high risk of arcing • Use hot sticks to keep as much distance as possible • Wear eye protection • Wear rubber gloves with leather protectors and/or other flash-proof gloves	• Use all specified safety equipment • Follow all safety procedures and requirements • Carefully inspect all equipment before placing it into service. This includes tools, test equipment, electrical distribution equipment, and safety equipment. • Make certain that all nonenergized equipment is properly grounded. This applies to both normal system grounding and temporary safety grounds
Blast	• NOMEX or other approved flash/flame-resistant work clothing. This will protect from splashed molten material • NOMEX or other approved flash suits when performing work with a high risk of arcing. This will protect from splashed molten material • Wear face shields	

Be aware that any given strategy may not be applicable in a given situation. For example,

• When troubleshooting equipment, de-energization may not be possible.
• De-energization may create an additional, unacceptable hazard. For example, if de-energization shuts down ventilation equipment in a hazardous area, workers may opt for working with energized equipment.
• Shutdown of an entire continuous process plan to work on or around one small auxiliary circuit may not be economically feasible.

If equipment cannot be deenergized, workers must use procedures and safety equipment that will minimize the safety hazards to the greatest extent possible.

CHAPTER 2

ELECTRICAL SAFETY EQUIPMENT

INTRODUCTION

The safety aspects of any job or procedure are greatly enhanced by the use of proper tools and equipment. This chapter outlines the construction and use of a variety of electrical safety equipment. Some of the equipment is used to actually perform work—items such as insulated tools or voltage-measuring devices fall into this category. Other safety products are used strictly to protect the worker, for example, flash suits and rubber goods.

Each specific piece of safety equipment is used to protect the worker from one or more of the three electrical safety hazards, and each piece of equipment should be employed when performing various types of jobs in the electric power system. Always make certain the equipment you are using is designed for the application and the voltage to which you will be exposed.

The guidelines for wearing and/or using the various types of equipment discussed in this chapter should be considered minimum guidelines. Requirements for specific locations should be determined on a case-by-case basis.

FLASH AND THERMAL PROTECTION

The extremely high temperatures and heat content of an electric arc can cause extremely painful and/or lethal burns. Since an electric arc can occur at any time, the worker must wear protection when exposed to potential arc hazards. Note that these sections address equipment for electrical hazard. Fire protection equipment has slightly different requirements and is not covered.

Table 2.1 itemizes the type of equipment required to protect the worker from the thermal hazards of electric arc. The next sections describe the type of equipment used and will identify when and how to use that equipment.

Clothing Materials

Materials used to make industrial clothing fall into four basic categories: synthetic materials, synthetic-cotton blends, 100 percent cotton, and specially designed, flame-retardant materials. These materials provide varying degrees of protection

TABLE 2.1 Equipment Used to Protect Workers from Arc Hazard

Area of body to be protected	Equipment used
Torso, arms, legs	Thermal work uniforms, flash suits
Eyes	Face shields, goggles, safety glasses
Head	Insulating hard hats, flash hoods
Hands	Rubber gloves with leather protectors

from electric arcing. The following paragraphs describe the various materials and combinations in ascending order of acceptability and safety.

Synthetic Materials. Untreated synthetic clothing materials such as polyester and nylon provide extremely poor thermal protection and should *never be used* when working in areas where an electric arc may occur. Some synthetic materials actually increase the danger of exposure to an electric arc. Synthetic materials have a tendency to melt into the skin when exposed to high temperatures. This melting causes three major difficulties.

1. The melted material forms a thermal seal which holds in heat and increases the severity of the burn.
2. Circulation is severely limited or cut off completely under the melted material. This slows healing and retards the flow of normal nutrients and infection-fighting white blood cells and antibodies.
3. The removal of the melted material is extremely painful and may increase the trauma already experienced by the burn victim.

Synthetic-Cotton Blends. Synthetic-cotton blends such as polyester-cotton are used to make clothing that is easier to care for. Although slightly less vulnerable to melting than pure polyester, the blends are still extremely vulnerable to the heat of an electric arc and the subsequent plasma cloud. Such blends provide poor thermal protection and should not be used in areas where the hazard of electric arc exists.

Cotton. Cotton work clothing made of materials such as denim and flannel is a better choice than clothing made from synthetic materials. Cotton does not melt into the skin when heated; rather, it burns and disintegrates, falling away from the skin. Thick, heavy cotton material provides a minimal barrier from arc temperatures and ignites quickly. At best, cotton provides only fair thermal protection.

Chemically Treated Materials. Cotton and synthetic-cotton blends for work clothing are available in chemically treated forms. Such materials are treated with a flame-retardant chemical which slows combustion and provides an additional level of protection from fire and heat. Chemically treated materials are often used in disposable, coverall-type clothing since the chemical treatment is degraded by repeated washing.

Although chemically treated materials are not flammable, they offer only minimal resistance to the radiation energy of an electric arc. Such materials provide fair to good thermal protection. Chemically treated materials are often referred to as flame-retardant materials.

NOMEX* IIIA. NOMEX is an aramid fiber made by the DuPont Company. It has a structure that thickens and carbonizes when exposed to heat. This unique characteristic provides NOMEX with excellent thermal protection.

NOMEX has been modified in the years since it was first introduced. NOMEX IIIA is made with an antistatic fiber and is, therefore, suitable for use in hazardous environments such as those with high concentrations of hydrocarbon gas.

Since the characteristics of NOMEX are inherent to the fiber, and not a chemical treatment, the thermal protection capabilities of NOMEX are not changed by repeated laundering.

Polybenzimidazole (PBI).[†] PBI is a product of the Hoechst Celanese Corporation. It is similar to NOMEX in that it is a synthetic fiber made especially to resist high temperatures. PBI is non-flammable, chemically resistant, and heat stable. This heat stability makes it less prone to shrinking or embrittlement when exposed to flame or high temperatures.

PBI does not ignite, melt or drip in Federal Vertical; Flame Tests FSTM 5903 and FSTM 5905. PBI's characteristics are permanent for the life of the garment. Hoescht Celanese performed tests indicate that PBI has heat protection characteristics which are equal to or superior than other materials.

Material Comparisons. Table 2.2 illustrates the relative properties of the various types of clothing materials. The information given in Table 2.2 is drawn from general industry experience and/or manufacturer experiments.

Figure 2.1 graphically illustrates the predicted, thermal performance of four of the commonly used materials. To generate these numbers, a specially instrumented

---

* NOMEX is a registered trademark of the E. I. Dupont de Nemours Company.
† PBI is a trademark of the Hoescht Celanese Corporation.

TABLE 2.2 Clothing Material Characteristics Comparison

Fiber property	Cotton	Polyester-cotton	FR* cotton	FR polyester-cotton	NOMEX
Flammable	Yes	Yes	No	No	No
Flame resistance	None	None	Topical treatment	Topical treatment	Inherent
Thermal protection	Poor	Poor	Fair	Fair to good	Excellent
Care	Requires ironing	Machine wash/dry	Requires ironing	Touch-up ironing	Machine wash/dry
Appearance after 10 washes	Poor	Good	Poor	Good	Good
Nominal life (years)	1	2–3	1	2	4–5
Relative cost	1	1	2	2.8	4
Cost per year	1	0.4	2	1.4	0.9

* FR = flame resistant.

Thermal performance of NOMEX® III flame retardant cotton,
flame retardant polyester/cotton blend, and untreated polyester/cotton blend.

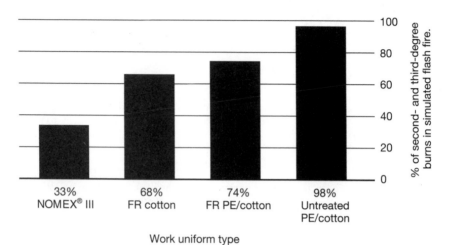

FIGURE 2.1   Relative thermal performance of various materials. (*Courtesy E.I. Dupont de Nemours.*)

FIGURE 2.2   Thermal manikin used to generate the graph shown in Fig. 2.1. (*Courtesy E.I. DuPont de Nemours.*)

manikin called Thermo-Man* is used (Fig. 2.2). The manikin is 6-ft, 1-in tall and has 122 heat sensors distributed over the entire body. The sensors measure the heat transmitted through the garments worn while a flash fire is applied to the manikin. A flash fire closely simulates the type of heat environment experienced during an electric arc and the resulting plasma cloud. The heat data recorded by these sensors was used to generate Fig. 2.1.

Work Clothing

Construction.   Work clothing used for routine, day-to-day electrical safety is employed primarily as flash protection. Flame-retardant cotton, flame-retardant synthetic-cotton blend, NOMEX, or PBI is preferred. The clothing should meet the following minimum requirements:

---

* Thermo-Man is a registered trademark of the E. I. DuPont de Nemours Company.

1. Long sleeves to provide full arm protection
2. Heavy weight for both thermal and mechanical protection

The suggested minimum is 4 ounces per square yard (oz/yd^2) if NOMEX or PBI is used and 7 to 8 oz/yd^2 if flame-retardant cloth or blends are used. Figure 2.3 shows several examples of NOMEX work clothing.

(a)

(b)

(c)

(d)

FIGURE 2.3 Nomex® work clothing. (*Courtesy Workrite Uniforms.*)

When to Use Thermally Protective Work Uniforms.   Thermally protective work uniforms should be required for all workers who are routinely exposed to the possibility of electric arc and/or flash. This applies especially to workers in the industries which have the added hazard of flash fire. At a minimum, all employees who are routinely exposed to 480 V and higher should use the thermally protective materials.

Care of Thermally Protective Work Uniforms.   The following information is necessarily general in nature. Always refer to the manufacturer's care and laundering instructions for specific information. Work uniforms should be kept clean and free of contaminants. Contaminated work clothing can be extremely hazardous. Table 2.3 lists typical care and use precautions for thermal work clothing and flash suits.

Flash Suits

Construction.   A flash suit is a thermal-protective garment made of a heavier-weight NOMEX, PBI or other flame-retardant material. The flash suit shown in Fig. 2.4 is made with 10 oz/yd² NOMEX. This garment provides protection for temperatures up to 450 degrees Fahrenheit (°F) [232 degrees Celsius (°C). (Note that the 450°F rating is a continuous ambient rating.) The flash suit has a short-term capability much in excess of this amount.

Flash suits are composed of a minimum of two parts—the face-shield/hood (Figs. 2.5 and 2.6) and the jacket (Fig. 2.4). Some flash suits are also supplied with pants. The jackets should be securely sealed to prevent the entry of the superheated plasma gas (see Fig. 2.7).

Using Flash Suits.   Flash suits should be used anytime an employee is exposed to a higher than normal possibility of electric arc. The procedures listed in Table 2.4 are typical of those in which many companies require the use of flash suits; however, specific rules should be developed for each company. *Flash suits should always be used in conjunction with adequate head, eye, and hand protection.* Note that all workers in the vicinity of the arc potential should be wearing a flash suit.

Some facilities impose a current limitation on the rule as well. For example, one large petrochemical company requires flash suits for the procedures listed in Table 2.2, but only when the circuit breaker feeding the circuit has an ampacity of 100 A or greater.

TABLE 2.3   Care and Use Guidelines for Thermal Protective Clothing

- Clothing should not be allowed to become greasy and/or impregnated with flammable liquids
- Launder according to manufacturer's instructions. Generally, home laundering in hot water with a heavy-duty detergent will be effective
- Do not mix flame resistant garments with items made of other materials in the same wash
- Do not use bleaches or other treatments unless recommended by the manufacturer
- Remember that laundering may degrade the chemical treatment on some flame-retardant materials. Observe manufacturer's recommendations as to how many washes constitute the life of the garment
- Inspect work uniforms and flash suits before each use. If they are contaminated, greasy, worn, or damaged in any way, they should be cleaned or replaced as required

FIGURE 2.4 Flash suits. (*Courtesy Encon Safety Products.*)

FIGURE 2.5 Face shield for flash suit. (*Courtesy Encon Safety Products.*)

FIGURE 2.6 Face shield open. (*Courtesy Encon Safety Products.*)

Head, Eye, and Hand Protection

When wearing flash suits, or whenever exposed to arc hazard, employees should wear full protection for the head, eyes, and hands. Head and eye protection will be provided if the employee is equipped with a flash suit. When not in a flash suit, however, employees should wear hard hats and eye shields or goggles. Hand protection should be provided by electrical insulating rubber gloves covered with leather protectors.

HEAD AND EYE PROTECTION

Hard Hats

Construction and Standards. In addition to wearing protection from falling objects and other blows, electrical workers should be equipped with and should wear hard hats that provide electrical insulating capabilities. Such hats should comply with the latest revision of the American National Standards Institute (ANSI) standard Z89.1 which classifies hard hats into three basic classes.

Class A hard hats are intended to reduce the force of impact of falling objects and to reduce the danger of contact with exposed low-voltage conductors. They are proof-tested by the manufacturer at 2200 V phase-to-ground.

Class B hard hats are intended to reduce the force of impact of falling objects and to reduce the danger of contact with exposed high-voltage conductors. They are proof-tested by the manufacturer at 20,000 V phase-to-ground.

FIGURE 2.7 Seals on jacket front and cuffs prevent plasma from entering the jacket. (*Courtesy Encon Safety Products.*)

TABLE 2.4 Procedures which Require the Use of Flash Suits

- Operating open-air switches on circuits of 480 V and higher
- Open-door switching and racking of circuit breakers—480 V and higher
- Removing and installing motor starters in motor control centers—208 V and higher
- Applying safety grounds—480 V and higher
- Measuring voltage in any circuit which is uncertain or has exhibited problems—208 V and higher
- Working on or near any exposed, energized conductors—208 V or higher

Class C hard hats are intended to reduce the force of impact of falling objects. They offer no electrical protection.

Figure 2.8 shows two examples of class B hard hats. Note that a hard hat must be a class A or class B hat to be used in areas where electrical shock may occur. The label for a class B hard hat is shown in Fig. 2.9.

Use and Care. Electrically insulating class A or B hard hats should be worn by workers anytime there is a possibility they will be exposed to shock, arc, blast, mechanical blows, or injuries. Table 2.5 lists typical working conditions in which workers should be wearing such protection.

All components of the hard hat should be inspected daily, before each use. This inspection should include the shell, suspension, headband, sweatband, and any accessories. If dents, cracks, penetrations, or any other damage is observed, the hard hat should be removed from service. Class A and B hard hats may be cleaned with warm water and soap. Solvents and other harsh cleaners should be avoided. Always refer to the manufacturer's instructions for specific cleaning information.

Safety Glasses, Goggles, and Face Shields

The plasma cloud and molten metal created by an electric arc are projected at high velocity by the blast. If the plasma or molten metal enters the eyes, the extremely high temperature will cause injury and possibly permanent blindness. Electrical workers exposed to the possibility of electric arc and blast should be equipped with and should wear eye protection. Such protection should comply with the latest revision of ANSI standard Z87.1 and should be nonconductive when used for electric arc and blast protection.

FIGURE 2.8 Hard hats suitable for use in electrical installations. (*Courtesy Mine Safety Appliances Company.*)

Shockgard ®

insulating safety headgear
adjustable head sizes 6½ thru 7¾
This hat or cap complies with
ANSI Z89.1 1986 CLASS "B"
& E.E.I. AP-1. 1961 safety require-
ments for industrial head protection

MFD BY
MSA MINE SAFETY APPLIANCES COMPANY
PITTSBURGH PENNSYLVANIA USA 15230
AP783 Rev 8   993618

FIGURE 2.9 Hard hat label for a class B hard hat. (*Courtesy Mine Safety Appliances Company.*)

FIGURE 2.10 Ultraviolet-resistant safety goggles. (*Courtesy Mine Safety Appliances Company.*)

Flash suit face shields (Figs. 2.4 through 2.6) will provide excellent face protection from molten metal and the plasma cloud. Goggles which reduce the ultraviolet light intensity (Fig. 2.10) are also recommended. Figure 2.11 is a photograph of a worker with an insulating hard hat and protective goggles.

Use and Care. Eye and face protection should be worn by workers anytime they are exposed to the possibility of electric arc and blast. Table 2.5 lists typical situations where such protection might be required.

Face protection should be cleaned before each use. Soft, lint-free cloths and warm water will normally provide the necessary cleaning action; however, most manufacturers supply cleaning materials for their specific apparatus.

FIGURE 2.11 Hard hat and goggles. (*Courtesy Mine Safety Appliances Company.*)

TABLE 2.5 Work Situations which Require Nonconductive Head Protection and Eye Protection

- Working close to exposed, overhead energized lines
- Working in switchgear, close to exposed energized conductors
- Anytime that a flash suit is recommended (see Table 2.4)
- When any local rules or recognized standards require the use of nonconductive hard hats or eye protection
- Anytime there is a danger of head, eye, or face injury from electric shock, arc, or blast

RUBBER-INSULATING EQUIPMENT

Rubber-insulating equipment includes rubber gloves, sleeves, line hose, blankets, covers, and mats. Employees should use such equipment when working in an area where the hazard of electric shock exists. This means anytime employees are working on or near an energized, exposed conductor, they should be using rubber-insulating equipment.

Rubber goods provide an insulating shield between the worker and the energized conductors. This insulation will save the workers' lives should they accidently contact the conductor. The American Society of Testing and Materials (ASTM) publishes recognized industry standards which cover rubber insulating goods.

FIGURE 2.12 Typical rubber glove set. (*Courtesy W.H. Salisbury and Co.*)

Rubber Gloves

Description. A complete rubber glove assembly is composed of a minimum of two parts—the rubber glove itself and a leather protective glove. In service, the leather protector fits over the outside of the rubber glove and protects it from physical damage and puncture. Sometimes the glove set will include a sheer, cotton insert that serves to absorb moisture and makes wearing the gloves more pleasant. Figure 2.12 shows a typical set of rubber gloves with leather protectors. *Caution: Rubber gloves should never be used without their protective leather shells unless specifically designed for such use.*

Construction and Standards. The ASTM publishes four standards which affect the construction and use of rubber gloves.

1. Standard D 120 establishes manufacturing and technical requirements for the rubber glove.

2. Standard F 696 establishes manufacturing and technical requirements for the leather protectors.

3. Standard F 496 specifies in-service care requirements.

4. Standard F 1236 is a guide for the visual inspection of gloves, sleeves, and other such rubber insulating equipment.

Rubber gloves are available in five basic voltage classes from class 0 to class 4 and two different types: types I and II. Table 2.6 identifies each class, its maximum use voltage, and the root-mean-square (rms) and direct current (dc) voltages that are used to proof-test the gloves. Figure 2.13 shows the general design and dimensions of rubber gloves. Rubber gloves are available in four standard lengths:

1. 10 in (267 mm)

2. 14 in (356 mm)

(a) Length Measurement on Standard Cuff Glove

(b) Length and Contour Measurements on Contour Cuff Gloves

FIGURE 2.13   Dimension measurements for standard and contour cuff rubber gloves. (*Courtesy ASTM.*)

TABLE 2.6 Rubber Insulating Equipment Classifications, Use Voltages, and Test Voltages

Class of insulating blankets	Nominal maximum-use voltage* phase-phase, ac, rms, max	AC proof-test voltage, rms, V	DC proof-test voltage, avg, V
0	1,000	5,000	20,000
1	7,500	10,000	40,000
2	17,000	20,000	50,000
3	26,500	30,000	60,000
4	36,000	40,000	70,000

* *Note:* The ac voltage (rms) classification of the protective equipment designates the maximum nominal design voltage of the energized system that may be safely worked. The nominal design voltage is equal to (1) the phase-to-phase voltage on multiphase circuits or (2) the phase-to-ground voltage on single-phase grounded circuits. Except for Class O equipment, the maximum-use voltage is based on the following formula: Maximum-use voltage (maximum nominal design voltage) = 0.95 ac proof-test voltage—2000.

3. 16 in (406 mm)

4. 18 in (457 mm)

Table 2.7 lists minimum and maximum thicknesses for the five classes of gloves.

In addition to the voltage classes, rubber gloves are available in two different types: type I which is *not* ozone-resistant and type II which is ozone-resistant.

All rubber goods must have an attached, color-coded label subject to the minimum requirements specified in Table 2.8. Figure 2.14 summarizes the voltage ratings for rubber goods and illustrates the labels which are applied by one manufacturer.

TABLE 2.7 Rubber Glove Thickness Standard

Class of Glove	Minimum thickness				Maximum thickness	
	In crotch		Other than crotch			
	mm	in	mm	in	mm	in
0	0.46	0.018	0.51	0.020	1.02	0.040
1	0.63	0.025	0.76	0.030	1.52	0.060
2	1.02	0.040	1.27	0.050	2.29	0.090
3	1.52	0.060	1.90	0.075	2.92	0.115
4	2.03	0.080	2.54	0.100	3.56	0.140

Source: Courtesy ASTM.

TABLE 2.8 Labeling Requirements for Rubber Goods

- Color coding according to voltage class: class 0—red, class 1—white, class 2—yellow, class 3—green, class 4—orange.
- Manufacturer's name
- Voltage class (0, 1, 2, 3, 4)
- Type
- Size (gloves only)

Class (Color Code)	Acceptance Proof Test Voltage		Blanket, Line Hose Sleeve, Covers Labels	Glove Labels	Max. Use Voltage
	A.C.	D.C.			
0 (RED)	5kV	20kV	SALISBURY & CO. CLASS 0 TYPE 1	W. H. SALISBURY & CO. ANSI/ASTM D120 CLASS 0 TYPE 1	1kV
1 (WHITE)	10kV	40kV	SALISBURY & CO. CLASS 1 TYPE 1	W. H. SALISBURY & CO. ANSI/ASTM D120 CLASS 1 TYPE 1	7.5kV
2 (YELLOW)	20kV	50kV	SALISBURY & CO. CLASS 2 TYPE 1 / W.H. SALISBURY & CO. SKOKIE, ILL U.S.A. "MAX. NOMINAL DESIGN VOLTAGE 17000V" CLASS 2 TYPE 1	W. H. SALISBURY & CO. ANSI/ASTM D120 CLASS 2 TYPE 1	17kV
3 (GREEN)	30kV	60kV	SALISBURY & CO. CLASS 3 TYPE 1 / W.H. SALISBURY & CO. SKOKIE, ILL U.S.A. "MAX. NOMINAL DESIGN VOLTAGE 26500V" CLASS 3 TYPE 1	W. H. SALISBURY & CO. ANSI/ASTM D120 CLASS 3 TYPE 1	26.5kV
4 (ORANGE)	40kV	70kV	SALISBURY & CO. CLASS 4 TYPE 1 / W.H. SALISBURY & CO. SKOKIE, ILL U.S.A. "MAX. NOMINAL DESIGN VOLTAGE 36000V" CLASS 4 TYPE 1	W. H. SALISBURY & CO. ANSI/ASTM D120 CLASS 4 TYPE 1	36kV

FIGURE 2.14   Rubber goods label and color code requirements. (*Courtesy W.H. Salisbury and Co.*)

When to Use Rubber Gloves. Rubber gloves and their leather protectors should be worn anytime there is danger of injury due to contact between the hands and energized parts of the power system. Each of the work situations described in Table 2.5 should require the use of rubber gloves and their leather protectors.

How to Use Rubber Gloves. Rubber gloves should be thoroughly inspected and air-tested before each use. They may be lightly dusted inside with talcum powder or manufacturer-supplied powder. This dusting helps to absorb perspiration and eases putting them on and removing them. *Caution: Do not use baby powder on rubber gloves. Some baby powder products contain additives which can damage the glove and reduce its life and effectiveness.*

Rubber gloves should be applied before any activity which exposes the worker to the possibility of contact with an energized conductor. Be certain to wear the leather protector with the glove. Always check the last test date marked on the glove and do not use it if the last test was more than 6 months earlier than the present date.

Rubber Mats

Description. Rubber mats are used to cover and insulate floors for personnel protection. Rubber insulating mats should not be confused with the rubber matting used to help prevent slips and falls. This type of mat is sold by many commercial retail outlets and is not intended for electrical insulation purposes. Rubber insulating mats will be clearly marked and labeled as such.

Insulating rubber matting has a smooth, corrugated, or diamond design on one surface and may be backed with fabric. The back of the matting may be finished with cloth imprint or other slip-resistant material.

Construction and Standards. The ASTM standard D-178 specifies the design, construction, and testing requirements for rubber matting.

Rubber mats are available in five basic voltage classes from class 0 to class 4, two different types, and three different subcategories. Table 2.6 identifies each class, its maximum use voltage, and ac rms and dc voltages that are used to test them. Table 2.9 identifies each of the types and special properties for insulating mats. Table 2.10 identifies the thickness requirements for insulating mats, Table 2.11 identifies the standard widths for insulating rubber matting.

Rubber mats must be clearly and permanently marked with the name of the manufacturer, type, and class. ASTM D-178 must also appear on the mat. This marking is to be placed a minimum of every 3 ft (1 m).

TABLE 2.9 Types and Special Property Specifications of Insulating Rubber Matting

	Type I	Type II
Composition	Made of any elastomer or combination of elastomeric compounds, properly vulcanized	Made of any elastomer or combination of elastomeric compounds with one or more of the special properties listed by subcategory
Subcategories	None	A: Ozone resistant B: Flame resistant C: Oil resistant

TABLE 2.10 Thickness Specifications for Insulating Rubber Mats

Class	Thickness		Tolerance	
	mm	in	mm	in
0	3.2	0.13	0.8	0.03
1	4.8	0.19	0.8	0.03
2	6.4	0.25	0.8	0.03
3	9.5	0.38	1.2	0.05
4	12.7	0.50	1.2	0.05

Source: Courtesy ASTM.

TABLE 2.11 Standard Widths for Insulating Rubber Matting

24 ± 0.5 in	(610 ± 13 mm)
30 ± 0.5 in	(760 ± 13 mm)
36 ± 1.0 in	(914 ± 25 mm)
48 ± 1.0 in	(1220 ± 25 mm)

When to Use Rubber Mats. Employers should use rubber mats in areas where there is an ongoing possibility of electric shock. Because permanently installed rubber mats are subject to damage, contamination, and embedding of foreign materials, they should not be relied upon as the sole source of electrical insulation.

How to Use Rubber Mats. Rubber mats are usually put in place on a permanent basis to provide both electrical insulation and slip protection. Mats should be carefully inspected before work is performed which may require their protection. Rubber mats should only be used as a backup type of protection. Rubber blankets, gloves, sleeves, and other such personal apparel should always be employed when electrical contact is likely.

Rubber Blankets

Description. Rubber blankets are rubber insulating devices that are used to cover conductive surfaces, energized or otherwise. They come in a variety of sizes and are used anytime employees are working in areas where they may be exposed to energized conductors.

Construction and Standards. The ASTM publishes three standards which affect the construction and use of rubber blankets.

1. Standard D 1048 specifies manufacturing and technical requirements for rubber blankets.

2. Standard F 479 specifies in-service care requirements.

3. Standard F 1236 is a guide for the visual inspection of blankets, gloves, sleeves, and other such rubber insulating equipment.

Rubber blankets are available in five basic voltage classes (0 to 4), two basic types (I and II), and two styles (A and B). Table 2.6 identifies each class, its maximum use voltage, and the ac rms and dc voltages that are used to proof-test the blankets. Table 2.12 lists standard blanket sizes, and Table 2.13 lists standard blanket thicknesses.

Type I blankets are made of an elastomer which is not ozone-resistant. Type II blankets are ozone-resistant. Both type I and type II blankets are further categorized into style A and style B. Style A is a nonreinforced construction, and style B

TABLE 2.12 Standard Blanket Sizes— Length and Width

Without slot mm (in.)	
457 by 910	(18 by 36)
560 by 560	(22 by 22)
690 by 910	(27 by 36)
910 by 910	(36 by 36)
910 by 2128	(36 by 84)
1160 by 1160	(45.5 by 45.5)
With slot mm (in.)	
560 by 560	(22 by 22)
910 by 910	(36 by 36)
1160 by 1160	(45.5 by 45.5)

Source: Courtesy ASTM.

TABLE 2.13 Rubber Blanket Thickness Measurements

Class	Thickness	
	mm	in.
0	1.6 to 2.2	0.06 to 0.09
1	2.6 to 3.6	0.10 to 0.14
2	2.8 to 3.8	0.11 to 0.15
3	3.0 to 4.0	0.12 to 0.16
4	3.2 to 4.3	0.13 to 0.17

Source: Courtesy ASTM.

has reinforcing members built-in. The reinforcing members may not adversely affect the insulating capabilities of the blanket.

Blankets have a bead around the entire periphery. The bead cannot be less than 0.31 in (8 mm) wide nor less than 0.06 in (1.5 mm) high. Blankets may have eyelets to facilitate securing the blanket to equipment; however, the eyelets must not be metal.

Rubber blankets must be marked either by molding the information directly into the blanket or by means of an attached, color-coded label. The labeling is subject to the minimum requirements specified in Table 2.8. Figure 2.14 summarizes the voltage ratings for rubber goods and illustrates the labels which are applied by one manufacturer.

When to Use Rubber Blankets. Rubber blankets should be used anytime there is danger of injury due to contact between any part of the body and energized parts of the power system. Rubber blankets may be used to cover switchgear, lines, buses, or concrete floors (Fig. 2.15). They differ from mats because they are not permanently installed.

FIGURE 2.15 Typical insulating rubber blanket.

How to Use Rubber Blankets. Rubber blankets should be thoroughly inspected before each use. They may then be draped over metal conductors or buses or hung to form insulating barriers.

Blankets should be applied before any activity which exposes the worker to the possibility of contact with an energized conductor. Always check the last test date marked on the blanket and do not use it if the last test was more than 1 year earlier than the present date.

Rubber Covers

Description. Rubber covers are rubber insulating devices that are used to cover specific pieces of equipment to protect workers from accidental contact. They include several classes of equipment such as insulator hoods, dead-end protectors, line hose connectors, cable end covers, and miscellaneous covers. Rubber covers are molded and shaped to fit the equipment for which they are intended.

Construction and Standards. The ASTM publishes three standards which affect the construction and use of rubber covers.

1. Standard D 1049 specifies manufacturing and technical requirements for rubber covers.
2. Standard F 478 specifies in-service care requirements.
3. Standard F 1236 is a guide for the visual inspection of blankets, gloves, sleeves, and other such rubber insulating equipment.

Rubber covers are available in five basic voltage classes (0 to 4), two basic types (I and II), and five styles (A, B, C, D, and E). Table 2.6 identifies each class, its maximum use voltage, and the ac rms and dc voltages that are used to proof-test the covers. Many varieties of rubber covers are available (Fig. 2.16). Their size and shape are determined by the equipment that they are designed to cover. Refer to ASTM standard D 1049 for complete listings of the various standard covers.

Type I covers are made of a properly vulcanized, cis-1,4-polyisoprene rubber compound which is not ozone-resistant. Type II covers are made of ozone-resistant elastomers. Both type I and II covers are further categorized into styles A, B, C, D, and E. Table 2.14 describes each of the five styles.

TABLE 2.14   Styles of Rubber Covers

Style	Description
A	Insulator hoods
B	Dead End Protectors
C	Line Hose Connectors
D	Cable End Covers
E	Miscellaneous Covers

Rubber covers must be marked either by molding the information directly into the cover or by means of an attached, color-coded label. The labeling is subject to the minimum requirements specified in Table 2.8. Figure 2.14 summarizes the voltage ratings for rubber goods and illustrates the labels which are applied by one manufacturer.

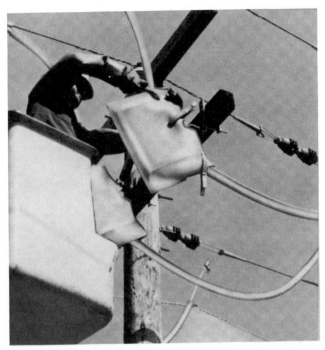

FIGURE 2.16 Typical insulating rubber covers. (*Courtesy W.H. Salisbury and Co.*)

When to Use Rubber Covers. Rubber covers should be used anytime there is danger of an injury due to contact between any part of the body and energized parts of the power system.

How to Use Rubber Covers. Rubber covers should be thoroughly inspected before each use. They may then be applied to the equipment which they are designed to cover. Any covers that appear to be defective or damaged should be taken out of service until they can be tested.

Covers should be applied before any activity which exposes the worker to the possibility of contact with an energized conductor. Covers which are used to connect line hose sections should always be used when multiple line hose sections are employed.

Line Hose

Description. Rubber insulating line hoses are portable devices used to cover exposed power lines and protect workers from accidental contact. Line hose segments are molded and shaped to completely cover the line to which they are affixed.

Construction and Standards. The ASTM publishes three standards which affect the construction and use of rubber line hose.

1. Standard D 1050 specifies manufacturing and technical requirements for rubber line hose.
2. Standard F 478 specifies in-service care requirements.
3. Standard F 1236 is a guide for the visual inspection of blankets, gloves, sleeves, and other such rubber insulating equipment.

Rubber line hose is available in five basic voltage classes (0 to 4), three basic types (I, II, and III), and four styles (A, B, C, and D). Table 2.6 identifies each class, its maximum-use voltage, and the ac rms and dc voltages that are used to proof-test them.

Type I line hose is made of a properly vulcanized, cis-1,4-polyisoprene rubber compound which is not ozone-resistant. Type II line hose is made of ozone-resistant elastomers. Type III line hose is made of an ozone-resistant combination of elastomer and thermoplastic polymers. Type III line hose is elastic. All three types are further categorized into styles A, B, C, and D. Table 2.15 lists the characteristics of each of the four styles.

TABLE 2.15 Characteristics of the Four Styles of Line Hose

Style	Description
A	Straight style, constant cross section
B	Connect end style. Similar to straight style with connection at one end
C	Extended lip style with major outward extending lips
D	Same as style C with a molded connector at one end

Rubber line hose must be marked either by molding the information directly into the hose or by means of an attached, color-coded label. The labeling is subject to the minimum requirements specified in Table 2.8. Figure 2.14 summarizes the voltage ratings for rubber goods and illustrates the labels which are applied by one manufacturer.

When to Use Rubber Line Hose.   Rubber line hose should be used anytime personnel are working on or close to energized lines or lines that could be energized.

How to Use Rubber Line Hose.   Line hoses should be thoroughly inspected before each use. They may then be applied to the lines which they are designed to cover. Any line hose that appears to be defective or damaged should be taken out of service until it can be tested.

Line hose should be applied before any activity which exposes the worker to the possibility of contact with an energized conductor. When more than one section of line hose is used, connecting line covers should be employed. The line hose should completely cover the line.

Rubber Sleeves

Description.   Rubber sleeves (Fig. 2.17) are worn by workers to protect their arms and shoulders from contact with exposed energized conductors. They fit over the arms and complement the rubber gloves to provide complete protection for the arms and hands. They are especially useful when work must be performed in a cramped environment.

FIGURE 2.17 Insulating rubber sleeves. (*Courtesy W.H. Salisbury and Co.*)

Construction and Standards.   The ASTM publishes three standards which affect the construction and use of rubber sleeves.

1. Standard D 1051 specifies manufacturing and technical requirements for rubber sleeves.
2. Standard F 496 specifies in-service care requirements.
3. Standard F 1236 is a guide for the visual inspection of blankets, gloves, sleeves, and other such rubber insulating equipment.

Insulating sleeves are available in five basic voltage classes (0 to 4), two basic types (I and II), and two styles (A and B). Table 2.6 identifies each class, its maximum use voltage, and the ac rms and dc voltages that are used to proof-test them.

Type I sleeves are made of properly vulcanized, cis-1,4-polyisoprene rubber compound which is not ozone-resistant. Type II sleeves are made of ozone-resistant elastomers.

Style A sleeves are made in a straight, tapered fashion (Fig. 2.18). Type B sleeves are of a curved elbow construction.

Rubber sleeves are manufactured with no seams. They have a smooth finish and self-reinforced edges. Sleeves are manufactured with holes used to strap or harness them onto the worker. The holes are nominally $\frac{5}{16}$ in (8 mm) in diameter and have nonmetallic, reinforced edges.

Rubber sleeves must be marked clearly and permanently with the name of the manufacturer or supplier, ASTM D 1051, type, class, size, and which arm they are to be used on (right or left). Such marking shall be confined to the shoulder flap area and shall be nonconducting and applied in such a manner as to not impair the required properties of the sleeve.

FIGURE 2.18   Style A, straight taper rubber insulating sleeves. (*Courtesy ASTM.*)

A sleeve shall have a color-coded label attached which identifies the voltage class. The labeling is subject to the minimum requirements specified in Table 2.8. Figure 2.14 summarizes the voltage ratings for rubber goods and illustrates the labels which are applied by one manufacturer. Table 2.16 shows standard thicknesses for rubber sleeves, and Table 2.17 lists standard dimensions and tolerances.

When to Use Rubber Sleeves.   Rubber sleeves should be used anytime personnel are working on or close to energized lines or lines that could be energized. They should be considered anytime rubber gloves are being worn and should be required for anyone working around or reaching through energized conductors.

TABLE 2.16   Standard Thickness for Rubber Insulating Sleeves

Class of sleeve	Minimum		Maximum	
	mm	in.	mm	in.
0	0.51	0.020	1.02	0.040
1	0.76	0.030	1.52	0.060
2	1.27	0.050	2.54	0.100
3	1.90	0.075	2.92	0.115
4	2.54	0.100	3.56	0.140

Source: Courtesy ASTM.

TABLE 2.17 Standard Dimensions and Tolerances for Rubber Insulating Sleeves

		Dimensions*							
		A		B		C		D	
Style	Size	mm	in.	mm	in.	mm	in.	mm	in.
Straight taper	regular	667	26¼	394	15½	286	11¼	140	5½
	large	724	28½	432	17	327	12⅞	175	6⅞
	extra large	762	30	483	19	337	13¼	175	6⅞
Curved elbow	regular	673	26½	394	15½	311	12¼	146	5¼
	large	705	27¾	406	16	327	12⅞	175	6⅞
	extra large	749	29½	445	17½	327	12⅞	178	7

* Tolerances shall be as follows:
A—±13 mm (±½ in)
B—Minimum allowable length
C—±13 mm (±½ in)
D—±6 mm (±¼ in)
Source: Courtesy ASTM.

How to Use Rubber Sleeves. Rubber sleeves should be inspected before each use. They may be worn to protect the worker from accidental contact with energized conductors. Be certain to check the last test date marked on the sleeve. If the date is more than 12 months earlier than the present date, the sleeve should not be used until it has been retested.

In-Service Inspection and Periodic Testing of Rubber Goods

Field Testing. Rubber goods should be inspected before each use. This inspection should include a thorough visual examination and, for rubber gloves, an air test. Table 2.18 is a synopsis of the inspection procedures defined in ASTM standard F 1236. Rolling is a procedure in which the rubber material is gently rolled between the hands or fingers of the inspector. This procedure is performed on both the inside and outside of the material. Figures 2.19 and 2.20 illustrate two types of rolling techniques.

Rubber gloves should be air tested before each use. First, the glove should be inflated with air pressure and visually inspected, and then it should be held close to the face to feel for air leaks through pinholes. Rubber gloves can be inflated by twirling, by rolling, or by using a mechanical glove inflater. Note that "rolling" in this situation is not the same as the rolling discussed earlier in the description of rubber goods inspection.

To inflate a glove by twirling, grasp the side edges of the glove (Fig. 2.21a), gently stretch the glove until the end closes and seals (Fig. 2.21b), and then twirl the glove in a rotating motion using the rolled edges of the glove opening as an axis (Fig. 2.21c). This will trap air in the glove and cause it to inflate.

Gloves that are too heavy to inflate by twirling may be inflated by rolling. To do this, lay the glove on a flat surface, palm up, and press the open end closed with the fingers (Fig. 2.22a). Then while holding the end closed, tightly roll up about 1½ in of the gauntlet (Fig. 2.22b). This will trap air in the glove and cause it to inflate. Gloves may also be inflated by commercially available mechanical inflaters (Fig. 2.23).

TABLE 2.18 Inspection Techniques for Rubber Insulating Equipment

Gloves and sleeves	Inspect glove and sleeve surface areas by gently rolling their entire outside and inside surface areas between the hands. This technique requires gently squeezing together the inside surfaces of the glove or sleeve to bend the outside surface areas and create sufficient stress to inside surfaces of the glove or sleeve to highlight cracks, cuts, or other irregularities. When the entire outside surface area has been inspected in this manner, turn the glove or sleeve inside-out and repeat the inspection on the inside surface (now the outside). If necessary, a more careful inspection of suspicious areas can be achieved by gently pinching and rolling the rubber between the fingers. Never leave a glove or sleeve in an inside-out condition. Stretch the thumb and finger crotches by pulling apart adjacent thumb and fingers to look for irregularities in those areas (Fig. 2.15)
Blankets and mats	Place rubber blankets on a clean, flat surface and roll up tightly starting at one corner and rolling toward the diagonally opposite corner. Inspect the entire surface for irregularities as it is rolled up. Unroll the blanket and roll it up again at right angles to the original direction of rolling. Repeat the rolling operations on the reverse side of the blanket (Fig. 2.16)
Line hose	Examine the inside surfaces of the insulating line hose by holding the hose at the far end from the lock and placing both hands side-by-side palms down around the hose. With the slot at the top and the long free end of the hose on the left, slowly bend the two ends of the hose downward while forcing the slot open with the thumbs. The hose should be open at the bend, exposing the inside surface. Slide the left hand about a foot down the hose and then, with both hands firmly gripping the hose, simultaneously move the left hand up and the right hand down to pass this section over the crown of the bend for inspection. Slide the right hand up the hose to the left hand. Hold the hose firmly with the right hand while the left hand again slides another foot down the hose. Repeat the inspection and, in this way, the entire length of hose passes through the hands from one end to the other

Source: This material is reproduced verbatim from ASTM standard F-1236. It appears with the permission of the American Society of Testing and Materials.

After the gloves are inflated, they may be visually inspected (Fig. 2.24) and then checked by holding them close to the face to listen and feel for air leaks through pinholes (Fig. 2.25).

Description of Irregularities in Rubber Goods. If damage or imperfections are discovered during inspections, the rubber goods may need to be removed from service. The following are typical of the types of problems that may be discovered.

1. *Abrasions and scratches* (Fig. 2.26). This is surface damage that normally occurs when the rubber material makes contact with an abrasive surface.
2. *Age cracks* (Fig. 2.27). Surface cracks that may look like crazing of glazed ceramics and may become progressively worse. Age cracks are due to slow oxidation caused by exposure to sunlight and ozone. It normally starts in areas of the rubber that are under stress.

3. *Chemical bloom* (Fig. 2.28).   A white or yellowish discoloration on the surface. It is caused by migration of chemical additives to the surface.

4. *Color splash* (Fig. 2.29).   This is a spot or blotch caused by a contrasting colored particle of unvulcanized rubber that became embedded into the finished product during the manufacturing process.

(a)

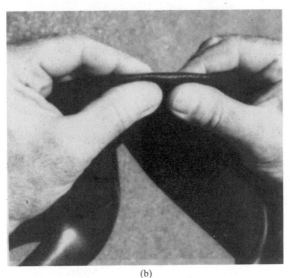

(b)

FIGURE 2.19   Inspection of gloves and blanket by rolling. (a) Hand rolling; (b) pinch rolling. (*Courtesy ASTM.*)

FIGURE 2.20 Inspection of rubber blanket by rolling.

(a)

FIGURE 2.21 Inflating rubber gloves by twirling. (a) Grasping; (b) streaching; (c) twirling. (*Courtesy ASTM.*)

(b)

(c)

FIGURE 2.21 (*Continued*) Inflating rubber gloves by twirling. (a) Grasping; (b) streaching; (c) twirling. (*Courtesy ASTM.*)

(a)

(b)

FIGURE 2.22   Inflating rubber gloves by rolling. (a) Pressing; (b) rolling. (*Courtesy ASTM.*)

5. *Cuts* (Fig. 2.30).   These are smooth incisions in the surface of the rubber caused by contact with sharp-edged objects.

6. *Depressions or indentations* (Fig. 2.31).   A shallow recess which exhibits a thinner rubber thickness at the bottom of the depression than in the surrounding areas.

7. *Detergent cracks.*   Cracks that appear on the inside surface of the glove or sleeve. The cracks form around a spot of detergent residue that was not removed during the cleaning and rinsing of the form prior to the dipping process.

8. *Embedded foreign matter* (Fig. 2.32).   This is a particle of nonrubber that has been embedded in the rubber during the manufacturing process. It normally shows up as a bump when the rubber is stretched.

9. *Form marks.*   This is a raised or indented section on the surface of the rubber. It is caused by an irregularity in the form that was used to mold the product.

10. *Hard spot* (Fig. 2.33).   A hardened spot caused by exposure to high heat or chemicals.

FIGURE 2.23   Mechanical inflation. (*Courtesy ASTM.*)

FIGURE 2.24   Visually inspecting inflated rubber gloves. (*Courtesy ASTM.*)

FIGURE 2.25 Inspecting rubber gloves by listening and feeling for air leaks through pinholes. (*Courtesy ASTM.*)

FIGURE 2.26 Scratches. (*Courtesy ASTM.*)

FIGURE 2.27 Age cracks. (*Courtesy ASTM.*)

11. *Mold mark* (Fig. 2.34).   A raised or indented section caused by an irregularity in the mold.
12. *Nicks, snags, and scratches* (Figs. 2.26, 2.35, 2.36).   Angular tears, notches, or chiplike injuries in the surface of the rubber caused by sharp objects such as wire, pointed tools, staples, or other similar sharp-edged hazards.
13. *Ozone cracks* (Fig. 2.37).   A series of interlacing cracks that start at stress points and worsen as a result of ozone-induced oxidation.

FIGURE 2.28 Chemical bloom. (*Courtesy ASTM.*)

FIGURE 2.29   Color splash. (*Courtesy ASTM.*)

FIGURE 2.30   Cuts. (*Courtesy ASTM.*)

FIGURE 2.31 Depression or indentations. (*Courtesy ASTM.*)

FIGURE 2.32 Embedded foreign material. (*Courtesy ASTM.*)

14. *Parting line or flash line.*   A ridge of rubber left on finished products. They occur at mold joints during manufacturing.

15. *Pitting* (Fig. 2.38).   A pockmark in the rubber surface. It is often created by the rupturing of an air bubble close to the surface during manufacturing.

16. *Protuberance* (Fig. 2.39).   A bulge or swelling above the surface of the rubber.

17. *Puncture* (Fig. 2.40).   Penetration by a sharp object through the entire thickness of the product.

18. *Repair marks* (Fig. 2.41).   An area of the rubber with a different texture. Usually caused by repair of the mold or form.

19. *Runs.*   Raised flow marks which occur on rubber glove fingers during the dipping process.

20. *Skin breaks.*   Cavities in the surface of the rubber. They have filmy ragged edges and smooth interior surfaces. They are usually caused by embedded dirt specks during the manufacturing process.

(a)

(b)

FIGURE 2.33 Hard spot. (*Courtesy ASTM.*)

(c)

(d)

FIGURE 2.33 (*Continued*) Hard spot. (*Courtesy ASTM.*)

(a)

(b)

FIGURE 2.34 Mold mark. (*Courtesy ASTM.*)

FIGURE 2.35 Nick. (*Courtesy ASTM.*)

FIGURE 2.36 Snag. (*Courtesy ASTM.*)

(a)

(b)

FIGURE 2.37 Ozone cracks. (*Courtesy ASTM.*)

FIGURE 2.38 Pitting. (*Courtesy ASTM.*)

FIGURE 2.39 Protuberance. (*Courtesy ASTM.*)

FIGURE 2.40 Puncture. (*Courtesy ASTM.*)

21. *Soft spots.* Areas of the rubber which have been soft or tacky as a result of heat, oils, or chemical solvents.

22. *Tears* (Fig. 2.42). A rip through the entire thickness of the rubber. Usually caused by forceful pulling at the edge.

Electrical Testing. Rubber insulating equipment should be electrically tested periodically. Table 2.19 summarizes the requirements and/or recommendations for such testing. Electrical testing of rubber goods is a relatively specialized procedure and should be performed only by organizations with the necessary equipment and

TABLE 2.19 In-service Electrical Tests for Rubber Insulating Goods

Product	Maximum test interval, months	ASTM standard	Notes
Gloves	6	F 496	Tested, unused gloves may be placed into service within 12 months of the previous tests without retesting
Mats	—	D 178	There is no regulatory requirement for in-service electrical testing of mats. They are tested by the manufacturer when new
Blankets	12	F 479	Tested, unused blankets may be placed into service within 12 months of the previous tests without being retested
Covers	—	F 478	Covers should be retested when in-service inspections indicate a need
Line hose	—	F 478	Line hose should be retested when in-service inspections indicate a need
Sleeves	12	F 496	Tested, unused sleeves may be placed into service within 12 months of the previous tests without being retested

experience. For detailed testing information refer to the ASTM standards referenced in Table 2.19. Note that all rubber goods are tested at the same voltages dependent upon their class (0, 1, 2, 3, or 4). See Table 2.6 for a listing of ASTM-required test voltages.

HOT STICKS

Description and Application

Hot sticks are poles made of an insulating material. They have tools and/or fittings on the ends which allow workers to manipulate energized conductors and equip-

FIGURE 2.41 Repair mark. (*Courtesy ASTM.*)

FIGURE 2.42 Tear. (*Courtesy ASTM.*)

ment from a safe distance. Hot sticks vary in length depending on the voltage level of the energized equipment and the work to be performed. Modern hot sticks are made of fiberglass or epoxiglass. Older designs were made of wood which was treated and painted with chemical-, moisture-, and temperature-resistant materials. Figure 2.43 is an example of a simple hot stick fitted with a tool suitable for operation of open-air disconnect switches.

Hot sticks can be fitted with a variety of tools and instruments. The most common fitting is the NEMA standard design shown in Fig. 2.44 as the *standard universal* fitting. This fitting allows a variety of tools and equipment to be connected to the hot stick. Figure 2.45 shows a voltage tester attached to a hot stick using a standard fitting.

Figure 2.44 also shows other attachments and extensions that can be used to increase the usefulness of hot sticks. In addition to the equipment shown in Fig. 2.44, hot sticks can also be equipped with wrenches, sockets, screwdrivers, cutters, saws, and other such tools.

FIGURE 2.43 Typical hot stick. (*Courtesy AB Chance Corp.*)

FIGURE 2.44 Various fittings, couplings, and tools for hot sticks. (*Courtesy AB Chance Corp.*)

FIGURE 2.45 Voltage tools attached to a hot stick. (*Courtesy W.H. Salisbury and Co.*)

FIGURE 2.46 Telescoping hot stick—shown collapsed. (*Courtesy AB Chance Corp.*)

Hot sticks can also be purchased in telescoping models (Fig. 2.46) and so-called shotgun models (Fig. 2.47). The telescoping type of hot stick is composed of several hollow, tubular sections which nest inside of each other. The topmost section is first extended and locked in place by means of a spring-loaded button which snaps into a hole. The user of the hot stick extends as many of the sections as are required to accomplish the job at hand. The telescoping hot stick makes very long hot stick lengths available which then collapse to a small, easy-to-carry assembly.

The shotgun hot stick (Fig. 2.47) has a sliding lever mechanism that allows the user to open and close a clamping hook mechanism at the end. In this way the user can attach the stick to a disconnect ring and then close it. After the switch is operated, the shotgun mechanism is operated to open the hook. The shotgun stick gets its name from its similarity to the pump-action shotgun.

Figure 2.48 shows a hot stick kit with several sections and various tools. This type of package provides a variety of configurations which will satisfy most of the day-to-day needs for the electrician and the overhead line worker. The kit includes the following components:

1. Six 4-ft sections of an Epoxiglas snap-together hot stick
2. Aluminum disconnect head for opening and closing switches and enclosed cutouts
3. Nonmetallic disconnect head for use in indoor substations where buswork and switches are in close proximity
4. Clamp stick head for use with 6-in-long eye-screw ground clamps. This is used to apply and remove safety grounds

FIGURE 2.47   Shotgun-type hot stick. (*Courtesy AB Chance Corp.*)

5. Tree trimmer attachment with $1\frac{1}{2}$ ft of additional stick and pull rope used to close jaws of the trimmer

6. Pruning saw

7. Pistol-grip saw handle for use when tree limbs can be reached and insulation is not required

8. Heavy-duty vinyl-impregnated storage case

Electricians involved primarily in indoor work might wish to substitute other tools for the tree trimming and pruning attachments.

When to Use

Hot sticks should be used to insulate and isolate the electrician from the possibility of electric shock, arc, or blast. Table 2.20 identifies the types of procedures for which hot sticks are recommended.

How to Use

The specifics of hot stick use will depend upon the task being performed and the location in which the worker is positioned. As a general rule, if hot sticks are being used, the worker should also wear other protective clothing. At a minimum, rubber gloves and face shields should be employed. However, many recommend that flash suits should also be worn, especially when safety grounds are being applied.

Before each use the hot stick should be closely inspected for signs of physical damage which may affect its insulating ability. If the hot stick is cracked, split, or otherwise damaged, it should be taken out of service.

Testing Requirements

ASTM standard F 711 requires that manufacturers test hot sticks to very stringent standards before they are sold; however, there is no standard requirement for peri-

FIGURE 2.48 Typical hot stick kit for electricians and line workers. (*Courtesy AB Chance Corp.*)

odic testing. It is suggested, however, that hot sticks be electrically tested annually or more often if physical inspections indicate a need.

INSULATED TOOLS

Description and Application

Insulated tools, such as those shown in Fig. 2.49, are standard hand tools with a complete covering of electrical insulation. Every part of the tool is fully insulated. Only the minimum amount of metallic work surface is left exposed. Such tools are used to prevent shock or arc in the event that the worker contacts the energized conductor.

When to Use

Insulated tools should be used anytime work is being performed on or near exposed, energized conductors.

TABLE 2.20 Typical Procedures Requiring Use of Hot Sticks

Medium voltage and higher
• Voltage measurement
• Any repairs or modifications to energized equipment
All voltages
• Operation of disconnects and cutouts
• Application of safety grounds

FIGURE 2.49   Insulated tool set. (*Courtesy CIP Insulated Products.*)

How to Use

Insulated tools are used in the same way that ordinary hand tools are used, and all the same cautions should be observed. Avoid using the tools in any application which may damage the insulation.

BARRIERS AND SIGNS

Whenever work is being performed which requires the temporary removal of normal protective barriers such as panels or doors, barriers and signs should be used to warn personnel of the hazard.

Barrier Tape

Barrier tape is a continuous length of abrasion-resistant plastic tape. It should be a minimum of 2 in wide and should be marked or colored to clearly indicate the nature of the hazard to which employees will be exposed if they cross the tape line. Figure 2.50 shows a type of barrier tape suitable for marking and barricading an area where an electrical hazard exists.

Such tape should be yellow or red to comply with Occupational Safety and Health Administration (OSHA) standards. Generally red tape, or red tape with a

FIGURE 2.50 Barrier tape styles suitable for electrical hazards. (*Courtesy Direct Safety Supply Co.*)

white stripe, is the preferred color for such applications. Whatever color is chosen should be a standard design that is used consistently for the same application.

Signs

Warning signs should be of standardized design and easily read. They should be placed in such a way to warn personnel of imminent hazard. Figure 2.51 shows a type of sign suitable for use as an electrical hazard warning.

FIGURE 2.51 Typical electrical hazard sign. (*Courtesy Ideal Industries, Inc.*)

When and How to Use

General Requirements. Table 2.21 lists the general procedures for using signs, barriers, and attendants to warn personnel of electrical hazards. Signs should be placed so that they are easily seen and read from all avenues of access to the hazardous area.

Temporary Hazard Barricades. Temporary hazard barricades should be constructed with a striped barrier tape using the following procedure:

1. The tape should be placed so that it completely encloses the hazardous area.
2. The tape should be clearly visible from all directions of approach.
3. The tape should be at a level such that it forms an effective barrier. Approximately 3 ft is suitable.
4. Allow an area of sufficient size to give adequate clearance between the hazard and any personnel outside the hazardous area.
5. If test equipment is being used on equipment inside the hazardous area, the tape should be arranged so that the equipment can be operated outside the area.
6. Do not use the same style and color of tape for any purpose other than marking temporary hazards.
7. Such a barricaded area should be considered to be the same as a metal enclosure; that is, *access is not possible.*
8. After the hazard has been eliminated, remove the tape.

Work Area Barricades. Work areas should be barricaded using solid-colored or striped tape. Use the following procedure:

1. The tape should completely enclose the area wherein work is going to occur.
2. The tape should be visible from all directions of approach.
3. Allow an area of sufficient size to give adequate clearance between the hazard and any personnel outside the hazardous area.
4. If test equipment is being used on equipment inside the hazardous area, the tape should be arranged so that the equipment can be operated outside the area.

TABLE 2.21 Summary of the Use of Warning Methods

Type of warning	When to use
Signs	Signs should be placed to warn employees about electrical hazards which may harm them
Barricades	Barricades should be used to prevent and limit employee access to work areas where they may be exposed to electrical hazards. Such barriers should be made of nonconductive material such as plastic barrier tape
Attendants	If signs and/or barricades cannot provide a level of safety sufficient to protect employees, attendants shall be placed to guard hazardous areas. Attendants shall be familiar with the nature and extent of the hazard so as to adequately warn other employees

5. Do not use the same style and color of tape for any purpose other than marking work areas.

6. Persons unfamiliar with the work being performed inside the barrier should not be allowed to enter.

7. After the hazard has been eliminated, remove the tape.

SAFETY TAGS, LOCKS, AND LOCKING DEVICES

Safety tags, locks, and locking devices are used to secure and mark equipment that has been taken out of service. They are applied in such a way that the equipment cannot be reenergized without first removing the tags and/or locks. For more information about lockout and tagout procedures refer to Chap. 3.

Safety Tags

Safety tags are applied to equipment to indicate that the equipment is not available for service. They are tags constructed of a durable, environment-proof material. They should be of standardized construction and include a warning that says Do Not Start, Do Not Open, Do Not Close, Do Not Operate, or other such warning. The tag must also indicate who placed it on the equipment and the nature of the problem with the equipment. Figure 2.52 shows tags which are suitable for such an application.

FIGURE 2.52 Typical tags suitable for tagout purposes. (*Courtesy Ideal Industries, Inc.*)

Some manufacturers supply tags with individual employee photographs on them. This type of tag helps to further identify who placed the tag and to personalize the installation.

Tags are to be applied using strong, self-locking fasteners. Nylon cable wraps are suitable for such an application. The fastener must have a breaking strength of not less than 50 lb.

Locks and Multiple-Lock Devices

Locks are used to prevent operation of equipment that has been de-energized. They must be strong enough to withstand all but the most forceful attempts to remove

FIGURE 2.53 Typical padlocks suitable for lockout purposes. (*Courtesy Ideal Industries, Inc.*)

them without the proper key. If a lock can be removed by any means other than a bolt cutter or the key that fits it, the lock should not be used.

Standard padlocks are normally applied for lockout purposes (Fig. 2.53). Each employee should have a set of padlocks which can be opened only by his or her key. A master key may be kept for emergency situations which require that the lock be opened by someone other than the one who placed it. See Chap. 3 for situations in which safety locks may be removed by someone other than the individual who placed it.

Departments may also have "group" padlocks which are placed by shift personnel and which are keyed to a departmental key. For example, the operations department may have shift operators who remove and restore equipment from service. Equipment may be removed from service during one shift and later returned to service during another shift. In such situations the group lock will be placed by one individual and removed by another. Thus, the group locks will have master keys so that any authorized shift operator can place or remove them.

Multiple-Lock Devices. Sometimes several workers will need to place a lock on one piece of equipment. This often happens when several crafts are working in the area secured by the lock. In these circumstances, a multiple-lock device is used (Fig. 2.54*a*). To lock out a piece of equipment, the multiple-lock device is first opened and applied as though it were a padlock. Then the padlock is inserted through one of the holes in the device. The padlock prevents opening of the multiple-lock device which, in turn, prevents operation of the equipment. The devices shown in Fig. 2.54*a* can accommodate up to six locks; however, multiple-lock devices can be "daisy chained" to allow as many locks as required.

The multiple-lock devices in Fig. 2.54*b* combine the multiple-lock device with a safety tag. The information required on the tag is written on the tag portion of the device which is then applied to the equipment.

(a)   (b)

FIGURE 2.54 Multiple-lock devices. (*Courtesy Ideal Industries, Inc.*)

Locking Devices

Some equipment, such as wall switches and molded case circuit breakers, do not readily accommodate locks. In these instances, when lockout is required, a locking device must be used. Figure 2.55a shows locking devices which may be placed over the handle of a molded case circuit breaker and clamped in place. The lock is then installed through the hole left for that purpose. The breaker cannot be operated until the device is removed, and the locking device cannot be removed until the padlock is open.

Figure 2.55b is a similar device which mounts on a standard wall switch. The locking device is first attached to the wall switch with the switch faceplate mounting screws. The switch is moved to the OFF position and the hinged cover of the device is closed. A padlock is placed through the flange supplied for that purpose.

Devices like the wall switch lockout device can be left in place permanently for switches that are frequently locked out. Although the device shown in Fig. 2.55b can be used to lock the switch in the ON position, this practice is not recommended.

(a)

(b)

FIGURE 2.55   Locking devices. (*Courtesy Ideal Industries, Inc.*)

When/Where to Use Lockout Tagout

Equipment should be locked out and tagged out when it is being serviced or maintained and an unexpected start-up could injure personnel who are working in the area. Thus tags and locks should be placed anytime an employee is exposed to contact with parts of the equipment which have been de-energized.

The locks and tags must be applied to all sources of power for the affected equipment. They must be applied in such a way that the equipment cannot be reenergized without first removing the locks and/or tags. See Chap. 3 for more complete information on lockout/tagout procedures. Figure 2.56 shows locks, tags, and multiple-lock devices being applied to electrical switching equipment.

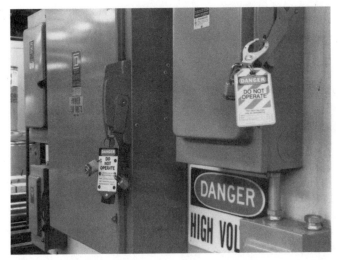

FIGURE 2.56 Typical application of locks, tags, and multiple-lock devices. (*Courtesy Ideal Industries, Inc.*)

VOLTAGE-MEASURING INSTRUMENTS

Safety Voltage Measurement

Safety voltage measurement actually involves measuring for no voltage. That is, a safety measurement is made to verify that the system has been de-energized and that no voltage is present. (See Chap. 3 for more details.) Because of this, the instruments that are used for safety voltage measurement do not need to be highly accurate. They need only be accurate enough to determine whether voltage is present in the system or not.

The instruments discussed in the following sections are intended primarily for safety voltage measurements and not as highly accurate devices. Some of them, however, are quite accurate. Contact the individual manufacturers for more specific information.

FIGURE 2.57 "AC Sensor" proximity voltage sensor for use on circuits up to 600 V alternating current. (*Courtesy Santronics, Inc., Sanford, NC.*)

Proximity Testers

Proximity testers do not require actual metal-to-metal contact to measure the voltage, or lack of voltage, in a given part of the system. They rely on the electrostatic field established by the electric potential to indicate the presence of voltage. Proximity testers will indicate voltage levels through insulation. They will not provide accurate results when cable is shielded.

Proximity testers are not accurate and do not indicate the actual level of the voltage that is present. Rather they indicate the presence of voltage by the illumination of a light and/or the sounding of a buzzer. Figures 2.57 through 2.59 are three different types of proximity detectors for various voltage levels.

Figure 2.57 shows a simple neon light proximity tester. The end of the unit is plastic and sized to fit into a standard 120-V duplex receptacle. It requires two AAA flashlight cells to operate. When placed in proximity to an energized circuit, the red neon, located in the white plastic tip, glows.

Figure 2.58 shows a proximity tester that uses a combination of audio and visual indicators. When turned on, the unit emits a slow beeping sound which is synchronized to a small flashing light. If

FIGURE 2.58 "TIC" tracer proximity voltage sensor for use on circuits up to 35,000 V. (*Courtesy TIF Electronics.*)

FIGURE 2.59 Audiovisual proximity voltage tester for use in circuits from 240 V to 500 kV. (*Courtesy W.H. Salisbury and Co.*)

the unit is placed close to an energized circuit, the number of beeps per second increases. The light flashes increase in frequency along with the beeps. The higher the voltage and/or the closer the voltage source, the faster the beeps. When the voltage is very high, the beeping sound turns into a steady tone. This unit has a three-position switch. One position turns the unit off, and the two others provide low- and high-voltage operation, respectively. If high voltages are being measured, the unit should be attached to a hot stick. The manufacturer supplies a hot stick for that purpose.

Figure 2.59 shows a proximity tester that is similar in some ways to the one shown in Fig. 2.58. It has both a light and a tone; however, the light and tone are steady when a voltage is sensed above the unit's operational threshold. The unit in Fig. 2.59 also has a multiposition switch which has an OFF position, a 240-V test position, a battery test position, and multiple voltage level positions from 4200 V up to the unit's maximum. This unit is shown attached to a hot stick in Fig. 2.45. It should not be used to measure higher voltages without the use of a hot stick and/or appropriate rubber insulating equipment.

FIGURE 2.60 Safety voltage and continuity tester. (*Courtesy Ideal Industries, Inc.*)

Contact Testers

Some personnel prefer the use of testers which make actual metal-to-metal contact with the circuit being energized. Such instruments are called *contact testers*. Contact testers may be simple indicators, but more often they are equipped with an analog or digital meter which indicates actual voltage level. Figures 2.60 through 2.63 illustrate various styles of contact testers that may be used for safety-related measurements.

Figure 2.60 shows one of the more popular models used for voltages up to 600 V alternating current or direct current. This unit is a solenoid type of instrument. That is, a spring-loaded solenoid plunger is connected to an indicator which aligns with a voltage scale. The distance that the plunger travels is proportional to the voltage level of the measured circuit. The voltage scale is read in volts. The instrument shown in Fig. 2.60 also indicates continuity and low voltage. It switches automatically between those functions. Note that this style of unit is one of the most popular styles in use for low-voltage measurements. Because of their solenoid mechanism, these styles are subject to small arcs when the contact is made with the measured circuit. This problem can be mitigated by using test leads equipped

(a)   (b)

FIGURE 2.61   Digital readout contact-type safety voltmeter. (*Courtesy Tegam, Inc.*)

FIGURE 2.62 Digital readout multimeter. (*Courtesy Fluke.*)

with fused resistors. Such resistors not only eliminate the arcing problem but also open in the event that an internal short circuit occurs in the meter.

Figure 2.61 shows a modern, digital readout safety voltmeter. This instrument is suitable for circuits up to 1000 V and is tested to 2300 V. It has an inherently high impedance; therefore, it is not prone to arcing when the leads make contact. The meter should only be used for voltage measurements. It has no continuity or ammeter scales.

Figure 2.62 shows a typical digital multimeter. These instruments are in common use by virtually all electricians and electrical and electronic technicians. Such instruments often have voltage ranges well above 1000 V; however, use of them in power circuits with voltages above 600 V is not recommended. Care should be taken when using this style of instrument in an electric power circuit.

The instrument shown in Fig. 2.63 is called a *phasing tester* because it is often

(a)

FIGURE 2.63 Phase tester extension handles.
(*Courtesy AB Chance Corp.*)

used to phase two circuits—that is, to check that A in circuit 1 is the same as A in circuit 2 and so on. Such units can also be used for safety-related voltage measurements. The instrument is composed of two high-resistance elements in series with an analog instrument. The resistances are selected in such a way that the meter tracks accurately up to 16 kV. To extend the range of the instrument up to 48 or 80 kV, extension resistors can be added.

Selecting Voltage-Measuring Instruments

Voltage-measuring instruments must be selected based on a variety of criteria. The following sections describe each of the steps that should be used in the selection of voltage-measuring instruments.

Voltage Level. The instrument used must have a voltage capability at least equal to the voltage of the circuit to be measured. Make certain that the manufacturer certifies the instrument for use at that level.

Application Location. Some instruments are designed for use solely on overhead lines or solely in metal-clad switchgear. Make certain that the manufacturer certifies the instrument for the application in which it will be used.

Internal Short Circuit Protection. If the measuring instrument should fail internally, it must not cause a short circuit to appear at the measuring probes. Instruments with resistance leads and/or internal fuses should be employed.

Sensitivity Requirements. The instrument must be capable of reading the lowest voltage which can be present. This is from all sources such as backfeed as well as normal voltage supply.

Circuit Loading. The instrument must be capable of measuring voltages that are inductively or capacitively coupled to the circuit. Therefore, it must have a high enough circuit impedance so that it does not load the circuit and reduce the system voltage to apparently safe levels.

(b)

FIGURE 2.63 (*Continued*)   Phase tester shown with carrying case.
(*Courtesy AB Chance Corp.*)

Instrument Condition

Before performing voltage measurements, the measuring instrument must be carefully inspected to ensure that it is in good mechanical and electrical condition.

Case Physical Condition.   The case and other mechanical assemblies of the instrument must be in good physical condition and not cracked, broken, or otherwise damaged. Any instrument with a broken case should be taken out of service and repaired or replaced.

Probe Exposure.   Only the minimum amount of lead should be exposed on contact-type instruments. This minimizes the chance of accidently causing a short circuit when the lead contacts more than one conductor at a time. Low-voltage instruments such as those shown in Figs. 2.60 and 2.61 have spring-loaded plastic sleeves which cover the entire probe until pushed by the pressure during the measurement. These types of probes should always be used for measurement of voltages in power systems.

Lead Insulation Quality.   The lead insulation should be closely inspected. If the insulation is frayed, scored, or otherwise damaged, the leads should be replaced before the instrument is used to measure voltage.

Fusing. If the instrument you are using is fused, the fuse should be checked to make certain that it is of the right size and capability. Instruments used to measure power system voltages should be equipped with high interrupting capacity fuses which will safely interrupt 200,000 A at rated voltage.

Operability. Make certain that the instrument is operable. If it uses batteries, they should be checked before the instrument is placed in service. Check the instrument on a known hot source before it is taken into the field. If it does not work, take it out of service until it can be repaired or replaced.

Three-Step Voltage Measurement Process

Since a safety-related voltage measurement is normally made to make certain that the circuit is dead, the measuring instrument must be checked both before and after the actual circuit is read. This ensures that a zero reading is, in fact, zero and not caused by a nonfunctional instrument. Note that this before-and-after check should be made in addition to the check that is given when the instrument is placed into service from the tool room or supply cabinet. This before-and-after measurement process is called the *three-step process.*

Step 1—Test the Instrument Before the Measurement. The measuring instrument should be applied to a source which is known to be hot. Ideally this source would be an actual power system circuit; however, this is not always possible, because a hot source is not always readily available—especially at medium voltages and higher.

Because of this problem manufacturers often have alternative means to check their instruments in the field. Some provide low-voltage positions on their instruments. Figure 2.64 shows the switch settings for the instrument of Fig. 2.16. This instrument may be verified in three different ways:

1. With the switch in the TEST-240V position, place the instrument head close to a live circuit in excess of 110 V.

2. With the switch in the TEST-240V position, rub the instrument head on cloth or clothing to obtain a static charge. The unit should indicate periodically.

3. Set the switch to the 35-KV overhead position and place the head close to a spark plug of a running engine.

FIGURE 2.64 Selective switch positions for the meter shown in Fig. 2.59. (*Courtesy W.H. Salisbury and Co.*)

After the instrument is verified, the BATTERY position can be used to verify the battery supply circuitry and the battery condition.

Figure 2.65 shows a test device and setup used to verify the type of instrument shown in Fig. 2.63. One lead from the test device (Fig. 2.65, inset) is plugged into a special jack mounted on the instrument. The other end is clipped to each of the measuring probes, one at a time. The reading on the instrument meter is used to determine the operability of the test instrument.

(a)

(b)

FIGURE 2.65 Field test unit for voltage testers similar to Fig. 2.63. (*Courtesy AB Chance Corp.*)

Of course, the best way to test an instrument is to check it on a known hot source using the scale position that will be used for the actual measurement.

Step 2—Measure the Circuit Being Verified. The instrument should then be used to actually verify the presence or absence of voltage in the circuit. See Chap. 3 for a detailed description of how to make such measurements.

Step 3—Retest the Instrument. Retest the instrument in the same way on the same hot source as was used in step 1. Table 2.22 summarizes the voltage-measuring steps discussed in this section. Because of the extreme importance of voltage measurement, this procedure is repeated in more detail in Chap. 3.

TABLE 2.22 Voltage-Measuring Instrument Selection and Use*

Instrument selection	• Voltage level
	• Application location
	• Internal short circuit protection
	• Sensitivity requirements
	• Circuit loading
Instrument condition	• Case physical condition
	• Probe exposure
	• Lead insulation quality
	• Fusing
	• Operability
Three-step process	• Check the meter
	• Check the circuit
	• Check the meter

* See text for details.

General Considerations for Low-Voltage–Measuring Instruments

Most general-purpose multimeters are not designed for power system use. This is certainly true of many of the small units that are available from some major retail companies. Table 2.23 lists specific requirements for test instruments used in power system voltage measurement.

SAFETY GROUNDING EQUIPMENT

The Need for Safety Grounding

Even circuits that have been properly locked and tagged can be accidently energized while personnel are working on or near exposed conductors. For example,

- If capacitors are not discharged and grounded, they could accidently be connected to the system.
- Voltages could be induced from adjacent circuits. Such voltages can be extremely high if the adjacent circuit experiences a short circuit.
- Switching errors could result in reenergizing of the circuit.
- An energized conductor can fall or be forced into the de-energized circuit, thereby energizing it and causing injury.
- Lightning strikes could induce extremely high voltages in the conductors.

Employees who are working on or near such exposed conductors could be severely injured from shock, arc, or blast which results when the conductors are accidently energized. Because of this, safety grounding equipment should be employed as one additional safety measure when employees must work near exposed conductors.

Whenever possible, safety grounds are applied to create a zone of equal potential around the employee. This means that the voltage is equal on all components within reach of the employee. Correct methods for applying safety grounds are discussed more fully in Chap. 3.

TABLE 2.23 Checklist for Low-Voltage–Measuring Equipment

- Instrument should be certified for use in electric power systems
- Leads should be of proper design
  - Secured permanently to instrument
  - Fully insulated probes with minimum metallic exposure
  - Insulation rated for voltage of circuits to be measured
- Internal fusing capable of interrupting fault current if short circuit occurs
- High resistance measurement to minimize arcing at probe tips
- Single-function (voltage readings) instrument preferred
  - If a multimeter is used, the resistance and current measurement circuits must be adequately fused
  - Auto-voltage detection is desirable
- Instrument insulation levels should be rated for voltage of the circuits to be measured

Safety Grounding Switches

Grounding switches are specially manufactured units designed to replace a circuit breaker in medium-voltage metal-clad switchgear. The switch rolls into the space normally occupied by the breaker, and the switch stabs connect to the bus and line connections which normally connect to the breaker stabs. Figures 2.66 through 2.68 show various views of a typical grounding switch.

Two different varieties of grounding switches are in common use. One type of switch has two sets of disconnect stabs: one set connects to the bus phase connections, and the other connects to the line connections. The other type of switch has only one set of stabs which can be moved to connect to either the bus or the line side of the switchgear connections.

For either variety of grounding switch, internal connections can be made to electrically ground the bus, the line, or both sides of the switch. Thus the switch grounds the circuit at the source.

Ground switches should be used very carefully and generally should not be relied on for 100 percent personal safety protection. Safety grounds (see next section) should be employed when secure personal protection is required.

Safety Grounding Jumpers

General Description.   Safety grounding jumpers (also called safety grounds) are lengths of insulated, highly conductive cable with suitable connectors at both ends. They are used to protect workers by short-circuiting and grounding de-energized conductors. Thus if a circuit is accidently energized, the safety grounds will short-circuit the current and protect the workers from injury. Safety grounds also drain static charges and prevent annoying or dangerous shocks. Figure 2.69 illustrates a typical set of safety grounds.

FIGURE 2.66   Front view of a 15-kV grounding switch. (*Courtesy UNO-VEN Refinery, Lemont, IL.*)

FIGURE 2.67   Rear view of a 15-kV grounding switch. (*Courtesy UNO-VEN Refinery, Lemont, IL.*)

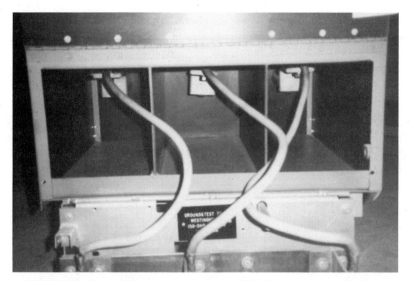

FIGURE 2.68 Closeup of jumper connections for 15-kV grounding switch. (*Courtesy UNO-VEN Refinery, Lemont, IL.*)

SAFETY GROUNDING JUMPERS
1. **Clamps: With Cable Strain Relief Sleeves**
2. **Ferrules: Per Cable size & Clamp mat'l.**
3. **Cable/s: Grounding: per system short circuit capacity. Length minimum required to reach.**

FIGURE 2.69 Typical safety ground jumpers with component parts marked. (*Courtesy W.H. Salisbury and Co.*)

Notice that the safety ground is composed of three major component parts: the clamp, the ferrule, and the cable. The entire assembly must be capable of withstanding the enormous thermal and magnetic forces that are applied when the circuit to which the jumper is applied becomes energized. The construction of safety grounds and their component parts are regulated by ASTM standard F 855.

Clamps. Clamps serve to connect the grounding jumper to the cable or bus system that it is being used to ground. ASTM standard F 855 defines three types of clamps (I, II, and III). Each of the three types is available in two basic classes (A and B). Table 2.24 describes the basic types and classes of clamp.

TABLE 2.24 Types and Classes of Grounding Jumper Clamps

Type I	Clamps for installation on de-energized conductors equipped with eyes for installation with removable hot sticks
Type II	Clamps for installation on de-energized conductors equipped with permanently mounted hot sticks
Type III	Clamps for installation on permanently grounded conductors of metal structures. These clamps are equipped with tee handles, eyes, or square or hexagon head screws, or both
Class A	Clamps equipped with smooth contact surfaces
Class B	Clamps equipped with serrated, cross-hatched, or other means used to abrade or bite through corrosion products on the conductor to which the jaw is clamped

Source: From ASTM Standard F 855.

Types I and II are used to connect the grounding jumper to the actual de-energized conductor. Type II has hot sticks which are permanently mounted to the clamp, and type I has only rings to which shotgun-type hot sticks can be connected. Type III clamps are used for connection to ground bus, tower steel, grounding clusters, and other such permanently grounded points. Figure 2.70*a* to *c* illustrates the three types of grounding clamp.

Each type of clamp can be purchased with either nonserrated (class A) or serrated (class B) jaws. Regardless of which type of jaw is purchased, the conductor sur-

(a)   (b)

FIGURE 2.70 ASTM type I, II, and III clamps. (a) Type I clamp; (b) Type II clamp; (c) Type III clamp. (*Courtesy AB Chance Corp.*)

(c)

FIGURE 2.70 (*Continued*) ASTM type I, II, and III clamps. (a) Type I clamp; (b) Type II clamp; (c) Type III clamp. (*Courtesy AB Chance Corp.*)

faces should be thoroughly cleaned before application of the clamp. The class B jaws provide additional assurance that adequate electric contact will be made.

Clamps are available in seven ASTM grades depending on the short circuit capability of the circuit to which they will be connected. Table 2.25 is taken from ASTM standard F 855 and identifies the seven grades and their associated electrical and mechanical characteristics.

Ferrules. Ferrules are used to connect the jumper cable to the clamp. ASTM standard F 855 identifies six basic types of ferrule as described in Table 2.26. Figure 2.71*a* through *d* illustrates each of the six basic types.

In addition to types, ferrules are manufactured in seven grades depending upon the short circuit currents which they are designed to withstand. Table 2.27 shows the electrical and mechanical characteristics for the seven grades of ferrule. Table 2.28 shows the physical specifications for grounding cable ferrules. Of course, ferrules must be attached to the clamp with a mechanically and electrically secure type of termination. Table 2.29 lists the ASTM standard types of terminations between ferrules and grounding clamps.

Typical
Type I
compression
ferrules

Typical
Type II
solder
ferrules

(a)

FIGURE 2.71 ASTM types I, II, III, IV, V, and VI ferrules. (*Courtesy ASTM.*)

(b)   (c)

FIGURE 2.71 (*Continued*)   ASTM types I, II, III, IV, V, and VI ferrules. (*Courtesy ASTM.*)

(d)

FIGURE 2.71 (*Continued*)   ASTM types I, II, III, IV, V, and VI ferrules. (*Courtesy ASTM.*)

Cables. The cables used for grounding jumpers are specified in three basic types (I, II, and III) as illustrated in Table 2.30. Note that the insulation can be of any color; however, most manufacturers use yellow, black, or clear insulation. Clear insulation has the advantage of allowing easy visual inspection to detect signs of conductor fusing after severe short circuits. Clear insulation, however, is sometimes sensitive to ultraviolet degradation. Yellow insulation has the advantage of being easily visible and indicating a potentially hazardous condition. Black insulation, while acceptable, can be easily mistaken for a normal conductor. Clear or yellow insulation is the preferred choice for grounding jumper cable.

Grounding jumper cable sizes are determined by the amount of available short circuit current that is present in the part of the system to which they are being applied. Table 2.31 lists the maximum current ratings and the size of cable required by ASTM standards. Table 2.31 also

TABLE 2.25 Grounding Clamp Ratings

	Grounding clamp torque strength, min				Short circuit properties*									
	Yield†		Ultimate		Withstand rating, symmetrical kA rms, 60 Hz			Ultimate rating/capacity,‡ symmetrical kA rms, 60 Hz					Continuous current rating, A RMS, 60 Hz	Minimum cable size with ferrule installed equal or larger than
Grade	lbf·in	n·m	lbf·in	n·m	15 cycles (250 ms)	30 cycles (500 ms)	Copper cable size	6 cycles (100 ms)	15 cycles (250 ms)	30 cycles (500 ms)	60 cycles (1 s)	Maximum copper test cable size		
1	280	32	330	37	14.5	10	#2	30	19	13	9	2/0	200	#2
2	280	32	330	37	21	15	1/0	48	30	21	15	4/0	250	1/0
3	280	32	330	37	27	20	2/0	60	38	27	19	4/0	300	2/0
4	330	37	400	45	36	25	3/0	76	48	34	24	250 kcmil	350	3/0
5	330	37	400	45	43	30	4/0	96	60	43	30	250 kcmil	400	4/0
6	330	37	400	45	54	39	250 kcmil or 2 2/0	113	71	50	35	350 kcmil	450	250 kcmil or 2 2/0
7	330	37	400	45	74	54	350 kcmil or 2 4/0	159	100	71	50	550 kcmil 550 kcmil	550	350 kcmil or 2 4/0

Note: lbf·in = foot-pound–inch, n·m = newton-meter, ms = millisecond, kcmil = thousand circular mil.
* Withstand and ultimate short circuit properties are based on performance with surges not exceeding 20% asymmetry factor.
† Yield shall mean no permanent deformation such that the clamp cannot be reused throughout its entire range of application.
‡ Ultimate rating represents a symmetrical current which the clamp shall carry for the specified time.
Source: Courtesy of ASTM.

TABLE 2.26 Types of Ferrules for Use on Safety Ground Jumpers

Type I	Compression ferrule. Cylindrical and made for installation on cable stranding by compression
Type II	Solder ferrule is tubular and made for installation on cable stranding with solder
Type III	Plain stud shrouded compression ferrule with a stepped bore that accepts the entire cable over the jacket
Type IV	Threaded stud shrouded compression ferrule with stepped bore that accepts entire cable over jacket and has male threads at forward end
Type V	Bolted shrouded compression ferrule with internal threads and a bolt at forward end
Type VI	Threaded stud compression ferrule with male threads at forward end

identifies the current ratings for commercially manufactured, complete jumpers described in the next section.

Complete Jumpers. While some users make their own safety ground jumpers using the ASTM specifications and buying the individual components, most prefer to buy a completely preassembled jumper set as illustrated in Fig. 2.72. The jumper illustrated in Fig. 2.72 is designed for use on live-front pad-mount underground distribution (UD) switchgear and transformers. It is rated at 15,000 A for 30 cycles and 21,000 A for 15 cycles. It has a three-way terminal block assembly, four bronze body grounding clamps, and three 6-ft lengths of 2/0 clear jacketed copper cable.

Many types of jumpers are available from the manufacturer's stock, and many more types can be quickly assembled by the manufacturer for specific applications.

Selecting Safety Grounding Jumpers

The selection of grounding jumpers may be performed with a relatively simple four-step process. The following four sections are provided courtesy of W.H. Salisbury and Company.

FIGURE 2.72 Commercially manufactured safety ground jumper. (*Courtesy AB Chance Corp.*)

TABLE 2.27 Grounding Cable Ferrule Ratings

		Short circuit properties*—Symmetrical kA rms, 60 Hz						Continuous current rating, rms 60 Hz
		Withstand rating		Ultimate rating/capacity†				
Grade	Cable size	15 cycles (250 ms)	30 cycles (500 ms)	6 cycles (100 ms)	15 cycles (250 ms)	30 cycles (500 ms)	60 cycles (1 s)	
1	2	14.5	10	30	19	13	9	200
2	1/0	21	15	48	30	21	15	250
3	2/0	27	20	60	38	27	19	300
4	3/0	36	25	76	48	34	24	350
5	4/0	43	30	96	60	43	30	400
6	250 kcmil	54	39	113	71	50	35	450
7	350 kcmil	74	54	159	100	71	50	550

* Withstand and ultimate short circuit properties are based on performance with surges not exceeding 20% asymmetry factor.
† Ultimate rating represents a symmetrical current which the ferrule shall carry for the time specified.
Source: Courtesy ASTM.

TABLE 2.28 Grounding Cable Ferrule Physical Specifications

Type	Description	Shape	Minimum Specifications to be Supplied by Manufacturers in Addition to Cable Capacity and Material
I	Compression	O. D. after Compression	Installing Die Code O. D. after Installation
II	Solder	O. D.	O. D.
III	Plain Stud Shrouded Compression	O. D.	Installing Die Codes Stud O. D.
IV	Threaded Stud Shrouded Compression	Thread Size A · 30°	Installing Die Codes Thread Size A
V	Bolted Shrouded Compression	O. D. · 30°	Installing Die Codes Bolt O. D. or Thread Size
VI	Threaded Compression	Thread Size A · 30°	Installing Die Codes Thread Size A

A Standard thread sizes are as follows:
  ½ in.–13 UNC ≈ M12 × 1.75, ⅝ in.–11 UNC ≈ M16 × 2.00, ¾ in.–10 UNC ≈ M20 × 2.50.
Note: Inspection or vent holes are optional for Types III, IV, V, and VI.
Source: Courtesy ASTM.

TABLE 2.29 Grounding Cable Ferrules and Compatible Grounding Clamp Terminations

CABLE FERRULES ASTM			MATCHING GROUNDING CLAMP CABLE TERMINATION ASTM		
ASTM Ferrule Type	Ferrule Description	Illustration of Ferrule Including Essential Interface Application Data Required	ASTM Termination Style	Termination Description	Essential Interface Application Data Required
I	Compression Ferrule	O. D. After Installation — Base Material	1.	Cable Retaining Eyebolt	
II	Solder Ferrule	O. D. — Base Material	2.	Eyebolt & Cable Support	Ferrule or Stud O. D. Accepted
			3.	Plain Bore Clamp and Cable Support	
III	Plain Stud Shrouded Compression Ferrule	O. D. — Base Material	4.	Plain Bore Tubular With Screws and Cable Support	
IV	Threaded Stud Shrouded Compression Ferrule	Thread Size ᴬ → 30° Base Material	5. 6. 7.	Plain Bore Boss Plain Bore Boss and Cable Support Threaded Bore Boss	Tap Boss I. D. or Thread Size ᴬ and Material
V	Bolted Shrouded Compression Ferrule	O. D. or Thread Size 30° Base Material	5. 6.	Plain Bore Boss Plain Bore Boss and Cable Support	Tap Boss I. D. and Material
VI	Threaded Compression Ferrule	Thread Size ᴬ 30° Base Material	6. 8. 9.	Plain Bore Boss and Cable Support Threaded Bore Boss and Cable Support Threaded Bore Clamp and Cable Support	Tap Boss Thread Size ᴬ and Material

ᴬ Standard thread sizes are as follows:
½ in.–13 UNC ≈ M12 × 1.75, ⅝ in.–11 UNC ≈ M16 × 2.00, ¾ in.–10 UNC ≈ M20 × 2.50.

Note: Inspection or vent holes are optional for Types III, IV, V, and VI.
Source: Courtesy ASTM.

TABLE 2.30 Cable Types for Use on Safety Ground Jumpers

Type I	Cables with stranded, soft drawn copper conductor with 665 or more strands of #30 American Wire Gauge (AWG) (0.0100 in) or #34 AWG (0.0063 in). Flexible elastomer jackets rated for installation and continuous service at temperatures from –40°F (–40°C) through +194°F (90°C)
Type II	Cables with stranded, soft drawn copper conductor with 133 wires or more for size #2 or 259 wires or more for size 1/0 and larger. Flexible elastomer jackets rated for installation and continuous service at temperatures from –13°F (–25°C) to +194°F (+90°C)
Type III	Cables with stranded, soft drawn copper conductor with 665 or more #30 AWG (0.0100 in). Flexible thermoplastic jackets rated for installation and continuous service at temperatures ranging from +14°F (–10°C) to +140°F (+60°C). *Caution:* The use of type III jacketed cables is restricted to open areas or spaces with adequate ventilation so that fumes which could be produced by overheating the jacket during a short circuit fault on the cable can be dispersed

TABLE 2.31 Grounding Jumper Ratings

| | Short circuit properties* | | | | | | |
| Grounding cable size (copper) | Withstand rating symmetrical kA rms, 60 Hz | | Ultimate capacity symmetrical kA rms, 60 Hz | | | | Continuous current rating, rms, 60 Hz |
	15 cycles (250 ms)	30 cycles (500 ms)	6 cycles (100 ms)	15 cycles (250 ms)	30 cycles (500 ms)	60 cycles (1 s)	
#2	14.5	10	29	18	13	9	200
1/0	21	15	47	29	21	14	250
2/0	27	20	59	37	26	18	300
3/0	36	25	74	47	33	23	350
4/0	43	30	94	59	42	29	400
250 kcmil	54	39	111	70	49	35	450
350 kcmil	74	54	155	98	69	49	550

* Withstand and ultimate short circuit properties are based on performance with surges not exceeding 20% asymmetry factor.
Source: Courtesy ASTM.

Short Circuit Capacity.   Determine the maximum short circuit capability at each typical grounding location. From this information the size of the cable can be determined from Table 2.31. (Table 2.31 is the same as table 5 in ASTM standard F 855.) Note that in selecting the cable size, it is perfectly acceptable to use smaller sizes of cable such as 2/0 and then double the cables when required for higher short circuit duties.

Grounding Clamps.   Grounding clamp types and styles must be determined for each conductor size and shape where grounding jumpers may be applied. If cable and/or bus is expected to be corroded and difficult to clean, serrated jaw clamps should be specified. Remember to specify clamps for both the conductor and the ground end of the grounding set.

Grounding Ferrules.   Selection of the grounding ferrules is based on the cable size and material and the cable termination style of the grounding clamp(s). Aluminum or copper-plated ferrules should be used with an aluminum clamp and copper cable. Bronze clamps should be used only with copper ferrules and copper cables. Some manufacturers simplify the ferrule selection by employing only one ferrule and cable termination design.

Complete Jumper Specification.   To simplify the selection of grounding sets, the user may first determine the short circuit capacity, conductor size and shape, and then refer the design of the jumper to the manufacturer. Most manufacturers have a variety of stock grounding jumpers and will design and build special systems on an as-needed basis.

Installation and Location

The actual procedures and methods for the installation of safety grounds are discussed in detail in Chap. 3. In general the following rules apply:

1. Always make a voltage measurement to verify the system is dead before installing safety grounds.

2. Grounds should be installed in such a way that they equalize the voltage on all equipment within reach of the worker. This equipotential grounding method is illustrated in Chap. 3.

3. When possible, safety grounds should be applied on both sides of the work area. Generally, the more grounding points, the better.

4. Application of safety grounds is considered to be a procedure with more than a normal risk of electric arc. Always wear face shields, rubber gloves, and—whenever possible—flash suits.

5. Safety grounds should be applied on systems of any voltage level to add additional protection for personnel when the system is out of service and conductors are exposed. Systems of 480 V and higher should always be safety-grounded when locked and tagged. Lower-voltage systems may be safety-grounded on an as-needed basis.

6. Of course, if the nature of the work precludes the use of safety grounds, they should not be applied. For example, the measurement of insulation resistance cannot be done when safety grounds are installed.

GROUND FAULT CIRCUIT INTERRUPTERS

Operating Principles

Most 120-V circuits are fed from standard thermal-magnetic molded-case circuit breakers. The circuit is similar to that shown in Fig. 2.73. In this configuration, the only protection from overcurrent is the circuit breaker, which requires a minimum of 15 A to even begin operation. Clearly, if a human being contacts the 120-V circuit, the circuit breaker will not operate unless a minimum of 15 A flows. Even then, it will operate slowly. Since current levels as low as 10 to 30 mA can be fatal to human beings, such installations are clearly not effective for personnel protection.

Figure 2.74 shows a system that has been in use since the late 1960s. This device, called a *ground fault circuit interrupter* (GFCI), has a current transformer which is applied to the hot and the neutral lead. The resulting output of the current transformer is proportional to the difference in the current between the two leads.

FIGURE 2.73 Standard protection schemes for 120-V circuits.

FIGURE 2.74 Standard 120-V supply with ground fault circuit interrupter. (*Courtesy AB Chance Corp.*)

To understand its operation, consider what happens when a normal load is attached to the duplex outlet of Fig. 2.74. Under such circumstances, all the current that flows through the hot wire will go to the load and return to the source on the neutral wire. Since the currents on the hot wire and the neutral wire are equal in magnitude, the output from the GFCI current transformer will be zero and the GFCI will not operate.

Now consider what happens when a grounded person contacts the hot wire downstream of the GFCI. Under these circumstances current will flow from the hot wire through the person and will return on the ground wire. Because of this the currents on the hot wire and the neutral wire will not be equal. The current transformer will produce an output to the sensor which will, in turn, cause the GFCI breaker contacts to open.

This operation occurs instantaneously, that is, with no intentional time delay. The circuit is disconnected very quickly and the person is spared the long-duration shock. While a GFCI does not guarantee the complete safety of personnel, it is set sensitively enough to save the life of the person an overwhelming percentage of the time.

Ground fault circuit interrupters are set to trip when the current difference between the hot lead and the neutral lead differ by more than 5 ± 1 mA.

Applications

The National Electrical Code (NEC) specifies locations which require the use of GFCIs. These locations include bathrooms, swimming pool outlets, and temporary power supplies for construction work. Refer to the most recent edition of the NEC for a detailed list of these requirements.

At a minimum, GFCI receptacles should be used in portable power cords used for temporary construction power during electrical system and other types of industrial work. Figure 2.75 shows a typical GFCI suitable for such use.

Ground fault circuit interrupters should be tested before each use. In addition to being visually inspected to check for frayed insulation and a damaged case, the GFCI circuit should be tested for proper operation. This test can be easily performed using a simple test device like that shown in Fig. 2.76. This device plugs into the duplex receptacle. When the receptacle is energized, the user can observe the

FIGURE 2.75 Portable ground fault circuit interrupter. (*Courtesy Direct Safety Supply Co.*)

lights on the end which will display in a certain pattern if the wiring to the receptacle is correct. The user then presses the test button and an intentional 5-mA ground is placed on the hot wire. If the GFCI is functional, it will operate and open the circuit. The user can then reset the GFCI and put it into service.

SAFETY ELECTRICAL ONE-LINE DIAGRAM

One-line diagrams are used in electric power systems for a variety of purposes including engineering, planning, short circuit analysis, and—most important—

FIGURE 2.76 Receptacle and GFCI tester. (*Courtesy Ideal Industries, Inc.*)

safety. The safety electrical one-line diagram (SEOLD) provides a roadmap for the electric power system. Figure 2.77 is an example of a typical SEOLD. Safety electrical one-line diagrams are used to ensure that switching operations are carried out in a safe, accurate, and efficient manner. *An accurate, up-to-date, legible SEOLD should be available for all parts of the electric power system.* Safety electrical one-line diagrams should be accurate, concise, and legible.

1. *Accuracy.* The SEOLD should be accurate and up to date. Regular revision reviews should be performed on the SEOLD, and any required changes or modifications should be implemented immediately. Personnel should be aware of the review process and should have easy access to suggesting changes on the SEOLD.

2. *Concise.* Because one-line diagrams are used for a variety of purposes, some facilities put a large amount of information on one diagram. Items such as cable lengths, sizes, and impedances; current transformer ratios; transformer impedances; protective relay logic circuits; and metering circuits are often found on one-line diagrams used for safety and operations. This practice is not acceptable. Table 2.32 lists the only items that should be included on a one-line diagram. Note that the use of computer-aided drafting systems makes the development of job-specific one-line diagrams quite simple.

3. *Legibility.* All too often, SEOLDs are allowed to become illegible. They may be sun-bleached, or they may simply be the product of an original diagram that has been allowed to become too old. The SEOLD should be easy to read even in subdued lighting.

FIGURE 2.77 Typical safety electrical one-line diagram (SEOLD). (*Courtesy Cadick Professional Services.*)

TABLE 2.32 Information Required to be Included on Safety Electrical One-Line Diagrams

Energy sources	All sources of energy in the power system should be included on the SEOLD. This includes the normal sources such as power company connections and generators, as well as possible sources of backfeed such as instrument transformers and foreign voltages brought in for remote-control purposes
Disconnect devices	The circuit breakers, switches, cutouts, fused disconnects, and any other devices which can be used to control the power system energy

Note: All energy sources and disconnect devices should be clearly marked with a unique identifying name and/or number. The device itself should be clearly marked with an identical name and/or number.

The SEOLD is the roadmap for the field electrician. Each electrical worker should have access to the SEOLD for day-to-day switching activities.

THE ELECTRICIAN'S SAFETY KIT

Each electrician should be supplied with a minimum list of electrical safety equipment. The list given in Table 2.33 should be considered the minimum. This represents the minimum requirement for an electrician's electrical safety. Other equipment should be added on an as-needed basis.

TABLE 2.33 Minimum Safety Equipment for Electricians*

- Rubber insulating gloves with leather protectors and protective carrying bags. Glove voltage classes should be consistent with the voltages around which the electrician is expected to work. Recommend one set of class 0 gloves and one set suitable for the highest voltage which the electrician will encounter
- Rubber insulating sleeves. Quantities and voltage classes consistent with the rubber gloves described above
- Rubber insulating blankets. Quantities and voltage classes consistent with the systems around which the electrician will be working
- Safety voltage tester. One each low-voltage plus one medium- or high-voltage unit
- Padlocks, multiple-lock devices, and lockout tags
- Hard hats, ANSI standard Z89.1 class B
- Safety glasses with full side shields, ANSI standard Z87.1 glasses suitable for thermal protection
- Warning signs—"Danger—High Voltage"—and others as required—red barrier tape with white stripe
- Safety ground cables as required
- Flame retardant work clothing—minimum 6 oz per yard
- Flame retardant flash suit—10 oz per yard with full head protection and three-quarter length coat
- Safety electrical one-line diagram

* *Note:* This listing is for electrical hazards only. Other protection such as ear protection, fire extinguishers, and flashlights should be supplied as required.

CHAPTER 3

SAFETY PROCEDURES AND METHODS

INTRODUCTION

The way work is performed in or around an electrical power system is just as important as the safety equipment that is used. Proper voltage measurement can mean the difference between life and death. Standing in the right place during switching operations can minimize or eliminate the effects of an electric arc and proper application of safety grounds can prevent an accidental reenergization from becoming a fatality.

This chapter summarizes many industry-accepted practices for working on or around energized electric power circuits. The methods and techniques covered in this section should be used as guidelines. Local work rules and regulatory standards always take precedence. Note that any and all safety procedures should be reviewed at least annually. System changes, employee reassignments, or accidents should be considered excellent reasons to modify existing procedures or to implement new procedures.

Safety is the one, truly personal concern in an electric power system. In the majority of electrical accidents, the injured victim was the so-called last link in the chain. The use of proper procedures and/or proper safety equipment could have prevented the accident. Equipment and procedures can be provided, but only the individual employee can make the decision to use them. Employees must be impressed with the knowledge that only they can make this final decision—a decision which may truly be life or death.

THE SIX-STEP SAFETY METHOD

Table 3.1 lists six important steps to practicing safe behavior and will serve as the foundation for a personnel safety philosophy. If implemented, this method will greatly enhance the safe and efficient performance of electrical work.

Each individual is most responsible for his or her own safety. The steps listed in Table 3.1 are all individual steps that can be taken by everyone who works on or around electric power circuits and conductors.

TABLE 3.1 Six-Step Safety Method

- Think—be aware
- Understand your procedures
- Follow your procedures
- Use appropriate safety equipment
- Ask if you are unsure
- Do not answer if you do not know

Think—Be Aware

Many accidents could have been prevented if the injured victim had concentrated on the safety aspects of the job. Thinking about personal or job-related problems while working on or near energized conductors is a one-way ticket to an accident. Always stay alert to the electrical hazards around the work area.

Understand Your Procedures

Every company has defined safety procedures which are to be followed. Each worker should be thoroughly familiar with all the safety procedures that affect his or her job. Knowledge of the required steps and the reasons for those steps can save a life.

Follow Your Procedures

Although, in the past, some facilities have allowed the violation of safety procedures in the name of production, such actions have invariably proven to be costly in terms of human suffering and/or death. Violation of safety procedures without good cause should be a discharge offense. What constitutes "good cause" must be decided on a local basis; however, excuses of lesser significance than immediate danger to life should not be acceptable.

Use Appropriate Safety Equipment

No matter how meticulous workers are, accidents—unpreventable accidents—do occasionally happen. Equipment failures, lightning strikes, switching surges, and other such events can cause shock, arc, or blast. Also, sometimes it becomes necessary for employees to work on or very close to energized conductors which increases the chance of accidental contact.

Because of these reasons appropriate safety equipment should be used anytime workers are exposed to the possibility of one of the three electrical hazards. Remember that nothing is sadder than an accident report which explains that the dead or injured worker was not wearing safety equipment.

Ask If You Are Unsure

Ignorance kills and injures many people each year. No one should ever get fired for asking a question—especially if it is a safety-related question. Anyone who is uncertain about a particular situation should be encouraged to ask questions which should then be answered by a qualified person immediately and to the fullest extent possible.

Do Not Answer If You Do Not Know

No one should answer a question if they are not certain of the answer. Self-proclaimed experts should keep their opinions to themselves.

SAFE SWITCHING OF POWER SYSTEMS

Introduction

The most basic safety procedure is to de-energize the parts of the system to which workers may be exposed. This procedure virtually eliminates the hazards of shock, arc, and blast. De-energizing, also called *clearing,* involves more than simply turning the switches off. To ensure maximum safety, de-energizing procedures that are precise for each situation should be written.

The following sections discuss the proper safety techniques for operation of various types of equipment and provide de-energizing and reenergizing procedures which may be used as the basis for the development of site-specific procedures. Please note that specific procedures may vary depending on the application and type of equipment. Refer to manufacturer's and/or local facility procedures for specific information. The methods given in these sections should be considered minimum requirements. Please note that these procedures assume that the device is being operated when one or both sides are energized.

Caution:

- Switching of electric power should only be carried out by qualified personnel who are familiar with the equipment and trained to recognize and compensate for the safety hazards associated with that equipment.
- Non-load-interrupting devices—that is, devices which are not intended to interrupt any current—should never be used to interrupt current flow.

When to De-energize

As a general rule, conductors should be de-energized anytime that personnel must work on or near them. However, this is not always possible. Conductors may be left energized under the following circumstances:

1. If de-energizing introduces an additional or greater safety hazard, the conductors may be left energized. If, for example, de-energizing the system turns off the lights or safety-related ventilation to the work area, the system may be left energized.
2. If the nature of the work requires that the system be energized, power may be left on. Troubleshooting a circuit is one example of such a situation.
3. If de-energization will shut down a major, continuous process system, the circuits may be worked while still energized. To satisfy this requirement, it must be

shown that the work to be performed must be done. Typical requirements for such energized work include safety- or hazard-related work.

If the employees must work on or around energized conductors, they must employ the requisite safety equipment and procedures to minimize the risk.

Operating Medium-Voltage Switchgear

General Description.   Figures 3.1 through 3.5 illustrate various types of medium-voltage switchgear and the breakers used in them. In this style of gear, the circuit breaker rolls into the switchgear on wheels as shown in Fig. 3.2 or on a sliding type of racking mechanism as shown in Fig. 3.5. The opening and closing of the breaker is performed electrically using a front-panel–mounted, pistol-grip type of control. Turning the grip in one direction (usually counterclockwise) opens the breaker, and turning it in the other direction closes it.

The breaker connects to the bus and the line via a set of disconnects, visible at the top of Fig. 3.2 and on the right side of Fig. 3.5. When the breaker is open, it can be moved toward the front of the cubicle so it disconnects from the bus and line. This action is referred to as *racking* the breaker. The breaker may be completely removed from the switchgear, or it may be put into two or more auxiliary positions. Racking a circuit breaker is accomplished using removable cranks. These cranks may be of a rotary type or a lever bar that is used to "walk" the breaker from the cubicle.

Most switchgear have two auxiliary positions: the *test* position and the *disconnected* position. In the test position, the breaker is disconnected from the bus; how-

FIGURE 3.1   Medium-voltage metal-clad switchgear. (*Courtesy Westinghouse Electric.*)

FIGURE 3.2   Circuit breaker used in switchgear shown in Fig. 3.1. (*Courtesy Westinghouse Electric.*)

FIGURE 3.3   Switchgear of Fig. 3.1 with door open showing circuit breaker cubicle. (*Courtesy Westinghouse Electric.*)

FIGURE 3.4 Metal-clad, medium-voltage switchgear for vacuum-type circuit breakers. (*Courtesy General Electric.*)

FIGURE 3.5 Medium-voltage, vacuum interrupter circuit breaker used in switchgear of Fig. 3.4. (*Courtesy General Electric.*)

ever, its control power is still applied through a set of secondary disconnects. This allows technicians to operate the breaker for maintenance purposes. In the disconnected position, the breaker is completely disconnected; however, it is still in the switchgear.

For many types of switchgear, the front panel provides worker protection from shock, arc, and blast. This means that the switchgear is designed to contain arc and blast as long as the door is properly closed and latched.

Closed-Door Operation. Table 3.2 lists the recommended safety equipment to be used by operators when performing both closed-door and open-door switching on medium-voltage switchgear. Note that both the primary operator and backup operator should be wearing the recommended clothing (Fig. 3.6). The primary operator is the worker who actually manipulates the handle which opens and/or closes the circuit breaker. The backup operator's responsibility is to back up the primary operator in the event there is a problem. The backup operator may be optional in some facilities.

TABLE 3.2 Recommended Minimum Safety Equipment for Operating Metal-clad Switchgear

---

Closed door
- Hard hat—ANSI type B
- Safety glasses with side shields
- Flame retardant work clothing (4 oz/yd or more)

Open door
- Hard hat—ANSI type A or B
- Rubber gloves with leather protectors
- Flame retardant flash suit with full head and face protection (7 oz/yd or more)

Note: Closed door means that the front safety panels are closed and latched. If the front panels are not designed to contain blast and arc, then *open-door* equipment should be worn.

To operate the switchgear with a closed door, the following steps apply:

1. The primary operator stands to the side of the cubicle containing the breaker to be operated. The side to which he or she stands should be determined by which side the operating handle is on. If the handle is in the middle, the operator should stand on the hinge or the handle side of the door depending on which side is stronger. (Refer to the manufacturer.)

2. The primary operator faces away from the gear.

3. The backup operator stands even farther from the cubicle, facing the primary operator.

4. The primary operator reaches across to the operating handle and turns it to open or close the breaker. Note that the primary operator continues to keep his or her face turned away from the gear. Some operators prefer to use a hot stick or a rope for this operation. This keeps the arms as far as possible from any hazard.

5. If the breaker can be racked with the door closed, and if the breaker is to be racked away, the primary operator inserts the racking handle. In this operation, the primary operator may have to face the breaker cubicle.

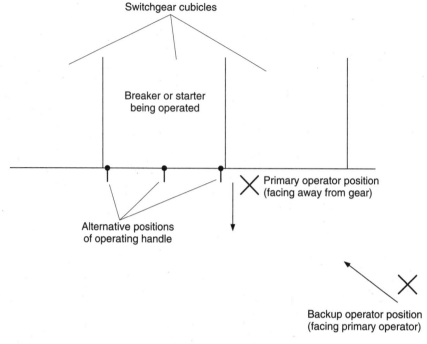

FIGURE 3.6   Proper position for operating electrical equipment (top view).

6. If lockout-tagout procedures are required, the primary operator places the necessary tags and/or locks.

Open-Door Operation.   Refer to Table 3.2 for a minimum listing of safety equipment for this operation. If the door must be open for racking the breaker away from or onto the bus, the following steps should be observed:

1. The breaker is opened as described earlier under Closed-Door Operation.
2. The primary operator opens the cubicle door and racks the breaker to the desired position.
3. If lockout-tagout procedures are required, the primary operator places the necessary tags and/or locks.

Operating Low-Voltage Switchgear

General Description.   With some exceptions, the operation of low-voltage switchgear is very similar to the operation of medium-voltage gear. Figures 3.7 through 3.10 illustrate various types of low-voltage switchgear and the breakers used in them.

In this style of gear, the circuit breaker rolls into the switchgear on a sliding type of racking mechanism as in Fig. 3.10. The circuit breaker is tripped by the release of a powerful set of springs. Depending on the breaker the springs are released either

FIGURE 3.7 Low-voltage metal-clad switchgear.
(*Courtesy General Electric.*)

manually or electrically using a front panel button or control switch. The springs may be charged manually or electrically, again depending on the breaker.

The breakers may be closed either with another set of springs or by means of a manual closing handle. The springs for spring-operated breakers may be charged either manually or electrically. For example, the breaker shown in Fig. 3.8c is a manually operated breaker. The large gray handle is cranked several times to charge the closing spring. When the spring is fully charged, the breaker may be closed by depressing a small, mechanical button on the face of the breaker. Tripping the breaker is accomplished by depressing another pushbutton. Other breakers have different means of opening and closing.

Low-voltage breakers connect to the bus and the line via a set of disconnects, visible on the right side of Fig. 3.8b. When the breaker is open, it can be moved toward the front of the cubicle so that it disconnects from the bus and line. This action is referred to as *racking* the breaker. Racking the larger-size low-voltage breakers is accomplished using removable cranks. These cranks are usually of a rotary type. The breaker may be completely removed from the switchgear, or it may be put into two or more auxiliary positions. Smaller low-voltage breakers are racked by simply pulling or pushing them.

Like medium-voltage switchgear, most low-voltage switchgear have two auxiliary positions (*test* and *disconnected*). In the test position, the breaker is discon-

AKR-6D-75
(a)

AKR-5C-75
(b)

AKS-5A-50
(c)

FIGURE 3.8 Low-voltage circuit breaker used in the switchgear shown in Fig. 3.7. (*Courtesy General Electric.*)

FIGURE 3.9 Low-voltage metal enclosed switchgear. (*Type R switchgear manufactured by Electrical Apparatus Division of Siemens Energy and Automation, Inc.*)

FIGURE 3.10 Low-voltage power circuit breaker racked completely away from the bus. (*Type RL circuit breaker manufactured by Electrical Apparatus Division of Siemens Energy and Automation, Inc.*)

nected from the bus; however, its control power and/or auxiliary switches are still applied through a set of secondary disconnects. This allows technicians to operate the breaker for maintenance purposes. In the disconnected position, the breaker is completely disconnected; however, it is still in the switchgear.

For many types of switchgear, the front panel provides worker protection from shock, arc, and blast. This means that the switchgear is designed to contain arc and blast as long as the door is properly closed and latched.

Closed-Door Operation. The closed-door operation of low-voltage breakers is virtually identical to the closed-door operation of medium-voltage circuit breakers. Table 3.2 lists the recommended safety equipment to be used by operators when performing both closed-door and open-door switching on low-voltage switchgear. Note that both the primary operator and backup operator should be wearing the recommended clothing (Fig. 3.6).

The primary operator is the worker who actually manipulates the handle which opens and/or closes the circuit breaker. The backup operator's responsibility is to back up the primary operator in the event there is a problem. The backup operator may be optional in some facilities.

To operate the switchgear with a closed door, the following steps apply:

1. If the breaker requires manual spring charging, the primary operator may face the breaker to obtain the necessary leverage on the cranking handle.

2. After the springs are charged, the primary operator stands to the side of the cubicle containing the breaker to be operated. The side to which he or she stands should be determined by which side the operating handle is on. If the handle is in the middle, the operator should stand on the hinge or the handle side of the door depending on which side is stronger. (Refer to the manufacturer.)

3. The primary operator faces away from the gear.

4. The backup operator stands even farther from the cubicle, facing the primary operator.

5. The primary operator reaches across to the operating buttons or handle and operates them to open or close the breaker. Note that the primary operator continues to keep his or her face turned away from the gear. Some operators prefer to use a hot stick or a rope for this operation. This keeps the arms as far as possible from any hazard.

6. If the breaker can be racked with the door closed, and if the breaker is to be racked in or out, the primary operator inserts the racking handle and turns it. Note that breakers which are racked manually cannot be racked with the door closed. In this operation the primary operator may have to face the breaker cubicle.

7. If lockout-tagout procedures are required, the primary operator places the necessary tags and/or locks.

Open-Door Operation.   Refer to Table 3.2 for a minimum listing of safety equipment for this operation. If the door must be open for racking the breaker, the following steps should be observed:

1. The breaker is opened as described earlier under Closed-Door Operation.

2. The primary operator opens the cubicle door and racks the breaker to the desired position.

3. If lockout-tagout procedures are required, the primary operator places the necessary tags and/or locks.

Operating Molded-Case Breakers and Panelboards

General Description.   Molded-case circuit breakers are designed with a case that completely contains the arc and blast of the interrupted current as shown in Fig. 3.11. Such breakers are permanently mounted in individual enclosures or panelboards (Fig. 3.12) along with many other such breakers.

Molded-case breakers have a three-position operating handle—open, closed, and tripped. When the operator opens the breaker, he or she does so by moving the operating handle to the open position. Likewise the close operation is accomplished by moving the handle to the close position.

When the breaker trips via its internal automatic protective devices, the handle moves to the tripped position. The trip position is normally an intermediate position between the full-closed and full-open positions. After a trip operation, the breaker cannot be operated until the handle is moved forcefully to the open position. This

FIGURE 3.11   Various molded-case circuit breakers. (*Courtesy Westing-house Electric*).

FIGURE 3.12   Panelboards equipped with molded-case circuit breakers. (*Courtesy McGraw-Hill, Inc.*)

action resets the internal tripping mechanism and reengages the manual operating mechanism.

Operation.   *Caution:* Circuit breakers should not be used for the routine energizing and de-energizing of circuits unless they are manufactured and marked for such purpose. They may be used for occasional or unusual disconnect service.

TABLE 3.3 Recommended Minimum Safety Equipment for Operating Molded-Case Circuit Breakers

---

- Hard hat—ANSI type A or B
- Safety glasses with side shields
- Flame retardant work clothing (4 oz/yd or more)
- Hand protection—leather or flame retardant gloves (do not need to be insulating)

Table 3.3 lists the minimum recommended safety equipment to be worn when operating molded-case circuit breakers, and Fig. 3.13 illustrates the proper position for the operation. Notice that a backup operator is not required for this procedure; however, secondary assistance is always a good practice. The procedure can be summarized as follows:

1. The operator stands to the side of the breaker and/or panel, facing the panel. The operator may stand to either side depending on the physical layout of the area.
2. The operator grasps the handle with the hand closest to the breaker.
3. The operator turns his or her head away from the breaker and then firmly moves the operating handle to the desired position.
4. If locks or tags are required, they are placed on the breaker using the types of equipment as described in Chap. 2.

Panel, switch, or control

X Operator

Note: Operator turns his/her head when operating the circuit breaker.

FIGURE 3.13   Proper position for operating molded-case circuit breakers, enclosed switches, and motor controls (top view).

Operating Enclosed Switches and Disconnects

General Description.   Figure 3.14 shows several basic types of enclosed switches. These devices are used to connect and/or disconnect circuits. Such devices may be load interrupting or non–load interrupting. If they are non–load interrupting, they must not be operated when current is flowing in the circuit. If you are uncertain as to whether the switches are load interrupting or not, look on the nameplate or check with the manufacturer. The presence of arc interrupters, such as those in Fig. 3.14d, is a good indication that the device is intended to interrupt load current.

These switches are operated by moving the handle. In some units, the handle is bolted or locked in place to prevent inadvertent operation. Enclosed switches have a mechanical interlock that prevents the case from being opened until the handle is in the open position. Qualified personnel may temporarily defeat the interlock if needed for maintenance or troubleshooting purposes. Such switches should not be

(a)

(b)

(c)

(d)

FIGURE 3.14 Various types of low- and medium-voltage, enclosed disconnect switches. (*Courtesy General Electric, Crouse-Hinds Co., and Enton Corporation, Cutler Hammer Products.*)

operated with the door open when load current if flowing. Be very cautious about opening medium-voltage switches.

Operation. The basic operating procedure for such switches is similar to the procedure given for molded-case circuit breakers. *Caution:* Switches should not be used to interrupt load current unless they are intended for that purpose. Refer to the manufacturer's information.

Table 3.4 lists the minimum recommended safety equipment to be worn when operating enclosed switches, and Fig. 3.13 illustrates the proper position for the operation. Notice that a backup operator is not required for this procedure; how-

TABLE 3.4   Recommended Minimum Safety Equipment for
Operating Enclosed Switches and Disconnects

• Hard hat—ANSI type B
• Safety glasses with side shields
• Flame retardant work clothing (4 oz/yd or more)
• Rubber gloves with leather protectors

ever, secondary assistance is always a good practice. The procedure can be summarized as follows:

1. The operator stands to the side of the switch and/or panel, facing the panel. The operator may stand to either side depending on the physical layout of the area.
2. The operator grasps the handle with the hand closest to the switch.
3. The operator turns his or her head away from the switch and then firmly moves the operating handle to the desired position.
4. If locks or tags are required, they are placed on the switch using the types of equipment described in Chap. 2.

Operating Open-Air Disconnects

General Description.   Open-air disconnects may be manually operated or mechanism-operated. Mechanism types (Fig. 3.15) are normally installed as overhead devices in medium-voltage substations or on pole lines. The switch has an operating handle close to the ground which is used to open or close the contacts. At ground level, a metal platform is often provided for the operator to stand on. This platform is bonded to the switch mechanism and to the ground grid or ground rod. The operator stands on the grid; thus the operator's hands and feet are at the same electric potential. Note that the operation of some switches is accomplished by moving the handle in the horizontal plane while others are moved in a vertical direction.

FIGURE 3.15   Mechanism-operated, three-phase, open-air switch. (*Courtesy Alan Mark Franks.*)

Manually operated switches are operated by physically pulling on the blade mechanism. In some cases, such as the one shown in Fig. 3.16, the switch blade is a fuse. The manual operation is accomplished by using a hot stick. Manually operated switches may be located overhead in outdoor installations, or they may be mounted indoors inside metal-clad switchgear.

FIGURE 3.16   Open-air, fused disconnect switch. (*Courtesy General Electric.*)

Operation.   Recommended protective clothing depends upon the type and location of the switch. Table 3.5 lists the minimum recommended safety equipment for operating overhead, mechanism-operated switches such as those shown in Fig. 3.15. Figure 3.17 shows the correct operating position for operating such a switch. *Caution:* Not all open-air switches are designed to interrupt load current. Do not use a non–load interrupting switch to interrupt load current.

TABLE 3.5   Recommended Minimum Safety Equipment for Operating Overhead Mechanism-Operated Switches

---

- Hard hat—ANSI type B
- Safety glasses with side shields
- Flame retardant work clothing (4 oz/yd or more)
- Rubber insulating gloves with leather protectors

FIGURE 3.17 Correct position for operating an overhead, mechanism-operated switch.

The basic operating procedure can be summarized as follows:

1. The operator stands on the metal platform (if available).
2. He or she grasps the operating handle firmly with both hands and moves it rapidly and firmly in the open or close direction as required.
3. If locks or tags are required, they are placed on the mechanism using the types of equipment described in Chap. 2.

Table 3.6 lists the recommended equipment for operation of manually operated open-air switches. Note that the use of flash suits is dependent on the location of the switch. If the switch is on an overhead construction that is outdoors, the worker may

TABLE 3.6   Recommended Minimum Safety Equipment for Operating Manually Operated Open-Air Disconnect Switches

---

- Hard hats—ANSI type B
- Safety glasses with side shields
- Flash suits with protective hood and face shield*
- Rubber insulating glove with leather protectors
- Hot stick of proper length with proper fittings

---

* Flash suit optional for outdoor, overhead switches.

opt to wear flame-resistant clothing instead of a flash suit. Because the operator must use a hot stick to operate this type of switch, he or she must stand directly in front of the switch.

The general operating procedure is as follows:

1. Stand in front of the switch.
2. Carefully insert the hot stick probe into the switch ring.
3. Look away from the switch and pull it open with a swift, firm motion.
4. Since one side of the switch may be hot, locks and tags are not always applied directly to the switch. If the switch is in an indoor, metal-clad enclosure, the lock and tag may be applied to the door of the gear.

Operating Motor Starters

General Description.   With some exceptions, the operation of motor starters is very similar to the operation of low- and medium-voltage gear. Figure 3.18 shows a single motor starter mounted in a cabinet suitable for mounting on a wall.

FIGURE 3.18   Combination motor starter in individual metal-clad cabinet.

In the motor control center, the starter moves on a mechanism specially designed for the purpose. In either type of construction, the motor is stopped and started by depressing the appropriate button. The starter also has a fused disconnect or a molded-case circuit breaker that is used to disconnect the motor and its circuitry from the power supply.

Motor starters used in motor control centers connect to the bus and the line via a set of disconnects. When the starter is open, it can be moved toward the front of the cubicle so that it disconnects from the bus and line. This action is referred to as *racking*. Racking starters is usually accomplished manually. The starter may be completely removed from the motor control center. Note that large medium-voltage contactors may be operated like medium-voltage circuit breakers.

For many types of motor control centers, the front panel provides worker protection from shock, arc, and blast. This means the motor control center is designed to contain arc and blast as long as the door is properly closed and latched.

Closed-Door Operation. The closed-door operation of motor starters is virtually identical to the closed-door operation of low-voltage circuit breakers. Table 3.2 lists the recommended safety equipment to be used by operators when performing both closed-door and open-door switching on motor starters. Note that both the primary operator and backup operator should be wearing the recommended clothing (Fig. 3.6). The primary operator is the worker who actually manipulates the handle that opens and/or closes the motor starter. The backup operator's responsibility is to back up the primary operator in the event there is a problem. The backup operator may be optional in some facilities.

To operate the starter with a closed door the following steps apply:

1. Depress the stop button to stop the motor.

2. After the motor is stopped, the primary operator stands to the side of the cubicle containing the starter to be operated. The side to which he or she stands should be determined by which side the operating handle is on. If the handle is in the middle, the operator should stand on the hinge side or the handle side of the door depending on which side is stronger. (Refer to the manufacturer.)

3. The primary operator faces away from the gear. *Note:* If the operating handle of the disconnect has a very tight operating mechanism, the primary operator may face the motor starter to obtain the necessary leverage on the cranking handle.

4. The backup operator stands even farther from the cubicle, facing the primary operator.

5. The primary operator reaches across to the operating handle and operates it to open or close the starter disconnect. Note that the primary operator continues to keep his or her face turned away from the gear. Some operators prefer to use a hot stick or a rope for this operation. This keeps the arms as far as from any hazard.

6. If the starter can be racked with the door closed (an unusual configuration), and if the starter is to be racked in or out, the primary operator inserts the racking handle and turns it. Note that starters which are racked manually cannot be racked with the door closed. In this operation, the primary operator may have to face the breaker cubicle.

7. If lockout-tagout procedures are required, the primary operator places the necessary tags and/or locks.

Open-Door Operation. Refer to Table 3.2 for a minimum listing of safety equipment for this operation. If the door must be open for racking the starter, the following steps should be observed:

1. The motor is stopped as described earlier under Closed-Door Operation.

2. The primary operator opens the cubicle door and racks the starter to the desired position.

3. If lockout-tagout procedures are required, the primary operator places the necessary tags and/or locks.

ENERGY CONTROL PROGRAMS

An energy control program is a procedure for the proper control of hazardous energy sources. It should include a listing of company-approved steps for the proper and safe energizing and de-energizing of energy isolation devices as well as general company policy statements on policies with respect to preferred methods of operation. Energy control programs fall into two categories—general and specific.

General Energy Control Programs

Overview.   A general energy program is one which is inherently generic in nature. Its steps are broad-based and designed in such a way that the program can be used as a procedure for a wide variety of equipment types. General energy programs should be used only when the equipment being isolated meets all the following criteria:

- The equipment can be disabled, so it has no potential for the release of stored or residual energy after shutdown.
- The equipment is supplied from a single energy source which can be readily identified and isolated.
- The equipment is completely de-energized and deactivated by the isolation and locking out procedure.
- No employees are allowed to work on or near the equipment until it has been tagged and locked. (See the Tagout-Lockout section later in this chapter.)
- A single lockout device will achieve a locked out condition.
- The isolating circuit breakers or switches are under the exclusive control of the employee(s) who placed the lock and tag.
- De-energizing and working on the equipment does not create a hazard for other employees.
- There have been no accidents involving unexpected activation or reenergization of the equipment during previous servicing.

Basic Energy Control Rules

- The safest and securest method to protect personnel from the electrical hazard is to de-energize the conductors which they must work on or near. De-energization is the preferred method.
- If conductors cannot be de-energized, safety equipment and safety-related work practices must be used to protect personnel exposed to the energized conductors.
- Before personnel are allowed to work on or near any exposed, de-energized conductors, the circuit breakers and/or disconnect switches must be locked and tagged to prevent their inadvertent operation.

- All personnel should be instructed to never operate or attempt to operate any circuit breaker and/or disconnect switch when it is tagged and/or locked.
- Only authorized, qualified, and trained personnel should be allowed to operate electric equipment.
- Locks and tags should be removed only by the personnel that placed them. Two exceptions may apply under the following situations:

    1. If the worker who placed the lock and tag is not available, his or her lock and tag may be removed by a qualified person who is authorized to perform such an action. This procedure is often called *bypassing control* as the person who removes the lock and tag is, in fact, bypassing the authority (control) of the person whose tag is being removed.
    2. Some facilities may authorize the concept of a group lock. A group lock is placed by an authorized shift worker, such as the shift operator, and may be removed by another authorized shift worker. This activity should not be used to prevent any employee from placing his or her tag and lock on energy-isolating devices that may feed conductors which they must work on or near.

De-energizing Equipment.   The general energy program for de-energizing equipment should include the following steps:

1. Before beginning the process, carefully identify the voltage levels and short circuit capabilities of the portion of the system which will be de-energized. This information serves to establish the level of the hazard to all personnel.
2. Notify all employees who will be affected by the de-energization that the system is to be de-energized.
3. Perform necessary checks and inspections to ensure that de-energizing the equipment will not introduce additional safety hazards, for example, de-energizing safety-related ventilation systems.
4. Shut down all processes being fed by the electric system which is to be de-energized.
5. Open the selected circuit breaker and/or switch.
6. Rack the circuit breaker away from the bus if it is of the type that can be manipulated in this manner.
7. Release stored energy from springs, hydraulic systems, or pneumatics.
8. Discharge and ground any capacitors located in the de-energized portions of the system.
9. Apply tags and/or locks.
10. Attempt to operate the breaker and/or switch to make certain that the locks are preventing operation. If a motor starter is involved, press the start button to make certain the motor will not start.
11. Measure the voltage on the conductors to which personnel will be exposed.
12. Notify personnel that the system is safely de-energized, locked, and tagged.

Reenergizing Equipment.   Reenergization of systems is considered to be more hazardous than de-energization. While the equipment has been out of service, personnel have grown used to its de-energized voltage status. In addition, tools and/or other equipment may have been inadvertently left on or near exposed conductors.

Because of these factors, the same type of rigorous steps should be followed during reenergization.

1. All personnel should be notified that the system is to be reenergized and warned to stay clear of circuits and equipment.

2. A trained, qualified person should conduct all tests and visual inspections necessary to verify that all tools, electric jumpers, shorts, grounds, and other such devices have been removed and that the circuits are ready to be reenergized.

3. Close and secure all cabinet doors and other safety-related enclosures.

4. Because the tests and inspections may have required some time, the personnel warnings should be repeated.

5. Locks and tags should be removed by the personnel that placed them.

6. If breakers were racked into disconnected positions, they should be racked in the connected position.

7. Make final checks and tests, and issue final warnings to all personnel.

8. Reenergize the system by closing and reconnecting breakers and switches. These operations are normally carried out in the reverse order of how they were opened.

Procedures Involving More than One Person.   When more than one person is required to lock and tag equipment, each person will place his or her own personal lock and tag on the circuit breakers and/or switches. The placement of multiple locks and tags on equipment is often called *ganging*. Since few circuit breakers or switches have the ability to accept multiple locks and tags, this procedure can take one of two common approaches.

1. A multiple-lock hasp may be applied to the breaker or switch. Such hasps will accept up to six locks. If more than six locks are required, multiple-lock hasps may be cascaded.

2. A lock box may be used. In such an operation, the lock is applied to the breaker or switch and the key is then placed inside the lock box. The lock box is then secured by the use of a multiple-lock hasp. This approach is used when the presence of many locks on the switch or breaker might cause operational problems.

After the work has been completed, each employee removes his or her lock from the lock box.

Specific Energy Control Programs

When a part of the system or piece of equipment does not meet all the criteria laid out in the overview to this section, a specific energy control program should be written. Although the procedures will vary depending on the specifics of the installation, at a minimum the program should include the following information:

- The description of the system and/or equipment which will be de-energized.
- Any controls, such as motor starter pushbuttons, which exist on the equipment.
- The voltages and short circuit capacities of the parts of the system which will be de-energized.
- The circuit breakers, switches, or contactors which are used to de-energize the system.
- The steps that must be used to de-energize the system. The steps should include:

1. The methods and order of operation of the circuit breakers, switches, etc.
2. Any special requirements for the lockout-tagout procedure.
3. Special notifications and safety requirements.

- Reenergizing requirements and procedures.

TAGOUT-LOCKOUT

Definition and Description

Tags are used to identify equipment that has been removed from service for mainte-nance or other purposes. They are uniquely designed and have clear warnings printed on them instructing personnel not to operate the equipment. Locks are applied to de-energized equipment to prevent accidental or unauthorized operation. Locks and tags are normally applied together; however, some special circumstances may require the use of a tag without a lock and/or a lock without a tag. See Chap. 2 for a detailed description of the construction of safety locks and tags.

Employers should develop a written specification which clearly defines the lockout-tagout rules for the facility. This specification should be kept on file and reviewed periodically to ensure that it is kept up to date. The following sections define some of the elements that should be included in the specification.

When to Use Locks and Tags

Locks and tags should be applied to circuit breakers, switches, or contactors when-ever personnel will be exposed to the conductors which are normally fed by those devices. The application of the tags will warn and inform other employees that the equipment is not available for service, who applied the tag, and why the tag was applied. The lock will prevent the operation of the breaker, switch, or contactor so that the circuit cannot be accidently reenergized.

Minor inspections, adjustments, measurements, and other such servicing activi-ties which are routine, repetitive, and integral to the use of the equipment do not require the placement of locks and tags unless one of the following conditions exist:

1. Guard, insulation, or other safety devices are required to be removed or bypassed.
2. An employee is required to place his or her body into close proximity with an exposed, energized electric conductor.

Locks and tags do not need to be used on plug and cord connected equipment as long as the cord and plug stay under the exclusive control of the employee who is exposed to the electrical hazard.

Locks without Tags or Tags without Locks

Tags may be used without locks under the following conditions:

1. The interrupting device is not designed to accept a lock.
2. An extra means of isolation is employed to provide one additional level of pro-tection. Such an extra procedure might take the form of an additional open point such as removing a fuse or disconnecting a wire or the placement of safety grounds to provide an equipotential work area.

Locks may be used without tags under the following conditions:

1. The de-energization is limited to only one circuit or piece of equipment.
2. The lockout lasts only as long as the employee who places the lock is on site and in the immediate area.

Rules for Using Locks and Tags

All electric equipment with the capability to be reenergized and harm employees shall be safely isolated by means of a lock and tag during maintenance, repair, or modification of the equipment.

When two or more crafts must both have access to the equipment, authorized employees from both crafts shall place locks and tags on behalf of the members of their craft. This practice is referred to as *ganging*. This should not be construed to limit the right of any employee to place his or her individual lock and tag on the equipment.

Responsibilities of Employees

Employees who are authorized to place locks and tags have certain responsibilities which they must exercise when placing those tags.

- The system must be surveyed to ensure that all sources of power to the system have been identified.
- All the isolating equipment (circuit breakers, switches, etc.) must be identified and correlated with the portions of the system to which they apply.
- The voltage level and short circuit magnitude for each part of the system to be de-energized must be determined. This step helps to assess the hazard to individuals who will be exposed to the de-energized system parts.
- All personnel who will be affected by the outage must be notified. This includes employees who may be served by the electric power or who may work on or around the equipment which will be affected by the outage.
- The employee(s) who place the locks and tags must maintain knowledge and control of the equipment to which they have affixed their locks and tags.

When locks and tags are removed, authorized, qualified employees must perform certain tasks, including the following:

1. Notify all affected personnel the system is going to be reenergized.
2. If appropriate, in a gang lock situation, make certain that all authorized employees are prepared to remove their locks and tags.
3. Inspect and/or test all parts of the system to make certain that they are ready to be reenergized.

Note: See the General Energy Control Program discussed previously for more information about these requirements.

Sequence

The following steps should be followed when shutting down an energized electric system:

1. Motors and other operational equipment should be shut down using normal or emergency procedures as required. During the shutdown process personnel safety must be the prime consideration.
2. All isolating equipment (circuit breakers, switches, and/or contactors) should be opened.
3. Isolating equipment that is capable of being racked out should be racked to the disconnected position.
4. Stored energy, such as closing/tripping springs, hydraulic pressure, pneumatic pressure, or other such mechanisms, should be discharged and released.
5. Discharge and ground capacitors.

Lock and Tag Application

Isolating equipment is capable of being locked out if either of the following conditions is met:

- The equipment has an attachment which is an integral part of the equipment, through which the locking device may be passed in such a way as to prevent operation of the isolating equipment.
- The lock can be attached in some other way to prevent operation without dismantling, rebuilding, or replacing the energy-isolating equipment. This might apply to a breaker which cannot be locked open but can be locked in the racked or disconnected position.

Locks and tags should be applied to all isolating equipment which are capable of being locked. Locks and tags should never be applied to selector switches, pushbuttons, or other such control devices.

Isolation Verification

After the locks and tags have been applied, the following steps should be employed to verify that the de-energization was successful:

1. Make certain that all employees are clear of the de-energized conductors.
2. Attempt to reenergize the system by operating the circuit breaker control handles, pushing the switch to close it, or whatever other procedure is appropriate.
3. Using proper procedures and test equipment, measure the voltage on conductors at the point(s) where employee exposure will take place. The voltage should be zero.

Removal of Locks and Tags

Normal Removal. When the work is finished and an employee is ready to remove his or her locks and tags, the following general approaches should be used:

- The work area should be inspected to ensure that nonessential items have been removed and all components are operationally intact.
- The work area should be inspected to ensure that all employees have been safely removed or positioned.

- Remove any specialized equipment such as safety grounds or spring tension blocks.
- Notify all affected employees that locks and tags are to be removed.
- Locks and tags should be removed by the personnel that placed them.

Control Bypass.   If the employee who placed the locks and tags is absent and not available to remove them, and if the locks and tags absolutely must be removed, another authorized employee should assume control of the equipment and remove the absent employee's locks and tags. The following steps should be employed:

1. The employee who is assuming control must make an assessment of the situation and determine that a genuine, critical need exists to remove the absent employee's locks and tags. Examples of such critical needs include:
   a. Immediate operation and/or production requires the equipment to resume operation and avoid general shutdown.
   b. Personnel safety requires restoration of power to the de-energized systems.
   c. Equipment must be temporarily returned to service to allow testing or other such evaluation.
2. The employee assuming control must make every reasonable attempt to contact the absent employee to obtain his or her assessment of the equipment.
3. The employee assuming control must contact other employees who may have knowledge of the availability of the equipment and the advisability of removing the absent employee's locks and tags.
4. The employee assuming control must develop and document a formal conclusion with regard to the decision to remove the absent employee's locks and tags.
5. The employee assuming control must follow the normal removal steps to remove the locks and tags and either reinstall his or her own locks and tags or reenergize the system.
6. The area where the absent employee's locks and tags were removed should be posted with large, easy-to-read signs indicating that the locks and tags have been removed.
7. The employee assuming control must contact the absent employee immediately upon his or her return. The returning employee must be told that his or her locks and tags have been removed and completely updated as to the status of the equipment. The absent employees shall remove the signs posted in step 6.

Figure 3.19 shows a form which may be used to document the control bypass procedure. In this figure the employee who is assuming control is referred to as the authorized controller. The absent employee is referred to as the authorized employee. Notice that each one of the major steps is documented on this form.

Temporary Removal.   Locks and tags may be temporarily removed by the employee who placed them. When doing so, the same steps used in normal removal should be observed.

Safety Ground Application

Safety grounds should be applied as an additional safety measure when equipment is removed from service. The only exception to this is when the nature of the work precludes the use of safety grounds. Procedures like insulation measurement cannot be performed when safety grounds are applied; therefore, they may not be used.

LOCKOUT/TAGOUT CONTROLLER'S BYPASS FORM

DATE _____ TIME _____

LOCATION _____

AUTHORIZED CONTROLLER _____

DEPARTMENT _____

AUTHORIZED EMPLOYEE _____

TO BE BY-PASSED DEPARTMENT _____

DESCRIPTION OF EQUIPMENT OR DEVICE(S) TO BE BY-PASSED _____

_____

NEED FOR BY PASS PROCEDURE _____

_____
_____
_____
_____
_____

EFFORTS TO CONTACT AUTHORIZED EMPLOYEE _____

_____
_____
_____
_____
_____

EFFORTS TO CONTACT OTHER PERSONNEL THAT MAY BE AWARE OF THE
APPLIED LOCKOUT/TAGOUT DETAILS _____

_____
_____
_____
_____
_____

CONTROLLER EVALUATION OF THE SITUATION _____

_____
_____
_____
_____

ACTION TAKEN BY THE CONTROLLER TO RELEASE EQUIPMENT FOR USE

_____
_____
_____
_____
_____

ACTIONS TAKEN TO PROPERLY MARK AND POST EQUIPMENT AND AREA AS
BEING RE-ENERGIZED _____

_____
_____
_____
_____
_____

FIGURE 3.19 Lockout-tagout control bypass form. (*Courtesy Cadick
Professional Services.*)

ACTIONS TAKEN TO NOTIFY EFFECTED EMPLOYEES _____

_____

_____

_____

_____

_____

AUTHORIZED CONTROLLER _____
DEPARTMENT _____ DATE _____

*AUTHORIZED EMPLOYEE _____
DEPARTMENT _____ DATE _____
* To be use after notification of By-Pass

FIGURE 3.19 *(Continued)* Lockout-tagout control bypass form. *(Courtesy Cadick Professional Services.)*

Control Transfer

Lockout-tagout control may be transferred from one employee to another as long as both employees are present. The following steps should be used:

1. The employee relinquishing control follows all steps involved in the normal removal of locks and tags.

2. The employee assuming control follows all steps involved in the normal application of locks and tags.

Nonemployees and Contractors

Nonemployees such as contractors should be required to use a lockout-tagout program which provides the same or greater protection as that afforded by the facilities procedure. Contractors should be required to submit their procedure for review and approval. No work should be allowed until the contractor's lockout-tagout program has been reviewed and approved.

All employees should be familiarized with the contractor's procedure and required to comply with it. Copies of the respective standards should be made available for both contractors and employees.

If the contractor is working on machines or equipment that have not yet been turned over to the facility, the contractor shall be required to lock and tag that equipment if it might operate and endanger employees. The contractor must guarantee the safety of the locked and tagged installation. As an alternative to this procedure, the contractor should be required to allow gang lockout and tagout with employees and contractor personnel.

Lockout-Tagout Training

All employees should be trained in the use, application, and removal of locks and tags. See Chap. 9 for more information on general employee safety training.

Procedural Reviews

The entire lockout-tagout procedure should be reviewed at intervals no longer than 1 year. A review report should be issued which identifies the portions of the procedure which were reviewed, changes which were considered, and changes which were implemented.

VOLTAGE-MEASUREMENT TECHNIQUES

Purpose

No circuit should ever be presumed dead until it has been measured using reliable, prechecked test equipment. Good safety practice and current regulatory standards require that circuits be certified de-energized by measurement as the last definitive step in the lockout-tagout procedure (see Chap. 4).

Instrument Selection

Voltage-measuring instruments should be selected for the voltage level, the application location, short circuit capacity, sensitivity requirements, and the circuit loading requirements of the circuit which is to be measured.

Voltage Level.   The instrument must be capable of withstanding the voltage of the circuit which is to be measured. Use of underrated instruments, even though the circuit is dead, is a violation of good safety practice.

Application Location.   Some instruments are designed for outdoor use only and should not be used in metal-clad switchgear. Always check the manufacturer's information and verify that the instrument is designed for the location in which it is being used.

Internal Short Circuit Protection.   Industrial-grade, safety-rated voltage-measuring instruments are equipped with internal fusing and/or high-resistance elements which will limit the short circuit current in the event the instrument fails internally. Be certain the instrument being used has internal protection with an interrupting/limiting rating that is at least equal to the short circuit capacity of the circuit that is being measured.

Sensitivity Requirements.   The instrument must be capable of measuring the lowest normal voltage that might be present in the circuit which is being measured. If the instrument has two ranges (high and low, for example), be certain to set it on the correct lowest range which applies to the voltage being measured.

Circuit Loading.   A real voltmeter can be represented by an ideal meter in parallel with a resistance. The resistance represents the amount of loading the meter places on the circuit (Fig. 3.20). In the diagram R_S represents that resistance of the system being measured and R_M is the internal resistance of the voltmeter. The voltmeter will read a voltage given by the formula:

$$V_M = V \times \frac{R_M}{R_M + R_S} \qquad (1)$$

If the meter internal resistance is high compared to system resistance, the voltage across the meter will be very close to the actual system voltage. If the meter resis-

Circuit being measured   Voltage measuring instrument

FIGURE 3.20   Equivalent circuit of voltage measurement.

tance is very low compared to the system resistance, the meter will read a lower voltage than actually exists because most of the voltage drop will be across the system resistance instead of the meter resistance. In this second situation, the meter is "loading" the circuit.

If a very low resistance meter is used, the meter may not read a potentially lethal static or inductively coupled voltage. This situation is unacceptable since an inductively coupled or static voltage can be lethal. The meter that is selected for a safety-related voltage measurement must have an internal resistance that is high enough to avoid this problem.

Instrument Condition

Before each use, an instrument must be closely inspected to ensure it is in proper working order and that insulation systems have not been damaged. The case physical condition, probe exposure, lead insulation, fusing, and the operability of the instrument should be verified.

Case Physical Condition.   The case must be free of breaks, cracks, or other damage that could create a safety hazard or misoperation. Broken instruments should be taken out of service until they can be repaired or replaced.

Probe Exposure.   Modern instrument probes have spring-loaded sleeves which cover the probe until forced back. Check to make certain that only the minimum amount of probe required to do the job is exposed.

Lead Insulation Quality.   Carefully inspect the lead insulation to make certain it is not damaged in any way.

Fusing.   Accessible fuses should be checked to be certain that they are correctly installed and have not been replaced by incorrect units.

Operability.   Before each usage, at the beginning of each shift for example, the instrument should be checked to make certain that it is operable. Do not substitute this check for the instrument checks required in the three-step process.

Three-Step Measurement Process

Step 1—Test the Instrument.   Immediately before each measurement, the instrument should be checked on a source which is known to be hot. This step confirms that the instrument is working before the actual circuit verification is made.

The preferred method is to use an actual power system conductor of the same voltage as that being verified. Finding such a circuit is easier when low-voltage measurements are being made; however, even then a hot circuit may not be available. Some manufacturers supply a device which creates a voltage that is sufficient for testing the instrument.

Some instruments intended for measurement of medium voltages have a low-voltage switch setting on them which allows them to be checked on low voltage.

Step 2—Measure the Circuit Being Verified.   After the instrument is tested, the worker then measures the circuit being verified to make certain it is de-energized. The actual wires that should be measured and the techniques to be used are discussed later in this chapter.

Step 3—Retest the Instrument.   After the circuit has been verified, the instrument should be rechecked. This ensures that the instrument was operable both before and after the measurement, thus affirming that a zero measurement is zero and not caused by an inoperable instrument.

What to Measure

As a general rule of thumb, all normally energized conductors should be measured to ground and to each other. The readings to ground should be made whether the system is grounded or not. Note that all readings should be made as close to the point of exposure as possible.

Single-Phase Systems.   The hot wire of single-phase systems should be measured both again neutral and ground. Figure 3.21 shows the points which should be measured.

Two-Phase Systems.   A voltage measurement should be taken between the two hot phases, between each hot phase and neutral (one at a time), and between each hot phase and ground. Figure 3.22 shows the measurement locations for a typical two-phase system.

Three-Phase Systems.   Measure between each of the hot wires, two at a time, between each hot wire and neutral, and between each hot wire and ground. Figure 3.23 shows the measurement locations for a typical three-phase system.

Using Voltage Transformer Secondaries for Voltage Measurements.   Many medium-voltage power systems are equipped with step-down voltage transformers which are used for metering or telemetering purposes. Because of the lower voltage on the secondary, some workers wish to measure the secondary winding voltage to

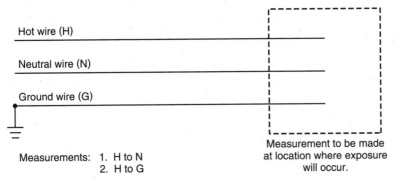

FIGURE 3.21 Measurement points for a single-phase system.

FIGURE 3.22 Measurement points for a single-phase power system.

FIGURE 3.23 Measurement points for a three-phase system.

verify that the primaries are de-energized. Such transformers may be used for safety-related voltage measurements under the following conditions:

1. The transformers can be visually traced and are known to be connected to the system where exposure will occur.

2. The transformers are located close to the part of the system where exposure will occur.

3. The transformer secondaries must be measured both before and after the circuit is de-energized. This verifies that the transformer fuses are not blown, resulting in an erroneous zero voltage reading.

4. A safety ground is applied to the primary circuit of the transformer after the measurement but before personnel contact occurs.

5. All other safety-related techniques should be used as described in the other parts of this chapter.

Caution: This procedure is considered a secondary, nonpreferred method. Do not use this approach unless absolutely necessary.

Using Panel Voltmeters for Voltage Measurements. Panel voltmeters may be used as a general indication of system energization; however, they should not be used for safety-related voltage measurements.

How to Measure

Preparation. Table 3.7 identifies the steps which should precede the actual measurement procedure. The area should be cleared of unnecessary personnel. This will prevent their exposure to arc or blast in the event that a problem occurs. The person making the measurement should wear and use appropriate safety equipment. (Safety equipment information will be covered later in this chapter.)

TABLE 3.7 Voltage Measurement Preparations

- Clear area of unnecessary personnel
- Wear appropriate safety equipment
- Expose conductors to be measured
- Position measuring instrument

After the safety equipment is on, the panels, doors, or other access means should be opened to expose the conductors that are to be measured. The measuring instrument is then carefully positioned. When making medium-voltage measurements with hot sticks, be certain that the hot stick is not contacting your body. The instrument should be securely positioned so that it does not fall to the floor if the leads are inadvertently overextended.

Safety Equipment. Table 3.8 lists the minimum recommended safety equipment to be worn when making low-voltage measurements. Table 3.9 lists equipment for medium-voltage measurements. The flash suit is identified as optional for outdoor, open-air measurements. Although many line personnel do not wear flash suits when performing overhead work, the use of these uniforms is strongly recommended.

TABLE 3.8 Recommended Minimum Safety Equipment for Making Low-Voltage Safety Measurements

---

- Hard hat—ANSI type B
- Safety glasses with side shields
- Low-voltage rubber gloves with leather protectors
- Rubber sleeves (if the measurement requires close proximity to conductors)
- Flame retardant work clothing (4 oz/yd or more)

TABLE 3.9 Recommended Minimum Safety Equipment for Making Medium- and High-Voltage Safety Measurements

---

- Hard hat—ANSI type B
- Safety glasses with side shields
- Rubber insulating gloves with leather protectors
- Rubber sleeves (if measurement requires close proximity to conductors)
- Flash suit with full head protection (7 oz/yd or more)*
- Flame retardant work clothing (4 oz/yd or more)

---

* For metal-clad switchgear indoor and outdoor. Optional for outdoor, open-air measurements.

Measurement.   After all preparations are made and the safety equipment is put on, the measuring instrument should be applied to the conductors. If a measurement to ground is being made, one lead should be connected to the ground first and then the phase connection made. When measuring between two hot wires, the order of connection is unimportant. If a contact instrument is being used, each lead should be carefully placed on the appropriate conductor. The meter or readout is then observed to see if the circuit is hot. If a proximity instrument is being used, it should be moved gradually toward the conductor until it indicates or until the conductor is touched.

PLACEMENT OF SAFETY GROUNDS

Safety Grounding Principles

Safety grounds are conductors which are temporarily applied to de-energized system conductors. They are used to provide a safe zone for personnel working on or around de-energized conductors and to ensure that an accidental reenergization will not cause injury. Power system components should be considered to be energized until safety grounds are in place. Safety grounds should never be placed until the conductors where they are to be installed have been measured and verified to be de-energized.

See Chap. 2 for a detailed description of the design and description of safety grounds. *Caution:* Safety grounds must be properly designed and sized for the conductors and short circuit capacity to which they may be subjected. Refer to Chap. 2 and/or manufacturer's information for specifics.

In the event that the system is accidently reenergized, enormous magnetic forces are exerted on the safety ground wires. The forces can cause the grounds to whip violently and cause injury to personnel. To minimize this effect the safety grounds should be as short as possible.

Safety Grounding Location

Equipotential Grounding.   Safety grounds should be applied in such a way that a
zone of equal potential is formed in the work area. This equipotential zone is formed
when fault current is bypassed around the work area by metallic conductors. Figure
3.24 shows the proper location of safety grounds for three different work situations.
In each of these situations, the worker is bypassed by the low-resistance metallic
conductors of the safety ground.

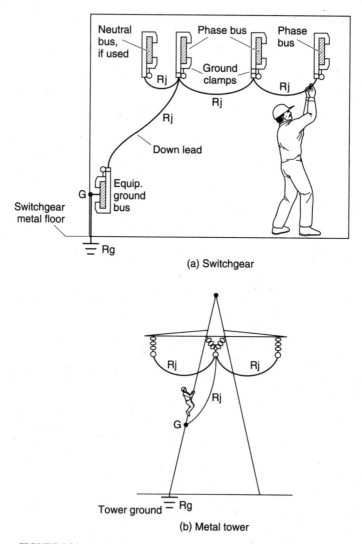

FIGURE 3.24   Application of safety grounds to provide a zone of equal potential.

(c) Wood pole

(d) Electrical equivalent

FIGURE 3.24 *(Continued)* Application of safety grounds to provide a zone of equal potential.

Assume the worker contacts the center phase. With a fault current capacity of 10,000 A, safety ground resistance (R_j) of 0.001 Ω, and worker resistance (R_w) of 500 Ω, the worker will receive only about 20 mA of current flow.

Figure 3.25a through d shows two nonpreferred or incorrect locations for the application of safety grounds. In these diagrams, the worker's body is in parallel with the series combination of the jumper resistance (R_j) and the ground resistance (R_g). The placement of grounds in this fashion greatly increases the voltage drop across the worker's body in the event the circuit is reenergized. Such placements should not be used.

(a)

(b)

FIGURE 3.25 Two incorrect, nonpreferred safety ground configurations.

FIGURE 3.25 *(Continued)* Two incorrect, nonpre-ferred safety ground configurations.

Single-Point versus Two-Point Grounding.   Single-point grounding is the place-ment of only one safety ground set. In this procedure, the safety grounds are placed as close to the point of work as is possible. When possible, the grounds are placed between the worker and the source of electric energy.

Two-point grounding is the placement of two safety ground sets. They are usually placed on opposite sides of the work area; that is, one set is placed "upstream" and one set is placed "downstream" from the workers.

In general, more safety ground sets are better than fewer; however, the safety ground system must provide a zone of equal potential as described in the previous section.

Application of Safety Grounds

Safety Equipment.   Table 3.10 lists the minimum recommended safety equipment that should be worn and used when applying safety grounds. Full shock, arc, and blast protective clothing is required. No matter how carefully the work area is pre-pared, the possibility still exists for error and/or inadvertent reenergization during the application process.

TABLE 3.10   Recommended Minimum Safety Equipment for Applications of Safety Grounds

---

- Hard hat—ANSI type B
- Safety glasses with side shields
- Rubber insulating gloves with leather protectors
- Flash suit with full head protection (7 oz/yd or more)*
- Hot stick with suitable fittings for application of safety ground clamps[†]

---

   * Flash suits may be optional in outdoor, overhead applications.
   [†] Hot sticks may not be usable in cramped switchgear applications. Workers should exercise best safety judgment in such applications.

Notice also that hot sticks are recommended for the actual application process. The use of hot sticks distances the worker from the point of contact and, therefore, minimizes the possibility of injury caused by arc or blast.

Procedure.   The actual application procedure will be different for each specific application. The following steps are recommended.

1. Thoroughly inspect the safety ground set which is to be used. Points to check include
   a. Insulation quality
   b. Condition of conductors
   c. Condition of clamps
   d. Condition of ferrule
   e. Condition of cable-to-ferrule connection
2. Identify the point at which each ground clamp will be connected to the system. Be certain to select points which minimize the amount of slack in the safety grounds. This will minimize the whipping action in the event the system is reenergized.

3. Put on required safety equipment.
4. Measure the system voltage to make certain that the system to be grounded is de-energized. (See the previous sections on voltage measurement.)
5. Make certain that all unnecessary personnel have been cleared from the area.
6. Apply the ground end of the safety ground sets first. (These points are labeled with the letter "G" in Fig. 3.24.)
7. Connect the phase-end safety ground clamp to the hot stick.
8. Firmly contact the de-energized conductor with the phase end of the safety ground.
9. Tighten the grounding clamp firmly. Remember the amount of resistance in the clamp connection can make the difference between a safe connection and a hazardous one.
10. Repeat steps 6 through 8 for each of the phases to be grounded.
11. Record the placement of each safety ground by identification number. (See Control of Safety Grounds in the next section.)

Figure 3.26 shows a worker applying safety grounds to a de-energized system.

Removal of Safety Grounds

Safety Equipment. The removal of safety grounds is no less hazardous than applying them. All the safety equipment listed in Table 3.10 should be worn. Safety grounds should be removed using hot sticks.

FIGURE 3.26 Worker applying safety grounds. (*Courtesy McGraw-Hill, Inc.*)

Procedure. Safety grounds should be removed as follows:

1. Put on all required safety equipment.
2. Remove each of the phase connections one at a time.
3. Remove the ground connection.
4. Check the ground off as being removed.

Remember that when safety grounds are not present, the system should be considered to be energized.

Control of Safety Grounds

Safety grounds must be removed before the power system is reenergized. They must also be inspected periodically and before each use. The following sections describe two methods of controlling the safety ground sets.

Inventory Method. Each safety ground set should be identified with its own unique serial number. The serial number should be etched or impressed on a metal tag which is permanently attached to the safety ground set.

A safety officer should be appointed to control the inventory of safety ground sets. This person will control the use of the safety grounds and is responsible for keeping lists of where the grounds are applied during an outage.

As each safety ground is applied, the safety officer notes its placement on a placement control sheet. As each ground is removed, the officer notes its removal on the sheet. No reenergization is allowed until the safety officer is satisfied that all safety grounds have been removed. Figure 3.27 is a typical safety ground placement control sheet.

The sheet shown in Fig. 3.27 has the minimum required information. Other columns—such as where the ground set is installed, who installed it, and who removed it—may be added as needed.

Visual Method. Some small facilities may not be able to justify the complexity of a control system such as that described in the previous section. A visual control system may suffice for facilities which have only one or two safety grounding sets. In such a system, a brightly colored rope is permanently attached to each grounding set. Nylon ski rope is ideal for this application. The length of the rope should be determined by the applications; however, 3 meters (m) (10 ft) is a good starting point.

At the remote end of the rope, attach a brightly colored warning sign stating "Grounds are Applied." After the safety grounds are attached to the system, the rope should be arranged on the switchgear so that it is easily seen. If it can be arranged, the rope should be placed so the gear cannot be closed up until the rope is removed. The green sign should be placed on the breaker control handle, start pushbutton, or other such device so that it is obviously visible.

When this procedure is used, it is very difficult to reenergize the system with the grounds in place. However, the inventory method is the preferred and recommended method.

SAFETY GROUND PLACEMENT CONTROL SHEET			
Safety Officer:		Outage Date:	
Ground Set ID Number	Date Applied:	Date Removed:	Safety Officer's Initials

FIGURE 3.27 Safety ground placement control sheet.

GENERAL WORK AREA SAFETY

Clearance Distances

Definitions. From time to time employees are required to work close to circuits which, for some reason, cannot be de-energized. In such instances the job should be planned so that workers are not required to approach the energized conductors any closer than is absolutely necessary. Workers who are familiar with the hazards of electricity and trained to avoid those hazards generally should be able to work safely at closer distances than other workers.

The approach distances defined in this section are for persons, any part of their bodies, tools, equipment, or any other conductive object which may make contact with both the conductor and the worker's body at the same time.

Qualified Persons. Qualified persons are those who are familiar with the hazards of electricity and trained to avoid those hazards. Table 3.11 is taken from the Occupational Safety and Health Administration's Safety Related Work Practices Rule. It defines how closely qualified persons are allowed to approach exposed, energized overhead conductors. Qualified persons should not routinely approach any closer than the values given in this table; furthermore, no tool, equipment, or metal object being held by the worker should be allowed any closer than the values in the table.

Note that this table applies to overhead lines. Although no regulatory standard currently applies to horizontal or enclosed conductor exposure, Table 3.11 may be used as a point of departure for the development of local rules.

TABLE 3.11 Approach Distances for Qualified Employees

Voltage range (phase to phase)	Minimum approach distance, in (cm)
300 V and less	Avoid contact
Over 300 V, not over 750 V	1 ft 0 in (30.5 cm)
Over 750 V, not over 2 kV	1 ft 6 in (46 cm)
Over 2 kV, not over 15 kV	2 ft 0 in (61 cm)
Over 15 kV, not over 37 kV	3 ft 0 in (91 cm)
Over 37 kV, not over 87.5 kV	3 ft 6 in (107 cm)
Over 87.5 kV, not over 121 kV	4 ft 0 in (122 cm)
Over 121 kV, not over 140 kV	4 ft 6 in (137 cm)

Unqualified Persons. Since unqualified persons are unable to recognize the hazards of electricity, they are therefore unable to avoid those hazards. Unqualified persons should maintain greater distances than qualified persons. Current regulatory standards specify 10 ft minimum from all overhead lines of 50,000 V or less, phase-to-phase. Table 3.12 identifies recommended clearance distances for unqualified persons.

Alternative Methods. Sometimes work cannot be planned to comply with the approach distance recommendations given in the previous sections. Personnel may be allowed to approach conductors more closely if one of the following conditions is met:

TABLE 3.12 Approach Distances for Unqualified Persons

Circuits 50,000 V and under*	10 ft
Circuits 50,001 to 150,000 V	15 ft

* Voltages are given in phase-to-phase volts.

1. The energized conductors are insulated using blankets, line hose, or other such insulating materials.
2. Insulating barricades are used to physically prevent the worker from contacting the energized conductors.
3. The workers are protected using rubber gloves, sleeves, flash suits, or other such protective equipment.

Barriers and Warning Signs

Barriers and warning signs should be placed to control entrance into a work area where there are exposed energized conductors. The installation of such equipment will vary depending on the layout of the work area. The following general criteria should be applied:

- The signs should be distinctive, easy to read, and posted at all entrances to the work area. The signs should clearly warn personnel of the hazardous or energized condition.
- Barriers and barrier tape should be placed at a height that is easy to see. Three feet or so is a good starting point. Adjust the height as dictated by the specific installation.
- Barriers and barrier tape should be placed so that equipment is not reachable from outside of the barrier. This will prevent the accidental or intentional operation of equipment by personnel not authorized to do so.
- If sufficient work room is not available when barriers are placed, attendants should be used to warn employees of the exposed hazards.

Figure 3.28a shows a sample arrangement for a work area in a switchgear room. The layout given here is for example only; however, the general principles may be used. Key points for this installation are

1. Stanchions are used to provide a firm structure for stringing the barrier tape.
2. Warning signs are placed at both entrances warning personnel that hazards exist inside.
3. Warning signs are also posted on the switchgear itself.
4. Five to ten feet of work clearance is allowed between the tape and the switchgear. This number may vary depending on the space available and the work to be performed.

Figure 3.28b shows a similar barrier system for a hallway lighting panel. The clearance distance here is less because of the need to allow passage down the hallway. Warning signs are used to alert personnel to the hazard.

Illumination

Personnel must not reach into or work in areas which do not have adequate illumination. Although de-energization is the preferred method of eliminating electrical hazards, if de-energization also eliminates illumination, alternative safety measures must be employed.

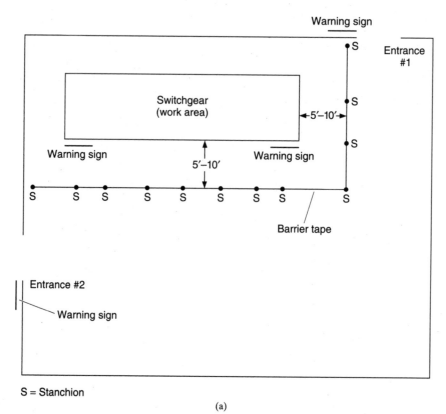

S = Stanchion

(a)

FIGURE 3.28 (*a*) Barriers and warning signs around a work area in a switchgear room with two entrances.

Conductive Clothing and Materials

When working on or around energized conductors, personnel should remove (preferred) and/or use insulating tape to wrap watches, rings, keys, knives, necklaces, and other such conductive items they have on their bodies.

Conductive materials such as wire, tools, and ladders should be handled in such a way that they do not come into contact with energized conductors. If such material cannot be kept at a safe clearance distance (see section on Approach Distances), they should be wrapped or insulated. Metal ladders should never be used in electrical installations.

Confined Work Spaces

A complete coverage of confined work spaces is beyond the scope of this handbook. Electrical safety hazards in confined work spaces should be avoided. The following steps should be employed:

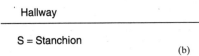

(b)

FIGURE 3.28 (*b*) Barriers and warning signs around a lighting panel which is open for work.

1. If safe approach distances cannot be maintained, energized conductors should be covered or barricaded so personnel cannot contact them.
2. Doors, hatches, and swinging panels should be secured so that they cannot swing open and push personnel into energized conductors.
3. Confined work spaces should be well ventilated to prevent the concentration of gases that may explode in the presence of an electric arc.
4. Exits should be clearly marked. Employees should be familiarized with the exits before entering the confined work space.
5. Confined work spaces must be well illuminated so that all hazards are clearly visible.

TOOLS AND TEST EQUIPMENT

General

Many electrical accidents involve failures of electric tools or test equipment. Such failures take a number of different forms including insulation failure, open ground return wires, internal shorts to ground, and overheating. These problems can be aggravated or even caused by using tools or test equipment improperly. For example, if extension cords not designed for use in wet areas are used in standing water, severe electric shock can result. The following general procedures should be employed when using electric tools or test equipment:

1. Tools and test equipment should be closely inspected before each use. (See section on Visual Inspection.)

2. Cord-connected tools should never be lifted or handled by their power cord. If tools must be lifted, a rope should be attached.

3. Grounded tools and equipment must have a continuous metallic connection from the tool ground to the supply ground.

4. If a grounded supply system is not available, double-insulated tools should be used.

5. Three-wire connection plugs should never be altered to fit into two-wire sockets.

6. So-called cheater plugs should not be used unless the third wire of the plug can be securely connected to the supply ground.

7. Locking types of plugs should be securely locked before the tool is energized.

8. Cords and tools should not be used in a wet environment unless they are specifically designed for such an application.

Authorized Users

Only authorized, trained persons should be allowed to use electric tools and test equipment. The training should include all the necessary inspection techniques for the tools that will be employed, plus recognition of the common types of safety hazards that are peculiar to the tool being used.

Visual Inspections

Tools and test equipment should be closely inspected before each use. This inspection should occur at the beginning of each work shift and again anytime a problem is suspected. The inspector should look for the following types of problems:

- Missing, corroded, or damaged prongs on connecting plugs
- Frayed, worn, or missing insulation on connecting cords and/or test leads
- Improperly exposed conductors
- Bent or damaged prongs or test probes
- Excessive exposure on test prongs
- Loose screws or other poorly made electrical connections
- Missing or mis-sized fuses
- Damaged or cracked cases
- Indication of burning, arcing, or overheating of any type

If any of these problems is noted, the tool or test equipment should be removed from service until the problem can be repaired. If repair is not feasible, the tool or test equipment should be replaced.

Electrical Tests

Tools and extension cords should be electrically tested on a monthly basis. The following tests should be performed:

1. *Ground continuity test.* A high current (25 A minimum) should be applied to the tool's ground circuit. The voltage drop on the ground circuit should be no more than 2.5 V.

2. *Leakage test.* This test determines how much current would flow through the operator in the event that the tool's ground circuit were severed.

3. *Insulation breakdown.* This test applies a high voltage (up to 3000 V) to the tools insulation system and then measures the amount of leakage current.

4. *Operational test.* This test applies rated voltage to the tool and determines how much current the tool draws.

If the tool fails any of the above tests, it should be removed from service until it can be repaired. If repair is not possible, the tool or cord should be replaced. Figure 3.29 is a test set designed especially to check the power circuits for cord-connected tools and extension cords.

Wet and Hazardous Environments

Tools and test equipment should only be used in the environments for which they have been designed. If the work area is wet, only tools which are rated for wet work should be used. Fully insulated, waterproof cords should be used if they will be exposed to water.

If work must be performed in explosive environments, the tools used should be sealed or otherwise designed so that electric arcs will not ignite the explosive materials.

FIGURE 3.29 Tool and appliance tester. (*Courtesy AVO Biddle Instruments.*)

THE ONE-MINUTE SAFETY AUDIT

Inattention is one of the major root causes of all accidents. Employees whose attention is distracted by work-related or personal problems are prone to miss obvious signs of impending hazards. To make certain that employees are constantly aware of potential hazards, the steps listed in Table 3.13 should be performed by each worker that enters an area where any of the electrical hazards may be present.

The following nine simple steps should not take more than 1 min to perform, even in a very large electrical facility. Of course, not every step will apply in each and every situation. For example, some electrical rooms have no transformers; therefore, step 5 would not be performed.

1. Notify responsible personnel of your presence in the area. In the event that a problem does occur you may not be able to summon the help that you need. If other personnel are aware of your presence in the area, they will know to come to your aid.

2. Listen for any abnormally loud or unusual noises. Sniff for unusual odors. Transformers and other electric equipment do make noise during normal operation. When such noises become too loud or change tone, trouble may be indicated. Burning odors or the smell of ozone can also be signs of incipient faults.

3. Locate all emergency exits. Electrical accidents are often accompanied by smoke, fire, and noise. Such conditions make it difficult or impossible to find the exits. If exit locations are committed to memory before any problems occur, the worker is more likely to remember them after the problem occurs.

4. Locate all fire alarms and telephones. The same reasoning applies here as locating emergency exits. During an emergency the location of fire alarms and telephones should be a reflex.

5. Inspect all transformer gauges. Transformers will often warn of impending failures by an increase in pressure, temperature, liquid level, or some combination of all these. An inspection of these elements can warn of a problem before it happens.

6. Locate the station one-line diagram. Switching and other such activities must be carried out in a safe manner. To do so requires that the system one-line diagram be accurate. Few things are more hazardous than opening a switch which is believed to be the source to an energized part of the system and then finding out later that, in fact, it was the wrong switch.

TABLE 3.13 The One-Minute Safety Audit

1. Notify responsible personnel of your presence in the area.
2. Listen for any abnormally loud or unusual noises. Sniff for unusual odors.
3. Locate all emergency exits.
4. Locate all fire alarms and telephones.
5. Inspect all transformer liquid level, temperature, and pressure gauges to make certain that they are within acceptable limits.
6. Locate the station one-line diagram and make certain that it is legible and correct.
7. Make certain that the room is neat and tidy. Generally, electrical facilities should not be used for the storage of equipment.
8. Be certain that all required safety equipment is readily available and easily reached.
9. Check to see that all protective relay and other operational flags are properly reset.

7. Make certain that the room is clean and tidy. Storage of some equipment in an electrical facility is a necessary and valuable procedure. For example, what better place to store electrical safety equipment than close to the gear where it may be needed. Ladders, tools, hot sticks, rubber insulating goods, replacement lights, and other such materials are all candidates for storage in the electrical facility. When such storage does take place, however, it should be done in an orderly and safe fashion. Storage cabinets should be procured for small equipment. Ladders should be hung on racks especially mounted for such a purpose. Wire reels and other such materials should not be in the exit paths.

8. Be certain that all safety equipment is readily available. Workers will often use the excuse that "the safety gear is too far away to justify using it for this short procedure." To eliminate such an excuse, the safety equipment should be readily available. Whether it is brought in with the work crew or stored in the electrical facility, it must be readily available.

9. Check all protective relay flags and other indicators. Operation indicators can often be a precursor of a safety problem. A pressure alarm that will not reset, for example, can indicate an impending explosion. Such indicators should be checked. Such an indicator should never be reset without first determining what caused the problem. Also, operations personnel should be contacted before resetting.

These nine, simple steps can be quickly accomplished by all personnel . . . and they may save a life.

CHAPTER 4

REGULATORY AND LEGAL SAFETY REQUIREMENTS AND STANDARDS

INTRODUCTION

The modern trend in electrical safety is toward more and more individual responsibility as employees are being held increasingly responsible for their actions. For individuals to successfully fulfill their responsibilities, they must be aware of the rules that apply to their performance. This means that company safety rules; national and international standards; and local, state, and federal laws must be part of an employee's knowledge base.

Electrical safety standards and/or requirements are produced by a variety of organizations. Some of the standards are voluntary and some are local or federal law. Whether voluntary or mandatory, these standards provide guidance for the proper way to work on or around electric energy. Much of the material covered in other parts of this handbook is drawn from the standards that will be covered in this chapter.

Since electrical standards are periodically reviewed and updated, the information included in this chapter is necessarily general. Always refer to the most recent addition of each of these standards when current information is required. Note that not all standards are covered in this chapter. The reader should refer to industry-specific literature for their own industries.

Because of the very critical role that standards organizations play, coverage of them is also included in this chapter. The organizational structure, the standard-making procedure, and the historical development of each standards organization is covered.

THE REGULATORY BODIES

The American National Standards Institute (ANSI)

Overview. Founded in 1918, the ANSI is a private, nonprofit, membership organization. The ANSI coordinates the United States voluntary consensus standards systems and approves American national standards. The ANSI membership includes over 1000 companies; hundreds of professional, technical, trade, labor, and consumer organizations; and dozens of government agencies. The ANSI's primary purpose is to ensure that a single set of nonconflicting American national standards are developed by ANSI-accredited standards developers and that all interests concerned have the opportunity to participate in the development process. Since all interested parties are able to participate in the standard-making process, ANSI standards are true consensus standards.

Functions.   The ANSI serves five extremely important functions for industry:

- *Coordinates voluntary standards activities.*   The ANSI assists standards developers and standards users from the private sector and government to reach agreement on the need for standards and to establish priorities. It accredits qualified organizations to develop standards, helps them avoid duplication of effort, and offers a neutral forum for resolving differences. The ANSI's Executive Standards Council and standards boards spearhead this function.
- *Approves American national standards.*   The ANSI administers the only recognized US system for establishing American national standards. The ANSI approval procedures ensure that any interested party can participate in a standard's development or comment on its provisions. These requirements for due process guarantee that American national standards earn high levels of confidence and credibility and achieve broad acceptance.
- *Represents US interests in international standardization.*   The ANSI is the sole US representative to two of the major, nontreaty standards organizations: the International Organization for Standardization (ISO) and the International Electrotechnical Commission (IEC). The ISO, founded in 1946, develops, coordinates, and promotes international standards with national standards organizations from over 70 countries around the world. The IEC, founded in 1906, develops and promotes electrotechnical standards with national committees from over 40 countries. The ANSI participates in almost the entire technical program of both organizations and administers many key committees and subgroups.
- *Provides information on and access to world standards.*   The ANSI maintains copies of approved and draft American national standards, ISO and IEC standards, proposals of regional groups tied to the European Community, and the specifications of 90 national standards organizations that belong to the ISO. These standards are available to interested parties.

Member Companies.   The ANSI is a membership organization and draws its principle revenue from the company members. Company members help to govern the ANSI by determining policies, procedures, and long-range plans for standards development. They identify commercial and industrial needs for standards, both nationally and internationally. Based on these needs, they encourage ANSI to initiate new activities for standards development and accelerate improvement of existing standards.

Standards Developers.   Standards developers are primarily national trade, technical, professional, consumer, and labor organizations. They voluntarily submit standards to the ANSI for recognition as national consensus standards. Many of these organizations are also members of the ANSI and are represented on the boards, councils, and committees that help govern the ANSI and coordinate national and international standardization activities.

Government Agencies.   The ANSI works with governmental agencies in the same way they work with other organizations. That is, government agencies are ANSI members, and government representatives serve on ANSI boards and councils.

Coordinating committees, formed with the Occupational Safety and Health Administration and the Consumer Product Safety Commission, provide forums to discuss activities affecting the voluntary and governmental standards communities.

The Institute of Electrical and Electronic Engineers (IEEE)

Overview.   The IEEE is the world's largest professional technical society, with over 300,000 members from approximately 150 countries around the world. The American Institute of Electrical Engineers (AIEE) was founded in 1884, and the Institute of Radio Engineers (IRE) was founded in 1912. These two organizations merged in 1963 to form the IEEE.

The IEEE is a membership society composed of electrical engineers and technicians. The interest areas of IEEE members covers the gamut of technical areas including computer engineering, biomedical technology, telecommunications, electric power, aerospace, and consumer products.

Functions.   Among the IEEE's primary activities are technical publishing, technical conferences, and development of technical standards. The IEEE is responsible for approximately 20 percent of the world's published literature in electrotechnology. Ranging from published papers, to textbooks, to technical journals, IEEE literature is typically on the cutting edge of technology.

The IEEE is divided into a variety of technical societies with a broad spectrum of technical interests. Primarily through these societies the IEEE holds more than 300 meetings annually which allow engineers and technicians to exchange information. The IEEE also develops and publishes voluntary technical standards which regulate a variety of electrical technical activities.

National Fire Protection Association (NFPA)

Overview.   The NFPA was founded in 1896 for the express purpose of protecting people, property, and the environment from the effects of fire. To fulfill its purposes, the NFPA focuses its efforts into intensive technical activities and extensive educational programs. The NFPA is a nonprofit organization and has a membership of approximately 60,000 from 85 nations.

The NFPA has an extremely well recognized and respected set of voluntary consensus codes and standards. These codes and standards, some 275 of them, are used extensively by the NFPA's network of fire service, industrial, health care, building code, and other professional members. The NFPA technical committees are staffed by more than 4500 volunteers from a balanced cross section of affected interests.

The NFPA is responsible for the National Electrical Code, a document which is one of the most recognized electrical safety standards in the world.

Functions. The NFPA is involved in a wide variety of functions and activities.

- The Learn Not to Burn Curriculum is for children from kindergarten through eighth grade. This program, introduced by the NFPA in 1979, has a documented record of saving hundreds of lives because of lessons remembered by children.
- Fire Prevention Week is observed each year on October 9—the anniversary of the great Chicago fire of 1871. The first Fire Prevention Week was proclaimed by President Warren G. Harding in 1922. The NFPA has sponsored the week ever since.
- The NFPA maintains one of the major fire safety literature collections.
- NFPA conducts investigations of major fires. These fires are investigated as a result of their technical or educational interest.

The NFPA Standards-Making System. The NFPA and its standards-making efforts grew from a meeting of a small group in Boston in 1895. That group was meeting to discuss sprinkler installation standards in the Boston area. From that initial standard has grown the NFPA standards-making system of today.

The standards-making procedure starts with the submission of a request for a new standard by an interested party. The request is reviewed by the NFPA Standards Council who publishes an announcement in the membership newsletter, *Fire News.* The announcement acknowledges the request for a standard and asks for comments on the need for the project, information on organizations that may be active in the subject matter of the proposed project, a listing of resource material that is available, and an indication of who would be willing to participate in the project if it is approved.

If the council determines a need for the proposed project, it either assigns the project to an existing technical committee or a new committee whose membership reflects a fair balance of concerned interests. Members of technical committees are appointed by the standards council and include volunteer experts representing the government, educational institutions, business, insurance companies, industry, and consumers. Each committee member is classified according to his or her interest, and each committee is structured so that no more than one-third of the membership is from a single interest.

Once the technical committee has been established, the NFPA issues public notices announcing the committee's next meeting date and calling for specific proposals from interested persons. Anyone may submit a proposal for text to be included in a new document or added to an existing document. The committee then meets to consider all proposals received and drafts a proposed document or amendments to an existing document. Submitters may address the committee on their proposals at the meeting. Letter ballot approval by at least two-thirds of all committee members eligible to vote is required to approve a proposal for inclusion in the document.

After suitable procedures to allow for objections, and a vote of the membership, the document is presented to the standards council for final issuance. If the standards council issues the standard, based on the vote of the membership, it is published in pamphlet form and is also included in the appropriate volume of NFPA's National Fire Codes. If the standard is to be an American national standard, it is submitted to the ANSI.

American Society for Testing and Materials (ASTM)

Overview. The ASTM was organized in 1898 and has grown to an extremely large, voluntary standards development organization. The organization develops standards in a variety of areas including materials, products, systems, and services. The ASTM has over 130 standards-writing committees which write standards in such diverse areas as metals, paints, plastics, textiles, petroleum, construction, energy, the environment, consumer products, medical services and devices, computerized systems, and electronics.

The ASTM headquarters has no technical research or testing facilities because such work is done voluntarily by over 30,000 technically qualified ASTM members located throughout the world. The ASTM publishes approximately 8500 standards each year in the 68 volumes of the *Annual Book of ASTM Standards.*

Function. The ASTM develops six principal types of full consensus standards including

- *Standard test method.* This is a definitive procedure for the identifications, measurement, and evaluation of one or more qualities, characteristics, or properties of a material, product, system, or service that produces a test result.

- *Standard specification.* This is a precise statement of a set of requirements to be satisfied by a material, product, system, or service that also indicates the procedures for determining whether each of the requirements is satisfied.

- *Standard practice.* A definitive procedure for performing one or more specific operations or functions that does not produce a test result.

- *Standard terminology.* A document comprising terms, definitions, descriptions of terms, explanations of symbols, abbreviations, or acronyms.

- *Standard guide.* A series of options or instructions that do not recommend a specific course of action.

- *Standard classification.* A systematic arrangement or division of materials, products, systems, or services into groups based on similar characteristics such as origin, composition, properties, or use.

The ASTM Standards-Making System. Like most consensus standards organizations, the ASTM begins its standards-making activities when a need is identified. Task group members prepare a draft standard, which is reviewed by its parent subcommittee through a letter ballot. After the subcommittee approves the document, it is submitted to a main committee letter ballot. Once approved at the main committee level, the document is submitted for balloting to the ASTM. All negative votes cast during the balloting process, which must include a written explanation of the voter's objections, must be fully considered before the document can be submitted to the next level in the process. Final approval of a standard depends on concurrence by the ASTM Committee on Standards that proper procedures were followed and due process was achieved.

American Society of Safety Engineers (ASSE)

Overview. The ASSE was founded in 1911. It is a membership organization composed of safety professionals throughout the world. The 27,000 members manage, supervise, and consult on safety, health, and environmental issues in industry, government, and education.

The ASSE's mission is to enhance the status and promote the advancement of the safety profession; and foster the technical, scientific, managerial, and ethical knowledge, skills, and competency of safety professionals.

The ASSE has a 25-member board of directors consisting of 13 region vice-presidents, one division vice-president, six appointed vice-presidents, and the society president, president-elect, first vice-president, past president, vice-president of finance, and the executive director. The board of directors is guided in decision making by 29 standing committees and task forces. The ASSE has over 130 chapters and over 40 student sections within 13 regions nationwide.

Function.   The ASSE meets its responsibilities by providing continuing education, membership services, standards-making activities, peer recognition awards, marketing, and safety public relations.

Continuing Education.   The ASSE sponsors professional development seminars, publications, conference proceedings, training packages, computer resources, and audiovisual aids.

Membership Services.   The ASSE provides a variety of related membership services including professional development seminars, technical publications, and leadership conferences.

ASSE Standards.   The ASSE serves as the secretariat for a number of American national standards. Those of special interest to electrical safety include Eye and Face Protection (Z87.1), Safety Requirements for confined Spaces (Z117.1), and Safety Requirements for Ladders (A14.1 to A14.8).

The Occupational Safety and Health Administration (OSHA)

Standards issued by the OSHA differ from other standards in one very significant aspect—they are enforceable under federal law. The following sections outline some of the more important facts about the OSHA and its standards. You should contact your local OSHA office if more detailed information is required.

The Occupational Safety and Health Act of 1970.   Part of the material in the following sections was drawn from the government publication OSHA 2056 entitled *All About OSHA*.

In 1970, the United States was faced with the following statistics:

- Job-related accidents accounted for more than 14,000 worker deaths per year.
- Nearly $2\frac{1}{2}$ million workers were disabled.
- Ten times as many person-days were lost from job-related disabilities than from strikes.
- Estimated new cases of occupational diseases totaled 300,000.

To address these problems, Congress passed The Occupational Safety and Health Act of 1970 (the Act). The execution of the Act is the responsibility of the Department of Labor under the Secretary of Labor. The Act created the OSHA to continually create, review, and redefine specific standards and practices.

Coverage under the Act extends to all employers and their employees in the 50 states, the District of Columbia, Puerto Rico, and all other territories under federal government jurisdiction. The Act exempts three important categories:

- Self-employed persons
- Farms at which only immediate members of the farm employer's family are employed

- Working conditions regulated by other federal agencies under other federal statutes

The Act has special provisions for some employees and employers. State and local governments and the federal government have special consideration under the Act. Employers and employees should contact their local OSHA office to determine what their obligations are.

The OSHA's Purpose. The OSHA is the administration that is given the principle responsibilities for implementation of the Act. A few of the OSHA's responsibilities include

- Encourage employers and employees to reduce workplace hazards and to implement new or improved existing safety and health programs.
- Establish separate but dependent responsibilities and rights for employers and employees with respect to achieving safe and healthful working conditions.
- Set and enforce mandatory occupational safety and health standards applicable to businesses affecting interstate commerce.
- Maintain a reporting and record keeping system to monitor job-related illnesses and injuries.
- Establish training programs to increase the number and competence of occupational safety and health personnel.
- Provide for the development, analysis, evaluation, and approval of state occupational safety and health programs.

The OSHA is a branch of the Department of Labor and is responsible to the Secretary of Labor.

Responsibilities and Rights of Employers. Employers have the principle responsibility to guarantee that all OSHA rules and regulations are properly and promptly administered in the workplace. Employers who do not carry out their responsibilities can be heavily fined. The following list identifies some of the more significant employer responsibilities. Employers must

- Meet their general responsibility to provide a workplace free from recognized hazards that are causing or are likely to cause death or serious physical harm to employees.
- Be familiar with mandatory OSHA standards and make copies available to employees for review upon request.
- Inform all employees about the OSHA.
- Examine workplace conditions to make sure they conform to applicable standards.
- Minimize or reduce hazards.
- Make sure that employees have, use, and maintain safe tools and equipment. These tools and equipment include appropriate personal protective equipment such as flash suits, rubber gloves, and hard hats.
- Use color codes, posters, labels, or signs when needed to warn employees of potential hazards.
- Establish or update operating procedures and communicate them so that employees follow safety and health requirements.

- Provide medical examinations when required by OSHA standards.
- Provide training required by OSHA standards. For example, the Safety Related Work Practices Rule and the Control of Hazardous Energy Source Rule both require a certain amount of employee training for complete implementation.
- Report to the nearest OSHA office within 48 h any fatal accident or one that results in the hospitalization of five or more employees.
- Keep OSHA-required records of work-related injuries and illnesses, and post a copy of the totals from the last page of OSHA No. 200 during the entire month of February of each year. *Note:* This applies only to employers with 11 or more employees and employers who are chosen by the Bureau of Labor Statistics.
- Post the OSHA poster (OSHA 2203) informing employees of their rights and responsibilities at a prominent location in the workplace. In states with OSHA-approved state job safety and health programs, the state's equivalent poster and/or the OSHA poster may be required.
- Provide employees, former employees, and their representatives access to the Log and Summary of Occupational Injuries and Illnesses (OSHA No. 200) at a reasonable time and in a reasonable manner.
- Provide access to employee medical records and exposure records to employees or their authorized representatives.
- Cooperate with the OSHA compliance officer by furnishing names of authorized employee representatives who may be asked to accompany the compliance officer during an inspection. (If none, the compliance officer will consult with a reasonable number of employees concerning safety and health in the workplace.)
- Not discriminate against employees who properly exercise their rights under the Act.
- Put OSHA citations at or near the work site involved.
- Abate cited violations within the prescribed period.

Employers also have rights under the OSHA act. The following items list some of the more important employer's rights. Employers have the right to

- Seek advice and off-site consultation as needed by writing, calling, or visiting the nearest OSHA office. The OSHA will not inspect merely because an employer requests assistance.
- Be active in their industry associations involvement in safety and health.
- Request and receive proper identification of the OSHA compliance officer prior to inspection.
- Be advised by the compliance officer of the reason for an inspection.
- Have an opening and closing conference with the compliance officer.
- Accompany the compliance officer on the inspection.
- File a Notice of Contest with the OSHA area director within 15 working days or receipt of a notice of citation and proposed penalty.
- Apply to the OSHA for a temporary variance from a standard if unable to comply because of the unavailability of materials, equipment, or personnel needed to make necessary changes within the required time.
- Apply to the OSHA for a permanent variance from a standard if they can furnish proof that their facilities or method of operation provide employee protection at least as effective as that required by the standard.

- Take an active role in developing safety and health standards through participation in OSHA standards and advisory committees, through nationally recognized standards-setting organizations and through evidence and views presented in writing or at hearings.
- Be assured of the confidentiality of any trade secrets observed by an OSHA compliance officer during inspection.
- Submit a written request to the National Institute of Occupational Safety and Health (NIOSH) for information on whether any substance in your workplace has potentially toxic effects in the concentrations being used.

Responsibilities and Rights of Employees. The Act was designed to establish workplace rules and regulations which will enhance the health and safety of employees. Because of this, the employers are considered to have principle responsibility for the implementation of OSHA rules. Employees, therefore, are not cited for violations. In spite of this, employees still have responsibilities under the Act. Employees must

- Read the OSHA poster at the job site.
- Comply with all applicable OSHA standards.
- Follow all employer safety and health rules and regulations, and wear or use prescribed protective equipment while engaged in work.
- Report hazardous conditions to the supervisor.
- Report any job-related injury or illness to the employer.
- Promptly seek treatment from job-related injuries or illnesses.
- Cooperate with the OSHA compliance officer conducting an inspection if he or she inquires about safety and health conditions in your workplace.
- Exercise their rights under the Act in a responsible manner.

Employees also have significant rights under the Act. Employees have a right to

- Seek safety and health on the job without fear of punishment.
- Complain to an employer, union, the OSHA, or any other government agency about job safety and health hazards.
- File safety or health grievances.
- Participate on a workplace safety and health committee or in union activities concerning job safety and health.
- Participate in OSHA inspections, conferences, hearings, or other OSHA-related activities.

OSHA'S Electrical Safety Standards. OSHA safety standards are published in the Code of Federal Regulations, Title 29, Subtitle B, Chapter XVII. The OSHA has issued or will issue electrical safety standards in at least four categories:

1. Design and installation safety
2. Safety-related work practices
3. Safety-related maintenance requirements
4. Special equipment

In addition, the OSHA has issued or will issue standards regulating a variety of related areas such as Control of Hazardous Energy. Electrical safety standards for general industry are found in Part 1910, Subpart S, which includes Paragraphs 1910-301 through 1910-399. Electrical safety standards for employees in the construction industry are found in Part 1926, Subpart K, which includes Paragraphs 1926-400 through 1926-449. Table 4.1 identifies the various locations for the standards.

Note that by its very nature, Table 4.1 is time-sensitive. Be certain to check the current edition of the OSHA standard for complete information. These standards can be procured from your local OSHA office. The various OSHA standards will be covered in more detail later in this chapter.

OSHA Technical Consultation.   The OSHA will provide technical support and consultation at no charge. The consultation services are provided by state government agencies or universities employing professional safety and health consultants. Although intended for smaller employers with more hazardous operations, the consultation service is available to companies of all sizes.

The technical consultation starts when the employer requests the service and makes a commitment to correct any possible violations discovered by the inspector. The complete consultation involves six basic steps: the request, the opening conference, the walk-through inspection, the closing conference, the written report, and the corrective actions. Table 4.2 lists and describes each of these six steps.

Employers are exempted from inspections or fines by OSHA compliance personnel during the consultation process. In some cases, if employers can demonstrate that an effective safety and health program is in operation, they may be exempted from OSHA general schedule enforcement inspections. This exemption does not apply to complaint or accident investigations.

Voluntary Protection Programs.   Voluntary protection programs (VPP) (Table 4.3) are designed to extend worker protection beyond the minimums required by the OSHA standards. These three programs are designed to

1. Recognize outstanding achievements of those who have successfully incorporated comprehensive safety and health programs into their total management system.
2. Motivate others to achieve excellent safety and health results in the same outstanding way.
3. Establish a relationship between employers, employees, and the OSHA that is based on cooperation rather than coercion or confrontation.

Voluntary protection programs are available in all states under federal jurisdiction, and some state OSHA agencies have similar programs. Employers should contact their local OSHA offices for details on the VPPs. The OSHA reevaluates VPPs on a regular basis—annually for Merit and Demonstration Programs and triennially for Star Programs.

Training and Education.   The OSHA can provide training and education in one of three basic ways. First, OSHA's area offices are full-service centers that provide a wealth of information in the form of pamphlets, brochures, publications, audiovisual aids, technical advice, and availability for speaking engagements.

Second, the OSHA Training Institute in Des Plaines, Illinois, provides both basic and advanced training in areas such as electrical hazards, machine guarding, ventilation, and ergonomics. The institute is a full-service training facility with all necessary classrooms, laboratories, library, and an audiovisual unit. Training courses at the

TABLE 4.1 Partial Listing of Applicable OSHA Safety Standards and the Industries to Which They Apply

Title	Industry	Paragraphs	Comments
Design Safety Standards for Electrical Equipment	General Industry & Maritime	1910.302–1910.308	
Safety-Related Work Practices	General Industry & Maritime	1910.331–1910.335	
Safety-Related Maintenance Requirements	General Industry & Maritime	1910.361–1910.380	Not implemented
Safety Requirements for Special Equipment	General Industry & Maritime	1910.381–1910.398	Not implemented
Installation Safety Requirements	Construction Industry	1926.402–1926.408	
Safety-Related Work Practices	Construction Industry	1926.416–1926.417	
Safety-Related Maintenance and Environmental Considerations	Construction Industry	1926.431–1926.432	
Safety Requirements for Special Equipment	Construction Industry	1926.441–1926.448	Only batteries implemented
Power Generation, Transmission, and Distribution	Construction Industry	1926.950–1926.960	
Power Transmission and Distribution	Power Generation, Transmission, and Distribution	1910.269	
Communications Safety	Telecommunications	1910.268	

TABLE 4.2 Six-Step OSHA Technical Consultation Process

Employer requests assistance	The employer contacts the state agency responsible for OSHA consultation services. Each state has its own agency. Phone numbers may be obtained by contacting the local OSHA office or requesting OSHA bulletins #2056 and #3047. Employer must make initial commitment to correct any observed discrepancies
Consultant holds on-site opening conference	In this conference the ground rules for the consultation are thoroughly explained to the employer, the plan for the walk-through visit is determined, and any preliminary questions are answered
Walk-through inspection	The employer representative and the consultant perform a walk-through inspection of the workplace. Specific hazards are noted and an examination of the aspects of the employer's safety and health program which relate to the scope of the visit are observed
Consultant holds an on-site closing conference	The closing conference is used to apprise the employer of any extremely serious violations which were observed. Generally only those hazards which represent an immediate and serious hazard to employees are itemized
Written report	A written report is issued by the consultant in which the hazards and/or violations of OSHA regulations are delineated
Corrective actions	The employer corrects those problems which were outlined by the consultant

TABLE 4.3 OSHA Voluntary Protection Programs

Star program	This is the most demanding and prestigious of the VPPs. It is open to any employer in any industry who has successfully managed a comprehensive safety and health program to reduce injury rates below the national average for the industry. Specific requirements for the program include: management commitment and employee participation; a high-quality work site analysis program; hazard prevention and control programs; and comprehensive safety and health training for all employees. These requirements must all be in place and operating effectively
Merit program	This is a stepping stone to the Star program. An employer with a basic safety and health program built around the Star requirements who is committed to improving the company's program and who has the resources to do so within a specified period of time may work with the OSHA to meet Star requirements
Demonstration program	This VPP is for companies that provide Star-quality worker protection in industries where certain Star requirements may not be appropriate or effective. It allows the OSHA both the opportunity to recognize outstanding safety and health programs that would otherwise be unreached by VPP and to determine if general Star requirements can be changed to include these companies as Star participants

institute are open to federal and state compliance officers; state consultants; federal agency personnel; private-sector employers, employees, and their representatives.

Finally, the OSHA provides funds in the form of grants to nonprofit organizations to conduct workplace training and education in subjects where the OSHA believes there is a lack of current workplace training.

State OSHA Organizations.   The Occupational Safety and Health Act encourages states to develop and operate state job safety and health plans. These plans are operated under OSHA guidance. The OSHA funds up to 50 percent of the state program's operating costs.

The requirements for development of a state program are beyond the scope of this book. The entire setup process is monitored by the OSHA with milestones and performance requirements established from the outset. At the end of the process, if the state program is operating at least as effectively as the federal OSHA program and other administrative requirements are met, the OSHA issues final approval and federal authority ends in the areas over which the state has jurisdiction.

THE NATIONAL ELECTRICAL SAFETY CODE (NESC)—ANSI C-2

General Description

The NESC was first developed in 1913 by the National Bureau of Standards as a consensus standard and remains so in the present. The NESC is an American national standard published by the IEEE, the secretariat for the NESC. It is intended to provide practical rules for safeguarding personnel during the installation, operation, or maintenance of electric supply and communications lines and associated equipment.

The code has three general rules as follows:

1. All electric supply and communication lines and equipment shall be designed, constructed, operated, and maintained to meet its requirements.

2. The utilities, authorized contractors, or other entities, as applicable, performing design, construction, operation, or maintenance tasks for electric supply or communication lines or equipment covered by the NESC are held responsible for meeting the applicable requirements.

3. For all particulars not specified in the NESC, construction and maintenance should be done in accordance with accepted good practice for the given local conditions.

Industries and Facilities Covered

The NESC rules cover supply and communication lines, equipment, and associated work practices used by both public and private electric supply, communications, railway, or similar utilities. The rules also cover similar systems which are under the control of qualified persons. This means that facilities such as co-generation plants, industrial complexes, or utility interactive systems are covered by the NESC.

Note that the NESC specifically states it does not cover installations in mines, ships, railway rolling equipment, aircraft, automotive equipment, or utilization wiring except in certain cases. It also specifies that building utilization requirements are covered by the National Electrical Code, ANSI/NFPA 70.

Technical/Safety Items Covered

The NESC covers five major areas in numerous parts. The following sections describe each of the major areas of coverage and lists the type of information included in each. The information provided in the following sections is intended to be general information only. Always refer to the most recent edition of the NESC for specific information.

Grounding Methods for Electric Supply and Communications Facilities. This section covers the methods to implement protective grounding for electric supply and communications facilities. The information is technical in nature and includes topics such as the point of connection, the composition of the grounding conductor, the means of connection, grounding electrodes, and many other grounding topics.

Rules for Installation and Maintenance of Electric Supply Stations and Equipment. This section covers those parts of the electrical supply system and associated structural arrangements which are accessible only to qualified personnel. It also covers the conductors and equipment employed primarily for the utilization of electric power when such conductors and equipment are used by the utility in the exercise of its function as a utility. Protective arrangements in electric supply stations, illumination, installation and maintenance of equipment, rotating equipment, storage batteries, transformers and regulators, conductors, circuit breakers, switchgear and enclosed metal bus, and surge arrestors are included in this section.

Safety Rules for the Installation and Maintenance of Overhead Electric Supply and Communications Lines. This section applies to overhead lines, associated structural assemblies, and extension of such lines into buildings. Typical examples of topics included in this part are inspection and tests of lines and equipment, grounding of circuits, arrangement of switches, relations between various classes of equipment, joint use of structures, clearances, grades of construction, line insulation, and other such topics.

Safety Rules for the Installation and Maintenance of Underground Electric Supply and Communication Lines. This part is similar to the previous part except the equipment it includes is underground equipment. Topics include general requirements applying to underground lines, underground conduit systems, supply cable, underground structures, direct buried cable, risers supply cable terminations, and installations in tunnels.

Rules for the Operation of Electric Supply and Communications Lines and Equipment. This final part of the NESC discusses rules for the operation of supply and communications lines and equipment. The first major section provides operational rules for both communications and supply employees. Personal general precautions, general operating routines, overhead line operating procedures, and underground line operating procedures are also included.

The second major section has additional rules which pertain to communications workers. Approaching energized conductors, joint-use structures, attendant on surface at joint-use manhole, and sheath continuity rules are included.

The final major part lists additional rules which pertain strictly to electrical supply employees. This section has six significant sections including energized conductors or parts, switching control procedures, working on energized lines, de-energizing equipment or lines, protective grounds, and live-line work.

THE NATIONAL ELECTRICAL CODE (NEC)— ANSI/NFPA 70

General Description

The NEC is arguably the oldest of all the various standards. It is an installation design standard that covers industrial, commercial, and residential electric utilization systems.

The NEC was first developed in 1897 by a variety of insurance, engineering, architectural, electrical, and other such interest groups. In 1911, the sponsorship of the Code was assumed by the NFPA. Later, the NEC was adopted as an American national standard by the ANSI. The NEC is only one of many fire safety codes that are published by the NFPA.

The NEC is unique among the other codes and standards in a very significant way—all or portions of it have been adopted as local law in many states, municipalities, cities, and other such areas. Many countries outside of the United States have adopted the NEC in its entirety, or in part, for their national installation codes. Note that both the NFPA and ANSI consider the NEC to be purely an advisory document.

The NEC has become a large document with a wealth of design, installation, and general technical information included. The principle objective of the NEC is to provide standardized, technically sound electrical installation standards to help minimize the possibility of electric fires.

Industries and Facilities Covered

The NEC covers four basic types of installations. Note that each of these installations are so-called utilization installations as opposed to transmission and distribution.

1. Installations of electric conductors and equipment within or on public and private buildings or other structures, including mobile homes, recreational vehicles, and floating buildings. This section also includes premises wiring for such facilities as yards, carnival lots, parking lots, and industrial substations.

2. Installation of conductors and equipment that connect to the supply of electricity.

3. Installations of other outside conductors and equipment on the premises.

4. Installations of optical fiber cable.

The NEC also lists several installations to which it does not apply including ships, railway rolling stock, underground mine installations, railway generation, communications equipment under the control of communications utilities, and certain facilities under the control of electric utilities. The utility facilities that are excluded are the communications, metering, generation, transformation, transmission, and distribution in buildings or substations used specifically for that purpose. The NEC does include utility office buildings and other such public and commercial structures.

Technical and Safety Items Included

The NEC includes technical specifications and requirements for virtually all electric lines and equipment. The Code has multiple chapters which include rules for wiring and protection, wiring methods and materials, equipment for general use, special occupancies, special equipment, special conditions, and communications systems.

Tables for conductor ampacities are included along with formulas for calculating the required size and number of conductors for special applications, as well as sizing requirements for protective devices. Grounding requirements including what, when, and how are included. Rules for interrupting capacities and other such information are also included. The NEC has become an engineering reference, an installation guide, a design standard, and a fire safety code all in one volume.

ELECTRICAL EQUIPMENT MAINTENANCE— ANSI/NFPA 70B

General Description

The Electrical Equipment Maintenance document (70B) is a companion publication to the NEC. Many interested parties had been requesting that safety-related maintenance requirements be added to the NEC. A special committee determined that the NEC, which is basically a design and installation standard, is not the correct vehicle for maintenance information.

In studying the need for this document, the committee determined that electrical safety concerns logically fall into four basic categories: product design standards, installation standards (covered by the NEC and the NESC), safety-related maintenance information, and usage instructions. Because of the high number of injuries and deaths related to improper or nonexistent equipment maintenance practices, the committee decided that an electric equipment maintenance document should be developed. To give the document as much prestige as possible, the decision was reached to make this new document a companion piece to the NEC. The final result, ANSI/NFPA 70B, contains recommended practice information for proper maintenance of electric equipment.

Industries and Facilities Covered

Document 70B covers maintenance of industrial-type electric systems and equipment. The covered systems and equipment are typical of those installed in commercial buildings, industrial plants, and large multifamily dwellings. Document 70B specifically states that it does not cover consumer appliances or home-type equipment. It also states that it is not intended to supersede manufacturer-recommended maintenance procedures.

Technical and Safety Items Covered

Document 70B includes 22 chapters and 10 appendices. One of the most important chapters develops a concise case for the implementation of proper preventive-maintenance procedures. Subsequent chapters cover maintenance fundamentals and how to plan a preventive-maintenance program. Then 12 chapters provide specific, detailed maintenance techniques and expected results for switchgear, circuit breakers, cables, motor control centers, rotating equipment, wiring devices, and other such electric equipment.

One chapter details the specifics of electrical testing in areas such as insulation resistance, protective device testing, infrared, fault-gas analysis, and many other such modern testing procedures. Still other chapters cover the maintenance of equipment which is subject to long intervals between shutdowns and methods to be used for de-energizing equipment in such a way that maintenance personnel are protected.

The appendices include information on walk-through inspections, instruction techniques, symbols, diagrams, and a variety of recommended test sheets and forms to be used for maintenance programs.

ELECTRICAL SAFETY REQUIREMENTS FOR EMPLOYEE WORKPLACES—ANSI/NFPA 70E

General Description

Consensus standards are developed by personnel who are intimately familiar with the safety hazards of any given discipline; therefore, they will be accurate and extremely useful to the purpose for which they were intended. Because of this, when the OSHA develops a safety standard, it prefers to work with existing consensus standards. In 1976, the NFPA formed a committee to assist the OSHA in the preparation of electrical safety standards.

The decision was made to develop a consensus standard which would embody four parts: Part I, Installation Safety Requirements; Part II, Safety-Related Work Practices; Part III, Safety-Related Maintenance Requirements; and Part IV, Safety Requirements for Special Equipment. These four parts are identical to the four major rules which the OSHA has developed or is developing. The first three major parts have been developed and have been through several revisions. Part IV has not been written as of early 1993; however, it is anticipated for later development.

The OSHA has published its installation safety standard and its safety-related work practices standard which are based, in part, on Parts I and II of NFPA 70E. The OSHA maintenance standard is expected to be available in the latter part of the 1990s.

Industries and Facilities Covered

NFPA 70E is a companion document to the NEC; therefore, it covers exactly the same industries as the NEC. Specifically NFPA 70E addresses electrical safety requirements that are necessary for safeguarding employees in the workplace. It covers three major installations:

1. Building electrical utilization installations including carnival and parking lots, mobile homes and recreational vehicles, and industrial substations
2. Conductors which connect installations to a supply of electricity
3. Other outside premises wiring

Document 70E specifically excludes five basic categories of installation:

1. Ships, watercraft, railway rolling stock, aircraft, and automotive vehicles other than mobile homes and recreational vehicles

2. Installations underground in mines

3. Installations of railways for generation, transformation, transmission, or distribution of power used exclusively for operation of rolling stock or installations used exclusively for signaling and communication purposes

4. Installation of communication equipment under the exclusive control of communications utilities, located outdoors or in building spaces used exclusively for such installations

5. Installations under the exclusive control of electric utilities used for communication, metering, or for the generation, control transformation, transmission, and distribution of electric energy located in buildings used exclusively by utilities for such purposes or located outdoors on property owned or leased by the utility or on public highways, streets, roads, etc., or outdoors by established rights on private property

Technical Safety Items Covered

Part I, Installation Safety Requirements. In developing document 70E, seven basic criteria were used:

1. The provisions should give employees protection from electrical hazards.

2. Its provisions should be excerpted from the NEC in such a way that they will maintain their intent as they apply to electrical safety.

3. The material should be selected so that frequent revision will not be required.

4. Compliance should be determined by means of an inspection during the normal state of employee inspection during normal work hours, without removal of parts requiring shutdown of the electric installation or by damaging the building structure.

5. The provisions should not have unnecessary details.

6. The provisions should be written so as to enhance their understanding by employers and employees.

7. The provisions must not add any requirements not found in the NEC.

Document 70E, Part I includes information on installing equipment, providing working clearances, guarding live parts, wiring design and protection, grounding connections, wiring methods, damp and wet locations, specific-purpose equipment, electric signs, cranes and hoists, electric welders, portable electric equipment, hazardous locations, and special systems. Part I is very similar to OSHA paragraphs 1910.302–1910.308 which will be covered in more detail later in this chapter.

Part II, Safety-Related Work Practices. Part II of 70E is intended to give directions to employees in how to perform their work in such a manner they can avoid electrical hazards. It includes information on working on or near energized parts, working on or near de-energized parts, safe de-energizing of systems, lockout-tagout procedures, safe use of tools and equipment, personal and other protective equipment, safe approach distances for overhead lines, switching of protective devices after operation, safety training, and safe voltage-measurement practices.

Virtually all the material in 70E was adopted by the OSHA in its safety-related work practices rule in Paragraphs 1910.331–1910.335.

Part III, Safety-Related Maintenance Requirements. Part III was added to the 1988 release of 70E and is currently being revised. The 1988 edition includes a variety of information on maintenance; for the most part it addresses the basic, common sense procedures for many common types of electric equipment. Included are substation and switchgear assemblies, premises wiring, controller equipment, fuses and molded-case circuit breakers, rotating electric equipment, portable electric tools and equipment, safety and protective equipment, hazardous (classified) locations, and batteries and battery rooms.

The 1988 edition of Part III has only minimal, broad recommendations. Specific maintenance techniques needed to meet the provisions of Part III are left to the employer to determine.

Part IV, Safety Requirements for Special Equipment. Nothing has been developed for this part as of the 1988 edition of 70E.

THE AMERICAN SOCIETY FOR TESTING AND MATERIALS (ASTM) STANDARDS

The ASTM publishes a variety of standards primarily associated with safety equipment design, usage, and testing. Table 4.4 summarizes some of the ASTM standards and briefly describes their coverage. Refer to Chap. 2 for many specific references and uses of the ASTM standards.

OCCUPATIONAL SAFETY AND HEALTH ADMINISTRATION (OSHA) STANDARDS

Overview

OSHA standards represent federal law and must be implemented by all covered industries except in those states which have adopted state safety programs which are approved by the OSHA. The OSHA has been developing many electrical and related safety standards since its creation in 1980. Table 4.1 lists several of those standards, the industry to which they apply, and their location in the Code of Federal Regulations.

Because the OSHA standards apply so universally, several of the more important ones are reproduced in their entirety in this section. *Note:* The standards reproduced in this section are the current standards at the date of publication of this handbook. The user should contact the OSHA for the current, up-to-date version of each standard.

TABLE 4.4 Summary of ASTM Standards for Electrical Protective Equipment

Standard number/name	Description
D 120/Specification for Rubber Insulating Gloves	Acceptance testing of rubber insulating gloves used for worker protection
D 178/Specification for Rubber Insulating Matting	Acceptance testing of rubber insulating matting used as floor covering
D 1048/Specification for Rubber Insulating Blankets	Acceptance testing of rubber insulating blankets
D 1049/Specification for Rubber Insulating Covers	Acceptance testing of rubber insulating covers. Insulator hoods, line hose connectors, etc.
D 1050/Specification for Rubber Insulating Line Hose	Acceptance testing of rubber line hose
D 1051/Specification for Rubber Insulating Sleeves	Acceptance testing of rubber insulating sleeves
F 478/In-Service Care of Insulating Line Hose & Covers	Care, inspection, testing, and use voltage of insulating line hose and covers
F 479/In-Service Care of Insulating Blankets	Care, inspection, testing, and use voltage of insulating blankets for shock protection
F 496/In-Service Care of Insulating Gloves and Sleeves	Care, inspection, testing, and use voltage of insulating gloves and sleeves for shock protection
F 696/Specification for Leather Protectors for Rubber Insulating Gloves and Mittens	Specification for the design and manufacture of leather protectors for rubber insulating goods. Note that the OSHA requires leather protectors over rubber insulating goods if they may be damaged
F 711/Specification for Fiberglass Reinforced Plastic Rod and Tube Used in Live Line Tools	Specification for the design and manufacture of insulating foam-filled tubes and rods made from fiberglass-reinforced plastic used for live line tools
F 712/Test Methods for Electrical Insulating Plastic Guard Equipment for Protection of Workers	Withstand voltage, flashover voltage, and leakage current test methods are defined for line guards, guard connectors, deadend covers, pole guards, and other such equipment
F 819/Definitions of Terms Relating to Electrical Protective Equipment	A concise definition list of key terms
F 855/Specifications for Temporary Grounding Systems to be Used on De-Energized Electric Power Lines and Equipment	Construction, testing, and materials used for temporary grounding systems
F 887/Specifications for Personal Climbing Equipment	Acceptance testing specifications for climbers, climber straps, body belts, and pole straps
F 914/Test Methods for Acoustic Emission for Insulated Aerial Personnel Devices	Acoustic emission testing methods for insulated aerial personnel devices
F 968/Specification for Electrically Insulating Plastic Guard Equipment for Protection of Workers	Construction and materials specification for line guards, guard connectors, deadend covers, and other such equipment
F 1116/Test Method for Determining Dielectric Strength of Overshoe Footwear	Recommended methods for determining the dielectric strength of insulating overshoe footwear
F 1117/Specification for Dielectric Overshoe Footwear	Acceptance testing of overshoe footwear
F 1236/Guide for Visual Inspection of Electrical Protective Rubber Products	Recommended methods and techniques for proper in-service inspection of electrical protective rubber products. Chapter 3 describes many of these methods

General Industry

At the time of this publication, the OSHA has not released proposed or final rules for maintenance requirements or for special equipment. Contact the OSHA for the status of these two standards.

Scope. The general industry OSHA standards apply to electric utilization systems installed or used within or on buildings, structures, and other premises. Other premises include

- Yards
- Carnivals
- Parking and other lots
- Mobile homes
- Recreational vehicles
- Industrial substations
- Conductors that connect the installations to a supply of electricity
- Other outside conductors on the premises

The OSHA has issued or will issue standards on design safety, safety-related work practices, lockout-tagout, maintenance-related safety, power transmission and distribution, and special equipment safety. All general industry electrical safety standards are published in Subpart S of Part 1910. Some related standards are published in Subpart J and others in Subpart R.

Design Safety Standards. The design safety standards cover all utilization systems which have been installed or undergone major modification since March 15, 1972. These standards provide design and installation requirements. The design safety standards are found in the United States Code of Federal Regulations, Title 29, Part 1910, Subpart S, Paragraphs 1910.303 through 1910.308. It is reproduced in Fig. 4.1.

Safety-Related Work Practices. This OSHA standard covers the procedures required to ensure that employees use optimum safety-related procedures when working around energized or potentially energized equipment. It covers a variety of topics including lockout-tagout procedures. Electrical lockout-tagout must follow the methods given in Paragraph 1910.333; however, with certain additions, 1910.333 does allow the use of the Control of Hazardous Energy Rule (1910.147).

The Electrical Safety-Related Work Practices Rule is found in the United States Code of Federal Regulations, Title 29, Part 1910, Subpart S, Paragraphs 1910.331 through 1910.335. It is reproduced in this text as Fig. 4.2.

Power Generation, Transmission, and Distribution. Employees involved in the operation or maintenance of equipment used for power generation, transmission, or distribution and under the control of an electric utility are covered by this rule. The rule is published in the United States Code of Federal Regulations, Title 29, Part 1910, Subpart R, Paragraph 1910.269. Figure 4.3 is the rule.

Control of Hazardous Energy Source (Lockout-Tagout). This rule is not an electrical standard; in fact, section (a)(1)(ii)(C) specifically excludes electrical hazards. However, the Safety-Related Work Practices Rule, Paragraph 1910.333(b)(2), Note 2 allows the use of the Lockout/Tagout rule with certain restriction. Because of its importance, it is reproduced here as Fig. 4.4. This rule is published in the United States Code of Federal Regulations, Title 29, Part 1910, Subpart J, Paragraph 1910.147.

Definitions. Figure 4.5 lists the definitions that the OSHA uses in Subpart S of Part 1910. It is published in the United States Code of Federal Regulations, Part 1910, Subpart S, Paragraph 1910.399.

Construction Industry

Scope. The OSHA publishes electrical safety standards for the construction industry in two subparts. Subpart K applies to construction sites and facilities exclusive of those intended exclusively for power generation, transmission, and distribution.

Installation Safety Requirements. Figure 4.6 is a reproduction of the Installation Safety Requirements for construction sites. This standard is published in the United States Code of Federal Regulations, Title 29, Part 1926, Subpart K, Paragraphs 1926.402 through 1926.408.

Safety-Related Work Practices. Because of the nature of electrical exposure of construction personnel, this rule is much shorter and less comprehensive than the safety-related work practices rule which applies to general industry. This standard is published in the United States Code of Federal Regulations, Title 29, Part 1926, Subpart K, Paragraphs 1926.416 and 1926.417. Figure 4.7 is a reproduction of the rule.

Safety-Related Maintenance and Environmental Considerations (Construction). This standard is published in the United States Code of Federal Regulations, Title 29, Part 1926, Subpart K, Paragraphs 431–432. Figure 4.8 is a reproduction of this standard.

Safety Requirements for Special Equipment (Construction). Batteries are the only apparatus included in this rule to date. It is published in the United States Code of Federal Regulations, Part 1926, Subpart K, Paragraph 1926.441. Figure 4.9 reproduces this standard.

Definitions. Figure 4.10 lists the definitions that the OSHA uses in Subpart K of Part 1926. It is published in the United States Code of Federal Regulations, Part 1926, Subpart K, Paragraph 1910.449.

DESIGN SAFETY STANDARDS FOR ELECTRICAL SYSTEMS

§ 1910.302   Electric utilization systems.

Sections 1910.302 through 1910.308 contain design safety standards for electric utilization systems.

(a) *Scope*—(1) *Covered.* The provisions of §§ 1910.302 through 1910.308 of this subpart cover electrical installations and utilization equipment installed or used within or on buildings, structures, and other premises including:

(i) Yards,

(ii) Carnivals,

(iii) Parking and other lots,

(iv) Mobile homes,

(v) Recreational vehicles,

(vi) Industrial substations,

(vii) Conductors that connect the installations to a supply of electricity, and

(viii) Other outside conductors on the premises.

(2) *Not covered.* The provisions of §§ 1910.302 through 1910.308 of this subpart do not cover:

(i) Installations in ships, watercraft, railway rolling stock, aircraft, or automotive vehicles other than mobile homes and recreational vehicles.

(ii) Installations underground in mines.

(iii) Installations of railways for generation, transformation, transmission, or distribution of power used exclusively for operation of rolling stock or installations used exclusively for signaling and communication purposes.

(iv) Installations of communication equipment under the exclusive control of communication utilities, located outdoors or in building spaces used exclusively for such installations.

(v) Installations under the exclusive control of electric utilities for the purpose of communication or metering: or for the generation, control, transformation, transmission, and distribution of electric energy located in buildings used exclusively by utilities for such purposes or located outdoors on property owned or leased by the utility or on public highways, streets, roads, etc., or outdoors by established rights on private property.

(b) *Extent of application.* (1) The requirements contained in the sections listed below shall apply to all electrical installations and utilization equipment, regardless of · when they were designed or installed.

Sections:

1910.303(b)	Examination, installation, and use of equipment.
1910.303(c)	Splices.
1910.303(d)	Arcing parts.
1910.303(e)	Marking.
1910.303(f)	Identification of disconnecting means.
1910.303(g)(2)	Guarding of live parts.
1910.304(e)(l)(i)	Protection of conductors and equipment.
1910.304(e)(l)(iv)	Location in or on premises.
1910.304(e)(l)(v)	Arcing or suddenly moving parts.
1910.304(f)(l)(ii)	2-Wire DC systems to be grounded:
1910.304(f)(l)(iii) and 1910.304(f)(l)(iv).	AC Systems to be grounded.
1910.304(f)(l)(v)	AC Systems 50 to 1000 volts not required to be grounded.
1910.304(f)(3)	Grounding connections.
1910.304(f)(4)	Grounding path.
1910.304(f)(5)(iv)(*a*) through 1910.304(f)(5)(iv)(*d*).	Fixed equipment required to be grounded.
1910.304(f)(5)(v)	Grounding of equipment connected by cord and plug.
1910.304(f)(5)(vi)	Grounding of nonelectrical equipment.
1910.304(f)(6)(i)	Methods of grounding fixed equipment.
1910.305(g)(l)(i) and 1910.305(g)(1)(ii).	Flexible cords and cables, uses.
1910.305(g)(l)(iii)	Flexible cords and cables prohibited.
1910.305(g)(2)(ii)	Flexible cords and cables, splices.
1910.305(g)(2)(iii)	Pull at joints and terminals of flexible cords and cables.
1910.307	Hazardous (classified) locations.

(2) Every electric utilization system and all utilization equipment installed after March 15, 1972, and every major replacement, modification, repair, or rehabilitation, after March 15, 1972, of any part of any electric utilization system or utilization equipment in-

FIGURE 4.1   Design Safety Standards for Electrical Systems (OSHA-CFR, Title 29, Part 1910, Subpart 1910, Paragraphs 302–308). (*Courtesy General Industry.*)

stalled before March 15, 1972, shall comply with the provisions of §§ 1910.302 through 1910.308.

NOTE: "Major replacements, modifications, repairs, or rehabilitations" include work similar to that involved when a new building or facility is built, a new wing is added, or an entire floor is renovated.

(3) The following provisions apply to electric utilization systems and utilization equipment installed after April 16, 1981:

§ 1910.303(h)(4) (i) and (ii).	Entrance and access to workspace (over 600 volts).
§ 1910.304(e)(1)(vi)(*b*)...	Circuit breakers operated vertically.
§ 1910.304(e)(1)(vi)(*c*)...	Circuit breakers used as switches.
§ 1910.304(f)(7)(ii)	Grounding of systems of 1000 volts or more supplying portable or mobile equipment.
§ 1910.305(j)(6)(ii)(*b*)....	Switching series capacitors over 600 volts.
§ 1910.306(c)(2)	Warning signs for elevators and escalators.
§ 1910.306(i)	Electrically controlled irrigation machines.
§ 1910.306(j)(5)...........	Ground-fault circuit interrupters for fountains.
§ 1910.308(a)(1)(ii)	Physical protection of conductors over 600 volts.
§ 1910.308(c)(2)	Marking of Class 2 and Class 3 power supplies.
§ 1910.308(d)...............	Fire protective signaling circuits.

[46 FR 4056, Jan. 16, 1981; 46 FR 40185, Aug. 7, 1981]

§ 1910.303 General requirements.

(a) *Approval.* The conductors and equipment required or permitted by this subpart shall be acceptable only if approved.

(b) *Examination, installation, and use of equipment*—(1) *Examination.* Electrical equipment shall be free from recognized hazards that are likely to cause death or serious physical harm to employees. Safety of equipment shall be determined using the following considerations:

(i) Suitability for installation and use in conformity with the provisions of this subpart. Suitability of equipment for an identified purpose may be evidenced by listing or labeling for that identified purpose.

(ii) Mechanical strength and durability, including, for parts designed to enclose and protect other equipment, the adequacy of the protection thus provided.

(iii) Electrical insulation.

(iv) Heating effects under conditions of use.

(v) Arcing effects.

(vi) Classification by type, size, voltage, current capacity, specific use.

(vii) Other factors which contribute to the practical safeguarding of employees using or likely to come in contact with the equipment.

(2) *Installation and use.* Listed or labeled equipment shall be used or installed in accordance with any instructions included in the listing or labeling.

(c) *Splices.* Conductors shall be spliced or joined with splicing devices suitable for the use or by brazing, welding, or soldering with a fusible metal or alloy. Soldered splices shall first be so spliced or joined as to be mechanically and electrically secure without solder and then soldered. All splices and joints and the free ends of conductors shall be covered with an insulation equivalent to that of the conductors or with an insulating device suitable for the purpose.

(d) *Arcing parts.* Parts of electric equipment which in ordinary operation produce arcs, sparks, flames, or molten metal shall be enclosed or separated and isolated from all combustible material.

(e) *Marking.* Electrical equipment may not be used unless the manufacturer's name, trademark, or other descriptive marking by which the organization responsible for the product may be identified is placed on the equipment. Other markings shall be provided giving voltage, current, wattage, or other ratings as necessary. The marking shall be of sufficient durability to withstand the environment involved.

(f) *Identification of disconnecting means and circuits.* Each disconnecting means required by this subpart for motors and appliances shall be legibly marked to indicate its purpose, unless located and arranged so the purpose is evident. Each service, feeder, and branch circuit, at its disconnecting means or overcurrent device, shall be legibly marked to indicate its purpose, unless located and arranged so the purpose is evident. These markings shall be of sufficient durability to withstand the environment involved.

FIGURE 4.1 (*Continued*) Design Safety Standards for Electrical Systems (OSHA-CFR, Title 29, Part 1910, Subpart 1910, Paragraphs 302–308). (*Courtesy General Industry.*)

(g) *600 Volts, nominal, or less*—(1) *Working space about electric equipment.* Sufficient access and working space shall be provided and maintained about all electric equipment to permit ready and safe operation and maintenance of such equipment.

(i) *Working clearances.* Except as required or permitted elsewhere in this subpart, the dimension of the working space in the direction of access to live parts operating at 600 volts or less and likely to require examination, adjustment, servicing, or maintenance while alive may not be less than indicated in Table S-1. In addition to the dimensions shown in Table S-1, workspace may not be less than 30 inches wide in front of the electric equipment. Distances shall be measured from the live parts if they are exposed, or from the enclosure front or opening if the live parts are enclosed. Concrete, brick, or tile walls are considered to be grounded. Working space is not required in back of assemblies such as dead-front switchboards or motor control centers where there are no renewable or adjustable parts such as fuses or switches on the back and where all connections are accessible from locations other than the back.

TABLE S-1—WORKING CLEARANCES

Nominal voltage to ground	Minimum clear distance for condition[2] (ft)		
	(a)	(b)	(c)
0-150	[1]3	[1]3	3
151-600	[1]3	3½	4

[1] Minimum clear distances may be 2 feet 6 inches for installations built prior to April 16, 1981.

[2] Conditions (a), (b), and (c), are as follows: (a) Exposed live parts on one side and no live or grounded parts on the other side of the working space, or exposed live parts on both sides effectively guarded by suitable wood or other insulating material. Insulated wire or insulated busbars operating at not over 300 volts are not considered live parts. (b) Exposed live parts on one side and grounded parts on the other side. (c) Exposed live parts on both sides of the workspace [not guarded as provided in Condition (a)] with the exposed between.

(ii) *Clear spaces.* Working space required by this subpart may not be used for storage. When normally enclosed live parts are exposed for inspection or servicing, the working space, if in a passageway or general open space, shall be suitably guarded.

(iii) *Access and entrance to working space.* At least one entrance of suffi-

cient area shall be provided to give access to the working space about electric equipment.

(iv) *Front working space.* Where there are live parts normally exposed on the front of switchboards or motor control centers, the working space in front of such equipment may not be less than 3 feet.

(v) *Illumination.* Illumination shall be provided for all working spaces about service equipment, switchboards, panelboards, and motor control centers installed indoors.

(vi) *Headroom.* The minimum headroom of working spaces about service equipment, switchboards, panelboards, or motor control centers shall be 6 feet 3 inches.

NOTE: As used in this section a motor control center is an assembly of one or more enclosed sections having a common power bus and principally containing motor control units.

(2) *Guarding of live parts.* (i) Except as required or permitted elsewhere in this subpart, live parts of electric equipment operating at 50 volts or more shall be guarded against accidental contact by approved cabinets or other forms of approved enclosures, or by any of the following means:

(A) By location in a room, vault, or similar enclosure that is accessible only to qualified persons.

(B) By suitable permanent, substantial partitions or screens so arranged that only qualified persons will have access to the space within reach of the live parts. Any openings in such partitions or screens shall be so sized and located that persons are not likely to come into accidental contact with the live parts or to bring conducting objects into contact with them.

(C) By location on a suitable balcony, gallery, or platform so elevated and arranged as to exclude unqualified persons.

(D) By elevation of 8 feet or more above the floor or other working surface.

(ii) In locations where electric equipment would be exposed to physical damage, enclosures or guards shall be so arranged and of such strength as to prevent such damage.

FIGURE 4.1 (*Continued*) Design Safety Standards for Electrical Systems (OSHA-CFR, Title 29, Part 1910, Subpart 1910, Paragraphs 302–308). (*Courtesy General Industry.*)

(iii) Entrances to rooms and other guarded locations containing exposed live parts shall be marked with conspicuous warning signs forbidding unqualified persons to enter.

(h) *Over 600 volts, nominal*—(1) *General.* Conductors and equipment used on circuits exceeding 600 volts, nominal, shall comply with all applicable provisions of paragraphs (a) through (g) of this section and with the following provisions which supplement or modify those requirements. The provisions of paragraphs (h)(2), (h)(3), and (h)(4) of this section do not apply to equipment on the supply side of the service conductors.

(2) *Enclosure for electrical installations.* Electrical installations in a vault, room, closet or in an area surrounded by a wall, screen, or fence, access to which is controlled by lock and key or other approved means, are considered to be accessible to qualified persons only. A wall, screen, or fence less than 8 feet in height is not considered to prevent access unless it has other features that provide a degree of isolation equivalent to an 8 foot fence. The entrances to all buildings, rooms, or enclosures containing exposed live parts or exposed conductors operating at over 600 volts, nominal, shall be kept locked or shall be under the observation of a qualified person at all times.

(i) *Installations accessible to qualified persons only.* Electrical installations having exposed live parts shall be accessible to qualified persons only and shall comply with the applicable provisions of paragraph (h)(3) of this section.

(ii) *Installations accessible to unqualified persons.* Electrical installations that are open to unqualified persons shall be made with metal-enclosed equipment or shall be enclosed in a vault or in an area, access to which is controlled by a lock. If metal-enclosed equipment is installed so that the bottom of the enclosure is less than 8 feet above the floor, the door or cover shall be kept locked. Metal-enclosed switchgear, unit substations, transformers, pull boxes, connection boxes, and other similar associated equipment shall be marked with appropriate caution signs. If equipment is exposed to physical damage from vehicular traffic, suitable guards shall be provided to prevent such damage. Ventilating or similar openings in metal-enclosed equipment shall be designed so that foreign objects inserted through these openings will be deflected from energized parts.

(3) *Workspace about equipment.* Sufficient space shall be provided and maintained about electric equipment to permit ready and safe operation and maintenance of such equipment. Where energized parts are exposed, the minimum clear workspace may not be less than 6 feet 6 inches high (measured vertically from the floor or platform), or less than 3 feet wide (measured parallel to the equipment). The depth shall be as required in Table S-2. The workspace shall be adequate to permit at least a 90-degree opening of doors or hinged panels.

(i) *Working space.* The minimum clear working space in front of electric equipment such as switchboards, control panels, switches, circuit breakers, motor controllers, relays, and similar equipment may not be less than specified in Table S-2 unless otherwise specified in this subpart. Distances shall be measured from the live parts if they are exposed, or from the enclosure front or opening if the live parts are enclosed. However, working space is not required in back of equipment such as deadfront switchboards or control assemblies where there are no renewable or adjustable parts (such as fuses or switches) on the back and where all connections are accessible from locations other than the back. Where rear access is required to work on de-energized parts on the back of enclosed equipment, a minimum working space of 30 inches horizontally shall be provided.

TABLE S-2—MINIMUM DEPTH OF CLEAR WORKING SPACE IN FRONT OF ELECTRIC EQUIPMENT

Nominal voltage to ground	Conditions [a] (ft)		
	(a)	(b)	(c)
601 to 2,500	3	4	5
2,501 to 9,000	4	5	6
9,001 to 25,000	5	6	9
25,001 to 75kV [1]	6	8	10

FIGURE 4.1 (*Continued*) Design Safety Standards for Electrical Systems (OSHA-CFR, Title 29, Part 1910, Subpart 1910, Paragraphs 302–308). (*Courtesy General Industry.*)

TABLE S-2—MINIMUM DEPTH OF CLEAR WORK-
ING SPACE IN FRONT OF ELECTRIC EQUIP-
MENT—Continued

Nominal voltage to ground	Conditions² (ft)		
	(a)	(b)	(c)
Above 75kV ¹	8	10	12

¹ Minimum depth of clear working space in front of electric equipment with a nominal voltage to ground above 25,000 volts may be the same as for 25,000 volts under Conditions (a), (b), and (c) for installations built prior to April 16, 1981.
² Conditions (a), (b), and (c) are as follows: (a) Exposed live parts on one side and no live or grounded parts on the other side of the working space, or exposed live parts on both sides effectively guarded by suitable wood or other insulating materials. Insulated wire or insulated busbars operating at not over 300 volts are not considered live parts. (b) Exposed live parts on one side and grounded parts on the other side. Concrete, brick, or tile walls will be considered as grounded surfaces. (c) Exposed live parts on both sides of the workspace not guarded as provided in Condition (a) with the operator between.

(ii) *Illumination.* Adequate illumination shall be provided for all working spaces about electric equipment. The lighting outlets shall be so arranged that persons changing lamps or making repairs on the lighting system will not be endangered by live parts or other equipment. The points of control shall be so located that persons are not likely to come in contact with any live part or moving part of the equipment while turning on the lights.

(iii) *Elevation of unguarded live parts.* Unguarded live parts above working space shall be maintained at elevations not less than specified in Table S-3.

TABLE S-3—ELEVATION OF UNGUARDED
ENERGIZED PARTS ABOVE WORKING SPACE

Nominal voltage between phases	Minimum elevation
601 to 7,500	*8 feet 6 inches.
7,501 to 35,000	9 feet.
Over 35kV...........................	9 feet + 0.37 inches per kV above 35kV.

*Note.—Minimum elevation may be 8 feet 0 inches for installations built prior to April 16, 1981 if the nominal voltage between phases is in the range of 601-6600 volts.

(4) *Entrance and access to work-space.* (See § 1910.302(b)(3).)

(i) At least one entrance not less than 24 inches wide and 6 feet 6 inches high shall be provided to give access to the working space about electric equipment. On switchboard and control panels exceeding 48 inches in width, there shall be one entrance at each end of such board where practicable. Where bare energized parts at any voltage or insulated energized parts above 600 volts are located adjacent to such entrance, they shall be suitably guarded.

(ii) Permanent ladders or stairways shall be provided to give safe access to the working space around electric equipment installed on platforms, balconies, mezzanine floors, or in attic or roof rooms or spaces.

[46 FR 4056, Jan. 16, 1981; 46 FR 40185, Aug. 7, 1981]

§ 1910.304   **Wiring design and protection.**

(a) *Use and identification of grounded and grounding conductors.* (1) *Identification of conductors.* A conductor used as a grounded conductor shall be identifiable and distinguishable from all other conductors. A conductor used as an equipment grounding conductor shall be identifiable and distinguishable from all other conductors.

(2) *Polarity of connections.* No grounded conductor may be attached to any terminal or lead so as to reverse designated polarity.

(3) *Use of grounding terminals and devices.* A grounding terminal or grounding-type device on a receptacle, cord connector, or attachment plug may not be used for purposes other than grounding.

(b) *Branch circuits*—(1) [Reserved]

(2) *Outlet devices.* Outlet devices shall have an ampere rating not less than the load to be served.

(c) *Outside conductors, 600 volts, nominal, or less.* Paragraphs (c)(1), (c)(2), (c)(3), and (c)(4) of this section apply to branch circuit, feeder, and service conductors rated 600 volts, nominal, or less and run outdoors as open conductors. Paragraph (c)(5) applies to lamps installed under such conductors.

(1) *Conductors on poles.* Conductors supported on poles shall provide a horizontal climbing space not less than the following:

(i) Power conductors below communication conductors—30 inches.

(ii) Power conductors alone or above communication conductors: 300 volts or less—24 inches; more than 300 volts—30 inches.

FIGURE 4.1 (*Continued*)   Design Safety Standards for Electrical Systems (OSHA-CFR, Title 29, Part 1910, Subpart 1910, Paragraphs 302–308). (*Courtesy General Industry.*)

(iii) Communication conductors below power conductors with power conductors 300 volts or less—24 inches; more than 300 volts—30 inches.

(2) *Clearance from ground.* Open conductors shall conform to the following minimum clearances:

(i) 10 feet—above finished grade, sidewalks, or from any platform or projection from which they might be reached.

(ii) 12 feet—over areas subject to vehicular traffic other than truck traffic.

(iii) 15 feet—over areas other than those specified in paragraph (c)(2)(iv) of this section that are subject to truck traffic.

(iv) 18 feet—over public streets, alleys, roads, and driveways.

(3) *Clearance from building openings.* Conductors shall have a clearance of at least 3 feet from windows, doors, porches, fire escapes, or similar locations. Conductors run above the top level of a window are considered to be out of reach from that window and, therefore, do not have to be 3 feet away.

(4) *Clearance over roofs.* Conductors shall have a clearance of not less than 8 feet from the highest point of roofs over which they pass, except that:

(i) Where the voltage between conductors is 300 volts or less and the roof has a slope of not less than 4 inches in 12, the clearance from roofs shall be at least 3 feet, or

(ii) Where the voltage between conductors is 300 volts or less and the conductors do not pass over more than 4 feet of the overhang portion of the roof and they are terminated at a through-the-roof raceway or approved support, the clearance from roofs shall be at least 18 inches.

(5) *Location of outdoor lamps.* Lamps for outdoor lighting shall be located below all live conductors, transformers, or other electric equipment, unless such equipment is controlled by a disconnecting means that can be locked in the open position or unless adequate clearances or other safeguards are provided for relamping operations.

(d) *Services—*(1) *Disconnecting means—*(i) *General.* Means shall be provided to disconnect all conductors in a building or other structure from the service-entrance conductors. The disconnecting means shall plainly indicate whether it is in the open or closed position and shall be installed at a readily accessible location nearest the point of entrance of the service-entrance conductors.

(ii) *Simultaneous opening of poles.* Each service disconnecting means shall simultaneously disconnect all ungrounded conductors.

(2) *Services over 600 volts, nominal.* The following additional requirements apply to services over 600 volts, nominal.

(i) *Guarding.* Service-entrance conductors installed as open wires shall be guarded to make them accessible only to qualified persons.

(ii) *Warning signs.* Signs warning of high voltage shall be posted where other than qualified employees might come in contact with live parts.

(e) *Overcurrent protection.* (1) *600 volts, nominal, or less.* The following requirements apply to overcurrent protection of circuits rated 600 volts, nominal, or less.

(i) *Protection of conductors and equipment.* Conductors and equipment shall be protected from overcurrent in accordance with their ability to safely conduct current.

(ii) *Grounded conductors.* Except for motor running overload protection, overcurrent devices may not interrupt the continuity of the grounded conductor unless all conductors of the circuit are opened simultaneously.

(iii) *Disconnection of fuses and thermal cutouts.* Except for service fuses, all cartridge fuses which are accessible to other than qualified persons and all fuses and thermal cutouts on circuits over 150 volts to ground shall be provided with disconnecting means. This disconnecting means shall be installed so that the fuse or thermal cutout can be disconnected from its supply without disrupting service to equipment and circuits unrelated to those protected by the overcurrent device.

(iv) *Location in or on premises.* Overcurrent devices shall be readily accessible to each employee or authorized building management personnel. These overcurrent devices may not be located where they will be exposed to

FIGURE 4.1 (*Continued*)   Design Safety Standards for Electrical Systems (OSHA-CFR, Title 29, Part 1910, Subpart 1910, Paragraphs 302–308). (*Courtesy General Industry.*)

physical damage nor in the vicinity of easily ignitible material.

(v) *Arcing or suddenly moving parts.* Fuses and circuit breakers shall be so located or shielded that employees will not be burned or otherwise injured by their operation.

(vi) *Circuit breakers.* (A) Circuit breakers shall clearly indicate whether they are in the open (off) or closed (on) position.

(B) Where circuit breaker handles on switchboards are operated vertically rather than horizontally or rotationally, the up position of the handle shall be the closed (on) position. (See § 1910.302(b)(3).)

(C) If used as switches in 120-volt, fluorescent lighting circuits, circuit breakers shall be approved for the purpose and marked "SWD." (See § 1910.302(b)(3).)

(2) *Over 600 volts, nominal.* Feeders and branch circuits over 600 volts, nominal, shall have short-circuit protection.

(f) *Grounding.* Paragraphs (f)(1) through (f)(7) of this section contain grounding requirements for systems, circuits, and equipment.

(1) *Systems to be grounded.* The following systems which supply premises wiring shall be grounded:

(i) All 3-wire DC systems shall have their neutral conductor grounded.

(ii) Two-wire DC systems operating at over 50 volts through 300 volts between conductors shall be grounded unless:

(A) They supply only industrial equipment in limited areas and are equipped with a ground detector; or

(B) They are rectifier-derived from an AC system complying with paragraphs (f)(1)(iii), (f)(1)(iv), and (f)(1)(v) of this section; or

(C) They are fire-protective signaling circuits having a maximum current of 0.030 amperes.

(iii) AC circuits of less than 50 volts shall be grounded if they are installed as overhead conductors outside of buildings or if they are supplied by transformers and the transformer primary supply system is ungrounded or exceeds 150 volts to ground.

(iv) AC systems of 50 volts to 1000 volts shall be grounded under any of the following conditions, unless ex-

empted by paragraph (f)(1)(v) of this section:

(A) If the system can be so grounded that the maximum voltage to ground on the ungrounded conductors does not exceed 150 volts;

(B) If the system is nominally rated 480Y/277 volt, 3-phase, 4-wire in which the neutral is used as a circuit conductor;

(C) If the system is nominally rated 240/120 volt, 3-phase, 4-wire in which the midpoint of one phase is used as a circuit conductor; or

(D) If a service conductor is uninsulated.

(v) AC systems of 50 volts to 1000 volts are not required to be grounded under any of the following conditions:

(A) If the system is used exclusively to supply industrial electric furnaces for melting, refining, tempering, and the like.

(B) If the system is separately derived and is used exclusively for rectifiers supplying only adjustable speed industrial drives.

(C) If the system is separately derived and is supplied by a transformer that has a primary voltage rating less than 1000 volts, provided all of the following conditions are met:

(*1*) The system is used exclusively for control circuits,

(*2*) The conditions of maintenance and supervision assure that only qualified persons will service the installation,

(*3*) Continuity of control power is required, and

(*4*) Ground detectors are installed on the control system.

(D) If the system is an isolated power system that supplies circuits in health care facilities.

(2) *Conductors to be grounded.* For AC premises wiring systems the identified conductor shall be grounded.

(3) *Grounding connections.* (i) For a grounded system, a grounding electrode conductor shall be used to connect both the equipment grounding conductor and the grounded circuit conductor to the grounding electrode. Both the equipment grounding conductor and the grounding electrode conductor shall be connected to the grounded circuit conductor on the supply side of the service disconnect-

FIGURE 4.1 (*Continued*)   Design Safety Standards for Electrical Systems (OSHA-CFR, Title 29, Part 1910, Subpart 1910, Paragraphs 302–308). (*Courtesy General Industry.*)

ing means, or on the supply side of the system disconnecting means or overcurrent devices if the system is separately derived.

(ii) For an ungrounded service-supplied system, the equipment grounding conductor shall be connected to the grounding electrode conductor at the service equipment. For an ungrounded separately derived system, the equipment grounding conductor shall be connected to the grounding electrode conductor at, or ahead of, the system disconnecting means or overcurrent devices.

(iii) On extensions of existing branch circuits which do not have an equipment grounding conductor, grounding-type receptacles may be grounded to a grounded cold water pipe near the equipment.

(4) *Grounding path.* The path to ground from circuits, equipment, and enclosures shall be permanent and continuous.

(5) *Supports, enclosures, and equipment to be grounded*—(i) *Supports and enclosures for conductors.* Metal cable trays, metal raceways, and metal enclosures for conductors shall be grounded, except that:

(A) Metal enclosures such as sleeves that are used to protect cable assemblies from physical damage need not be grounded; or

(B) Metal enclosures for conductors added to existing installations of open wire, knob-and-tube wiring, and nonmetallic-sheathed cable need not be grounded if all of the following conditions are met: (1) Runs are less than 25 feet; (2) enclosures are free from probable contact with ground, grounded metal, metal laths, or other conductive materials; and (3) enclosures are guarded against employee contact.

(ii) *Service equipment enclosures.* Metal enclosures for service equipment shall be grounded.

(iii) *Frames of ranges and clothes dryers.* Frames of electric ranges, wall-mounted ovens, counter-mounted cooking units, clothes dryers, and metal outlet or junction boxes which are part of the circuit for these appliances shall be grounded.

(iv) *Fixed equipment.* Exposed non-current-carrying metal parts of fixed equipment which may become energized shall be grounded under any of the following conditions:

(A) If within 8 feet vertically or 5 feet horizontally of ground or grounded metal objects and subject to employee contact.

(B) If located in a wet or damp location and not isolated.

(C) If in electrical contact with metal.

(D) If in a hazardous (classified) location.

(E) If supplied by a metal-clad, metal-sheathed, or grounded metal raceway wiring method.

(F) If equipment operates with any terminal at over 150 volts to ground; however, the following need not be grounded:

(1) Enclosures for switches or circuit breakers used for other than service equipment and accessible to qualified persons only;

(2) Metal frames of electrically heated appliances which are permanently and effectively insulated from ground; and

(3) The cases of distribution apparatus such as transformers and capacitors mounted on wooden poles at a height exceeding 8 feet above ground or grade level.

(v) *Equipment connected by cord and plug.* Under any of the conditions described in paragraphs (f)(5)(v)(A) through (f)(5)(v)(C) of this section, exposed non-current-carrying metal parts of cord- and plug-connected equipment which may become energized shall be grounded.

(A) If in hazardous (classified) locations (see § 1910.307).

(B) If operated at over 150 volts to ground, except for guarded motors and metal frames of electrically heated appliances if the appliance frames are permanently and effectively insulated from ground.

(C) If the equipment is of the following types:

(1) Refrigerators, freezers, and air conditioners;

(2) Clothes-washing, clothes-drying and dishwashing machines, sump pumps, and electrical aquarium equipment;

(3) Hand-held motor-operated tools;

(4) Motor-operated appliances of the following types: hedge clippers, lawn

FIGURE 4.1 (*Continued*)   Design Safety Standards for Electrical Systems (OSHA-CFR, Title 29, Part 1910, Subpart 1910, Paragraphs 302–308). (*Courtesy General Industry.*)

mowers, snow blowers, and wet scrubbers;

(5) Cord- and plug-connected appliances used in damp or wet locations or by employees standing on the ground or on metal floors or working inside of metal tanks or boilers;

(6) Portable and mobile X-ray and associated equipment;

(7) Tools likely to be used in wet and conductive locations; and

(8) Portable hand lamps.

Tools likely to be used in wet and conductive locations need not be grounded if supplied through an isolating transformer with an ungrounded secondary of not over 50 volts. Listed or labeled portable tools and appliances protected by an approved system of double insulation, or its equivalent, need not be grounded. If such a system is employed, the equipment shall be distinctively marked to indicate that the tool or appliance utilizes an approved system of double insulation.

(vi) *Nonelectrical equipment.* The metal parts of the following nonelectrical equipment shall be grounded: frames and tracks of electrically operated cranes; frames of nonelectrically driven elevator cars to which electric conductors are attached; hand operated metal shifting ropes or cables of electric elevators, and metal partitions, grill work, and similar metal enclosures around equipment of over 750 volts between conductors.

(6) *Methods of grounding fixed equipment.* (i) Non-current-carrying metal parts of fixed equipment, if required to be grounded by this subpart, shall be grounded by an equipment grounding conductor which is contained within the same raceway, cable, or cord, or runs with or encloses the circuit conductors. For DC circuits only, the equipment grounding conductor may be run separately from the circuit conductors.

(ii) Electric equipment is considered to be effectively grounded if it is secured to, and in electrical contact with, a metal rack or structure that is provided for its support and the metal rack or structure is grounded by the method specified for the non-current-carrying metal parts of fixed equipment in paragraph (f)(6)(i) of this section. For installations made before April 16, 1981, only, electric equipment is also considered to be effectively grounded if it is secured to, and in metallic contact with, the grounded structural metal frame of a building. Metal car frames supported by metal hoisting cables attached to or running over metal sheaves or drums of grounded elevator machines are also considered to be effectively grounded.

(7) *Grounding of systems and circuits of 1000 volts and over (high voltage.)*—(i) *General.* If high voltage systems are grounded, they shall comply with all applicable provisions of paragraphs (f)(1) through (f)(6) of this section as supplemented and modified by this paragraph (f)(7).

(ii) *Grounding of systems supplying portable or mobile equipment.* (See § 1910.302(b)(3).) Systems supplying portable or mobile high voltage equipment, other than substations installed on a temporary basis, shall comply with the following:

(A) Portable and mobile high voltage equipment shall be supplied from a system having its neutral grounded through an impedance. If a delta-connected high voltage system is used to supply the equipment, a system neutral shall be derived.

(B) Exposed non-current-carrying metal parts of portable and mobile equipment shall be connected by an equipment grounding conductor to the point at which the system neutral impedance is grounded.

(C) Ground-fault detection and relaying shall be provided to automatically de-energize any high voltage system component which has developed a ground fault. The continuity of the equipment grounding conductor shall be continuously monitored so as to de-energize automatically the high voltage feeder to the portable equipment upon loss of continuity of the equipment grounding conductor.

(D) The grounding electrode to which the portable or mobile equipment system neutral impedance is connected shall be isolated from and separated in the ground by at least 20 feet from any other system or equipment grounding electrode, and there shall be no direct connection between the

FIGURE 4.1 (*Continued*)   Design Safety Standards for Electrical Systems (OSHA-CFR, Title 29, Part 1910, Subpart 1910, Paragraphs 302–308). (*Courtesy General Industry.*)

grounding electrodes, such as buried pipe, fence, etc.

(iii) *Grounding of equipment.* All non-current-carrying metal parts of portable equipment and fixed equipment including their associated fences, housings, enclosures, and supporting structures shall be grounded. However, equipment which is guarded by location and isolated from ground need not be grounded. Additionally, pole-mounted distribution apparatus at a height exceeding 8 feet above ground or grade level need not be grounded.

[46 FR 4056, Jan. 16, 1981; 46 FR 40185, Aug. 7, 1981, as amended at 55 FR 32015, Aug. 6, 1990]

§ 1910.305 **Wiring methods, components, and equipment for general use.**

(a) *Wiring methods.* The provisions of this section do not apply to the conductors that are an integral part of factory-assembled equipment.

(1) *General requirements*—(i) *Electrical continuity of metal raceways and enclosures.* Metal raceways, cable armor, and other metal enclosures for conductors shall be metallically joined together into a continuous electric conductor and shall be so connected to all boxes, fittings, and cabinets as to provide effective electrical continuity.

(ii) *Wiring in ducts.* No wiring systems of any type shall be installed in ducts used to transport dust, loose stock or flammable vapors. No wiring system of any type may be installed in any duct used for vapor removal or for ventilation of commercial-type cooking equipment, or in any shaft containing only such ducts.

(2) *Temporary wiring.* Temporary electrical power and lighting wiring methods may be of a class less than would be required for a permanent installation. Except as specifically modified in this paragraph, all other requirements of this subpart for permanent wiring shall apply to temporary wiring installations.

(i) *Uses permitted, 600 volts, nominal, or less.* Temporary electrical power and lighting installations 600 volts, nominal, or less may be used only:

(A) During and for remodeling, maintenance, repair, or demolition of buildings, structures, or equipment, and similar activities;

(B) For experimental or development work, and

(C) For a period not to exceed 90 days for Christmas decorative lighting, carnivals, and similar purposes.

(ii) *Uses permitted, over 600 volts, nominal.* Temporary wiring over 600 volts, nominal, may be used only during periods of tests, experiments, or emergencies.

(iii) *General requirements for temporary wiring.* (A) Feeders shall originate in an approved distribution center. The conductors shall be run as multiconductor cord or cable assemblies, or, where not subject to physical damage, they may be run as open conductors on insulators not more than 10 feet apart.

(B) Branch circuits shall originate in an approved power outlet or panelboard. Conductors shall be multiconductor cord or cable assemblies or open conductors. If run as open conductors they shall be fastened at ceiling height every 10 feet. No branch-circuit conductor may be laid on the floor. Each branch circuit that supplies receptacles or fixed equipment shall contain a separate equipment grounding conductor if run as open conductors.

(C) Receptacles shall be of the grounding type. Unless installed in a complete metallic raceway, each branch circuit shall contain a separate equipment grounding conductor and all receptacles shall be electrically connected to the grounding conductor.

(D) No bare conductors nor earth returns may be used for the wiring of any temporary circuit.

(E) Suitable disconnecting switches or plug connectors shall be installed to permit the disconnection of all ungrounded conductors of each temporary circuit.

(F) Lamps for general illumination shall be protected from accidental contact or breakage. Protection shall be provided by elevation of at least 7 feet from normal working surface or by a suitable fixture or lampholder with a guard.

(G) Flexible cords and cables shall be protected from accidental damage. Sharp corners and projections shall be

FIGURE 4.1 (*Continued*)   Design Safety Standards for Electrical Systems (OSHA-CFR, Title 29, Part 1910, Subpart 1910, Paragraphs 302–308). (*Courtesy General Industry.*)

avoided. Where passing through doorways or other pinch points, flexible cords and cables shall be provided with protection to avoid damage.

(3) *Cable trays.* (i) *Uses permitted.* (a) Only the following may be installed in cable tray systems:

(1) Mineral-insulated metal-sheathed cable (Type MI);

(2) Armored cable (Type AC);

(3) Metal-clad cable (Type MC);

(4) Power-limited tray cable (Type PLTC);

(5) Nonmetallic-sheathed cable (Type NM or NMC);

(6) Shielded nonmetallic-sheathed cable (Type SNM);

(7) Multiconductor service-entrance cable (Type SE or USE);

(8) Multiconductor underground feeder and branch-circuit cable (Type UF);

(9) Power and control tray cable (Type TC);

(10) Other factory-assembled, multiconductor control, signal, or power cables which are specifically approved for installation in cable trays; or

(11) Any approved conduit or raceway with its contained conductors.

(b) In industrial establishments only, where conditions of maintenance and supervision assure that only qualified persons will service the installed cable tray system, the following cables may also be installed in ladder, ventilated trough, or 4 inch ventilated channeltype cable trays:

(1) Single conductor cables which are 250 MCM or larger and are Types RHH, RHW, USE, or THW, and other 250 MCM or larger single conductor cables if specifically approved for installation in cable trays. Where exposed to direct rays of the sun, cables shall be sunlight-resistant.

(2) Type MV cables, where exposed to direct rays of the sun, shall be sunlight-resistant.

(c) Cable trays in hazardous (classified) locations shall contain only the cable types permitted in such locations.

(ii) *Uses not permitted.* Cable tray systems may not be used in hoistways or where subjected to severe physical damage.

(4) *Open wiring on insulators*—(i) *Uses permitted.* Open wiring on insulators is only permitted on systems of 600 volts, nominal, or less for industrial or agricultural establishments and for services.

(ii) *Conductor supports.* Conductors shall be rigidly supported on noncombustible, nonabsorbent insulating materials and may not contact any other objects.

(iii) *Flexible nonmetallic tubing.* In dry locations where not exposed to severe physical damage, conductors may be separately enclosed in flexible nonmetallic tubing. The tubing shall be in continuous lengths not exceeding 15 feet and secured to the surface by straps at intervals not exceeding 4 feet 6 inches.

(iv) *Through walls, floors, wood cross members, etc.* Open conductors shall be separated from contact with walls, floors, wood cross members, or partitions through which they pass by tubes or bushings of noncombustible, nonabsorbent insulating material. If the bushing is shorter than the hole, a waterproof sleeve of nonconductive material shall be inserted in the hole and an insulating bushing slipped into the sleeve at each end in such a manner as to keep the conductors absolutely out of contact with the sleeve. Each conductor shall be carried through a separate tube or sleeve.

(v) *Protection from physical damage.* Conductors within 7 feet from the floor are considered exposed to physical damage. Where open conductors cross ceiling joists and wall studs and are exposed to physical damage, they shall be protected.

(b) *Cabinets, boxes, and fittings*—(1) *Conductors entering boxes, cabinets, or fittings.* Conductors entering boxes, cabinets, or fittings shall also be protected from abrasion, and openings through which conductors enter shall be effectively closed. Unused openings in cabinets, boxes, and fittings shall be effectively closed.

(2) *Covers and canopies.* All pull boxes, junction boxes, and fittings shall be provided with covers approved for the purpose. If metal covers are used they shall be grounded. In completed installations each outlet box shall have a cover, faceplate, or fixture canopy. Covers of outlet boxes having holes through which flexible

FIGURE 4.1 (*Continued*) Design Safety Standards for Electrical Systems (OSHA-CFR, Title 29, Part 1910, Subpart 1910, Paragraphs 302–308). (*Courtesy General Industry.*)

cord pendants pass shall be provided with bushings designed for the purpose or shall have smooth, well-rounded surfaces on which the cords may bear.

(3) *Pull and junction boxes for systems over 600 volts, nominal.* In addition to other requirements in this section for pull and junction boxes, the following shall apply to these boxes for systems over 600 volts, nominal:

(i) Boxes shall provide a complete enclosure for the contained conductors or cables.

(ii) Boxes shall be closed by suitable covers securely fastened in place. Underground box covers that weigh over 100 pounds meet this requirement. Covers for boxes shall be permanently marked "HIGH VOLTAGE." The marking shall be on the outside of the box cover and shall be readily visible and legible.

(c) *Switches—*(1) *Knife switches.* Single-throw knife switches shall be so connected that the blades are dead when the switch is in the open position. Single-throw knife switches shall be so placed that gravity will not tend to close them. Single-throw knife switches approved for use in the inverted position shall be provided with a locking device that will ensure that the blades remain in the open position when so set. Double-throw knife switches may be mounted so that the throw will be either vertical or horizontal. However, if the throw is vertical a locking device shall be provided to ensure that the blades remain in the open position when so set.

(2) *Faceplates for flush-mounted snap switches.* Flush snap switches that are mounted in ungrounded metal boxes and located within reach of conducting floors or other conducting surfaces shall be provided with faceplates of nonconducting, noncombustible material.

(d) *Switchboards and panelboards.* Switchboards that have any exposed live parts shall be located in permanently dry locations and accessible only to qualified persons. Panelboards shall be mounted in cabinets, cutout boxes, or enclosures approved for the purpose and shall be dead front. However, panelboards other than the dead front externally-operable type are per-

mitted where accessible only to qualified persons. Exposed blades of knife switches shall be dead when open.

(e) *Enclosures for damp or wet locations.* (1) Cabinets, cutout boxes, fittings, boxes, and panelboard enclosures in damp or wet locations shall be installed so as to prevent moisture or water from entering and accumulating within the enclosures. In wet locations the enclosures shall be weatherproof.

(2) Switches, circuit breakers, and switchboards installed in wet locations shall be enclosed in weatherproof enclosures.

(f) *Conductors for general wiring.* All conductors used for general wiring shall be insulated unless otherwise permitted in this Subpart. The conductor insulation shall be of a type that is approved for the voltage, operating temperature, and location of use. Insulated conductors shall be distinguishable by appropriate color or other suitable means as being grounded conductors, ungrounded conductors, or equipment grounding conductors.

(g) *Flexible cords and cables—*(1) *Use of flexible cords and cables.* (i) Flexible cords and cables shall be approved and suitable for conditions of use and location. Flexible cords and cables shall be used only for:

(A) Pendants;
(B) Wiring of fixtures;
(C) Connection of portable lamps or appliances;
(D) Elevator cables;
(E) Wiring of cranes and hoists;
(F) Connection of stationary equipment to facilitate their frequent interchange;
(G) Prevention of the transmission of noise or vibration;
(H) Appliances where the fastening means and mechanical connections are designed to permit removal for maintenance and repair; or
(i) Data processing cables approved as a part of the data processing system.

(ii) If used as permitted in paragraphs (g)(1)(i)(c), (g)(1)(i)(f), or (g)(1)(i)(h) of this section, the flexible cord shall be equipped with an attachment plug and shall be energized from an approved receptacle outlet.

FIGURE 4.1 (*Continued*)   Design Safety Standards for Electrical Systems (OSHA-CFR, Title 29, Part 1910, Subpart 1910, Paragraphs 302–308). (*Courtesy General Industry.*)

(iii) Unless specifically permitted in paragraph (g)(1)(i) of this section, flexible cords and cables may not be used:

(A) As a substitute for the fixed wiring of a structure;

(B) Where run through holes in walls, ceilings, or floors;

(C) Where run through doorways, windows, or similar openings;

(D) Where attached to building surfaces; or

(E) Where concealed behind building walls, ceilings, or floors.

(iv) Flexible cords used in show windows and showcases shall be Type S, SO, SJ, SJO, ST, STO, SJT, SJTO, or AFS except for the wiring of chain-supported lighting fixtures and supply cords for portable lamps and other merchandise being displayed or exhibited.

(2) *Identification, splices, and terminations.* (i) A conductor of a flexible cord or cable that is used as a grounded conductor or an equipment grounding conductor shall be distinguishable from other conductors. Types SJ, SJO, SJT, SJTO, S, SO, ST, and STO shall be durably marked on the surface with the type designation, size, and number of conductors.

(ii) Flexible cords shall be used only in continuous lengths without splice or tap. Hard service flexible cords No. 12 or larger may be repaired if spliced so that the splice retains the insulation, outer sheath properties, and usage characteristics of the cord being spliced.

(iii) Flexible cords shall be connected to devices and fittings so that strain relief is provided which will prevent pull from being directly transmitted to joints or terminal screws.

(h) *Portable cables over 600 volts, nominal.* Multiconductor portable cable for use in supplying power to portable or mobile equipment at over 600 volts, nominal, shall consist of No. 8 or larger conductors employing flexible stranding. Cables operated at over 2,000 volts shall be shielded for the purpose of confining the voltage stresses to the insulation. Grounding conductors shall be provided. Connectors for these cables shall be of a locking type with provisions to prevent their opening or closing while ener-

gized. Strain relief shall be provided at connections and terminations. Portable cables may not be operated with splices unless the splices are of the permanent molded, vulcanized, or other approved type. Termination enclosures shall be suitably marked with a high voltage hazard warning, and terminations shall be accessible only to authorized and qualified personnel.

(i) *Fixture wires*—(1) *General.* Fixture wires shall be approved for the voltage, temperature, and location of use. A fixture wire which is used as a grounded conductor shall be identified.

(2) *Uses permitted.* Fixture wires may be used:

(i) For installation in lighting fixtures and in similar equipment where enclosed or protected and not subject to bending or twisting in use; or

(ii) For connecting lighting fixtures to the branch-circuit conductors supplying the fixtures.

(3) *Uses not permitted.* Fixture wires may not be used as branch-circuit conductors except as permitted for Class 1 power limited circuits.

(j) *Equipment for general use*—(1) *Lighting fixtures, lampholders, lamps, and receptacles.* (i) Fixtures, lampholders, lamps, rosettes, and receptacles may have no live parts normally exposed to employee contact. However, rosettes and cleat-type lampholders and receptacles located at least 8 feet above the floor may have exposed parts.

(ii) Handlamps of the portable type supplied through flexible cords shall be equipped with a handle of molded composition or other material approved for the purpose, and a substantial guard shall be attached to the lampholder or the handle.

(iii) Lampholders of the screw-shell type shall be installed for use as lampholders only. Lampholders installed in wet or damp locations shall be of the weatherproof type.

(iv) Fixtures installed in wet or damp locations shall be approved for the purpose and shall be so constructed or installed that water cannot enter or accumulate in wireways, lampholders, or other electrical parts.

(2) *Receptacles, cord connectors, and attachment plugs (caps).* (i) Recepta-

FIGURE 4.1 (*Continued*)   Design Safety Standards for Electrical Systems (OSHA-CFR, Title 29, Part 1910, Subpart 1910, Paragraphs 302–308). (*Courtesy General Industry.*)

cles, cord connectors, and attachment plugs shall be constructed so that no receptacle or cord connector will accept an attachment plug with a different voltage or current rating than that for which the device is intended. However, a 20-ampere T-slot receptacle or cord connector may accept a 15-ampere attachment plug of the same voltage rating.

(ii) A receptacle installed in a wet or damp location shall be suitable for the location.

(3) *Appliances.* (i) Appliances, other than those in which the current-carrying parts at high temperatures are necessarily exposed, may have no live parts normally exposed to employee contact.

(ii) A means shall be provided to disconnect each appliance.

(iii) Each appliance shall be marked with its rating in volts and amperes or volts and watts.

(4) *Motors.* This paragraph applies to motors, motor circuits, and controllers.

(i) *In sight from.* If specified that one piece of equipment shall be "in sight from" another piece of equipment, one shall be visible and not more than 50 feet from the other.

(ii) *Disconnecting means.* (A) A disconnecting means shall be located in sight from the controller location. However, a single disconnecting means may be located adjacent to a group of coordinated controllers mounted adjacent to each other on a multi-motor continuous process machine. The controller disconnecting means for motor branch circuits over 600 volts, nominal, may be out of sight of the controller, if the controller is marked with a warning label giving the location and identification of the disconnecting means which is to be locked in the open position.

(B) The disconnecting means shall disconnect the motor and the controller from all ungrounded supply conductors and shall be so designed that no pole can be operated independently.

(C) If a motor and the driven machinery are not in sight from the controller location, the installation shall comply with one of the following conditions:

(1) The controller disconnecting means shall be capable of being locked in the open position.

(2) A manually operable switch that will disconnect the motor from its source of supply shall be placed in sight from the motor location.

(D) The disconnecting means shall plainly indicate whether it is in the open (off) or closed (on) position.

(E) The disconnecting means shall be readily accessible. If more than one disconnect is provided for the same equipment, only one need be readily accessible.

(F) An individual disconnecting means shall be provided for each motor, but a single disconnecting means may be used for a group of motors under any one of the following conditions:

(1) If a number of motors drive special parts of a single machine or piece of apparatus, such as a metal or woodworking machine, crane, or hoist;

(2) If a group of motors is under the protection of one set of branch-circuit protective devices; or

(3) If a group of motors is in a single room in sight from the location of the disconnecting means.

(iii) *Motor overload, short-circuit, and ground-fault protection.* Motors, motor-control apparatus, and motor branch-circuit conductors shall be protected against overheating due to motor overloads or failure to start, and against short-circuits or ground faults. These provisions shall not require overload protection that will stop a motor where a shutdown is likely to introduce additional or increased hazards, as in the case of fire pumps, or where continued operation of a motor is necessary for a safe shutdown of equipment or process and motor overload sensing devices are connected to a supervised alarm.

(iv) *Protection of live parts—all voltages.* (A) Stationary motors having commutators, collectors, and brush rigging located inside of motor end brackets and not conductively connected to supply circuits operating at more than 150 volts to ground need not have such parts guarded. Exposed live parts of motors and controllers operating at 50 volts or more between termi-

---

FIGURE 4.1 (*Continued*)   Design Safety Standards for Electrical Systems (OSHA-CFR, Title 29, Part 1910, Subpart 1910, Paragraphs 302–308). (*Courtesy General Industry.*)

nals shall be guarded against accidental contact by any of the following:

(*1*) By installation in a room or enclosure that is accessible only to qualified persons;

(*2*) By installation on a suitable balcony, gallery, or platform, so elevated and arranged as to exclude unqualified persons; or

(*3*) By elevation 8 feet or more above the floor.

(B) Where live parts of motors or controllers operating at over 150 volts to ground are guarded against accidental contact only by location, and where adjustment or other attendance may be necessary during the operation of the apparatus, suitable insulating mats or platforms shall be provided so that the attendant cannot readily touch live parts unless standing on the mats or platforms.

(5) *Transformers.* (i) The following paragraphs cover the installation of all transformers except the following:

(A) Current transformers;

(B) Dry-type transformers installed as a component part of other apparatus;

(C) Transformers which are an integral part of an X-ray, high frequency, or electrostatic-coating apparatus;

(D) Transformers used with Class 2 and Class 3 circuits, sign and outline lighting, electric discharge lighting, and power-limited fire-protective signalling circuits; and

(E) Liquid-filled or dry-type transformers used for research, development, or testing, where effective safeguard arrangements are provided.

(ii) The operating voltage of exposed live parts of transformer installations shall be indicated by warning signs or visible markings on the equipment or structure.

(iii) Dry-type, high fire point liquid-insulated, and askarel-insulated transformers installed indoors and rated over 35kV shall be in a vault.

(iv) If they present a fire hazard to employees, oil-insulated transformers installed indoors shall be in a vault.

(v) Combustible material, combustible buildings and parts of buildings, fire escapes, and door and window openings shall be safeguarded from fires which may originate in oil-insulated transformers attached to or adjacent to a building or combustible material.

(vi) Transformer vaults shall be constructed so as to contain fire and combustible liquids within the vault and to prevent unauthorized access. Locks and latches shall be so arranged that a vault door can be readily opened from the inside.

(vii) Any pipe or duct system foreign to the vault installation may not enter or pass through a transformer vault.

(viii) Materials may not be stored in transformer vaults.

(6) *Capacitors.* (i) All capacitors, except surge capacitors or capacitors included as a component part of other apparatus, shall be provided with an automatic means of draining the stored charge after the capacitor is disconnected from its source of supply.

(ii) Capacitors rated over 600 volts, nominal, shall comply with the following additional requirements:

(A) Isolating or disconnecting switches (with no interrupting rating) shall be interlocked with the load interrupting device or shall be provided with prominently displayed caution signs to prevent switching load current.

(B) For series capacitors (see § 1910.302(b)(3)), the proper switching shall be assured by use of at least one of the following:

(*1*) Mechanically sequenced isolating and bypass switches,

(*2*) Interlocks, or

(*3*) Switching procedure prominently displayed at the switching location.

(7) *Storage batteries.* Provisions shall be made for sufficient diffusion and ventilation of gases from storage batteries to prevent the accumulation of explosive mixtures.

[46 FR 4056, Jan. 16, 1981; 46 FR 40185, Aug. 7, 1981]

§ 1910.306 Specific purpose equipment and installations.

(a) *Electric signs and outline lighting*—(1) *Disconnecting means.* Signs operated by electronic or electromechanical controllers located outside the sign shall have a disconnecting means located inside the controller enclosure or within sight of the controller location, and it shall be capable of

FIGURE 4.1 (*Continued*)   Design Safety Standards for Electrical Systems (OSHA-CFR, Title 29, Part 1910, Subpart 1910, Paragraphs 302–308). (*Courtesy General Industry.*)

being locked in the open position. Such disconnecting means shall have no pole that can be operated independently, and it shall open all ungrounded conductors that supply the controller and sign. All other signs, except the portable type, and all outline lighting installations shall have an externally operable disconnecting means which can open all ungrounded conductors and is within the sight of the sign or outline lighting it controls.

(2) Doors or covers giving access to uninsulated parts of indoor signs or outline lighting exceeding 600 volts and accessible to other than qualified persons shall either be provided with interlock switches to disconnect the primary circuit or shall be so fastened that the use of other than ordinary tools will be necessary to open them.

(b) *Cranes and hoists.* This paragraph applies to the installation of electric equipment and wiring used in connection with cranes, monorail hoists, hoists, and all runways.

(1) *Disconnecting means.* A readily accessible disconnecting means (i) shall be provided between the runway contact conductors and the power supply.

(ii) Another disconnecting means, capable of being locked in the open position, shall be provided in the leads from the runway contact conductors or other power supply on any crane or monorail hoist.

(A) If this additional disconnecting means is not readily accessible from the crane or monorail hoist operating station, means shall be provided at the operating station to open the power circuit to all motors of the crane or monorail hoist.

(B) The additional disconnect may be omitted if a monorail hoist or hand-propelled crane bridge installation meets all of the following:

(*1*) The unit is floor controlled;

(*2*) The unit is within view of the power supply disconnecting means; and

(*3*) No fixed work platform has been provided for servicing the unit.

(2) *Control.* A limit switch or other device shall be provided to prevent the load block from passing the safe upper limit of travel of any hoisting mechanism.

(3) *Clearance.* The dimension of the working space in the direction of access to live parts which may require examination, adjustment, servicing, or maintenance while alive shall be a minimum of 2 feet 6 inches. Where controls are enclosed in cabinets, the door(s) shall either open at least 90 degrees or be removable.

(c) *Elevators, dumbwaiters, escalators, and moving walks—*(1) *Disconnecting means.* Elevators, dumbwaiters, escalators, and moving walks shall have a single means for disconnecting all ungrounded main power supply conductors for each unit.

(2) *Warning signs.* If interconnections between control panels are necessary for operation of the system on a multicar installation that remains energized from a source other than the disconnecting means, a warning sign shall be mounted on or adjacent to the disconnecting means. The sign shall be clearly legible and shall read "Warning—Parts of the control panel are not de-energized by this switch." (See § 1910.302(b)(3).)

(3) *Control panels.* If control panels are not located in the same space as the drive machine, they shall be located in cabinets with doors or panels capable of being locked closed.

(d) *Electric welders—disconnecting means.* (1) A disconnecting means shall be provided in the supply circuit for each motor-generator arc welder, and for each AC transformer and DC rectifier arc welder which is not equipped with a disconnect mounted as an intergral part of the welder.

(2) A switch or circuit breaker shall be provided by which each resistance welder and its control equipment can be isolated from the supply circuit. The ampere rating of this disconnecting means may not be less than the supply conductor ampacity.

(e) *Data processing systems—disconnecting means.* A disconnecting means shall be provided to disconnect the power to all electronic equipment in data processing or computer rooms. This disconnecting means shall be controlled from locations readily accessible to the operator at the principal exit doors. There shall also be a similar disconnecting means to disconnect

FIGURE 4.1 (*Continued*)   Design Safety Standards for Electrical Systems (OSHA-CFR, Title 29, Part 1910, Subpart 1910, Paragraphs 302–308). (*Courtesy General Industry.*)

the air conditioning system serving this area.

(f) *X-Ray equipment.* This paragraph applies to X-ray equipment for other than medical or dental use.

(1) *Disconnecting means.* (i) A disconnecting means shall be provided in the supply circuit. The disconnecting means shall be operable from a location readily accessible from the X-ray control. For equipment connected to a 120-volt branch circuit of 30 amperes or less, a grounding-type attachment plug cap and receptacle of proper rating may serve as a disconnecting means.

(ii) If more than one piece of equipment is operated from the same high-voltage circuit, each piece or each group of equipment as a unit shall be provided with a high-voltage switch or equivalent disconnecting means. This disconnecting means shall be constructed, enclosed, or located so as to avoid contact by employees with its live parts.

(2) *Control*—(i) *Radiographic and fluoroscopic types.* Radiographic and fluoroscopic-type equipment shall be effectively enclosed or shall have interlocks that de-energize the equipment automatically to prevent ready access to live current-carrying parts.

(ii) *Diffraction and irradiation types.* Diffraction- and irradiation-type equipment shall be provided with a means to indicate when it is energized unless the equipment or installation is effectively enclosed or is provided with interlocks to prevent access to live current-carrying parts during operation.

(g) *Induction and dielectric heating equipment*—(1) *Scope.* Paragraphs (g)(2) and (g)(3) of this section cover induction and dielectric heating equipment and accessories for industrial and scientific applications, but not for medical or dental applications or for appliances.

(2) *Guarding and grounding.* (i) *Enclosures.* The converting apparatus (including the DC line) and high-frequency electric circuits (excluding the output circuits and remote-control circuits) shall be completely contained within enclosures of noncombustible material.

(ii) *Panel controls.* All panel controls shall be of dead-front construction.

(iii) *Access to internal equipment.* Where doors are used for access to voltages from 500 to 1000 volts AC or DC, either door locks or interlocks shall be provided. Where doors are used for access to voltages of over 1000 volts AC or DC, either mechanical lockouts with a disconnecting means to prevent access until voltage is removed from the cubicle, or both door interlocking and mechanical door locks, shall be provided.

(iv) *Warning labels.* "Danger" labels shall be attached on the equipment and shall be plainly visible even when doors are open or panels are removed from compartments containing voltages of over 250 volts AC or DC.

(v) *Work applicator shielding.* Protective cages or adequate shielding shall be used to guard work applicators other than induction heating coils. Induction heating coils shall be protected by insulation and/or refractory materials. Interlock switches shall be used on all hinged access doors, sliding panels, or other such means of access to the applicator. Interlock switches shall be connected in such a manner as to remove all power from the applicator when any one of the access doors or panels is open. Interlocks on access doors or panels are not required if the applicator is an induction heating coil at DC ground potential or operating at less than 150 volts AC.

(vi) *Disconnecting means.* A readily accessible disconnecting means shall be provided by which each unit of heating equipment can be isolated from its supply circuit.

(3) *Remote control.* If remote controls are used for applying power, a selector switch shall be provided and interlocked to provide power from only one control point at a time. Switches operated by foot pressure shall be provided with a shield over the contact button to avoid accidental closing of the switch.

(h) *Electrolytic cells.* (1) *Scope.* These provisions for electrolytic cells apply to the installation of the electrical components and accessory equipment of electrolytic cells, electrolytic cell lines, and process power supply for the production of aluminum, cadmium, chlorine, copper, fluorine, hydro-

FIGURE 4.1 (*Continued*)   Design Safety Standards for Electrical Systems (OSHA-CFR, Title 29, Part 1910, Subpart 1910, Paragraphs 302–308). (*Courtesy General Industry.*)

gen peroxide, magnesium, sodium, sodium chlorate, and zinc. Cells used as a source of electric energy and for electroplating processes and cells used for production of hydrogen are not covered by these provisions.

(2) *Definitions applicable to this paragraph.*

Cell line: An assembly of electrically interconnected electrolytic cells supplied by a source of direct-current power.

Cell line attachments and auxiliary equipment: Cell line attachments and auxiliary equipment include, but are not limited to: auxiliary tanks; process piping; duct work; structural supports; exposed cell line conductors; conduits and other raceways; pumps; positioning equipment and cell cutout or bypass electrical devices. Auxiliary equipment also includes tools, welding machines, crucibles, and other portable equipment used for operation and maintenance within the electrolytic cell line working zone. In the cell line working zone, auxiliary equipment includes the exposed conductive surfaces of ungrounded cranes and crane-mounted cell-servicing equipment.

Cell line working zone: The cell line working zone is the space envelope wherein operation or maintenance is normally performed on or in the vicinity of exposed energized surfaces of cell lines or their attachments.

Electrolytic Cells: A receptacle or vessel in which electrochemical reactions are caused by applying energy for the purpose of refining or producing usable materials.

(3) *Application.* Installations covered by paragraph (h) of this section shall comply with all applicable provisions of this subpart, except as follows:

(i) Overcurrent protection of electrolytic cell DC process power circuits need not comply with the requirements of § 1910.304(e).

(ii) Equipment located or used within the cell line working zone or associated with the cell line DC power circuits need not comply with the provisions of § 1910.304(f).

(iii) Electrolytic cells, cell line conductors, cell line attachments, and the wiring of auxiliary equipment and devices within the cell line working zone

need not comply with the provisions of §§ 1910.303, and 1910.304 (b) and (c).

(4) *Disconnecting means.* (i) If more than one DC cell line process power supply serves the same cell line, a disconnecting means shall be provided on the cell line circuit side of each power supply to disconnect it from the cell line circuit.

(ii) Removable links or removable conductors may be used as the disconnecting means.

(5) *Portable electric equipment.* (i) The frames and enclosures of portable electric equipment used within the cell line working zone may not be grounded. However, these frames and enclosures may be grounded if the cell line circuit voltage does not exceed 200 volts DC or if the frames are guarded.

(ii) Ungrounded portable electric equipment shall be distinctively marked and may not be interchangeable with grounded portable electric equipment.

(6) *Power supply circuits and receptacles for portable electric equipment.* (i) Circuits supplying power to ungrounded receptacles for hand-held, cord- and plug-connected equipment shall be electrically isolated from any distribution system supplying areas other than the cell line working zone and shall be ungrounded. Power for these circuits shall be supplied through isolating transformers.

(ii) Receptacles and their mating plugs for ungrounded equipment may not have provision for a grounding conductor and shall be of a configuration which prevents their use for equipment required to be grounded.

(iii) Receptacles on circuits supplied by an isolating transformer with an ungrounded secondary shall have a distinctive configuration, shall be distinctively marked, and may not be used in any other location in the plant.

(7) *Fixed and portable electric equipment.* (i) AC systems supplying fixed and portable electric equipment within the cell line working zone need not be grounded.

(ii) Exposed conductive surfaces, such as electric equipment housings, cabinets, boxes, motors, raceways and the like that are within the cell line working zone need not be grounded.

FIGURE 4.1 (*Continued*)   Design Safety Standards for Electrical Systems (OSHA-CFR, Title 29, Part 1910, Subpart 1910, Paragraphs 302–308). (*Courtesy General Industry.*)

(iii) Auxiliary electrical devices, such as motors, transducers, sensors, control devices, and alarms, mounted on an electrolytic cell or other energized surface, shall be connected by any of the following means:

(A) Multiconductor hard usage or extra hard usage flexible cord;

(B) Wire or cable in suitable raceways; or

(C) Exposed metal conduit, cable tray, armored cable, or similar metallic systems installed with insulating breaks such that they will not cause a potentially hazardous electrical condition.

(iv) Fixed electric equipment may be bonded to the energized conductive surfaces of the cell line, its attachments, or auxiliaries. If fixed electric equipment is mounted on an energized conductive surface, it shall be bonded to that surface.

(8) *Auxiliary nonelectric connections.* Auxiliary nonelectric connections, such as air hoses, water hoses, and the like, to an electrolytic cell, its attachments, or auxiliary equipment may not have continuous conductive reinforcing wire, armor, braids, and the like. Hoses shall be of a nonconductive material.

(9) *Cranes and hoists.* (i) The conductive surfaces of cranes and hoists that enter the cell line working zone need not be grounded. The portion of an overhead crane or hoist which contacts an energized electrolytic cell or energized attachments shall be insulated from ground.

(ii) Remote crane or hoist controls which may introduce hazardous electrical conditions into the cell line working zone shall employ one or more of the following systems:

(A) Insulated and ungrounded control circuit;

(B) Nonconductive rope operator;

(C) Pendant pushbutton with nonconductive supporting means and having nonconductive surfaces or ungrounded exposed conductive surfaces; or

(D) Radio.

(i) *Electrically driven or controlled irrigation machines.* (See § 1910.302(b)(3).)

(1) *Lightning protection.* If an electrically driven or controlled irrigation machine has a stationary point, a driven ground rod shall be connected to the machine at the stationary point for lightning protection.

(2) *Disconnecting means.* The main disconnecting means for a center pivot irrigation machine shall be located at the point of connection of electrical power to the machine and shall be readily accessible and capable of being locked in the open position. A disconnecting means shall be provided for each motor and controller.

(j) *Swimming pools, fountains, and similar installations*—(1) *Scope.* Paragraphs (j)(2) through (j)(5) of this section apply to electric wiring for and equipment in or adjacent to all swimming, wading, therapeutic, and decorative pools and fountains, whether permanently installed or storable, and to metallic auxiliary equipment, such as pumps, filters, and similar equipment. Therapeutic pools in health care facilities are exempt from these provisions.

(2) *Lighting and receptacles*—(i) *Receptacles.* A single receptacle of the locking and grounding type that provides power for a permanently installed swimming pool recirculating pump motor may be located not less than 5 feet from the inside walls of a pool. All other receptacles on the property shall be located at least 10 feet from the inside walls of a pool. Receptacles which are located within 15 feet of the inside walls of the pool shall be protected by ground-fault circuit interrupters.

NOTE: In determining these dimensions, the distance to be measured is the shortest path the supply cord of an appliance connected to the receptacle would follow without piercing a floor, wall, or ceiling of a building or other effective permanent barrier.

(ii) *Lighting fixtures and lighting outlets.* (A) Unless they are 12 feet above the maximum water level, lighting fixtures and lighting outlets may not be installed over a pool or over the area extending 5 feet horizontally from the inside walls of a pool. However, a lighting fixture or lighting outlet which has been installed before April 16, 1981, may be located less than 5 feet measured horizontally from the inside walls of a pool if it is at least 5

FIGURE 4.1 (*Continued*) Design Safety Standards for Electrical Systems (OSHA-CFR, Title 29, Part 1910, Subpart 1910, Paragraphs 302–308). (*Courtesy General Industry.*)

feet above the surface of the maximum water level and shall be rigidly attached to the existing structure. It shall also be protected by a ground-fault circuit interrupter installed in the branch circuit supplying the fixture.

(B) Unless installed 5 feet above the maximum water level and rigidly attached to the structure adjacent to or enclosing the pool, lighting fixtures and lighting outlets installed in the area extending between 5 feet and 10 feet horizontally from the inside walls of a pool shall be protected by a ground-fault circuit interrupter.

(3) *Cord- and plug-connected equipment.* Flexible cords used with the following equipment may not exceed 3 feet in length and shall have a copper equipment grounding conductor with a grounding-type attachment plug.

(i) Cord- and plug-connected lighting fixtures installed within 16 feet of the water surface of permanently installed pools.

(ii) Other cord- and plug-connected, fixed or stationary equipment used with permanently installed pools.

(4) *Underwater equipment.* (i) A ground-fault circuit interrupter shall be installed in the branch circuit supplying underwater fixtures operating at more than 15 volts. Equipment installed underwater shall be approved for the purpose.

(ii) No underwater lighting fixtures may be installed for operation at over 150 volts between conductors.

(5) *Fountains.* All electric equipment operating at more than 15 volts, including power supply cords, used with fountains shall be protected by ground-fault circuit interrupters. (See § 1910.302(b)(3).)

[46 FR 4056, Jan. 16, 1981; 46 FR 40185, Aug. 7, 1981]

§ 1910.307 **Hazardous (classified) locations.**

(a) *Scope.* This section covers the requirements for electric equipment and wiring in locations which are classified depending on the properties of the flammable vapors, liquids or gases, or combustible dusts or fibers which may be present therein and the likelihood that a flammable or combustible concentration or quantity is present. Haz-

ardous (classified) locations may be found in occupancies such as, but not limited to, the following: aircraft hangars, gasoline dispensing and service stations, bulk storage plants for gasoline or other volatile flammable liquids, paint-finishing process plants, health care facilities, agricultural or other facilities where excessive combustible dusts may be present, marinas, boat yards, and petroleum and chemical processing plants. Each room, section or area shall be considered individually in determining its classification. These hazardous (classified) locations are assigned six designations as follows:

Class I, Division 1
Class I, Division 2
Class II, Division 1
Class II, Division 2
Class III, Division 1
Class III, Division 2

For definitions of these locations see § 1910.399(a). All applicable requirements in this subpart shall apply to hazardous (classified) locations, unless modified by provisions of this section.

(b) *Electrical installations.* Equipment, wiring methods, and installations of equipment in hazardous (classified) locations shall be intrinsically safe, approved for the hazardous (classified) location, or safe or for the hazardous (classified) location. Requirements for each of these options are as follows:

(1) *Intrinsically safe.* Equipment and associated wiring approved as intrinsically safe shall be permitted in any hazardous (classified) location for which it is approved.

(2) *Approved for the hazardous (classified) location.* (i) Equipment shall be approved not only for the class of location but also for the ignitible or combustible properties of the specific gas, vapor, dust, or fiber that will be present.

NOTE: NFPA 70, the National Electrical Code, lists or defines hazardous gases, vapors, and dusts by "Groups" characterized by their ignitible or combustible properties.

(ii) Equipment shall be marked to show the class, group, and operating temperature or temperature range, based on operation in a 40 degrees C

FIGURE 4.1 (*Continued*) Design Safety Standards for Electrical Systems (OSHA-CFR, Title 29, Part 1910, Subpart 1910, Paragraphs 302–308). (*Courtesy General Industry.*)

ambient, for which it is approved. The temperature marking may not exceed the ignition temperature of the specific gas or vapor to be encountered. However, the following provisions modify this marking requirement for specific equipment:

(A) Equipment of the non-heat-producing type, such as junction boxes, conduit, and fittings, and equipment of the heat-producing type having a maximum temperature not more than 100 degrees C (212 degrees F) need not have a marked operating temperature or temperature range.

(B) Fixed lighting fixtures marked for use in Class I, Division 2 locations only, need not be marked to indicate the group.

(C) Fixed general-purpose equipment in Class I locations, other than lighting fixtures, which is acceptable for use in Class I, Division 2 locations need not be marked with the class, group, division, or operating temperature.

(D) Fixed dust-tight equipment, other than lighting fixtures, which is acceptable for use in Class II, Division 2 and Class III locations need not be marked with the class, group, division, or operating temperature.

(3) *Safe for the hazardous (classified) location.* Equipment which is safe for the location shall be of a type and design which the employer demonstrates will provide protection from the hazards arising from the combustibility and flammability of vapors, liquids, gases, dusts, or fibers.

NOTE: The National Electrical Code, NFPA 70, contains guidelines for determining the type and design of equipment and installations which will meet this requirement. The guidelines of this document address electric wiring, equipment, and systems installed in hazardous (classified) locations and contain specific provisions for the following: wiring methods, wiring connections; conductor insulation, flexible cords, sealing and drainage, transformers, capacitors, switches, circuit breakers, fuses, motor controllers, receptacles, attachment plugs, meters, relays, instruments, resistors, generators, motors, lighting fixtures, storage battery charging equipment, electric cranes, electric hoists and similar equipment, utilization equipment, signaling systems, alarm systems, remote control systems, local loud speaker and communication systems, ventilation piping, live parts, lightning surge protection, and grounding. Compliance with these guidelines will constitute one means, but not the only means, of compliance with this paragraph.

(c) *Conduits.* All conduits shall be threaded and shall be made wrench-tight. Where it is impractical to make a threaded joint tight, a bonding jumper shall be utilized.

(d) *Equipment in Division 2 locations.* Equipment that has been approved for a Division 1 location may be installed in a Division 2 location of the same class and group. General-purpose equipment or equipment in general-purpose enclosures may be installed in Division 2 locations if the equipment does not constitute a source of ignition under normal operating conditions.

[46 FR 4056, Jan. 16, 1981; 46 FR 40185, Aug. 7, 1981]

§ 1910.308 **Special systems.**

(a) *Systems over 600 volts, nominal.* Paragraphs (a) (1) through (4) of this section cover the general requirements for all circuits and equipment operated at over 600 volts.

(1) *Wiring methods for fixed installations.* (i) Above-ground conductors shall be installed in rigid metal conduit, in intermediate metal conduit, in cable trays, in cablebus, in other suitable raceways, or as open runs of metal-clad cable suitable for the use and purpose. However, open runs of non-metallic-sheathed cable or of bare conductors or busbars may be installed in locations accessible only to qualified persons. Metallic shielding components, such as tapes, wires, or braids for conductors, shall be grounded. Open runs of insulated wires and cables having a bare lead sheath or a braided outer covering shall be supported in a manner designed to prevent physical damage to the braid or sheath.

(ii) Conductors emerging from the ground shall be enclosed in approved raceways. (See § 1910.302(b)(3).)

(2) *Interrupting and isolating devices.* (i) Circuit breaker installations located indoors shall consist of metal-enclosed units or fire-resistant cell-mounted units. In locations accessible only to qualified personnel, open

FIGURE 4.1 (*Continued*)   Design Safety Standards for Electrical Systems (OSHA-CFR, Title 29, Part 1910, Subpart 1910, Paragraphs 302–308). (*Courtesy General Industry.*)

mounting of circuit breakers is permitted. A means of indicating the open and closed position of circuit breakers shall be provided.

(ii) Fused cutouts installed in buildings or tranformer vaults shall be of a type approved for the purpose. They shall be readily accessible for fuse replacement.

(iii) A means shall be provided to completely isolate equipment for inspection and repairs. Isolating means which are not designed to interrupt the load curent of the circuit shall be either interlocked with an approved circuit interrupter or provided with a sign warning against opening them under load.

(3) *Mobile and portable equipment.* (i) *Power cable connections to mobile machines.* A metallic enclosure shall be provided on the mobile machine for enclosing the terminals of the power cable. The enclosure shall include provisions for a solid connection for the ground wire(s) terminal to effectively ground the machine frame. The method of cable termination used shall prevent any strain or pull on the cable from stressing the electrical connections. The enclosure shall have provision for locking so only authorized qualified persons may open it and shall be marked with a sign warning of the presence of energized parts.

(ii) *Guarding live parts.* All energized switching and control parts shall be enclosed in effectively grounded metal cabinets or enclosures. Circuit breakers and protective equipment shall have the operating means projecting through the metal cabinet or enclosure so these units can be reset without locked doors being opened. Enclosures and metal cabinets shall be locked so that only authorized qualified persons have access and shall be marked with a sign warning of the presence of energized parts. Collector ring assemblies on revolving-type machines (shovels, draglines, etc.) shall be guarded.

(4) *Tunnel installation*—(i) *Application.* The provisions of this paragraph apply to installation and use of high-voltage power distribution and utilization equipment which is portable and/or mobile, such as substations, trailers, cars, mobile shovels, draglines, hoists,

drills, dredges, compressors, pumps, conveyors, and underground excavators.

(ii) *Conductors.* Conductors in tunnels shall be installed in one or more of the following:

(A) Metal conduit or other metal raceway,

(B) Type MC cable, or

(C) Other approved multiconductor cable.

Conductors shall also be so located or guarded as to protect them from physical damage. Multiconductor portable cable may supply mobile equipment. An equipment grounding conductor shall be run with circuit conductors inside the metal raceway or inside the multiconductor cable jacket. The equipment grounding conductor may be insulated or bare.

(iii) *Guarding live parts.* Bare terminals of transformers, switches, motor controllers, and other equipment shall be enclosed to prevent accidental contact with energized parts. Enclosures for use in tunnels shall be drip-proof, weatherproof, or submersible as required by the environmental conditions.

(iv) *Disconnecting means.* A disconnecting means that simultaneously opens all ungrounded conductors shall be installed at each transformer or motor location.

(v) *Grounding and bonding.* All non-energized metal parts of electric equipment and metal raceways and cable sheaths shall be effectively grounded and bonded to all metal pipes and rails at the portal and at intervals not exceeding 1000 feet throughout the tunnel.

(b) *Emergency power systems*—(1) *Scope.* The provisions for emergency systems apply to circuits, systems, and equipment intended to supply power for illumination and special loads, in the event of failure of the normal supply.

(2) *Wiring methods.* Emergency circuit wiring shall be kept entirely independent of all other wiring and equipment and may not enter the same raceway, cable, box, or cabinet or other wiring except either where common circuit elements suitable for the purpose are required, or for trans-

FIGURE 4.1 (*Continued*)   Design Safety Standards for Electrical Systems (OSHA-CFR, Title 29, Part 1910, Subpart 1910, Paragraphs 302–308). (*Courtesy General Industry.*)

ferring power from the normal to the emergency source.

(3) *Emergency illumination.* Where emergency lighting is necessary, the system shall be so arranged that the failure of any individual lighting element, such as the burning out of a light bulb, cannot leave any space in total darkness.

(c) *Class 1, Class 2, and Class 3 remote control, signaling, and power-limited circuits*—(1) *Classification.* Class 1, Class 2, or Class 3 remote control, signaling, or power-limited circuits are characterized by their usage and electrical power limitation which differentiates them from light and power circuits. These circuits are classified in accordance with their respective voltage and power limitations as summarized in paragraphs (c)(1)(i) through (c)(1)(iii) of this section.

(i) *Class 1 circuits.* (A) A Class 1 power-limited circuit is supplied from a source having a rated output of not more than 30 volts and 1000 volt-amperes.

(B) A Class 1 remote control circuit or a Class 1 signaling circuit has a voltage which does not exceed 600 volts; however, the power output of the source need not be limited.

(ii) *Class 2 and Class 3 circuits.* (A) Power for Class 2 and Class 3 circuits is limited either inherently (in which no overcurrent protection is required) or by a combination of a power source and overcurrent protection.

(B) The maximum circuit voltage is 150 volts AC or DC for a Class 2 inherently limited power source, and 100 volts AC or DC for a Class 3 inherently limited power source.

(C) The maximum circuit voltage is 30 volts AC and 60 volts DC for a Class 2 power source limited by overcurrent protection, and 150 volts AC or DC for a Class 3 power source limited by overcurrent protection.

(iii) The maximum circuit voltages in paragraphs (c)(1)(i) and (c)(1)(ii) of this section apply to sinusoidal AC or continuous DC power sources, and where wet contact occurence is not likely.

(2) *Marking.* A Class 2 or Class 3 power supply unit shall be durably marked where plainly visible to indi-

cate the class of supply and its electrical rating. (See § 1910.302(b)(3).)

(d) *Fire protective signaling systems.* (See § 1910.302(b)(3).)

(1) *Classifications.* Fire protective signaling circuits shall be classified either as non-power limited or power limited.

(2) *Power sources.* The power sources for use with fire protective signaling circuits shall be either power limited or nonlimited as follows:

(i) The power supply of non-power-limited fire protective signaling circuits shall have an output voltage in excess of 600 volts.

(ii) The power for power-limited fire protective signaling circuits shall be either inherently limited, in which no overcurrent protection is required, or limited by a combination of a power source and overcurrent protection.

(3) *Non-power-limited conductor location.* Non-power-limited fire protective signaling circuits and Class 1 circuits may occupy the same enclosure, cable, or raceway provided all conductors are insulated for maximum voltage of any conductor within the enclosure, cable, or raceway. Power supply and fire protective signaling circuit conductors are permitted in the same enclosure, cable, or raceway only if connected to the same equipment.

(4) *Power-limited conductor location.* Where open conductors are installed, power-limited fire protective signaling circuits shall be separated at least 2 inches from conductors of any light, power, Class 1, and non-power-limited fire protective signaling circuits unless a special and equally protective method of conductor separation is employed. Cables and conductors of two or more power-limited fire protective signaling circuits or Class 3 circuits are permitted in the same cable, enclosure, or raceway. Conductors of one or more Class 2 circuits are permitted within the same cable, enclosure, or raceway with conductors of power-limited fire protective signaling circuits provided that the insulation of Class 2 circuit conductors in the cable, enclosure, or raceway is at least that needed for the power-limited fire protective signaling circuits.

(5) *Identification.* Fire protective signaling circuits shall be identified at

FIGURE 4.1 (*Continued*)   Design Safety Standards for Electrical Systems (OSHA-CFR, Title 29, Part 1910, Subpart 1910, Paragraphs 302–308). (*Courtesy General Industry.*)

terminal and junction locations in a manner which will prevent unintentional interference with the signaling circuit during testing and servicing. Power-limited fire protective signaling circuits shall be durably marked as such where plainly visible at terminations.

(e) *Communications systems*—(1) *Scope.* These provisions for communication systems apply to such systems as central-station-connected and non-central-station-connected telephone circuits, radio and television receiving and transmitting equipment, including community antenna television and radio distribution systems, telegraph, district messenger, and outside wiring for fire and burglar alarm, and similar central station systems. These installations need not comply with the provisions of §§ 1910.303 through 1910.308(d), except § 1910.304(c)(1) and § 1910.307(b).

(2) *Protective devices.* (i) Communication circuits so located as to be exposed to accidental contact with light or power conductors operating at over 300 volts shall have each circuit so exposed provided with a protector approved for the purpose.

(ii) Each conductor of a lead-in from an outdoor antenna shall be provided with an antenna discharge unit or other suitable means that will drain static charges from the antenna system.

(3) *Conductor location*—(i) *Outside of buildings.* (a) Receiving distribution lead-in or aerial-drop cables attached to buildings and lead-in conductors to radio transmitters shall be so installed as to avoid the possibility of accidental contact with electric light or power conductors.

(b) The clearance between lead-in conductors and any lightning protection conductors may not be less than 6 feet.

(ii) *On poles.* Where practicable, communication conductors on poles shall be located below the light or power conductors. Communications conductors may not be attached to a crossarm that carries light or power conductors.

(iii) *Inside of buildings.* Indoor antennas, lead-ins, and other communication conductors attached as open conductors to the inside of buildings shall be located at least 2 inches from conductors of any light or power or Class 1 circuits unless a special and equally protective method of conductor separation, approved for the purpose, is employed.

(4) *Equipment location.* Outdoor metal structures supporting antennas, as well as self-supporting antennas such as vertical rods or dipole structures, shall be located as far away from overhead conductors of electric light and power circuits of over 150 volts to ground as necessary to avoid the possibility of the antenna or structure falling into or making accidental contact with such circuits.

(5) *Grounding*—(i) *Lead-in conductors.* If exposed to contact with electric light and power conductors, the metal sheath of aerial cables entering buildings shall be grounded or shall be interrupted close to the entrance to the building by an insulating joint or equivalent device. Where protective devices are used, they shall be grounded in an approved manner.

(ii) *Antenna structures.* Masts and metal structures supporting antennas shall be permanently and effectively grounded without splice or connection in the grounding conductor.

(iii) *Equipment enclosures.* Transmitters shall be enclosed in a metal frame or grill or separated from the operating space by a barrier, all metallic parts of which are effectively connected to ground. All external metal handles and controls accessible to the operating personnel shall be effectively grounded. Unpowered equipment and enclosures shall be considered grounded where connected to an attached coaxial cable with an effectively grounded metallic shield.

FIGURE 4.1 (*Continued*)   Design Safety Standards for Electrical Systems (OSHA-CFR, Title 29, Part 1910, Subpart 1910, Paragraphs 302–308). (*Courtesy General Industry.*)

Safety-Related Work Practices

§ 1910.331 Scope.

(a) *Covered work by both qualified and unqualified persons.* The provisions of §§ 1910.331 through 1910.335 cover electrical safety-related work practices for both qualified persons (those who have training in avoiding the electrical hazards of working on or near exposed energized parts) and unqualified persons (those with little or no such training) working on, near, or with the following installations:

(1) *Premises wiring.* Installations of electric conductors and equipment within or on buildings or other structures, and on other premises such as yards, carnival, parking, and other lots, and industrial substations;

(2) *Wiring for connection to supply.* Installations of conductors that connect to the supply of electricity; and

(3) *Other wiring.* Installations of other outside conductors on the premises.

(4) *Optical fiber cable.* Installations of optical fiber cable where such installations are made along with electric conductors.

Note: See § 1910.399 for the definition of "qualified person." See § 1910.332 for training requirements that apply to qualified and unqualified persons.

(b) *Other covered work by unqualified persons.* The provisions of §§ 1910.331 through 1910.335 also cover work performed by unqualified persons on, near, or with the installations listed in paragraphs (c)(1) through (c)(4) of this section.

(c) *Excluded work by qualified persons.* The provisions of §§ 1910.331 through 1910.335 do not apply to work performed by qualified persons on or directly associated with the following installations:

(1) *Generation, transmission, and distribution installations.* Installations for the generation, control, transformation, transmission, and distribution of electric energy (including communication and metering) located in buildings used for such purposes or located outdoors.

Note 1: Work on or directly associated with installations of utilization equipment used for purposes other than generating, transmitting, or distributing electric energy (such as installations which are in office buildings, warehouses, garages, machine shops, or recreational buildings, or other utilization installations which are not an integral part of a generating installation, substation, or control center) is covered under paragraph (a)(1) of this section.

Note 2: Work on or directly associated with generation, transmission, or distribution installations includes:

(1) Work performed directly on such installations, such as repairing overhead or underground distribution lines or repairing a feed-water pump for the boiler in a generating plant.

(2) Work directly associated with such installations, such as line-clearance tree trimming and replacing utility poles.

(3) Work on electric utilization circuits in a generating plant provided that:

(A) Such circuits are commingled with installations of power generation equipment or circuits, and

(B) The generation equipment or circuits present greater electrical hazards than those posed by the utilization equipment or circuits (such as exposure to higher voltages or lack of overcurrent protection).

(2) *Communications installations.* Installations of communication equipment to the extent that the work is covered under § 1910.268.

(3) *Installations in vehicles.* Installations in ships, watercraft, railway rolling stock, aircraft, or automotive vehicles other than mobile homes and recreational vehicles.

(4) *Railway installations.* Installations of railways for generation, transformation, transmission, or distribution of power used exclusively for operation of rolling stock or installations of railways used exclusively for signaling and communication purposes.

§ 1910.332 Training.

(a) *Scope.* The training requirements contained in this section apply to employees who face a risk of electric shock that is not reduced to a safe level by the electrical installation requirements of §§ 1910.303 through 1910.308.

Note: Employees in occupations listed in Table S-4 face such a risk and are required to be trained. Other employees who also may reasonably be expected to face a comparable risk of injury due to electric shock or other electrical hazards must also be trained.

(b) *Content of training.* (1) *Practices addressed in this standard.* Employees shall be trained in and familiar with the safety-related work practices required by §§ 1910.331 through 1910.335 that pertain to their respective job assignments.

(2) *Additional requirements for unqualified persons.* Employees who are covered by paragraph (a) of this section but who are not qualified persons shall also be trained in and familiar with any electrically related safety practices not specifically addressed by §§ 1910.331 through 1910.335 but which are necessary for their safety.

(3) *Additional requirements for qualified persons.* Qualified persons (i.e., those permitted to work on or near exposed energized parts) shall, at a minimum, be trained in and familiar with the following:

(i) The skills and techniques necessary to distinguish exposed live parts from other parts of electric equipment.

(ii) The skills and techniques necessary to determine the nominal voltage of exposed live parts, and

(iii) The clearance distances specified in § 1910.333(c) and the corresponding voltages to which the qualified person will be exposed.

Note 1: For the purposes of §§ 1910.331 through 1910.335, a person must have the training required by paragraph (b)(3) of this section in order to be considered a qualified person.

Note 2: Qualified persons whose work on energized equipment involves either direct contact or contact by means of tools or materials must also have the training needed to meet § 1910.333(c)(2).

(c) *Type of training.* The training required by this section shall be of the classroom or on-the-job type. The degree of training provided shall be determined by the risk to the employee.

TABLE S-4.—TYPICAL OCCUPATIONAL CATEGORIES OF EMPLOYEES FACING A HIGHER THAN NORMAL RISK OF ELECTRICAL ACCIDENT

Occupation
Blue collar supervisors.[1]
Electrical and electronic engineers.[1]
Electrical and electronic equipment assemblers.[1]
Electrical and electronic technicians.[1]
Electricians.
Industrial machine operators.[1]
Material handling equipment operators.[1]
Mechanics and repairers.[1]
Painters.[1]
Riggers and roustabouts.[1]
Stationary engineers.[1]
Welders.

[1] Workers in these groups do not need to be trained if their work or the work of those they supervise does not bring them or the employees they supervise close enough to exposed parts of electric circuits operating at 50 volts or more to ground for a hazard to exist.

§ 1910.333 Selection and use of work practices.

(a) *General.* Safety-related work practices shall be employed to prevent electric shock or other injuries resulting from either direct or indirect electrical contacts, when work is performed near or on equipment or circuits which are or may be energized. The specific safety-related work practices shall be

FIGURE 4.2 Electrical Safety-Related Work Practices (OSHA-CFR, Title 29, Part 1910, Subpart S, Paragraphs 331–335). (*Courtesy General Industry.*)

consistent with the nature and extent of the associated electrical hazards.

(1) *Deenergized parts.* Live parts to which an employee may be exposed shall be deenergized before the employee works on or near them, unless the employer can demonstrate that deenergizing introduces additional or increased hazards or is infeasible due to equipment design or operational limitations. Live parts that operate at less than 50 volts to ground need not be deenergized if there will be no increased exposure to electrical burns or to explosion due to electric arcs.

Note 1: Examples of increased or additional hazards include interruption of life support equipment, deactivation of emergency alarm systems, shutdown of hazardous location ventilation equipment, or removal of illumination for an area.

Note 2: Examples of work that may be performed on or near energized circuit parts because of infeasibility due to equipment design or operational limitations include testing of electric circuits that can only be performed with the circuit energized and work on circuits that form an integral part of a continuous industrial process in a chemical plant that would otherwise need to be completely shut down in order to permit work on one circuit or piece of equipment.

Note 3: Work on or near deenergized parts is covered by paragraph (b) of this section.

(2) *Energized parts.* If the exposed live parts are not deenergized (i.e., for reasons of increased or additional hazards or infeasibility), other safety-related work practices shall be used to protect employees who may be exposed to the electrical hazards involved. Such work practices shall protect employees against contact with energized circuit parts directly with any part of their body or indirectly through some other conductive object. The work practices that are used shall be suitable for the conditions under which the work is to be performed and for the voltage level of the exposed electric conductors or circuit parts. Specific work practice requirements are detailed in paragraph (c) of this section.

(b) *Working on or near exposed deenergized parts.* (1) *Application.* This paragraph applies to work on exposed deenergized parts or near enough to them to expose the employee to any electrical hazard they present. Conductors and parts of electric equipment that have been deenergized but have not been locked out or tagged in accordance with paragraph (b) of this section shall be treated as energized parts, and paragraph (c) of this section applies to work on or near them.

(2) *Lockout and tagging.* While any employee is exposed to contact with parts of fixed electric equipment or circuits which have been deenergized,

the circuits energizing the parts shall be locked out or tagged or both in accordance with the requirements of this paragraph. The requirements shall be followed in the order in which they are presented (i.e., paragraph (b)(2)(i) first, then paragraph (b)(2)(ii), etc.).

Note 1: As used in this section, fixed equipment refers to equipment fastened in place or connected by permanent wiring methods.

Note 2: Lockout and tagging procedures that comply with paragraphs (c) through (f) of § 1910.147 will also be deemed to comply with paragraph (b)(2) of this section provided that:

(1) The procedures address the electrical safety hazards covered by this Subpart; and

(2) The procedures also incorporate the requirements of paragraphs (b)(2)(iii)(D) and (b)(2)(iv)(B) of this section.

(i) *Procedures.* The employer shall maintain a copy of the procedures outlined in paragraph (b)(2) and shall make it available for inspection by employees and by the Assistant Secretary of Labor and his or her authorized representatives.

Note: The written procedures may be in the form of a copy of paragraph (b) of this section.

(ii) *Deenergizing equipment.* (A) Safe procedures for deenergizing circuits and equipment shall be determined before circuits or equipment are deenergized.

(B) The circuits and equipment to be worked on shall be disconnected from all electric energy sources. Control circuit devices, such as push buttons, selector switches, and interlocks, may not be used as the sole means for deenergizing circuits or equipment. Interlocks for electric equipment may not be used as a substitute for lockout and tagging procedures.

(C) Stored electric energy which might endanger personnel shall be released. Capacitors shall be discharged and high capacitance elements shall be short-circuited and grounded, if the stored electric energy might endanger personnel.

Note: If the capacitors or associated equipment are handled in meeting this requirement, they shall be treated as energized.

(D) Stored non-electrical energy in devices that could reenergize electric circuit parts shall be blocked or relieved to the extent that the circuit parts could not be accidentally energized by the device.

(iii) *Application of locks and tags.* (A) A lock and a tag shall be placed on each disconnecting means used to deenergize circuits and equipment on which work is to be performed, except as provided in paragraphs (b)(2)(iii)(C) and (b)(2)(iii)(E)

of this section. The lock shall be attached so as to prevent persons from operating the disconnecting means unless they resort to undue force or the use of tools.

(B) Each tag shall contain a statement prohibiting unauthorized operation of the disconnecting means and removal of the tag.

(C) If a lock cannot be applied, or if the employer can demonstrate that tagging procedures will provide a level of safety equivalent to that obtained by the use of a lock, a tag may be used without a lock.

(D) A tag used without a lock, as permitted by paragraph (b)(2)(iii)(C) of this section, shall be supplemented by at least one additional safety measure that provides a level of safety equivalent to that obtained by the use of a lock. Examples of additional safety measures include the removal of an isolating circuit element, blocking of a controlling switch, or opening of an extra disconnecting device.

(E) A lock may be placed without a tag only under the following conditions:

(1) Only one circuit or piece of equipment is deenergized, and

(2) The lockout period does not extend beyond the work shift, and

(3) Employees exposed to the hazards associated with reenergizing the circuit or equipment are familiar with this procedure.

(iv) Verification of deenergized condition. The requirements of this paragraph shall be met before any circuits or equipment can be considered and worked as deenergized.

(A) A qualified person shall operate the equipment operating controls or otherwise verify that the equipment cannot be restarted.

(B) A qualified person shall use test equipment to test the circuit elements and electrical parts of equipment to which employees will be exposed and shall verify that the circuit elements and equipment parts are deenergized. The test shall also determine if any energized condition exists as a result of inadvertently induced voltage or unrelated voltage backfeed even though specific parts of the circuit have been deenergized and presumed to be safe. If the circuit to be tested is over 600 volts, nominal, the test equipment shall be checked for proper operation immediately before and immediately after this test.

(v) Reenergizing equipment. These requirements shall be met, in the order given, before circuits or equipment are re-energized, even temporarily.

(A) A qualified person shall conduct tests and visual inspections, as

FIGURE 4.2 (*Continued*)   Electrical Safety-Related Work Practices (OSHA-CFR, Title 29, Part 1910, Subpart S, Paragraphs 331–335). (*Courtesy General Industry.*)

necessary, to verify that all tools, electrical jumpers, shorts, grounds, and other such devices have been removed, so that the circuits and equipment can be safely energized.

(B) Employees exposed to the hazards associated with reenergizing the circuit or equipment shall be warned to stay clear of circuits and equipment.

(C) Each lock and tag shall be removed by the employee who applied it or under his or her direct supervision. However, if this employee is absent from the workplace, then the lock or tag may be removed by a qualified person designated to perform this task provided that:

(*1*) The employer ensures that the employee who applied the lock or tag is not available at the workplace, and

(*2*) The employer ensures that the employee is aware that the lock or tag has been removed before he or she resumes work at that workplace.

(D) There shall be a visual determination that all employees are clear of the circuits and equipment.

(c) *Working on or near exposed energized parts. (1) Application.* This paragraph applies to work performed on exposed live parts (involving either direct contact or contact by means of tools or materials) or near enough to them for employees to be exposed to any hazard they present.

(2) *Work on energized equipment.* Only qualified persons may work on electric circuit parts or equipment that have not been deenergized under the procedures of paragraph (b) of this section. Such persons shall be capable of working safely on energized circuits and shall be familiar with the proper use of special precautionary techniques, personal protective equipment, insulating and shielding materials, and insulated tools.

(3) *Overhead lines.* If work is to be performed near overhead lines, the lines shall be deenergized and grounded, or other protective measures shall be provided before work is started. If the lines are to be deenergized, arrangements shall be made with the person or organization that operates or controls the electric circuits involved to deenergize and ground them. If protective measures are provided such as guarding, isolating, or insulating, these precautions shall prevent employees from contacting such lines directly with any part of their body or indirectly through conductive materials, tools, or equipment.

Note: The work practices used by qualified persons installing insulating devices on overhead power transmission or distribution lines are not covered by §§ 1910.332 through 1910.335. Under paragraph (c)(2) of this

section, unqualified persons are prohibited from performing this type of work.

(i) *Unqualified persons.* (A) When an unqualified person is working in an elevated position near overhead lines, the location shall be such that the person and the longest conductive object he or she may contact cannot come closer to any unguarded, energized overhead line than the following distances:

(*1*) For voltages to ground 50kV or below—10 ft. (305 cm);

(*2*) For voltages to ground over 50kV—10 ft. (305 cm) plus 4 in. (10 cm) for every 10kV over 50kV.

(B) When an unqualified person is working on the ground in the vicinity of overhead lines, the person may not bring any conductive object closer to unguarded, energized overhead lines than the distances given in paragraph (c)(3)(i)(A) of this section.

Note: For voltages normally encountered with overhead power lines, objects which do not have an insulating rating for the voltage involved are considered to be conductive.

(ii) *Qualified persons.* When a qualified person is working in the vicinity of overhead lines, whether in an elevated position or on the ground, the person may not approach or take any conductive object without an approved insulating handle closer to exposed energized parts than shown in Table S–5 unless:

(A) The person is insulated from the energized part (gloves, with sleeves if necessary, rated for the voltage involved are considered to be insulation of the person from the energized part on which work is performed), or

(B) The energized part is insulated both from all other conductive objects at a different potential and from the person, or

(C) The person is insulated from all conductive objects at a potential different from that of the energized part.

TABLE S–5.—APPROACH DISTANCES FOR QUALIFIED EMPLOYEES ALTERNATING CURRENT

Voltage range (phase to phase)	Minimum approach distance
300V and less	Avoid contact.
Over 300V, not over 750V.	1 ft. 0 in. (30.5 cm).
Over 750V, not over 2kV ..	1 ft. 6 in. (46 cm).
Over 2kV, not over 15kV ..	2 ft. 0 in. (61 cm).
Over 15kV, not over 37kV.	3 ft. 0 in. (91 cm).
Over 37kV, not over 87.5kV.	3 ft. 6 in. (107 cm).
Over 87.5kV, not over 121kV.	4 ft. 0 in. (122 cm).

TABLE S–5.—APPROACH DISTANCES FOR QUALIFIED EMPLOYEES ALTERNATING CURRENT—Continued

Voltage range (phase to phase)	Minimum approach distance
Over 121kV, not over 140kV.	4 ft. 6 in. (137 cm).

(iii) *Vehicular and mechanical equipment.* (A) Any vehicle or mechanical equipment capable of having parts of its structure elevated near energized overhead lines shall be operated so that a clearance of 10 ft. (305 cm) is maintained. If the voltage is higher than 50kV, the clearance shall be increased 4 in. (10 cm) for every 10kV over that voltage. However, under any of the following conditions, the clearance may be reduced:

(*1*) If the vehicle is in transit with its structure lowered, the clearance may be reduced to 4 ft. (122 cm). If the voltage is higher than 50kV, the clearance shall be increased 4 in. (10 cm) for every 10kV over that voltage.

(*2*) If insulating barriers are installed to prevent contact with the lines, and if the barriers are rated for the voltage of the line being guarded and are not a part of or an attachment to the vehicle or its raised structure, the clearance may be reduced to a distance within the designed working dimensions of the insulating barrier.

(*3*) If the equipment is an aerial lift insulated for the voltage involved, and if the work is performed by a qualified person, the clearance (between the uninsulated portion of the aerial lift and the power line) may be reduced to the distance given in Table S–5.

(B) Employees standing on the ground may not contact the vehicle or mechanical equipment or any of its attachments, unless:

(*1*) The employee is using protective equipment rated for the voltage; or

(*2*) The equipment is located so that no uninsulated part of its structure (that portion of the structure that provides a conductive path to employees on the ground) can come closer to the line than permitted in paragraph (c)(3)(iii) of this section.

(C) If any vehicle or mechanical equipment capable of having parts of its structure elevated near energized overhead lines is intentionally grounded, employees working on the ground near the point of grounding may not stand at the grounding location whenever there is a possibility of overhead line contact. Additional precautions, such as the use of barricades or insulation, shall be taken to protect employees from

FIGURE 4.2 (*Continued*)   Electrical Safety-Related Work Practices (OSHA-CFR, Title 29, Part 1910, Subpart S, Paragraphs 331–335). (*Courtesy General Industry.*)

hazardous ground potentials, depending on earth resistivity and fault currents, which can develop within the first few feet or more outward from the grounding point.

(4) *Illumination.* (i) Employees may not enter spaces containing exposed energized parts, unless illumination is provided that enables the employees to perform the work safely.

(ii) Where lack of illumination or an obstruction precludes observation of the work to be performed, employees may not perform tasks near exposed energized parts. Employees may not reach blindly into areas which may contain energized parts.

(5) *Confined or enclosed work spaces.* When an employee works in a confined or enclosed space (such as a manhole or vault) that contains exposed energized parts, the employer shall provide, and the employee shall use, protective shields, protective barriers, or insulating materials as necessary to avoid inadvertent contact with these parts. Doors, hinged panels, and the like shall be secured to prevent their swinging into an employee and causing the employee to contact exposed energized parts.

(6) *Conductive materials and equipment.* Conductive materials and equipment that are in contact with any part of an employee's body shall be handled in a manner that will prevent them from contacting exposed energized conductors or circuit parts. If an employee must handle long dimensional conductive objects (such as ducts and pipes) in areas with exposed live parts, the employer shall institute work practices (such as the use of insulation, guarding, and material handling techniques) which will minimize the hazard.

(7) *Portable ladders.* Portable ladders shall have nonconductive siderails if they are used where the employee or the ladder could contact exposed energized parts.

(8) *Conductive apparel.* Conductive articles of jewelry and clothing (such as watch bands, bracelets, rings, key chains, necklaces, metalized aprons, cloth with conductive thread, or metal headgear) may not be worn if they might contact exposed energized parts. However, such articles may be worn if they are rendered nonconductive by covering, wrapping, or other insulating means.

(9) *Housekeeping duties.* Where live parts present an electrical contact hazard, employees may not perform housekeeping duties at such close distances to the parts that there is a possibility of contact, unless adequate safeguards (such as insulating equipment or barriers) are provided.

Electrically conductive cleaning materials (including conductive solids such as steel wool, metalized cloth, and silicon carbide, as well as conductive liquid solutions) may not be used in proximity to energized parts unless procedures are followed which will prevent electrical contact.

(10) *Interlocks.* Only a qualified person following the requirements of paragraph (c) of this section may defeat an electrical safety interlock, and then only temporarily while he or she is working on the equipment. The interlock system shall be returned to its operable condition when this work is completed.

§ 1910.334 Use of equipment.

(a) *Portable electric equipment.* This paragraph applies to the use of cord- and plug-connected energized equipment, including flexible cord sets (extension cords).

(1) *Handling.* Portable equipment shall be handled in a manner which will not cause damage. Flexible electric cords connected to equipment may not be used for raising or lowering the equipment. Flexible cords may not be fastened with staples or otherwise hung in such a fashion as could damage the outer jacket or insulation.

(2) *Visual inspection.* (i) Portable cord- and plug-connected equipment and flexible cord sets (extension cords) shall be visually inspected before use on any shift for external defects (such as loose parts, deformed and missing pins, or damage to outer jacket or insulation) and for evidence of possible internal damage (such as pinched or crushed outer jacket). Cord- and plug-connected equipment and flexible cord sets (extension cords) which remain connected once they are put in place and are not exposed to damage need not be visually inspected until they are relocated.

(ii) If there is a defect or evidence of damage that might expose an employee to injury, the defective or damaged item shall be removed from service, and no employee may use it until necessary repairs and tests to render the equipment safe have been made.

(iii) When an attachment plug is to be connected to a receptacle (including any on a cord set), the relationship of the plug and receptacle contacts shall first be checked to ensure that they are of proper mating configurations.

(3) *Grounding-type equipment.* (i) A flexible cord used with grounding-type equipment shall contain an equipment grounding conductor.

(ii) Attachment plugs and receptacles may not be connected or altered in a manner which would prevent proper continuity of the equipment grounding

conductor at the point where plugs are attached to receptacles. Additionally, these devices may not be altered to allow the grounding pole of a plug to be inserted into slots intended for connection to the current-carrying conductors.

(iii) Adapters which interrupt the continuity of the equipment grounding connection may not be used.

(4) *Conductive work locations.* Portable electric equipment and flexible cords used in highly conductive work locations (such as those inundated with water or other conductive liquids), or in job locations where employees are likely to contact water or conductive liquids, shall be approved for those locations.

(5) *Connecting attachment plugs.* (i) Employees' hands may not be wet when plugging and unplugging flexible cords and cord- and plug-connected equipment, if energized equipment is involved.

(ii) Energized plug and receptacle connections may be handled only with insulating protective equipment if the condition of the connection could provide a conducting path to the employee's hand (if, for example, a cord connector is wet from being immersed in water).

(iii) Locking-type connectors shall be properly secured after connection.

(b) *Electric power and lighting circuits.* (1) *Routine opening and closing of circuits.* Load rated switches, circuit breakers, or other devices specifically designed as disconnecting means shall be used for the opening, reversing, or closing of circuits under load conditions. Cable connectors not of the load-break type, fuses, terminal lugs, and cable splice connections may not be used for such purposes, except in an emergency.

(2) *Reclosing circuits after protective device operation.* After a circuit is deenergized by a circuit protective device, the circuit may not be manually reenergized until it has been determined that the equipment and circuit can be safely energized. The repetitive manual reclosing of circuit breakers or reenergizing circuits through replaced fuses is prohibited.

Note: When it can be determined from the design of the circuit and the overcurrent devices involved that the automatic operation of a device was caused by an overload rather than a fault condition, no examination of the circuit or connected equipment is needed before the circuit is reenergized.

(3) *Overcurrent protection modification.* Overcurrent protection of circuits and conductors may not be modified, even on a temporary basis, beyond that allowed by § 1910.304(e).

FIGURE 4.2 (*Continued*)   Electrical Safety-Related Work Practices (OSHA-CFR, Title 29, Part 1910, Subpart S, Paragraphs 331–335). (*Courtesy General Industry.*)

the installation safety requirements for overcurrent protection.

(c) *Test instruments and equipment.* (1) *Use.* Only qualified persons may perform testing work on electric circuits or equipment.

(2) *Visual inspection.* Test instruments and equipment and all associated test leads, cables, power cords, probes, and connectors shall be visually inspected for external defects and damage before the equipment is used. If there is a defect or evidence of damage that might expose an employee to injury, the defective or damaged item shall be removed from service, and no employee may use it until necessary repairs and tests to render the equipment safe have been made.

(3) *Rating of equipment.* Test instruments and equipment and their accessories shall be rated for the circuits and equipment to which they will be connected and shall be designed for the environment in which they will be used.

(d) *Occasional use of flammable or ignitible materials.* Where flammable materials are present only occasionally, electric equipment capable of igniting them shall not be used, unless measures are taken to prevent hazardous conditions from developing. Such materials include, but are not limited to: flammable gases, vapors, or liquids; combustible dust; and ignitible fibers or flyings.

Note: Electrical installation requirements for locations where flammable materials are present on a regular basis are contained in § 1910.307.

§ 1910.335 **Safeguards for personnel protection.**

(a) *Use of protective equipment.* (1) *Personal protective equipment.* (i) Employees working in areas where there are potential electrical hazards shall be provided with, and shall use, electrical protective equipment that is appropriate for the specific parts of the body to be protected and for the work to be performed.

Note: Personal protective equipment requirements are contained in subpart I of this part.

(ii) Protective equipment shall be maintained in a safe, reliable condition and shall be periodically inspected or tested, as required by § 1910.137.

(iii) If the insulating capability of protective equipment may be subject to damage during use, the insulating material shall be protected. (For example, an outer covering of leather is sometimes used for the protection of rubber insulating material.)

(iv) Employees shall wear nonconductive head protection wherever there is a danger of head injury from electric shock or burns due to contact with exposed energized parts.

(v) Employees shall wear protective equipment for the eyes or face wherever there is danger of injury to the eyes or face from electric arcs or flashes or from flying objects resulting from electrical explosion.

(2) *General protective equipment and tools.* (i) When working near exposed energized conductors or circuit parts, each employee shall use insulated tools or handling equipment if the tools or handling equipment might make contact with such conductors or parts. If the insulating capability of insulated tools or handling equipment is subject to damage, the insulating material shall be protected.

(A) Fuse handling equipment, insulated for the circuit voltage, shall be used to remove or install fuses when the fuse terminals are energized.

(B) Ropes and handlines used near exposed energized parts shall be nonconductive.

(ii) Protective shields, protective barriers, or insulating materials shall be used to protect each employee from shock, burns, or other electrically related injuries while that employee is working near exposed energized parts which might be accidentally contacted or where dangerous electric heating or arcing might occur. When normally enclosed live parts are exposed for maintenance or repair, they shall be guarded to protect unqualified persons from contact with the live parts.

(b) *Alerting techniques.* The following alerting techniques shall be used to warn and protect employees from hazards which could cause injury due to electric shock, burns, or failure of electric equipment parts:

(1) *Safety signs and tags.* Safety signs, safety symbols, or accident prevention tags shall be used where necessary to warn employees about electrical hazards which may endanger them, as required by § 1910.145.

(2) *Barricades.* Barricades shall be used in conjunction with safety signs where it is necessary to prevent or limit employee access to work areas exposing employees to uninsulated energized conductors or circuit parts. Conductive barricades may not be used where they might cause an electrical contact hazard.

(3) *Attendants.* If signs and barricades do not provide sufficient warning and protection from electrical hazards, an attendant shall be stationed to warn and protect employees.

FIGURE 4.2 (*Continued*)   Electrical Safety-Related Work Practices (OSHA-CFR, Title 29, Part 1910, Subpart S, Paragraphs 331–335). (*Courtesy General Industry.*)

§ 1910.269 Electric power generation, transmission, and distribution.

(a) *General.* (1) *Application.* (i) This section covers the operation and maintenance of electric power generation, control, transformation, transmission, and distribution lines and equipment. These provisions apply to:

(A) Power generation, transmission, and distribution installations, including related equipment for the purpose of communication or metering, which are accessible only to qualified employees;

Note: The types of installations covered by this paragraph include the generation, transmission, and distribution installations of electric utilities, as well as equivalent installations of industrial establishments. Supplementary electric generating equipment that is used to supply a workplace for emergency, standby, or similar purposes only is covered under Subpart S of this Part. (See paragraph (a)(1)(ii)(B) of this section.)

(B) Other installations at an electric power generating station, as follows:

(1) Fuel and ash handling and processing installations, such as coal conveyors,

(2) Water and steam installations, such as penstocks, pipelines, and tanks, providing a source of energy for electric generators,

(3) Chlorine and hydrogen systems.

(C) Test sites where electrical testing involving temporary measurements associated with electric power generation, transmission, and distribution is performed in laboratories, in the field, in substations, and on lines, as opposed to metering, relaying, and routine line work; and

(D) Work on or directly associated with the installations covered in paragraphs (a)(1)(i)(A) through (a)(1)(i)(C) of this section.

(E) Line-clearance tree-trimming operations, as follows:

(1) Entire § 1910.269 of this Part, except paragraph (r)(1) of this section, applies to line-clearance tree-trimming operations performed by qualified employees (those who are knowledgeable in the construction and operation of electric power generation, transmission, or distribution equipment involved, along with the associated hazards).

(2) Paragraphs (a)(2), (b), (c), (g), (k), (p), and (r) of this section apply to line-clearance tree-trimming operations performed by line-clearance tree trimmers who are not qualified employees.

(ii) Notwithstanding paragraph (A)(1)(I) of this section, § 1910.269 of this Part does not apply:

(A) To construction work, as defined in § 1910.12 of this Part; or

(B) To electrical installations, electrical safety-related work practices, or electrical maintenance considerations covered by Subpart S of this Part.

Note 1: Work practices conforming to §§ 1910.332 through 1910.335 of this Part are considered as complying with the electrical safety-related work practice requirements of this section identified in Table 1 of Appendix A-2 to this section, provided the work is being performed on a generation or distribution installation meeting §§ 1910.303 through 1910.308 of this Part. This table also identifies provisions in this section that apply to work by qualified persons directly on or associated with installations of electric power generation, transmission, and distribution lines or equipment, regardless of compliance with §§ 1910.332 through 1910.335 of this Part.

Note 2: Work practices performed by qualified persons and conforming to § 1910.269 of this Part are considered as complying with § 1910.333(c) and § 1910.335 of this Part.

(iii) This section applies in addition to all other applicable standards contained in this Part 1910. Specific references in this section to other sections of Part 1910 are provided for emphasis only.

(2) *Training.* Employees shall be trained in and familiar with the safety-related work practices, safety procedures, and other safety requirements in this section that pertain to their respective job assignments. Employees shall also be trained in and familiar with any other safety practices, including applicable emergency procedures (such as pole top and manhole rescue), that are not specifically addressed by this section but that are related to their work and are necessary for their safety.

(ii) Qualified employees shall also be trained and competent in:

(A) The skills and techniques necessary to distinguish exposed live parts from other parts of electric equipment,

(B) The skills and techniques necessary to determine the nominal voltage of exposed live parts,

(C) The minimum approach distances specified in this section corresponding to the voltages to which the qualified employee will be exposed, and

(D) The proper use of the special precautionary techniques, personal protective equipment, insulating and shielding materials, and insulated tools for working on or near exposed energized parts of electric equipment.

Note: For the purposes of this section, a person must have this training in order to be considered a qualified person.

(iii) The employer shall determine, through regular supervision and through inspections conducted on at least an annual basis, that each employee is complying with the safety-related work practices required by this section.

(iv) An employee shall receive additional training (or retraining) under any of the following conditions:

(A) If the supervision and annual inspections required by paragraph (a)(2)(iii) of this section indicate that the employee is not complying with the safety-related work practices required by this section, or

(B) If new technology, new types of equipment, or changes in procedures necessitate the use of safety-related work practices that are different from those which the employee would normally use, or

(C) If he or she must employ safety-related work practices that are not normally used during his or her regular job duties.

Note: OSHA would consider tasks that are performed less often than once per year to necessitate retraining before the performance of the work practices involved.

(v) The training required by paragraph (a)(2) of this section shall be of the classroom or on-the-job type.

(vi) The training shall establish employee proficiency in the work practices required by this section and shall introduce the procedures necessary for compliance with this section.

(vii) The employer shall certify that each employee has received the training required by paragraph (a)(2) of this section. This certification shall be made when the employee demonstrates proficiency in the work practices involved and shall be maintained for the duration of the employee's employment.

Note: Employment records that indicate that an employee has received the required training are an acceptable means of meeting this requirement.

(3) *Existing conditions.* Existing conditions related to the safety of the

---

FIGURE 4.3 Electric Power Generation, Transmission, and Distribution Rule. This rule is reproduced as issued in the Monday, January 31, 1994 issue of the Federal Register. Appendixes are included.

work to be performed shall be determined before work on or near electric lines or equipment is started. Such conditions include, but are not limited to, the nominal voltages of lines and equipment, the maximum switching transient voltages, the presence of hazardous induced voltages, the presence and condition of protective grounds and equipment grounding conductors, the condition of poles, environmental conditions relative to safety, and the locations of circuits and equipment, including power and communication lines and fire protective signaling circuits.

(b) *Medical services and first aid.* The employer shall provide medical services and first aid as required in § 1910.151 of this Part. In addition to the requirements of § 1910.151 of this Part, the following requirements also apply:

(1) *Cardiopulmonary resuscitation and first aid training.* When employees are performing work on or associated with exposed lines or equipment energized at 50 volts or more, persons trained in first aid including cardiopulmonary resuscitation (CPR) shall be available as follows:

(i) For field work involving two or more employees at a work location, at least two trained persons shall be available. However, only one trained person need be available if all new employees are trained in first aid, including CPR, within 3 months of their hiring dates.

(ii) For fixed work locations such as generating stations, the number of trained persons available shall be sufficient to ensure that each employee exposed to electric shock can be reached within 4 minutes by a trained person. However, where the existing number of employees is insufficient to meet this requirement (at a remote substation, for example), all employees at the work location shall be trained.

(2) *First aid supplies.* First aid supplies required by § 1910.151(b) of this Part shall be placed in weatherproof containers if the supplies could be exposed to the weather.

(3) *First aid kits.* Each first aid kit shall be maintained, shall be readily available for use, and shall be inspected frequently enough to ensure that expended items are replaced but at least once per year.

(c) *Job briefing.* The employer shall ensure that the employee in charge conducts a job briefing with the employees involved before they start each job. The briefing shall cover at least the following subjects: hazards associated with the job, work procedures involved, special precautions, energy source controls, and personal protective equipment requirements.

(1) *Number of briefings.* If the work or operations to be performed during the work day or shift are repetitive and similar, at least one job briefing shall be conducted before the start of the first job of each day or shift. Additional job briefings shall be held if significant changes, which might affect the safety of the employees, occur during the course of the work.

(2) *Extent of briefing.* A brief discussion is satisfactory if the work involved is routine and if the employee, by virtue of training and experience, can reasonably be expected to recognize and avoid the hazards involved in the job. A more extensive discussion shall be conducted:

(i) If the work is complicated or particularly hazardous, or

(ii) If the employee cannot be expected to recognize and avoid hazards involved in the job.

Note: The briefing is always required to touch on all the subjects listed in the introductory text to paragraph (c) of this section.

(3) *Working alone.* An employee working alone need not conduct a job briefing. However, the employer shall ensure that the tasks to be performed are planned as if a briefing were required.

(d) *Hazardous energy control (lockout/tagout) procedures.* (1) *Application.* The provisions of paragraph (d) of this section apply to the use of lockout/tagout procedures for the control of energy sources in installations for the purpose of electric power generation, including related equipment for communication or metering. Locking and tagging procedures for the deenergizing of electric energy sources which are used exclusively for purposes of transmission and distribution are addressed by paragraph (m) of this section.

Note 1: Installations in electric power generation facilities that are not an integral part of, or inextricably commingled with, power generation processes or equipment are covered under § 1910.147 and Subpart S of this Part.

Note 2: Lockout and tagging procedures that comply with paragraphs (c) through (f) of § 1910.147 of this Part will also be deemed to comply with para-

graph of this section if the procedures address the hazards covered by paragraph (d) of this section.

(2) *General.* (i) The employer shall establish a program consisting of energy control procedures, employee training, and periodic inspections to ensure that, before any employee performs any servicing or maintenance on a machine or equipment where the unexpected energizing, start up, or release of stored energy could occur and cause injury, the machine or equipment is isolated from the energy source and rendered inoperative.

(ii) The employer's energy control program under paragraph (d)(2) of this section shall meet the following requirements:

(A) If an energy isolating device is not capable of being locked out, the employer's program shall use a tagout system.

(B) If an energy isolating device is capable of being locked out, the employer's program shall use lockout, unless the employer can demonstrate that the use of a tagout system will provide full employee protection as follows:

(1) When a tagout device is used on an energy isolating device which is capable of being locked out, the tagout device shall be attached at the same location that the lockout device would have been attached, and the employer shall demonstrate that the tagout program will provide a level of safety equivalent to that obtained by the use of a lockout program.

(2) In demonstrating that a level of safety is achieved in the tagout program equivalent to the level of safety obtained by the use of a lockout program, the employer shall demonstrate full compliance with all tagout-related provisions of this standard together with such additional elements as are necessary to provide the equivalent safety available from the use of a lockout device. Additional means to be considered as part of the demonstration of full employee protection shall include the implementation of additional safety measures such as the removal of an isolating circuit element, blocking of a controlling switch, opening of an extra disconnecting device, or the removal of a valve handle to reduce the likelihood of inadvertent energizing.

(C) After [insert date 120 days after publication], whenever replacement or major repair, renovation, or modification of a machine or equipment is

---

FIGURE 4.3 (*Continued*)   Electric Power Generation, Transmission, and Distribution Rule. This rule is reproduced as issued in the Monday, January 31, 1994 issue of the Federal Register. Appendixes are included.

performed, and whenever new machines or equipment are installed, energy isolating devices for such machines or equipment shall be designed to accept a lockout device.

(iii) Procedures shall be developed, documented, and used for the control of potentially hazardous energy covered by paragraph (d) of this section.

(iv) The procedure shall clearly and specifically outline the scope, purpose, responsibility, authorization, rules, and techniques to be applied to the control of hazardous energy, and the measures to enforce compliance including, but not limited to, the following:

(A) A specific statement of the intended use of this procedure;

(B) Specific procedural steps for shutting down, isolating, blocking and securing machines or equipment to control hazardous energy;

(C) Specific procedural steps for the placement, removal, and transfer of lockout devices or tagout devices and the responsibility for them; and

(D) Specific requirements for testing a machine or equipment to determine and verify the effectiveness of lockout devices, tagout devices, and other energy control measures.

(v) The employer shall conduct a periodic inspection of the energy control procedure at least annually to ensure that the procedure and the provisions of paragraph (d) of this section are being followed.

(A) The periodic inspection shall be performed by an authorized employee who is not using the energy control procedure being inspected.

(B) The periodic inspection shall be designed to identify and correct any deviations or inadequacies.

(C) If lockout is used for energy control, the periodic inspection shall include a review, between the inspector and each authorized employee, of that employee's responsibilities under the energy control procedure being inspected.

(D) Where tagout is used for energy control, the periodic inspection shall include a review, between the inspector and each authorized and affected employee, of that employee's responsibilities under the energy control procedure being inspected, and the elements set forth in paragraph (d)(2)(vii) of this section.

(E) The employer shall certify that the inspections required by paragraph (d)(2)(v) of this section have been accomplished. The certification shall identify the machine or equipment on which the energy control procedure

was being used, the date of the inspection, the employees included in the inspection, and the person performing the inspection.

Note: If normal work schedule and operation records demonstrate adequate inspection activity and contain the required information, no additional certification is required.

(vi) The employer shall provide training to ensure that the purpose and function of the energy control program are understood by employees and that the knowledge and skills required for the safe application, usage, and removal of energy controls are acquired by employees. The training shall include the following:

(A) Each authorized employee shall receive training in the recognition of applicable hazardous energy sources, the type and magnitude of energy available in the workplace, and in the methods and means necessary for energy isolation and control.

(B) Each affected employee shall be instructed in the purpose and use of the energy control procedure.

(C) All other employees whose work operations are or may be in an area where energy control procedures may be used shall be instructed about the procedures and about the prohibition relating to attempts to restart or reenergize machines or equipment that are locked out or tagged out.

(vii) When tagout systems are used, employees shall also be trained in the following limitations of tags:

(A) Tags are essentially warning devices affixed to energy isolating devices and do not provide the physical restraint on those devices that is provided by a lock.

(B) When a tag is attached to an energy isolating means, it is not to be removed without authorization of the authorized person responsible for it, and it is never to be bypassed, ignored, or otherwise defeated.

(C) Tags must be legible and understandable by all authorized employees, affected employees, and all other employees whose work operations are or may be in the area, in order to be effective.

(D) Tags and their means of attachment must be made of materials which will withstand the environmental conditions encountered in the workplace.

(E) Tags may evoke a false sense of security, and their meaning needs to be understood as part of the overall energy control program.

(F) Tags must be securely attached to energy isolating devices so that they cannot be inadvertently or accidentally detached during use.

(viii) Retraining shall be provided by the employer as follows:

(A) Retraining shall be provided for all authorized and affected employees whenever there is a change in their job assignments, a change in machines, equipment, or processes that present a new hazard or whenever there is a change in the energy control procedures.

(B) Retraining shall also be conducted whenever a periodic inspection under paragraph (d)(2)(v) of this section reveals, or whenever the employer has reason to believe, that there are deviations from or inadequacies in an employee's knowledge or use of the energy control procedures.

(C) The retraining shall reestablish employee proficiency and shall introduce new or revised control methods and procedures, as necessary.

(ix) The employer shall certify that employee training has been accomplished and is being kept up to date. The certification shall contain each employee's name and dates of training.

(3) *Protective materials and hardware.* (i) Locks, tags, chains, wedges, key blocks, adapter pins, self-locking fasteners, or other hardware shall be provided by the employer for isolating, securing, or blocking of machines or equipment from energy sources.

(ii) Lockout devices and tagout devices shall be singularly identified; shall be the only devices used for controlling energy; may not be used for other purposes; and shall meet the following requirements:

(A) Lockout devices and tagout devices shall be capable of withstanding the environment to which they are exposed for the maximum period of time that exposure is expected.

(1) Tagout devices shall be constructed and printed so that exposure to weather conditions or wet and damp locations will not cause the tag to deteriorate or the message on the tag to become illegible.

(2) Tagout devices shall be so constructed as not to deteriorate when used in corrosive environments.

(B) Lockout devices and tagout devices shall be standardized within the facility in at least one of the following criteria: color, shape, size. Additionally, in the case of tagout devices, print and format shall be standardized.

FIGURE 4.3 (*Continued*)   Electric Power Generation, Transmission, and Distribution Rule. This rule is reproduced as issued in the Monday, January 31, 1994 issue of the Federal Register. Appendixes are included.

(C) Lockout devices shall be substantial enough to prevent removal without the use of excessive force or unusual techniques, such as with the use of bolt cutters or metal cutting tools.

(D) Tagout devices, including their means of attachment, shall be substantial enough to prevent inadvertent or accidental removal. Tagout device attachment means shall be of a nonreusable type, attachable by hand, self-locking, and non-releasable with a minimum unlocking strength of no less than 50 pounds and shall have the general design and basic characteristics of being at least equivalent to a one-piece, all-environment-tolerant nylon cable tie.

(E) Each lockout device or tagout device shall include provisions for the identification of the employee applying the device.

(F) Tagout devices shall warn against hazardous conditions if the machine or equipment is energized and shall include a legend such as the following: Do Not Start, Do Not Open, Do Not Close, Do Not Energize, Do Not Operate.

Note: For specific provisions covering accident prevention tags, see § 1910.145 of this Part.

(4) *Energy isolation.* Lockout and tagout device application and removal may only be performed by the authorized employees who are performing the servicing or maintenance.

(5) *Notification.* Affected employees shall be notified by the employer or authorized employee of the application and removal of lockout or tagout devices. Notification shall be given before the controls are applied and after they are removed from the machine or equipment.

Note: See also paragraph (d)(7) of this section, which requires that the second notification take place before the machine or equipment is reenergized.

(6) *Lockout/tagout application.* The established procedures for the application of energy control (the lockout or tagout procedures) shall include the following elements and actions, and these procedures shall be performed in the following sequence:

(i) Before an authorized or affected employee turns off a machine or equipment, the authorized employee shall have knowledge of the type and magnitude of the energy, the hazards of the energy to be controlled, and the

method or means to control the energy.

(ii) The machine or equipment shall be turned off or shut down using the procedures established for the machine or equipment. An orderly shutdown shall be used to avoid any additional or increased hazards to employees as a result of the equipment stoppage.

(iii) All energy isolating devices that are needed to control the energy to the machine or equipment shall be physically located and operated in such a manner as to isolate the machine or equipment from energy sources.

(iv) Lockout or tagout devices shall be affixed to each energy isolating device by authorized employees.

(A) Lockout devices shall be attached in a manner that will hold the energy isolating devices in a "safe" or "off" position.

(B) Tagout devices shall be affixed in such a manner as will clearly indicate that the operation or movement of energy isolating devices from the "safe" or "off" position is prohibited.

(1) Where tagout devices are used with energy isolating devices designed with the capability of being locked out, the tag attachment shall be fastened at the same point at which the lock would have been attached.

(2) Where a tag cannot be affixed directly to the energy isolating device, the tag shall be located as close as safely possible to the device, in a position that will be immediately obvious to anyone attempting to operate the device.

(v) Following the application of lockout or tagout devices to energy isolating devices, all potentially hazardous stored or residual energy shall be relieved, disconnected, restrained, or otherwise rendered safe.

(vi) If there is a possibility of reaccumulation of stored energy to a hazardous level, verification of isolation shall be continued until the servicing or maintenance is completed or until the possibility of such accumulation no longer exists.

(vii) Before starting work on machines or equipment that have been locked out or tagged out, the authorized employee shall verify that isolation and deenergizing of the machine or equipment have been accomplished. If normally energized parts will be exposed to contact by an employee while the machine or equipment is deenergized, a test shall be

performed to ensure that these parts are deenergized.

(7) *Release from lockout/tagout.* Before lockout or tagout devices are removed and energy is restored to the machine or equipment, procedures shall be followed and actions taken by the authorized employees to ensure the following:

(i) The work area shall be inspected to ensure that nonessential items have been removed and that machine or equipment components are operationally intact.

(ii) The work area shall be checked to ensure that all employees have been safely positioned or removed.

(iii) After lockout or tagout devices have been removed and before a machine or equipment is started, affected employees shall be notified that the lockout or tagout devices have been removed.

(iv) Each lockout or tagout devices shall be removed from each energy isolating device by the authorized employee who applied the lockout or tagout device. However, if that employee is not available to remove it, the device may be removed under the direction of the employer, provided that specific procedures and training for such removal have been developed, documented, and incorporated into the employer's energy control program. The employer shall demonstrate that the specific procedure provides a degree of safety equivalent to that provided by the removal of the device by the authorized employee who applied it. The specific procedure shall include at least the following elements:

(A) Verification by the employer that the authorized employee who applied the device is not at the facility;

(B) Making all reasonable efforts to contact the authorized employee to inform him or her that his or her lockout or tagout device has been removed; and

(C) Ensuring that the authorized employee has this knowledge before he or she resumes work at that facility.

(8) *Additional requirements.* (i) If the lockout or tagout devices must be temporarily removed from energy isolating devices and the machine or equipment must be energized to test or position the machine, equipment, or component thereof, the following sequence of actions shall be followed:

(A) Clear the machine or equipment of tools and materials in accor-

---

FIGURE 4.3 (*Continued*)   Electric Power Generation, Transmission, and Distribution Rule. This rule is reproduced as issued in the Monday, January 31, 1994 issue of the Federal Register. Appendixes are included.

dance with paragraph (d)(7)(i) of this section;

(B) Remove employees from the machine or equipment area in accordance with paragraphs (d)(7)(ii) and (d)(7)(iii) of this section;

(C) Remove the lockout or tagout devices as specified in paragraph (d)(7)(iv) of this section;

(D) Energize and proceed with the testing or positioning; and

(E) Deenergize all systems and reapply energy control measures in accordance with paragraph (d)(6) of this section to continue the servicing or maintenance.

(ii) When servicing or maintenance is performed by a crew, craft, department, or other group, they shall use a procedure which affords the employees a level of protection equivalent to that provided by the implementation of a personal lockout or tagout device. Group lockout or tagout devices shall be used in accordance with the procedures required by paragraphs (d)(2)(iii) and (d)(2)(iv) of this section including, but not limited to, the following specific requirements:

(A) Primary responsibility shall be vested in an authorized employee for a set number of employees working under the protection of a group lockout or tagout device (such as an operations lock);

(B) Provision shall be made for the authorized employee to ascertain the exposure status of all individual group members with regard to the lockout or tagout of the machine or equipment;

(C) When more than one crew, craft, department, or other group is involved, assignment of overall job-associated lockout or tagout control responsibility shall be given to an authorized employee designated to coordinate affected work forces and ensure continuity of protection; and

(D) Each authorized employee shall affix a personal lockout or tagout device to the group lockout device, group lockbox, or comparable mechanism when he or she begins work and shall remove those devices when he or she stops working on the machine or equipment being serviced or maintained.

(iii) Procedures shall be used during shift or personnel changes to ensure the continuity of lockout or tagout protection, including provision for the orderly transfer of lockout or tagout device protection between off-going and on-coming employees, to minimize their exposure to hazards

from the unexpected energizing or start-up of the machine or equipment or from the release of stored energy.

(iv) Whenever outside servicing personnel are to be engaged in activities covered by paragraph (d) of this section, the on-site employer and the outside employer shall inform each other of their respective lockout or tagout procedures, and each employer shall ensure that his or her personnel understand and comply with restrictions and prohibitions of the energy control procedures being used.

(v) If energy isolating devices are installed in a central location under the exclusive control of a system operator, the following requirements apply:

(A) The employer shall use a procedure that affords employees a level of protection equivalent to that provided by the implementation of a personal lockout or tagout device.

(B) The system operator shall place and remove lockout and tagout devices in place of the authorized employee under paragraphs (d)(4), (d)(6)(iv) and (d)(7)(iv) of this section.

(C) Provisions shall be made to identify the authorized employee who is responsible for (that is, being protected by) the lockout or tagout device, to transfer responsibility for lockout and tagout devices, and to ensure that an authorized employee requesting removal or transfer of a lockout or tagout device is the one responsible for it before the device is removed or transferred.

(e) *Enclosed spaces.* This paragraph covers enclosed spaces that may be entered by employees. It does not apply to vented vaults if a determination is made that the ventilation system is operating to protect employees before they enter the space. This paragraph applies to routine entry into enclosed spaces in lieu of the permit-space entry requirements contained in paragraphs (d) through (k) of § 1910.146 of this Part. If, after the precautions given in paragraphs (e) and (t) of this section are taken, the hazards remaining in the enclosed space endanger the life of an entrant or could interfere with escape from the space, then entry into the enclosed space shall meet the permit-space entry requirements of paragraphs (d) through (k) of § 1910.146 of this Part.

Note: Entries into enclosed spaces conducted in accordance with the permit-space entry requirements of paragraphs (d) through (k) of § 1910.146 of this Part

are considered as complying with paragraph (e) of this section.

(1) *Safe work practices.* The employer shall ensure the use of safe work practices for entry into and work in enclosed spaces and for rescue of employees from such spaces.

(2) *Training.* Employees who enter enclosed spaces or who serve as attendants shall be trained in the hazards of enclosed space entry, in enclosed space entry procedures, and in enclosed space rescue procedures.

(3) *Rescue equipment.* Employers shall provide equipment to ensure the prompt and safe rescue of employees from the enclosed space.

(4) *Evaluation of potential hazards.* Before any entrance cover to an enclosed space is removed, the employer shall determine whether it is safe to do so by checking for the presence of any atmospheric pressure or temperature differences and by evaluating whether there might be a hazardous atmosphere in the space. Any conditions making it unsafe to remove the cover shall be eliminated before the cover is removed.

Note: The evaluation called for in this paragraph may take the form of a check of the conditions expected to be in the enclosed space. For example, the cover could be checked to see if it is hot and, if it is fastened and placed, could be loosened gradually to release any residual pressure. A determination must also be made of whether conditions at the site could cause a hazardous atmosphere, such as an oxygen deficient or flammable atmosphere, to develop within the space.

(5) *Removal of covers.* When covers are removed from enclosed spaces, the opening shall be promptly guarded by a railing, temporary cover, or other barrier intended to prevent an accidental fall through the opening and to protect employees working in the space from objects entering the space.

(6) *Hazardous atmosphere.* Employees may not enter any enclosed space while it contains a hazardous atmosphere, unless the entry conforms to the generic permit-required confined spaces standard in § 1910.146 of this Part.

Note: The term "entry" is defined in § 1910.146(b) of this Part.

(7) *Attendants.* While work is being performed in the enclosed space, a person with first aid training meeting paragraph (b) of this section shall be immediately available outside the

---

FIGURE 4.3 (*Continued*) Electric Power Generation, Transmission, and Distribution Rule. This rule is reproduced as issued in the Monday, January 31, 1994 issue of the Federal Register. Appendixes are included.

enclosed space to render emergency assistance if there is reason to believe that a hazard may exist in the space or if a hazard exists because of traffic patterns in the area of the opening used for entry. That person is not precluded from performing other duties outside the enclosed space if these duties do not distract the attendant from monitoring employees within the space.

Note: See paragraph of this section for additional requirements on attendants for work in manholes.

(8) *Calibration of test instruments.* Test instruments used to monitor atmospheres in enclosed spaces shall be kept in calibration, with a minimum accuracy of ±10 percent.

(9) *Testing for oxygen deficiency.* Before an employee enters an enclosed space, the internal atmosphere shall be tested for oxygen deficiency with a direct-reading meter or similar instrument, capable of collection and immediate analysis of data samples without the need for off-site evaluation. If continuous forced air ventilation is provided, testing is not required provided that the procedures used ensure that employees are not exposed to the hazards posed by oxygen deficiency.

(10) *Testing for flammable gases and vapors.* Before an employee enters an enclosed space, the internal atmosphere shall be tested for flammable gases and vapors with a direct-reading meter or similar instrument capable of collection and immediate analysis of data samples without the need for off-site evaluation. This test shall be performed after the oxygen testing and ventilation required by paragraph (e)(9) of this section demonstrate that there is sufficient oxygen to ensure the accuracy of the test for flammability.

(11) *Ventilation and monitoring.* If flammable gases or vapors are detected or if an oxygen deficiency is found, forced air ventilation shall be used to maintain oxygen at a safe level and to prevent a hazardous concentration of flammable gases and vapors from accumulating. A continuous monitoring program to ensure that no increase in flammable gas or vapor concentration occurs may be followed in lieu of ventilation, if flammable gases or vapors are detected at safe levels.

Note: See the definition of hazardous atmosphere for guidance in determining whether or not a given concentration of a substances is considered to be hazardous.

(12) *Specific ventilation requirements.* If continuous forced air ventilation is used, it shall begin before entry is made and shall be maintained long enough to ensure that a safe atmosphere exists before employees are allowed to enter the work area. The forced air ventilation shall be so directed as to ventilate the immediate area where employees are present within the enclosed space and shall continue until all employees leave the enclosed space.

(13) *Air supply.* The air supply for the continuous forced air ventilation shall be from a clean source and may not increase the hazards in the enclosed space.

(14) *Open flames.* If open flames are used in enclosed spaces, a test for flammable gases and vapors shall be made immediately before the open flame device is used and at least once per hour while the device is used in the space. Testing shall be conducted more frequently if conditions present in the enclosed space indicate that once per hour is insufficient to detect hazardous accumulations of flammable gases or vapors.

Note: See the definition of hazardous atmosphere for guidance in determining whether or not a given concentration of a substances is considered to be hazardous.

(f) *Excavations.* Excavation operations shall comply with Subpart P of Part 1926 of this chapter.

(g) *Personal protective equipment.* (1) *General.* Personal protective equipment shall meet the requirements of Subpart I of this Part.

(2) *Fall protection.* (i) Personal fall arrest equipment shall meet the requirements of Subpart E of Part 1926 of this Chapter.

(ii) Body belts and safety straps for work positioning shall meet the requirements of § 1926.959 of this Chapter.

(iii) Body belts, safety straps, lanyards, lifelines, and body harnesses shall be inspected before use each day to determine that the equipment is in safe working condition. Defective equipment may not be used.

(iv) Lifelines shall be protected against being cut or abraded.

(v) Fall arrest equipment, work positioning equipment, or travel restricting equipment shall be used by employees working at elevated locations more than 4 feet (1.2 m) above the ground on poles, towers, or similar structures if other fall protection has not been provided. The use of fall protection equipment is not required to be used by a qualified employee climbing or changing location on poles, towers, or similar structures, unless conditions, such as, but not limited to, ice, high winds, the design of the structure (for example, no provision for holding on with hands), or the presence of contaminants on the structure, could cause the employee to lose his or her grip or footing.

Note 1: This paragraph applies to structures that support overhead electric power generation, transmission, and distribution lines and equipment. It does not apply to portions of buildings, such as loading docks, to electric equipment, such as transformers and capacitors, nor to aerial lifts. Requirements for fall protection associated with walking and working surfaces are contained in Subpart D of this Part; requirements for fall protection associated with aerial lifts are contained in § 1910.67 of this Part.

Note 2: Employees undergoing training are not considered "qualified employees" for the purposes of this provision. Unqualified employees (including trainees) are required to use fall protection any time they are more than 4 feet (1.2 m) above the ground.

(vi) The following requirements apply to personal fall arrest systems:
(A) When stopping or arresting a fall, personal fall arrest systems shall limit the maximum arresting force on an employee to 900 pounds (4 kN) if used with a body belt.

(B) When stopping or arresting a fall, personal fall arrest systems shall limit the maximum arresting force on an employee to 1800 pounds (8 kN) if used with a body harness.

(C) Personal fall arrest systems shall be rigged such that an employee can neither free fall more than 6 feet (1.8 m) nor contact any lower level.

(vii) If vertical lifelines or droplines are used, not more than one employee may be attached to any one lifeline.

(viii) Snaphooks may not be connected to loops made in webbing-type lanyards.

(ix) Snaphooks may not be connected to each other.

(h) *Ladders, platforms, step bolts, and manhole steps.* (1) *General.* Requirements for ladders contained in Subpart D of this Part apply, except as specifically noted in paragraph (h)(2) of this section.

(2) *Special ladders and platforms.* Portable ladders and platforms used

FIGURE 4.3 (*Continued*)   Electric Power Generation, Transmission, and Distribution Rule. This rule is reproduced as issued in the Monday, January 31, 1994 issue of the Federal Register. Appendixes are included.

on structures or conductors in conjunction with overhead line work need not meet paragraphs (d)(2)(i) and (d)(2)(iii) of § 1910.25 of this Part or paragraph (c)(3)(iii) of § 1910.26 of this Part. However, these ladders and platforms shall meet the following requirements:

(i) Ladders and platforms shall be secured to prevent their becoming accidentally dislodged.

(ii) Ladders and platforms may not be loaded in excess of the working loads for which they are designed.

(iii) Ladders and platforms may be used only in applications for which they were designed.

(iv) In the configurations in which they are used, ladders and platforms shall be capable of supporting without failure at least 2.5 times the maximum intended load.

(3) *Conductive ladders.* Portable metal ladders and other portable conductive ladders may not be used near exposed energized lines or equipment. However, in specialized high-voltage work, conductive ladders shall be used where the employer can demonstrate that nonconductive ladders would present a greater hazard than conductive ladders.

(i) *Hand and portable power tools.* (1) *General.* Paragraph (i)(2) of this section applies to electric equipment connected by cord and plug. Paragraph (i)(3) of this section applies to portable and vehicle-mounted generators used to supply cord- and plug-connected equipment. Paragraph (i)(4) of this section applies to hydraulic and pneumatic tools.

(2) *Cord- and plug-connected equipment.* (1) Cord- and plug-connected equipment supplied by premises wiring is covered by Subpart S of this Part.

(ii) Any cord- and plug-connected equipment supplied by other than premises wiring shall comply with one of the following in lieu of § 1910.243(a)(5) of this Part:

(A) It shall be equipped with a cord containing an equipment grounding conductor connected to the tool frame and to a means for grounding the other end (however, this option may not be used where the introduction of the ground into the work environment increases the hazard to an employee); or

(B) It shall be of the double-insulated type conforming to Subpart S of this Part; or

(C) It shall be connected to the power supply through an isolating

transformer with an ungrounded secondary.

(3) *Portable and vehicle-mounted generators.* Portable and vehicle-mounted generators used to supply cord- and plug-connected equipment shall meet the following requirements:

(i) The generator may only supply equipment located on the generator or the vehicle and cord- and plug-connected equipment through receptacles mounted on the generator or the vehicle.

(ii) The non-current-carrying metal parts of equipment and the equipment grounding conductor terminals of the receptacles shall be bonded to the generator frame.

(iii) In the case of vehicle-mounted generators, the frame of the generator shall be bonded to the vehicle frame.

(iv) Any neutral conductor shall be bonded to the generator frame.

(4) *Hydraulic and pneumatic tools.* (i) Safe operating pressures for hydraulic and pneumatic tools, hoses, valves, pipes, filters, and fittings may not be exceeded.

Note: If any hazardous defects are present, no operating pressure would be safe, and the hydraulic or pneumatic equipment involved may not be used. In the absence of defects, the maximum rated operating pressure is the maximum safe pressure.

(ii) A hydraulic or pneumatic tool used where it may contact exposed live parts shall be designed and maintained for such use.

(iii) The hydraulic system supplying a hydraulic tool used where it may contact exposed live parts shall provide protection against loss of insulating value for the voltage involved due to the formation of a partial vacuum in the hydraulic line.

Note: Hydraulic lines without check valves having a separation of more than 35 feet (10.7 m) between the oil reservoir and the upper end of the hydraulic system promote the formation of a partial vacuum.

(iv) A pneumatic tool used on energized electrical lines or equipment or used where it may contact exposed live parts shall provide protection against the accumulation of moisture in the air supply.

(v) Pressure shall be released before connections are broken, unless quick acting, self-closing connectors are used. Hoses may not be kinked.

(vi) Employees may not use any part of their bodies to locate or attempt to stop a hydraulic leak.

(j) *Live-line tools.* (1) *Design of tools.* Live-line tool rods, tubes, and poles shall be designed and constructed to withstand the following minimum tests:

(i) 100,000 volts per foot (3281 volts per centimeter) of length for 5 minutes if the tool is made of fiberglass-reinforced plastic (FRP), or

(ii) 75,000 volts per foot (2461 volts per centimeter) of length for 3 minutes if the tool is made of wood, or

(iii) Other tests that the employer can demonstrate are equivalent.

Note: Live-line tools using rod and tube that meet ASTM F711-89, Standard Specification for Fiberglass-Reinforced Plastic (FRP) Rod and Tube Used in Live-Line Tools, conform to paragraph (j)(1)(i) of this section.

(2) *Condition of tools.* (i) Each live-line tool shall be wiped clean and visually inspected for defects before use each day.

(ii) If any defect or contamination that could adversely affect the insulating qualities or mechanical integrity of the live-line tool is present after wiping, the tool shall be removed from service and examined and tested according to paragraph (j)(2)(iii) of this section before being returned to service.

(iii) Live-line tools used for primary employee protection shall be removed from service every 2 years and whenever required under paragraph (j)(2)(ii) of this section for examination, cleaning, repair, and testing as follows:

(A) Each tool shall be thoroughly examined for defects.

(B) If a defect or contamination that could adversely affect the insulating qualities or mechanical integrity of the live-line tool is found, the tool shall be repaired and refinished or shall be permanently removed from service. If no such defect or contamination is found, the tool shall be cleaned and waxed.

(C) The tool shall be tested in accordance with paragraphs (j)(2)(iii)(D) and (j)(2)(iii)(E) of this section under the following conditions:

(1) After the tool has been repaired or refinished; and

(2) After the examination if repair or refinishing is not performed, unless the tool is made of FRP rod or foam-filled FRP tube and the employer can demonstrate that the tool has no defects that could cause it to fail in use.

FIGURE 4.3 (*Continued*)   Electric Power Generation, Transmission, and Distribution Rule. This rule is reproduced as issued in the Monday, January 31, 1994 issue of the Federal Register. Appendixes are included.

(D) The test method used shall be designed to verify the tool's integrity along its entire working length and, if the tool is made of fiberglass-reinforced plastic, its integrity under wet conditions.

(E) The voltage applied during the tests shall be as follows:

(1) 75,000 volts per foot (2461 volts per centimeter) of length for 1 minute if the tool is made of fiberglass, or

(2) 50,000 volts per foot (1640 volts per centimeter) of length for 1 minute if the tool is made of wood, or

(3) Other tests that the employer can demonstrate are equivalent.

Note: Guidelines for the examination, cleaning, repairing, and in-service testing of live-line tools are contained in the Institute of Electrical and Electronics Engineers Guide for In-Service Maintenance and Electrical Testing of Live-Line Tools, IEEE Std. 978-1984.

(k) *Materials handling and storage.*
(1) *General.* Material handling and storage shall conform to the requirements of Subpart N of this Part.

(2) *Materials storage near energized lines or equipment.* (i) In areas not restricted to qualified persons only, materials or equipment may not be stored closer to energized lines or exposed energized parts of equipment than the following distances plus an amount providing for the maximum sag and side swing of all conductors and providing for the height and movement of material handling equipment:

(A) For lines and equipment energized at 50 kV or less, the distance is 10 feet (305 cm).

(B) For lines and equipment energized at more than 50 kV, the distance is 10 feet (305 cm) plus 4 inches (10 cm) for every 10 kV over 50 kV.

(ii) In areas restricted to qualified employees, material may not be stored within the working space about energized lines or equipment.

Note: Requirements for the size of the working space are contained in paragraphs (u)(1) and (v)(3) of this section.

(1) *Working on or near exposed energized parts.* This paragraph applies to work on exposed live parts, or near enough to them, to expose the employee to any hazard they present.

(1) *General.* Only qualified employees may work on or with exposed energized lines or parts of equipment. Only qualified employees may work in areas containing unguarded, uninsulated energized lines or parts of

equipment operating at 50 volts or more. Electric lines and equipment shall be considered and treated as energized unless the provisions of paragraph (d) or paragraph (m) of this section have been followed.

(i) Except as provided in paragraph (l)(1)(ii) of this section, at least two employees shall be present while the following types of work are being performed:

(A) Installation, removal, or repair of lines that are energized at more than 600 volts,

(B) Installation, removal, or repair of deenergized lines if an employee is exposed to contact with other parts energized at more than 600 volts,

(C) Installation, removal, or repair of equipment, such as transformers, capacitors, and regulators, if an employee is exposed to contact with parts energized at more than 600 volts,

(D) Work involving the use of mechanical equipment, other than insulated aerial lifts, near parts energized at more than 600 volts, and

(E) Other work that exposes an employee to electrical hazards greater than or equal to those posed by operations that are specifically listed in paragraphs (l)(1)(i)(A) through (l)(1)(i)(D) of this section.

(ii) Paragraph (l)(1)(i) of this section does not apply to the following operations:

(A) Routine switching of circuits, if the employer can demonstrate that conditions at the site allow this work to be performed safely,

(B) Work performed with live-line tools if the employee is positioned so that he or she is neither within reach of nor otherwise exposed to contact with energized parts, and

(C) Emergency repairs to the extent necessary to safeguard the general public.

(2) *Minimum approach distances.* The employer shall ensure that no employee approaches or takes any conductive object closer to exposed energized parts than set forth in Table R-6 through Table R-10, unless:

(i) The employee is insulated from the energized part (insulating gloves or insulating gloves and sleeves worn in accordance with paragraph (l)(3) of this section are considered insulation of the employee only with regard to the energized part upon which work is being performed), or

(ii) The energized part is insulated from the employee and from any other conductive object at a different potential, or

(iii) The employee is insulated from any other exposed conductive object, as during live-line bare-hand work.

Note: Paragraphs (v)(5)(i) and of this section contain requirements for the guarding and isolation of live parts. Parts of electric circuits that meet these two provisions are not considered as "exposed" unless a guard is removed or an employee enters the space intended to provide isolation from the live parts.

(3) *Type of insulation.* If the employee is to be insulated from energized parts by the use of insulating gloves (under paragraph (l)(2)(i) of this section), insulating sleeves shall also be used. However, insulating sleeves need not be used under the following conditions:

(i) If exposed energized parts on which work is not being performed are insulated from the employee and

(ii) If such insulation is placed from a position not exposing the employee's upper arm to contact with other energized parts.

(4) *Working position.* The employer shall ensure that each employee, to the extent that other safety-related conditions at the worksite permit, works in a position from which a slip or shock will not bring the employee's body into contact with exposed, uninsulated parts energized at a potential different from the employee.

(5) *Making connections.* The employer shall ensure that connections are made as follows:

(i) In connecting deenergized equipment or lines to an energized circuit by means of a conducting wire or device, an employee shall first attach the wire to the deenergized part;

(ii) When disconnecting equipment or lines from an energized circuit by means of a conducting wire or device, an employee shall remove the source end first; and

(iii) When lines or equipment are connected to or disconnected from energized circuits, loose conductors shall be kept away from exposed energized parts.

(6) *Apparel.* (i) When work is performed within reaching distance of exposed energized parts of equipment, the employer shall ensure that each employee removes or renders nonconductive all exposed conductive articles, such as key or watch chains, rings, or wrist watches or bands, unless such articles do not increase the hazards associated with contact with the energized parts.

FIGURE 4.3 (*Continued*)   Electric Power Generation, Transmission, and Distribution Rule. This rule is reproduced as issued in the Monday, January 31, 1994 issue of the Federal Register. Appendixes are included.

(ii) The employer shall train each employee who is exposed to the hazards of flames or electric arcs in the hazards involved.

(iii) The employer shall ensure that each employee who is exposed to the hazards of flames or electric arcs does not wear clothing that, when exposed to flames or electric arcs, could increase the extent of injury that would be sustained by the employee.

Note: Clothing made from the following types of fabrics, either alone or in blends, is prohibited by this paragraph, unless the employer can demonstrate that the fabric has been treated to withstand the conditions that may be encountered or that the clothing is worn in such a manner as to eliminate the hazard involved: acetate, nylon, polyester, rayon.

(7) *Fuse handling.* When fuses must be installed or removed with one or both terminals energized at more than 300 volts with exposed parts energized at more than 50 volts, the employer shall ensure that tools or gloves rated for the voltage are used. When expulsion-type fuses are installed with one or both terminals energized at more than 300 volts, the employer shall ensure that each employee wears eye protection meeting the requirements of Subpart I of this Part, uses a tool rated for the voltage, and is clear of the exhaust path of the fuse barrel.

(8) *Covered (noninsulated) conductors.* The requirements of this section which pertain to the hazards of exposed live parts also apply when work is performed in the proximity of covered (noninsulated) wires.

(9) *Noncurrent-carrying metal parts.* Noncurrent-carrying metal parts of equipment or devices, such as transformer cases and circuit breaker housings, shall be treated as energized at the highest voltage to which they are exposed, unless the employer inspects the installation and determines that these parts are grounded before work is performed.

(10) *Opening circuits under load.* Devices used to open circuits under load conditions shall be designed to interrupt the current involved.

TABLE R-6.—AC Live-Line Work Minimum Approach Distance

Nominal voltage in kilovolts phase to phase	Distance			
	Phase to ground exposure		Phase to phase exposure	
	(ft-in)	(m)	(ft-in)	(m)
0.05 to 1.0	(4)	(4)	(4)	(4)
1.1 to 15.0	2–1	0.64	2–2	0.66
15.1 to 36.0	2–4	0.72	2–7	0.77
36.1 to 46.0	2–7	0.77	2–10	0.85
46.1 to 72.5	3–0	0.90	3–6	1.05
72.6 to 121	3–2	0.95	4–3	1.29
138 to 145	3–7	1.09	4–11	1.50
161 to 169	4–0	1.22	5–8	1 71
230 to 242	5–3	1.59	7–6	2.27
345 to 362	8–6	2.59	12–6	3.80
500 to 550	11–3	3.42	18–1	5.50
765 to 800	14–11	4.53	26–0	7.91

NOTE 1: These distances take into consideration the highest switching surge an employee will be exposed to on any system with air as the insulating medium and the maximum voltages shown.
NOTE 2: The clear live-line tool distance shall equal or exceed the values for the indicated voltage ranges.
NOTE 3: See Appendix B of this part for information on how the minimum approach distances listed in the tables were derived.
4 Avoid contact.

(m) *Deenergizing lines and equipment for employee protection.* (1) *Application.* Paragraph (m) of this section applies to the deenergizing of transmission and distribution lines and equipment for the purpose of protecting employees. Control of hazardous energy sources used in the generation of electric energy is covered in paragraph (d) of this section. Conductors and parts of electric equipment that have been deenergized under procedures other than those required by paragraphs (d) or (m) of this section, as applicable, shall be treated as energized.

(2) *General.* (i) If a system operator is in charge of the lines or equipment and their means of disconnection, all of the requirements of paragraph (m)(3) of this section shall be observed, in the order given, before work is begun.

(ii) If no system operator is in charge of the lines or equipment and their means of disconnection, one employee in the crew shall be designated as being in charge of the clearance. All of the requirements of paragraph (m)(3) of this section apply, in the order given, except as provided in paragraph (m)(2)(iii) of this section. The employee in charge of the clearance shall take the place of the system operator, as necessary.

(iii) If only one crew will be working on the lines or equipment and if the means of disconnection is accessible and visible to and under the sole control of the employee in charge of the clearance, paragraphs (m)(3)(i), (m)(3)(iii), (m)(3)(iv), (m)(3)(viii) and (m)(3)(xii) of this section do not

TABLE R-7.—AC LIVE-LINE WORK MINIMUM APPROACH DISTANCE WITH OVERVOLTAGE FACTOR PHASE-TO-GROUND EXPOSRUE

Maximum anticipated per-unit transient overvoltage	Distance in feet-inches						
	Maximum phase-to-phase voltage in kilovolts						
	121	145	169	242	362	552	800
1.5	....	....	....	....	....	6–0	9–8
1.6	....	....	....	....	....	6–6	10–8
1.7	....	....	....	....	....	7–0	11–8
1.8	....	....	....	....	....	7–7	12–8
1.9	....	....	....	....	....	8–1	13–9
2.0	2–5	2–9	3–0	3–10	5–3	8–9	14–11
2.1	2–6	2–10	3–2	4–0	5–5	9–4	....
2.2	2–7	2–11	3–3	4–1	5–9	9–11	....
2.3	2–8	3–0	3–4	4–3	6–1	10–6	....
2.4	2–9	3–1	3–5	4–5	6–4	11–3	....
2.5	2–9	3–2	3–6	4–6	6–8	....	....
2.6	2–10	3–3	3–8	4–8	7–1	....	....
2.7	2–11	3–4	3–9	4–10	7–5	....	....
2.8	3–0	3–5	3–10	4–11	7–9	....	....
2.9	3–1	3–6	3–11	5–1	8–2	....	....

FIGURE 4.3 (*Continued*)   Electric Power Generation, Transmission, and Distribution Rule. This rule is reproduced as issued in the Monday, January 31, 1994 issue of the Federal Register. Appendixes are included.

TABLE R–7 —AC LIVE-LINE WORK MINIMUM APPROACH DISTANCE WITH OVERVOLTAGE FACTOR PHASE-TO-GROUND EXPOSURE—CONTINUED

Maximum anticipated per-unit transient overvoltage	Distance in feet-inches						
	Maximum phase-to-phase voltage in kilovolts						
	121	145	169	242	362	552	800
3.0	3–2	3–7	4–0	5–3	8–6	....	....

NOTE 1: The distance specified in this table may be applied only where the maximum anticipated per-unit transient overvoltage has been determined by engineering analysis and has been supplied by the employer. Table R–6 applies otherwise.
NOTE 2: The distances specified in this table are the air, bare-hand, and live-line tool distances.
NOTE 3: See Appendix B of this part for information on how the minimum approach distances listed in the tables were derived and on how to calculate revised minimum approach distances based on the control of transient overvoltages.

TABLE R–8.—AC LIVE-LINE WORK MINIMUM APPROACH DISTANCE WITH OVERVOLTAGE FACTOR PHASE-TO-PHASE EXPOSURE

Maximum anticipated per-unit transient overvoltage	Distance in feet-inches						
	Maximum phase-to-phase voltage in kilovolts						
	121	145	169	242	362	552	800
1.5	....	....	....	....	....	7–4	12–1
1.6	....	....	....	....	....	8–9	14–6
1.7	....	....	....	....	....	10–2	17–2
1.8	....	....	....	....	....	11–7	19–11
1.9	....	....	....	....	....	13–2	22–11
2.0	3–7	4–1	4–8	6–1	8–7	14–10	26–0
2.1	3–7	4–2	4–9	6–3	8–10	15–7	....
2.2	3–8	4–3	4–10	6–4	9–2	16–4	....
2.3	3–9	4–4	4–11	6–6	9–6	17–2	....
2.4	3–10	4–5	5–0	6–7	9–11	18–1	....
2.5	3–11	4–6	5–2	6–9	10–4	....	....
2.6	4–0	4–7	5–3	6–11	10–9	....	....
2.7	4–1	4–8	5–4	7–0	11–2	....	....
2.8	4–1	4–9	5–5	7–2	11–7	....	....
2.9	4–2	4–10	5–6	7–4	12–1	....	....
3.0	4–3	4–11	5–8	7–6	12–6	....	....

NOTE 1: The distance specified in this table may be applied only where the maximum anticipated per-unit transient overvoltage has been determined by engineering analysis and has been supplied by the employer. Table R–6 applies otherwise.
NOTE 2: The distances specified in this table are the air, bare-hand, and live-line tool distances.
NOTE 3: See Appendix B of this part for information on how the minimum approach distances listed in the tables were derived and on how to calculate revised minimum approach distances based on the control of transient overvoltages.

TABLE R–9.—DC Live-Line Work Minimum Approach Distance With Overvoltage Factor

Maximum anticipated per-unit transient overvoltage	Distance in feet-inches				
	Maximum line-to-ground voltage in kilovolts				
	250	400	500	600	750
1.5 or lower	3–8	5–3	6–9	8–7	11–10
1.6	3–10	5–7	7–4	9–5	13–1
1.7	4–1	6–0	7–11	10–3	14–4
1.8	4–3	6–5	8–7	11–2	15–9

NOTE 1: The distances specified in this table may be applied only where the maximum anticipated per-unit transient overvoltage has been determined by engineering analysis and has been supplied by the employer. However, if the transient overvoltage factor is not known, a factor of 1.8 shall be assumed.
NOTE 2: The distances specified in this table are the air, bare-hand, and live-line tool distances.

TABLE R–10.—ALTITUDE CORRECTION FACTOR

Altitude				Correction factor
ft	ft	m	m	
3000	10000	900	3000	1.00 / 1.20
4000	12000	1200	3600	1.02 / 1.25
5000	14000	1500	4200	1.05 / 1.30
6000	16000	1800	4800	1.08 / 1.35
7000	18000	2100	5400	1.11 / 1.39
8000	20000	2400	6000	1.14 / 1.44
9000		2700		1.17

NOTE: If the work is performed at elevations greater than 3000 ft (900 m) above mean sea level, the minimum approach distance shall be determined by multiplying the distances in Table R–6 through Table R–9 by the correction factor corresponding to the altitude at which work is performed.

FIGURE 4.3 (*Continued*) Electric Power Generation, Transmission, and Distribution Rule. This rule is reproduced as issued in the Monday, January 31, 1994 issue of the Federal Register. Appendixes are included.

apply. Additionally, tags required by the remaining provisions of paragraph (m)(3) of this section need not be used.

(iv) Any disconnecting means that are accessible to persons outside the employer's control (for example, the general public) shall be rendered inoperable while they are open for the purpose of protecting employees.

(3) *Deenergizing lines and equipment.* (i) A designated employee shall make a request of the system operator to have the particular section of line or equipment deenergized. The designated employee becomes the employee in charge (as this term is used in paragraph (m)(3) of this section) and is responsible for the clearance.

(ii) All switches, disconnectors, jumpers, taps, and other means through which known sources of electric energy may be supplied to the particular lines and equipment to be deenergized shall be opened. Such means shall be rendered inoperable, unless its design does not so permit, and tagged to indicate that employees are at work.

(iii) Automatically and remotely controlled switches that could cause the opened disconnecting means to close shall also be tagged at the point of control. The automatic or remote control feature shall be rendered inoperable, unless its design does not so permit.

(iv) Tags shall prohibit operation of the disconnecting means and shall indicate that employees are at work.

(v) After the applicable requirements in paragraphs (m)(3)(i) through (m)(3)(iv) of this section have been followed and the employee in charge of the work has been given a clearance by the system operator, the lines and equipment to be worked shall be tested to ensure that they are deenergized.

(vi) Protective grounds shall be installed as required by paragraph (n) of this section.

(vii) After the applicable requirements of paragraphs (m)(3)(i) through (m)(3)(vi) of this section have been followed, the lines and equipment involved may be worked as deenergized.

(viii) If two or more independent crews will be working on the same lines or equipment, each crew shall independently comply with the requirements in paragraph (m)(3) of this section.

(ix) To transfer the clearance, the employee in charge (or, if the employee in charge is forced to leave the worksite due to illness or other emergency, the employee's supervisor) shall inform the system operator; employees in the crew shall be informed of the transfer; and the new employee in charge shall be responsible for the clearance.

(x) To release a clearance, the employee in charge shall:

(A) Notify employees under his or her direction that the clearance is to be released;

(B) Determine that all employees in the crew are clear of the lines and equipment;

(C) Determine that all protective grounds installed by the crew have been removed; and

(D) Report this information to the system operator and release the clearance.

(xi) The person releasing a clearance shall be the same person that requested the clearance, unless responsibility has been transferred under paragraph (m)(3)(ix) of this section.

(xii) Tags may not be removed unless the associated clearance has been released under paragraph (m)(3)(x) of this section.

(xiii) Only after all protective grounds have been removed, after all crews working on the lines or equipment have released their clearances, after all employees are clear of the lines and equipment, and after all protective tags have been removed from a given point of disconnection, may action be initiated to reenergize the lines or equipment at that point of disconnection.

(n) *Grounding for the protection of employees.* (1) *Application.* Paragraph (n) of this section applies to the grounding of transmission and distribution lines and equipment for the purpose of protecting employees. Paragraph (n)(4) of this section also applies to the protective grounding of other equipment as required elsewhere in this section.

(2) *General.* For the employee to work lines or equipment as deenergized, the lines or equipment shall be deenergized under the provisions of paragraph (m) of this section and shall be grounded as specified in paragraphs (n)(3) through (n)(9) of this section. However, if the employer can demonstrate that installation of a ground is impracticable or that the conditions resulting from the installation of a

ground would present greater hazards than working without grounds, the lines and equipment may be treated as deenergized provided all of the following conditions are met:

(i) The lines and equipment have been deenergized under the provisions of paragraph (m) of this section.

(ii) There is no possibility of contact with another energized source.

(iii) The hazard of induced voltage is not present.

(3) *Equipotential zone.* Temporary protective grounds shall be placed at such locations and arranged in such a manner as to prevent each employee from being exposed to hazardous differences in electrical potential.

(4) *Protective grounding equipment.* (i) Protective grounding equipment shall be capable of conducting the maximum fault current that could flow at the point of grounding for the time necessary to clear the fault. This equipment shall have an ampacity greater than or equal to that of No. 2 AWG copper.

Note: Guidelines for protective grounding equipment are contained in American Society for Testing and Materials Standard Specifications for Temporary Grounding Systems to be Used on De-Energized Electric Power Lines and Equipment, ASTM F855-1990.

(ii) Protective grounds shall have an impedance low enough to cause immediate operation of protective devices in case of accidental energizing of the lines or equipment.

(5) *Testing.* Before any ground is installed, lines and equipment shall be tested and found absent of nominal voltage, unless a previously installed ground is present.

(6) *Order of connection.* When a ground is to be attached to a line or to equipment, the ground-end connection shall be attached first, and then the other end shall be attached by means of a live-line tool.

(7) *Order of removal.* When a ground is to be removed, the grounding device shall be removed from the line or equipment using a live-line tool before the ground-end connection is removed.

(8) *Additional precautions.* When work is performed on a cable at a location remote from the cable terminal, the cable may not be grounded at the cable terminal if there is a possibility of hazardous transfer of potential should a fault occur.

(9) *Removal of grounds for test.* Grounds may be removed temporar-

---

FIGURE 4.3 (*Continued*)   Electric Power Generation, Transmission, and Distribution Rule. This rule is reproduced as issued in the Monday, January 31, 1994 issue of the Federal Register. Appendixes are included.

ily during tests. During the test procedure, the employer shall ensure that each employee uses insulating equipment and is isolated from any hazards involved, and the employer shall institute any additional measures as may be necessary to protect each exposed employee in case the previously grounded lines and equipment become energized.

(o) *Testing and test facilities.* (1) *Application.* Paragraph (o) of this section provides for safe work practices for high-voltage and high-power testing performed in laboratories, shops, and substations, and in the field and on electric transmission and distribution lines and equipment. It applies only to testing involving interim measurements utilizing high voltage, high power, or combinations of both, and not to testing involving continuous measurements as in routine metering, relaying, and normal line work.

Note: Routine inspection and maintenance measurements made by qualified employees are considered to be routine line work and are not included in the scope of paragraph (o) of this section, as long as the hazards related to the use of intrinsic high-voltage or high-power sources require only the normal precautions associated with routine operation and maintenance work required in the other paragraphs of this section. Two typical examples of such excluded test work procedures are "phasing-out" testing and testing for a "no-voltage" condition.

(2) *General requirements.* (i) The employer shall establish and enforce work practices for the protection of each worker from the hazards of high-voltage or high-power testing at all test areas, temporary and permanent. Such work practices shall include, as a minimum, test area guarding, grounding, and the safe use of measuring and control circuits. A means providing for periodic safety checks of field test areas shall also be included. (See paragraph (o)(6) of this section.)

(ii) Employees shall be trained in safe work practices upon their initial assignment to the test area, with periodic reviews and updates provided as required by paragraph (a)(2) of this section.

(3) *Guarding of test areas.* (i) Permanent test areas shall be guarded by walls, fences, or barriers designed to keep employees out of the test areas.

(ii) In field testing, or at a temporary test site where permanent fences and gates are not provided, one of the following means shall be used to prevent unauthorized employees from entering:

(A) The test area shall be guarded by the use of distinctively colored safety tape that is supported approximately waist high and to which safety signs are attached,

(B) The test area shall be guarded by a barrier or barricade that limits access to the test area to a degree equivalent, physically and visually, to the barricade specified in paragraph (o)(3)(ii)(A) of this section, or

(C) The test area shall be guarded by one or more test observers stationed so that the entire area can be monitored.

(iii) The barriers required by paragraph (o)(3)(ii) of this section shall be removed when the protection they provide is no longer needed.

(iv) Guarding shall be provided within test areas to control access to test equipment or to apparatus under test that may become energized as part of the testing by either direct or inductive coupling, in order to prevent accidental employee contact with energized parts.

(4) *Grounding practices.* (i) The employer shall establish and implement safe grounding practices for the test facility.

(A) All conductive parts accessible to the test operator during the time the equipment is operating at high voltage shall be maintained at ground potential except for portions of the equipment that are isolated from the test operator by guarding.

(B) Wherever ungrounded terminals of test equipment or apparatus under test may be present, they shall be treated as energized until determined by tests to be deenergized.

(ii) Visible grounds shall be applied, either automatically or manually with properly insulated tools, to the high-voltage circuits after they are deenergized and before work is performed on the circuit or item or apparatus under test. Common ground connections shall be solidly connected to the test equipment and the apparatus under test.

(iii) In high-power testing, an isolated ground-return conductor system shall be provided so that no intentional passage of current, with its attendant voltage rise, can occur in the ground grid or in the earth. However, an isolated ground-return conductor need not be provided if the employer can demonstrate that both the following conditions are met:

(A) An isolated ground-return conductor cannot be provided due to the distance of the test site from the electric energy source, and

(B) Employees are protected from any hazardous step and touch potentials that may develop during the test.

Note: See Appendix C of this part for information on measures that can be taken to protect employees from hazardous step and touch potentials.

(iv) In tests in which grounding of test equipment by means of the equipment grounding conductor located in the equipment power cord cannot be used due to increased hazards to test personnel or the prevention of satisfactory measurements, a ground that the employer can demonstrate affords equivalent safety shall be provided, and the safety ground shall be clearly indicated in the test set-up.

(v) When the test area is entered after equipment is deenergized, a ground shall be placed on the high-voltage terminal and any other exposed terminals.

(A) High capacitance equipment or apparatus shall be discharged through a resistor rated for the available energy.

(B) A direct ground shall be applied to the exposed terminals when the stored energy drops to a level at which it is safe to do so.

(vi) If a test trailer or test vehicle is used in field testing, its chassis shall be grounded. Protection against hazardous touch potentials with respect to the vehicle, instrument panels, and other conductive parts accessible to employees shall be provided by bonding, insulation, or isolation.

(5) *Control and measuring circuits.* (i) Control wiring, meter connections, test leads and cables may not be run from a test area unless they are contained in a grounded metallic sheath and terminated in a grounded metallic enclosure or unless other precautions are taken that the employer can demonstrate as ensuring equivalent safety.

(ii) Meters and other instruments with accessible terminals or parts shall be isolated from test personnel to protect against hazards arising from such terminals and parts becoming energized during testing. If this isolation is provided by locating test equipment in metal compartments with viewing windows, interlocks shall be provided to interrupt the power supply if the compartment cover is opened.

FIGURE 4.3 (*Continued*)   Electric Power Generation, Transmission, and Distribution Rule. This rule is reproduced as issued in the Monday, January 31, 1994 issue of the Federal Register. Appendixes are included.

(iii) The routing and connections of temporary wiring shall be made secure against damage, accidental interruptions and other hazards. To the maximum extent possible, signal, control, ground, and power cables shall be kept separate.

(iv) If employees will be present in the test area during testing, a test observer shall be present. The test observer shall be capable of implementing the immediate deenergizing of test circuits for safety purposes.

(6) *Safety check.* (i) Safety practices governing employee work at temporary or field test areas shall provide for a routine check of such test areas for safety at the beginning of each series of tests.

(ii) The test operator in charge shall conduct these routine safety checks before each series of tests and shall verify at least the following conditions:

(A) That barriers and guards are in workable condition and are properly placed to isolate hazardous areas;

(B) That system test status signals, if used, are in operable condition;

(C) That test power disconnects are clearly marked and readily available in an emergency;

(D) That ground connections are clearly identifiable;

(E) That personal protective equipment is provided and used as required by Subpart I of this Part and by this section; and

(F) That signal, ground, and power cables are properly separated.

(p) *Mechanical equipment.* (1) *General requirements.* (i) The critical safety components of mechanical elevating and rotating equipment shall receive a thorough visual inspection before use on each shift.

Note: Critical safety components of mechanical elevating and rotating equipment are components whose failure would result in a free fall or free rotation of the boom.

(ii) No vehicular equipment having an obstructed view to the rear may be operated on off-highway jobsites where any employee is exposed to the hazards created by the moving vehicle, unless:

(A) The vehicle has a reverse signal alarm audible above the surrounding noise level, or

(B) The vehicle is backed up only when a designated employee signals that it is safe to do so.

(iii) The operator of an electric line truck may not leave his or her position at the controls while a load is suspended, unless the employer can demonstrate that no employee (including the operator) might be endangered.

(iv) Rubber-tired, self-propelled scrapers, rubber-tired front-end loaders, rubber-tired dozers, wheel-type agricultural and industrial tractors, crawler-type tractors, crawler-type loaders, and motor graders, with or without attachments, shall have rollover protective structures that meet the requirements of Subpart W of Part 1926 of this chapter.

(2) *Outriggers.* (i) Vehicular equipment, if provided with outriggers, shall be operated with the outriggers extended and firmly set as necessary for the stability of the specific configuration of the equipment. Outriggers may not be extended or retracted outside of clear view of the operator unless all employees are outside the range of possible equipment motion.

(ii) If the work area or the terrain precludes the use of outriggers, the equipment may be operated only within its maximum load ratings for the particular configuration of the equipment without outriggers.

(3) *Applied loads.* Mechanical equipment used to lift or move lines or other material shall be used within its maximum load rating and other design limitations for the conditions under which the work is being performed.

(4) *Operations near energized lines or equipment.* (i) Mechanical equipment shall be operated so that the minimum approach distances of Table R-6 through Table R‑10 are maintained from exposed energized lines and equipment. However, the insulated portion of an aerial lift operated by a qualified employee in the lift is exempt from this requirement.

(ii) A designated employee other than the equipment operator shall observe the approach distance to exposed lines and equipment and give timely warnings before the minimum approach distance required by paragraph (p)(4)(i) is reached, unless the employer can demonstrate that the operator can accurately determine that the minimum approach distance is being maintained.

(iii) If, during operation of the mechanical equipment, the equipment could become energized, the operation shall also comply with at least one of paragraphs (p)(4)(iii)(A) through (p)(4)(iii)(C) of this section.

(A) The energized lines exposed to contact shall be covered with insulating protective material that will withstand the type of contact that might be made during the operation.

(B) The equipment shall be insulated for the voltage involved. The equipment shall be positioned so that its uninsulated portions cannot approach the lines or equipment any closer than the minimum approach distances specified in Table R-6 through Table R-10.

(C) Each employee shall be protected from hazards that might arise from equipment contact with the energized lines. The measures used shall ensure that employees will not be exposed to hazardous differences in potential. Unless the employer can demonstrate that the methods in use protect each employee from the hazards that might arise if the equipment contacts the energized line, the measures used shall include all of the following techniques:

(1) Using the best available ground to minimize the time the lines remain energized,

(2) Bonding equipment together to minimize potential differences,

(3) Providing ground mats to extend areas of equipotential, and

(4) Employing insulating protective equipment or barricades to guard against any remaining hazardous potential differences.

Note: Appendix C of this part contains information on hazardous step and touch potentials and on methods of protecting employees from hazards resulting from such potentials.

(q) *Overhead lines.* This paragraph provides additional requirements for work performed on or near overhead lines and equipment.

(1) *General.* (i) Before elevated structures, such as poles or towers, are subjected to such stresses as climbing or the installation or removal of equipment may impose, the employer shall ascertain that the structures are capable of sustaining the additional or unbalanced stresses. If the pole or other structure cannot withstand the loads which will be imposed, it shall be braced or otherwise supported so as to prevent failure.

Note: Appendix D of this part contains test methods that can be used in ascertaining whether a wood pole is capable of sustaining the forces that would be imposed by an employee climbing the pole. This paragraph also requires the employer to ascertain that the pole

FIGURE 4.3 (*Continued*) Electric Power Generation, Transmission, and Distribution Rule. This rule is reproduced as issued in the Monday, January 31, 1994 issue of the Federal Register. Appendixes are included.

can sustain all other forces that will be imposed by the work to be performed.

(ii) When poles are set, moved, or removed near exposed energized overhead conductors, the pole may not contact the conductors.

(iii) When a pole is set, moved, or removed near an exposed energized overhead conductor, the employer shall ensure that each employee wears electrical protective equipment or uses insulated devices when handling the pole and that no employee contacts the pole with uninsulated parts of his or her body.

(iv) To protect employees from falling into holes into which poles are to be placed, the holes shall be attended by employees or physically guarded whenever anyone is working nearby.

(2) *Installing and removing overhead lines.* The following provisions apply to the installation and removal of overhead conductors or cable.

(i) The employer shall use the tension stringing method, barriers, or other equivalent measures to minimize the possibility that conductors and cables being installed or removed will contact energized power lines or equipment.

(ii) The protective measures required by paragraph (p)(4)(iii) of this section for mechanical equipment shall also be provided for conductors, cables, and pulling and tensioning equipment when the conductor or cable is being installed or removed close enough to energized conductors that any of the following failures could energize the pulling or tensioning equipment or the wire or cable being installed or removed:

(A) Failure of the pulling or tensioning equipment,

(B) Failure of the wire or cable being pulled, or

(C) Failure of the previously installed lines or equipment.

(iii) If the conductors being installed or removed cross over energized conductors in excess of 600 volts and if the design of the circuit-interrupting devices protecting the lines so permits, the automatic-reclosing feature of these devices shall be made inoperative.

(iv) Before lines are installed parallel to existing energized lines, the employer shall make a determination of the approximate voltage to be induced in the new lines, or work shall proceed on the assumption that the induced voltage is hazardous. Unless the employer can demonstrate that

the lines being installed are not subject to the induction of a hazardous voltage or unless the lines are treated as energized, the following requirements also apply:

(A) Each bare conductor shall be grounded in increments so that no point along the conductor is more than 2 miles (3.22 km) from a ground.

(B) The grounds required in paragraph (q)(2)(iv)(A) of this section shall be left in place until the conductor installation is completed between dead ends.

(C) The grounds required in paragraph (q)(2)(iv)(A) of this section shall be removed as the last phase of aerial cleanup.

(D) If employees are working on bare conductors, grounds shall also be installed at each location where these employees are working, and grounds shall be installed at all open dead-end or catch-off points or the next adjacent structure.

(E) If two bare conductors are to be spliced, the conductors shall be bonded and grounded before being spliced.

(v) Reel handling equipment, including pulling and tensioning devices, shall be in safe operating condition and shall be leveled and aligned.

(vi) Load ratings of stringing lines, pulling lines, conductor grips, load-bearing hardware and accessories, rigging, and hoists may not be exceeded.

(vii) Pulling lines and accessories shall be repaired or replaced when defective.

(viii) Conductor grips may not be used on wire rope, unless the grip is specifically designed for this application.

(ix) Reliable communications, through two-way radios or other equivalent means, shall be maintained between the reel tender and the pulling rig operator.

(x) The pulling rig may only be operated when it is safe to do so.

Note: Examples of unsafe conditions include employees in locations prohibited by paragraph (q)(2)(xi) of this section, conductor and pulling line hang-ups, and slipping of the conductor grip.

(xi) While the conductor or pulling line is being pulled (in motion) with a power-driven device, employees are not permitted directly under overhead operations or on the cross arm, except as necessary to guide the stringing sock or board over or through the stringing sheave.

(3) *Live-line bare-hand work.* In addition to other applicable provisions contained in this section, the following requirements apply to live-line bare-hand work:

(i) Before using or supervising the use of the live-line bare-hand technique on energized circuits, employees shall be trained in the technique and in the safety requirements of paragraph (q)(3) of this section. Employees shall receive refresher training as required by paragraph (a)(2).

(ii) Before any employee uses the live-line bare-hand technique on energized high-voltage conductors or parts, the following information shall be ascertained:

(A) The nominal voltage rating of the circuit on which the work is to be performed,

(B) The minimum approach distance to ground of lines and other energized parts on which work is to be performed and

(C) The voltage limitations of equipment to be used.

(iii) The insulated equipment, insulated tools, and aerial devices and platforms used shall be designed, tested, and intended for live-line bare-hand work. Tools and equipment shall be kept clean and dry while they are in use.

(iv) The automatic-reclosing feature of circuit-interrupting devices protecting the lines shall be made inoperative, if the design of the devices permits.

(v) Work may not be performed when adverse weather conditions would make the work hazardous even after the work practices required by this section are employed. Additionally, work may not be performed when winds reduce the phase-to-phase or phase-to-ground minimum approach distances at the work location below that specified in paragraph (q)(3)(xiii) of this section, unless the grounded objects and other lines and equipment are covered by insulating guards.

Note: Thunderstorms in the immediate vicinity, high winds, snow storms, and ice storms are examples of adverse weather conditions that are presumed to make live-line bare-hand work too hazardous to perform safely.

(vi) A conductive bucket liner or other conductive device shall be provided for bonding the insulated aerial device to the energized line or equipment.

FIGURE 4.3 (*Continued*)   Electric Power Generation, Transmission, and Distribution Rule. This rule is reproduced as issued in the Monday, January 31, 1994 issue of the Federal Register. Appendixes are included.

(A) The employee shall be connected to the bucket liner or other conductive device by the use of conductive shoes, leg clips, or other means.

(B) Where differences in potentials at the worksite pose a hazard to employees, electrostatic shielding designed for the voltage being worked shall be provided.

(vii) Before the employee contacts the energized part, the conductive bucket liner or other conductive device shall be bonded to the energized conductor by means of a positive connection. This connection shall remain attached to the energized conductor until the work on the energized circuit is completed.

(viii) Aerial lifts to be used for live-line bare-hand work shall have dual controls (lower and upper) as follows:

(A) The upper controls shall be within easy reach of the employee in the basket. On a two-basket-type lift, access to the controls shall be within easy reach from either basket.

(B) The lower set of controls shall be located near the base of the boom, and they shall be so designed that they can override operation of the equipment at any time.

(ix) Lower (ground-level) lift controls may not be operated with an employee in the lift, except in case of emergency.

(x) Before employees are elevated into the work position, all controls (ground level and bucket) shall be checked to determine that they are in proper working condition.

(xi) Before the boom of an aerial lift is elevated, the body of the truck shall be grounded, or the body of the truck shall be barricaded and treated as energized.

(xii) A boom-current test shall be made before work is started each day, each time during the day when higher voltage is encountered, and when changed conditions indicate a need for an additional test. This test shall consist of placing the bucket in contact with an energized source equal to the voltage to be encountered for a minimum of 3 minutes. The leakage current may not exceed 1 microampere per kilovolt of nominal phase-to-ground voltage. Work from the aerial lift shall be immediately suspended upon indication of a malfunction in the equipment.

(xiii) The minimum approach distances specified in Table R-6 through Table R-10 shall be maintained from all grounded objects and from lines and equipment at a potential different from that to which the live-line bare-hand equipment is bonded, unless such grounded objects and other lines and equipment are covered by insulating guards.

(xiv) While an employee is approaching, leaving, or bonding to an energized circuit, the minimum distances in Table R-6 through Table R-10 shall be maintained between the employee and any grounded parts, including the lower boom and portions of the truck.

(xv) While the bucket is positioned alongside an energized bushing or insulator string, the phase-to-ground minimum approach distances of Table R-6 through Table R-10 shall be maintained between all parts of the bucket and the grounded end of the bushing or insulator string or any other grounded surface.

(xvi) Hand lines may not be used between the bucket and the boom or between the bucket and the ground. However, non-conductive-type hand lines may be used from conductor to ground if not supported from the bucket. Ropes used for live-line bare-hand work may not be used for other purposes.

(xvii) Uninsulated equipment or material may not be passed between a pole or structure and an aerial lift while an employee working from the bucket is bonded to an energized part.

(xviii) A minimum approach distance table reflecting the minimum approach distances listed in Table R-6 through Table R-10 shall be printed on a plate of durable non-conductive material. This table shall be mounted so as to be visible to the operator of the boom.

(xix) A non-conductive measuring device shall be readily accessible to assist employees in maintaining the required minimum approach distance.

(4) *Towers and structures.* The following requirements apply to work performed on towers or other structures which support overhead lines.

(i) The employer shall ensure that no employee is under a tower or structure while work is in progress, except where the employer can demonstrate that such a working position is necessary to assist employees working above.

(ii) Tag lines or other similar devices shall be used to maintain control of tower sections being raised or positioned, unless the employer can demonstrate that the use of such devices would create a greater hazard.

(iii) The loadline may not be detached from a member or section until the load is safely secured.

(iv) Except during emergency restoration procedures, work shall be discontinued when adverse weather conditions make the work hazardous in spite of the work practices required by this section.

Note: Thunderstorms in the immediate vicinity, high winds, snow storms, and ice storms are examples of adverse weather conditions that are presumed to make this work too hazardous to perform, except under emergency conditions.

(r) *Line-clearance tree trimming operations.* This paragraph provides additional requirements for line-clearance tree-trimming operations and for equipment used in these operations.

(1) *Electrical hazards.* This paragraph does not apply to qualified employees.

(i) Before an employee climbs, enters, or works around any tree, a determination shall be made of the nominal voltage of electric power lines posing a hazard to employees. However, a determination of the maximum nominal voltage to which an employee will be exposed may be made instead, if all lines are considered as energized at this maximum voltage.

(ii) There shall be a second line-clearance tree trimmer within normal (that is, unassisted) voice communication under any of the following conditions:

(A) If a line-clearance tree trimmer is to approach more closely than 10 feet (305 cm) any conductor or electrical apparatus energized at more than 750 volts or

(B) If branches or limbs being removed are closer to lines energized at more than 750 volts than the distances listed in Table R-6, Table R-9, and Table R-10 or

(C) If roping is necessary to remove branches or limbs from such conductors or apparatus.

(iii) Line-clearance tree trimmers shall maintain the minimum approach distances from energized conductors given in Table R-6, Table R-9, and Table R-10.

(iv) Branches that are contacting exposed energized conductors or equipment or that are within the distances specified in Table R-6, Table R-9, and Table R-10 may be removed only through the use of insulating equipment.

FIGURE 4.3 (*Continued*) Electric Power Generation, Transmission, and Distribution Rule. This rule is reproduced as issued in the Monday, January 31, 1994 issue of the Federal Register. Appendixes are included.

Note: A tool constructed of a material that the employer can demonstrate has insulating qualities meeting paragraph (j)(1) of this section are considered as insulated under this paragraph if the tool is clean and dry.

(v) Ladders, platforms, and aerial devices may not be brought closer to an energized part than the distances listed in Table R-6, Table R-9, and Table R-10.

(vi) Line-clearance tree-trimming work may not be performed when adverse weather conditions make the work hazardous in spite of the work practices required by this section. Each employee performing line-clearance tree trimming work in the aftermath of a storm or under similar emergency conditions shall be trained in the special hazards related to this type of work.

Note: Thunderstorms in the immediate vicinity, high winds, snow storms, and ice storms are examples of adverse weather conditions that are presumed to make line-clearance tree trimming work too hazardous to perform safely.

(2) *Brush chippers.* (i) Brush chippers shall be equipped with a locking device in the ignition system.

(ii) Access panels for maintenance and adjustment of the chipper blades and associated drive train shall be in place and secure during operation of the equipment.

(iii) Brush chippers not equipped with a mechanical infeed system shall be equipped with an infeed hopper of length sufficient to prevent employees from contacting the blades or knives of the machine during operation.

(iv) Trailer chippers detached from trucks shall be chocked or otherwise secured.

(v) Each employee in the immediate area of an operating chipper feed table shall wear personal protective equipment as required by Subpart I of this Part.

(3) *Sprayers and related equipment.* (i) Walking and working surfaces of sprayers and related equipment shall be covered with slip-resistant material. If slipping hazards cannot be eliminated, slip-resistant footwear or handrails and stair rails meeting the requirements of Subpart D may be used instead of slip-resistant material.

(ii) Equipment on which employees stand to spray while the vehicle is in motion shall be equipped with guardrails around the working area. The guardrail shall be constructed in accordance with Subpart D of this Part.

(4) *Stump cutters.* (i) Stump cutters shall be equipped with enclosures or guards to protect employees.

(ii) Each employee in the immediate area of stump grinding operations (including the stump cutter operator) shall wear personal protective equipment as required by Subpart I of this Part.

(5) *Gasoline-engine power saws.* Gasoline-engine power saw operations shall meet the requirements of § 1910.266(c)(5) of this Part and the following:

(i) Each power saw weighing more than 15 pounds (6.8 kilograms, service weight) that is used in trees shall be supported by a separate line, except when work is performed from an aerial lift and except during topping or removing operations where no supporting limb will be available.

(ii) Each power saw shall be equipped with a control that will return the saw to idling speed when released.

(iii) Each power saw shall be equipped with a clutch and shall be so adjusted that the clutch will not engage the chain drive at idling speed.

(iv) A power saw shall be started on the ground or where it is otherwise firmly supported. Drop starting of saws over 15 pounds (6.8 kg) is permitted outside of the bucket of an aerial lift only if the area below the lift is clear of personnel.

(v) A power saw engine may be started and operated only when all employees other than the operator are clear of the saw.

(vi) A power saw may not be running when the saw is being carried up into a tree by an employee.

(vii) Power saw engines shall be stopped for all cleaning, refueling, adjustments, and repairs to the saw or motor, except as the manufacturer's servicing procedures require otherwise.

(6) *Backpack power units for use in pruning and clearing.* (i) While a backpack power unit is running, no one other than the operator may be within 10 feet (305 cm) of the cutting head of a brush saw.

(ii) A backpack power unit shall be equipped with a quick shutoff switch readily accessible to the operator.

(iii) Backpack power unit engines shall be stopped for all cleaning, refueling, adjustments, and repairs to the saw or motor, except as the manufacturer's servicing procedures require

otherwise.

(7) *Rope.* (i) Climbing ropes shall be used by employees working aloft in trees. These ropes shall have a minimum diameter of 0.5 inch (1.2 cm) with a minimum breaking strength of 2300 pounds (10.2 kN). Synthetic rope shall have elasticity of not more than 7 percent.

(ii) Rope shall be inspected before each use and, if unsafe (for example, because of damage or defect), may not be used.

(iii) Rope shall be stored away from cutting edges and sharp tools. Rope contact with corrosive chemicals, gas, and oil shall be avoided.

(iv) When stored, rope shall be coiled and piled, or shall be suspended, so that air can circulate through the coils.

(v) Rope ends shall be secured to prevent their unraveling.

(vi) Climbing rope may not be spliced to effect repair.

(vii) A rope that is wet, that is contaminated to the extent that its insulating capacity is impaired, or that is otherwise not considered to be insulated for the voltage involved may not be used near exposed energized lines.

(8) *Fall protection.* Each employee shall be tied in with a climbing rope and safety saddle when the employee is working above the ground in a tree, unless he or she is ascending into the tree.

(s) *Communication facilities.* (1) *Microwave transmission.* (i) The employer shall ensure that no employee looks into an open waveguide or antenna that is connected to an energized microwave source.

(ii) If the electromagnetic radiation level within an accessible area associated with microwave communications systems exceeds the radiation protection guide given in § 1910.97(a)(2) of this Part, the area shall be posted with the warning symbol described in § 1910.97(a)(3) of this Part. The **lower** half of the warning symbol shall include the following statements or ones that the employer can demonstrate are equivalent:

Radiation in this area may exceed hazard limitations and special precautions are required. Obtain specific instruction before entering.

(iii) When an employee works in an area where the electromagnetic radiation could exceed the radiation protection guide, the employer shall institute measures that ensure that the employee's exposure is not greater than that permitted by that guide.

FIGURE 4.3 (*Continued*)   Electric Power Generation, Transmission, and Distribution Rule. This rule is reproduced as issued in the Monday, January 31, 1994 issue of the Federal Register. Appendixes are included.

Such measures may include administrative and engineering controls and personal protective equipment.

(2) *Power line carrier.* Power line carrier work, including work on equipment used for coupling carrier current to power line conductors, shall be performed in accordance with the requirements of this section pertaining to work on energized lines.

(t) *Underground electrical installations.* This paragraph provides additional requirements for work on underground electrical installations.

(1) *Access.* A ladder or other climbing device shall be used to enter and exit a manhole or subsurface vault exceeding 4 feet (122 cm) in depth. No employee may climb into or out of a manhole or vault by stepping on cables or hangers.

(2) *Lowering equipment into manholes.* Equipment used to lower materials and tools into manholes or vaults shall be capable of supporting the weight to be lowered and shall be checked for defects before use. Before tools or material are lowered into the opening for a manhole or vault, each employee working in the manhole or vault shall be clear of the area directly under the opening.

(3) *Attendants for manholes.* (i) While work is being performed in a manhole containing energized electric equipment, an employee with first aid and CPR training meeting paragraph (b)(1) of this section shall be available on the surface in the immediate vicinity to render emergency assistance.

(ii) Occasionally, the employee on the surface may briefly enter a manhole to provide assistance, other than emergency.

Note 1: An attendant may also be required under paragraph (e)(7) of this section. One person may serve to fulfill both requirements. However, attendants required under paragraph (e)(7) of this section are not permitted to enter the manhole.

Note 2: Employees entering manholes containing unguarded, uninsulated energized lines or parts of electric equipment operating at 50 volts or more are required to be qualified under paragraph (l)(1) of this section.

(iii) For the purpose of inspection, housekeeping, taking readings, or similar work, an employee working alone may enter, for brief periods of time, a manhole where energized cables or equipment are in service, if the employer can demonstrate that the employee will be protected from all electrical hazards.

(iv) Reliable communications, through two-way radios or other equivalent means, shall be maintained among all employees involved in the job.

(4) *Duct rods.* If duct rods are used, they shall be installed in the direction presenting the least hazard to employees. An employee shall be stationed at the far end of the duct line being rodded to ensure that the required minimum approach distances are maintained.

(5) *Multiple cables.* When multiple cables are present in a work area, the cable to be worked shall be identified by electrical means, unless its identity is obvious by reason of distinctive appearance or location or by other readily apparent means of identification. Cables other than the one being worked shall be protected from damage.

(6) *Moving cables.* Energized cables that are to be moved shall be inspected for defects.

(7) *Defective cables.* Where a cable in a manhole has one or more abnormalities that could lead to or be an indication of an impending fault, the defective cable shall be deenergized before any employee may work in the manhole, except when service load conditions and a lack of feasible alternatives require that the cable remain energized. In that case, employees may enter the manhole provided they are protected from the possible effects of a failure by shields or other devices that are capable of containing the adverse effects of a fault in the joint.

Note: Abnormalities such as oil or compound leaking from cable or joints, broken cable sheaths or joint sleeves, hot localized surface temperatures of cables or joints, or joints that are swollen beyond normal tolerance are presumed to lead to or be an indication of an impending fault.

(8) *Sheath continuity.* When work is performed on buried cable or on cable in manholes, metallic sheath continuity shall be maintained or the cable sheath shall be treated as energized.

(u) *Substations.* This paragraph provides additional requirements for substations and for work performed in them.

(1) *Access and working space.* Sufficient access and working space shall be provided and maintained about electric equipment to permit ready and safe operation and maintenance of such equipment.

Note: Guidelines for the dimensions of access and workspace about electric equipment in substations are contained in American National Standard— National Electrical Safety Code, ANSI C2-1987. Installations meeting the ANSI

provisions comply with paragraph (u)(1) of this section. An installation that does not conform to this ANSI standard will, nonetheless, be considered as complying with paragraph (u)(1) of this section if the employer can demonstrate that the installation provides ready and safe access based on the following evidence:

(1) That the installation conforms to the edition of ANSI C2 that was in effect at the time the installation was made,

(2) That the configuration of the installation enables employees to maintain the minimum approach distances required by paragraph (l)(2) of this section while they are working on exposed, energized parts, and

(3) That the precautions taken when work is performed on the installation provide protection equivalent to the protection that would be provided by access and working space meeting ANSI C2-1987.

(2) *Draw-out-type circuit breakers.* When draw-out-type circuit breakers are removed or inserted, the breaker shall be in the open position. The control circuit shall also be rendered inoperative, if the design of the equipment permits.

(3) *Substation fences.* Conductive fences around substations shall be grounded. When a substation fence is expanded or a section is removed, fence grounding continuity shall be maintained, and bonding shall be used to prevent electrical discontinuity.

(4) *Guarding of rooms containing electric supply equipment.* (i) Rooms and spaces in which electric supply lines or equipment are installed shall meet the requirements of paragraphs (u)(4)(ii) through (u)(4)(v) of this section under the following conditions:

(A) If exposed live parts operating at 50 to 150 volts to ground are located within 8 feet of the ground or other working surface inside the room or space,

(B) If live parts operating at 151 to 600 volts and located within 8 feet of the ground or other working surface inside the room or space are guarded only by location, as permitted under paragraph (u)(5)(i) of this section, or

(C) If live parts operating at more than 600 volts are located within the room or space, unless:

(1) The live parts are enclosed within grounded, metal-enclosed equipment whose only openings are designed so that foreign objects inserted in these openings will be deflected from energized parts, or

(2) The live parts are installed at a height above ground and any other working surface that provides protection at the voltage to which they are

---

FIGURE 4.3 (*Continued*)   Electric Power Generation, Transmission, and Distribution Rule. This rule is reproduced as issued in the Monday, January 31, 1994 issue of the Federal Register. Appendixes are included.

energized corresponding to the protection provided by an 8-foot height at 50 volts.

(ii) The rooms and spaces shall be so enclosed within fences, screens, partitions, or walls as to minimize the possibility that unqualified persons will enter.

(iii) Signs warning unqualified persons to keep out shall be displayed at entrances to the rooms and spaces.

(iv) Entrances to rooms and spaces that are not under the observation of an attendant shall be kept locked.

(v) Unqualified persons may not enter the rooms or spaces while the electric supply lines or equipment are energized.

(5) *Guarding of energized parts.* (i) Guards shall be provided around all live parts operating at more than 150 volts to ground without an insulating covering, unless the location of the live parts gives sufficient horizontal or vertical or a combination of these clearances to minimize the possibility of accidental employee contact.

Note: Guidelines for the dimensions of clearance distances about electric equipment in substations are contained in American National Standard— National Electrical Safety Code, ANSI C2-1987. Installations meeting the ANSI provisions comply with paragraph (u)(5)(i) of this section. An installation that does not conform to this ANSI standard will, nonetheless, be considered as complying with paragraph (u)(5)(i) of this section if the employer can demonstrate that the installation provides sufficient clearance based on the following evidence:

(1) That the installation conforms to the edition of ANSI C2 that was in effect at the time the installation was made,

(2) That each employee is isolated from energized parts at the point of closest approach, and

(3) That the precautions taken when work is performed on the installation provide protection equivalent to the protection that would be provided by horizontal and vertical clearances meeting ANSI C2-1987.

(ii) Except for fuse replacement and other necessary access by qualified persons, the guarding of energized parts within a compartment shall be maintained during operation and maintenance functions to prevent accidental contact with energized parts and to prevent tools or other equipment from being dropped on energized parts.

(iii) When guards are removed from energized equipment, barriers shall be installed around the work area to prevent employees who are not working on the equipment, but

who are in the area, from contacting the exposed live parts.

(6) *Substation entry.* (i) Upon entering an attended substation, each employee other than those regularly working in the station shall report his or her presence to the employee in charge in order to receive information on special system conditions affecting employee safety.

(ii) The job briefing required by paragraph (c) of this section shall cover such additional subjects as the location of energized equipment in or adjacent to the work area and the limits of any deenergized work area.

(v) *Power generation.* This paragraph provides additional requirements and related work practices for power generating plants.

(1) *Interlocks and other safety devices.* (i) Interlocks and other safety devices shall be maintained in a safe, operable condition.

(ii) No interlock or other safety device may be modified to defeat its function, except for test, repair, or adjustment of the device.

(2) *Changing brushes.* Before exciter or generator brushes are changed while the generator is in service, the exciter or generator field shall be checked to determine whether a ground condition exists. The brushes may not be changed while the generator is energized if a ground condition exists.

(3) *Access and working space.* Sufficient access and working space shall be provided and maintained about electric equipment to permit ready and safe operation and maintenance of such equipment.

Note: Guidelines for the dimensions of access and workspace about electric equipment in generating stations are contained in American National Standard—National Electrical Safety Code, ANSI C2-1987. Installations meeting the ANSI provisions comply with paragraph (v)(3) of this section. An installation that does not conform to this ANSI standard will, nonetheless, be considered as complying with paragraph (v)(3) of this section if the employer can demonstrate that the installation provides ready and safe access based on the following evidence:

(1) That the installation conforms to the edition of ANSI C2 that was in effect at the time the installation was made,

(2) That the configuration of the installation enables employees to maintain the minimum approach distances required by paragraph (l)(2) of this section while they work on exposed, energized parts, and

(3) That the precautions taken when work is performed on the installation provide protection equivalent to the pro-

tection that would be provided by access and working space meeting ANSI C2-1987.

(4) *Guarding of rooms containing electric supply equipment.* (i) Rooms and spaces in which electric supply lines or equipment are installed shall meet the requirements of paragraphs (v)(4)(ii) through (v)(4)(v) of this section under the following conditions:

(A) If exposed live parts operating at 50 to 150 volts to ground are located within 8 feet of the ground or other working surface inside the room or space.

(B) If live parts operating at 151 to 600 volts and located within 8 feet of the ground or other working surface inside the room or space are guarded only by location, as permitted under paragraph (v)(5)(i) of this section, or

(C) If live parts operating at more than 600 volts are located within the room or space, unless:

(1) The live parts are enclosed within grounded, metal-enclosed equipment whose only openings are designed so that foreign objects inserted in these openings will be deflected from energized parts, or

(2) The live parts are installed at a height above ground and any other working surface that provides protection at the voltage to which they are energized corresponding to the protection provided by an 8-foot height at 50 volts.

(ii) The rooms and spaces shall be so enclosed within fences, screens, partitions, or walls as to minimize the possibility that unqualified persons will enter.

(iii) Signs warning unqualified persons to keep out shall be displayed at entrances to the rooms and spaces.

(iv) Entrances to rooms and spaces that are not under the observation of an attendant shall be kept locked.

(v) Unqualified persons may not enter the rooms or spaces while the electric supply lines or equipment are energized.

(5) *Guarding of energized parts.* (i) Guards shall be provided around all live parts operating at more than 150 volts to ground without an insulating covering, unless the location of the live parts gives sufficient horizontal or vertical or a combination of these clearances to minimize the possibility of accidental employee contact.

Note: Guidelines for the dimensions of clearance distances about electric equipment in generating stations are contained in American National Standard— National Electrical Safety Code, ANSI

FIGURE 4.3 (*Continued*) Electric Power Generation, Transmission, and Distribution Rule. This rule is reproduced as issued in the Monday, January 31, 1994 issue of the Federal Register. Appendixes are included.

C2-1987. Installations meeting the ANSI provisions comply with paragraph (v)(5)(i) of this section. An installation that does not conform to this ANSI standard will, nonetheless, be considered as complying with paragraph (v)(5)(i) of this section if the employer can demonstrate that the installation provides sufficient clearance based on the following evidence:

(1) That the installation conforms to the edition of ANSI C2 that was in effect at the time the installation was made,

(2) That each employee is isolated from energized parts at the point of closest approach, and

(3) That the precautions taken when work is performed on the installation provide protection equivalent to the protection that would be provided by horizontal and vertical clearances meeting ANSI C2-1987.

(ii) Except for fuse replacement or other necessary access by qualified persons, the guarding of energized parts within a compartment shall be maintained during operation and maintenance functions to prevent accidental contact with energized parts and to prevent tools or other equipment from being dropped on energized parts.

(iii) When guards are removed from energized equipment, barriers shall be installed around the work area to prevent employees who are not working on the equipment, but who are in the area, from contacting the exposed live parts.

(6) *Water or steam spaces.* The following requirements apply to work in water and steam spaces associated with boilers:

(i) A designated employee shall inspect conditions before work is permitted and after its completion. Eye protection, or full face protection if necessary, shall be worn at all times when condenser, heater, or boiler tubes are being cleaned.

(ii) Where it is necessary for employees to work near tube ends during cleaning, shielding shall be installed at the tube ends.

(7) *Chemical cleaning of boilers and pressure vessels.* The following requirements apply to chemical cleaning of boilers and pressure vessels:

(i) Areas where chemical cleaning is in progress shall be cordoned off to restrict access during cleaning. If flammable liquids, gases, or vapors or combustible materials will be used or might be produced during the cleaning process, the following requirements also apply:

(A) The area shall be posted with signs restricting entry and warning of the hazards of fire and explosion; and

(B) Smoking, welding, and other possible ignition sources are prohibited in these restricted areas.

(ii) The number of personnel in the restricted area shall be limited to those necessary to accomplish the task safely.

(iii) There shall be ready access to water or showers for emergency use.

Note: See § 1910.141 of this Part for requirements that apply to the water supply and to washing facilities.

(iv) Employees in restricted areas shall wear protective equipment meeting the requirements of Subpart I of this Part and including, but not limited to, protective clothing, boots, goggles, and gloves.

(8) *Chlorine systems.* (i) Chlorine system enclosures shall be posted with signs restricting entry and warning of the hazard to health and the hazards of fire and explosion.

Note: See Subpart Z of this Part for requirements necessary to protect the health of employees from the effects of chlorine.

(ii) Only designated employees may enter the restricted area. Additionally, the number of personnel shall be limited to those necessary to accomplish the task safely.

(iii) Emergency repair kits shall be available near the shelter or enclosure to allow for the prompt repair of leaks in chlorine lines, equipment, or containers.

(iv) Before repair procedures are started, chlorine tanks, pipes, and equipment shall be purged with dry air and isolated from other sources of chlorine.

(v) The employer shall ensure that chlorine is not mixed with materials that would react with the chlorine in a dangerously exothermic or other hazardous manner.

(9) *Boilers.* (i) Before internal furnace or ash hopper repair work is started, overhead areas shall be inspected for possible falling objects. If the hazard of falling objects exists, overhead protection such as planking or nets shall be provided.

(ii) When opening an operating boiler door, employees shall stand clear of the opening of the door to avoid the heat blast and gases which may escape from the boiler.

(10) *Turbine generators.* (i) Smoking and other ignition sources are prohibited near hydrogen or hydrogen sealing systems, and signs warning of the danger of explosion and fire shall be posted.

(ii) Excessive hydrogen makeup or abnormal loss of pressure shall be

considered as an emergency and shall be corrected immediately.

(iii) A sufficient quantity of inert gas shall be available to purge the hydrogen from the largest generator.

(11) *Coal and ash handling.* (i) Only designated persons may operate railroad equipment.

(ii) Before a locomotive or locomotive crane is moved, a warning shall be given to employees in the area.

(iii) Employees engaged in switching or dumping cars may not use their feet to line up drawheads.

(iv) Drawheads and knuckles may not be shifted while locomotives or cars are in motion.

(v) When a railroad car is stopped for unloading, the car shall be secured from displacement that could endanger employees.

(vi) An emergency means of stopping dump operations shall be provided at railcar dumps.

(vii) The employer shall ensure that employees who work in coal- or ash-handling conveyor areas are trained and knowledgeable in conveyor operation and in the requirements of paragraphs (v)(11)(viii) through (v)(11)(xii) of this section.

(viii) Employees may not ride a coal- or ash-handling conveyor belt at any time. Employees may not cross over the conveyor belt, except at walkways, unless the conveyor's energy source has been deenergized and has been locked out or tagged in accordance with paragraph (d) of this section.

(ix) A conveyor that could cause injury when started may not be started until personnel in the area are alerted by a signal or by a designated person that the conveyor is about to start.

(x) If a conveyor that could cause injury when started is automatically controlled or is controlled from a remote location, an audible device shall be provided that sounds an alarm that will be recognized by each employee as a warning that the conveyor will start and that can be clearly heard at all points along the conveyor where personnel may be present. The warning device shall be actuated by the device starting the conveyor and shall continue for a period of time before the conveyor starts that is long enough to allow employees to move clear of the conveyor system. A visual warning may be used in place of the audible device if the employer can demonstrate that it will provide an equally effective warning in the particular circumstances involved.

Note: *Exception:* If the employer can demonstrate that the system's function

---

FIGURE 4.3 (*Continued*) Electric Power Generation, Transmission, and Distribution Rule. This rule is reproduced as issued in the Monday, January 31, 1994 issue of the Federal Register. Appendixes are included.

would be seriously hindered by the required time delay, warning signs may be provided in place of the audible warning device. If the system was installed before [insert date 1 year after publication date], warning signs may be provided in place of the audible warning device until such time as the conveyor or its control system is rebuilt or rewired. These warning signs shall be clear, concise, and legible and shall indicate that conveyors and allied equipment may be started at any time, that danger exists, and that personnel must keep clear. These warning signs shall be provided along the conveyor at areas not guarded by position or location.

(xi) Remotely and automatically controlled conveyors, and conveyors that have operating stations which are not manned or which are beyond voice and visual contact from drive areas, loading areas, transfer points, and other locations on the conveyor path not guarded by location, position, or guards shall be furnished with emergency stop buttons, pull cords, limit switches, or similar emergency stop devices. However, if the employer can demonstrate that the design, function, and operation of the conveyor do not expose an employee to hazards, an emergency stop device is not required.

(A) Emergency stop devices shall be easily identifiable in the immediate vicinity of such locations.

(B) An emergency stop device shall act directly on the control of the conveyor involved and may not depend on the stopping of any other equipment.

(C) Emergency stop devices shall be installed so that they cannot be overridden from other locations.

(xii) Where coal-handling operations may produce a combustible atmosphere from fuel sources or from flammable gases or dust, sources of ignition shall be eliminated or safely controlled to prevent ignition of the combustible atmosphere.

Note: Locations that are hazardous because of the presence of combustible dust are classified as Class II hazardous locations. See § 1910.307 of this Part.

(xiii) An employee may not work on or beneath overhanging coal in coal bunkers, coal silos, or coal storage areas, unless the employee is protected from all hazards posed by shifting coal.

(xiv) An employee entering a bunker or silo to dislodge the contents shall wear a body harness with lifeline attached. The lifeline shall be secured to a fixed support outside the bunker and shall be attended at all times by an employee located outside the bunker or facility.

(12) *Hydroplants and equipment.* Employees working on or close to water gates, valves, intakes, forebays, flumes, or other locations where increased or decreased water flow or levels may pose a significant hazard shall be warned and shall vacate such dangerous areas before water flow changes are made.

(w) *Special conditions.* (1) *Capacitors.* The following additional requirements apply to work on capacitors and on lines connected to capacitors.

Note: See paragraphs (m) and (n) of this section for requirements pertaining to the deenergizing and grounding of capacitor installations.

(i) Before employees work on capacitors, the capacitors shall be disconnected from energized sources and, after a wait of at least 5 minutes from the time of disconnection, short-circuited.

(ii) Before the units are handled, each unit in series-parallel capacitor banks shall be short-circuited between all terminals and the capacitor case or its rack. If the cases of capacitors are on ungrounded substation racks, the racks shall be bonded to ground.

(iii) Any line to which capacitors are connected shall be short-circuited before it is considered deenergized.

(2) *Current transformer secondaries.* The secondary of a current transformer may not be opened while the transformer is energized. If the primary of the current transformer cannot be deenergized before work is performed on an instrument, a relay, or other section of a current transformer secondary circuit, the circuit shall be bridged so that the current transformer secondary will not be opened.

(3) *Series streetlighting.* If the open-circuit voltage exceeds 600 volts, the series streetlighting circuit shall be worked in accordance with paragraph (q) or (t) of this section, as appropriate. A series loop may only be opened after the streetlighting transformer has been deenergized and isolated from the source of supply or after the loop is bridged to avoid an open-

circuit condition.

(4) *Illumination.* Sufficient illumination shall be provided to enable the employee to perform the work safely.

(5) *Protection against drowning.* (i) Whenever an employee may be pulled or pushed or may fall into water where the danger of drowning exists, the employee shall be provided with and shall use U.S. Coast Guard approved personal flotation devices.

(ii) Each personal flotation device shall be maintained in safe condition and shall be inspected frequently enough to ensure that it does not have rot, mildew, water saturation, and or any other condition that could render the device unsuitable for use.

(iii) An employee may cross streams or other bodies of water only if a safe means of passage, such as a bridge, is provided.

(6) *Employee protection in public work areas.*

(i) Traffic control signs and traffic control devices used for the protection of employees shall meet the requirements of § 1926.200(g)(2) of this Chapter.

(ii) Before work is begun in the vicinity of vehicular or pedestrian traffic that may endanger employees, warning signs or flags and other traffic control devices shall be placed in conspicuous locations to alert and channel approaching traffic.

(iii) Where additional employee protection is necessary, barricades shall be used.

(iv) Excavated areas shall be protected with barricades.

(v) At night, warning lights shall be prominently displayed.

(7) *Backfeed.* If there is a possibility of voltage backfeed from sources of cogeneration or from the secondary system (for example, backfeed from more than one energized phase feeding a common load), the requirements of paragraph (1) of this section apply if the lines or equipment are to be worked as energized, and the requirements of paragraphs (m) and (n) of this section apply if the lines or equipment are to be worked as deenergized.

(8) *Lasers.* Laser equipment shall be installed, adjusted, and operated in accordance with § 1926.54 of this Chapter.

(9) *Hydraulic fluids.* Hydraulic fluids used for the insulated sections of equipment shall provide insulation for the voltage involved.

FIGURE 4.3 (*Continued*)   Electric Power Generation, Transmission, and Distribution Rule. This rule is reproduced as issued in the Monday, January 31, 1994 issue of the Federal Register. Appendixes are included.

Appendix A-1 to Section 1910.269—Application of Section 1910.269 and Subpart S of this Part to Electrical Installations.

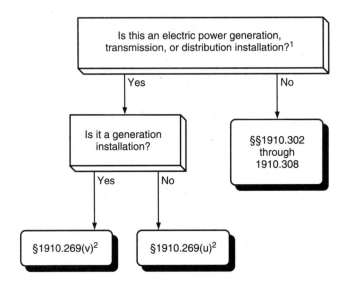

[1]Electrical installation design requirements only. See Appendix A-2 of this section for electrical safety-related work practices. Supplementary electric generating equipment that is used to supply a workplace for emergency, standby, or similar purposes only is not considered to be an electric power generation installation.

[2]See Table 1 of Appendix A-2 of this section for requirements that can be met through compliance with subpart S of this part.

FIGURE 4.3 (*Continued*) Electric Power Generation, Transmission, and Distribution Rule. This rule is reproduced as issued in the Monday, January 31, 1994 issue of the Federal Register. Appendixes are included.

Appendix A-2 to Section 1910.269—Application of Section 1910.269 and Subpart S of this Part to Electrical Safety-Related Work Practices.

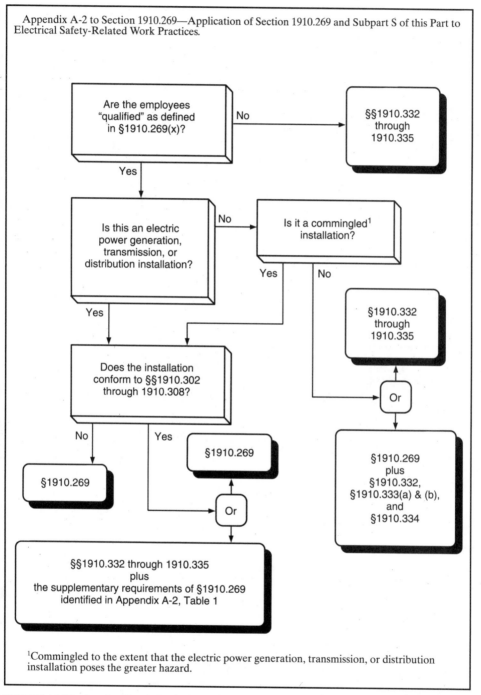

¹Commingled to the extent that the electric power generation, transmission, or distribution installation poses the greater hazard.

FIGURE 4.3 (*Continued*)   Electric Power Generation, Transmission, and Distribution Rule. This rule is reproduced as issued in the Monday, January 31, 1994 issue of the Federal Register. Appendixes are included.

TABLE 1.—ELECTRICAL SAFETY-RELATED WORK PRACTICES IN SECTION 1910.269

Compliance with subpart S is considered as compliance with § 1910.269[1]	Paragraphs that apply regardless of compliance with subpart S
(d), electric shock hazards only	$(a)(2)^2$ and $(a)(3)^2$.
(h)(3)	$(b)^2$.
(i)(2)	$(c)^2$.
(k)	(d), other than electric shock hazards.
(l)(1) through (l)(4), (l)(6)(i), and (l)(8) through (l)(10)	(e).
(m)	(f).
(p)(4)	(g).
(s)(2)	(h)(1) and (h)(2).
(u)(1) and (u)(3) through (u)(5)	$(i)(3)^2$ and $(i)(4)^2$.
(v)(3) through (v)(5)	$(j)^2$.
(w)(1) and (w)(7)	$(l)(5)^2$, $(l)(6)(iii)^2$, $(l)(6)(iii)^2$, and $(l)(7)^2$.
	$(n)^2$.
	$(o)^2$.
	(p)(1) through (p)(3).
	$(q)^2$.
	(r).
	(s)(1).
	$(t)^2$.
	$(u)(2)^2$ and $(u)(6)^2$.
	(v)(1), $(v)(2)^2$, and (v)(6) through (v)(12).
	(w)(2) through $(w)(6)^2$, (w)(8), and $(w)(9)^2$.

[1]If the electrical installation meets the requirements of §§ 1910.332 through 1910.308 of this Part, then the electrical installation and any associated electrical safety-related work practices conforming to §§ 1910.332 through 1910.335 of this Part are considered to comply with these provisions of § 1910.269 of this Part.

[2]These provisions include electrical safety requirements that must be met regardless of compliance with Subpart S of this Part.

FIGURE 4.3 (*Continued*) Electric Power Generation, Transmission, and Distribution Rule. This rule is reproduced as issued in the Monday, January 31, 1994 issue of the Federal Register. Appendixes are included.

Appendix A-3 to Section 1910.269—Application of Section 1910.269 and Subpart S of This Part to Tree-Trimming Operations.

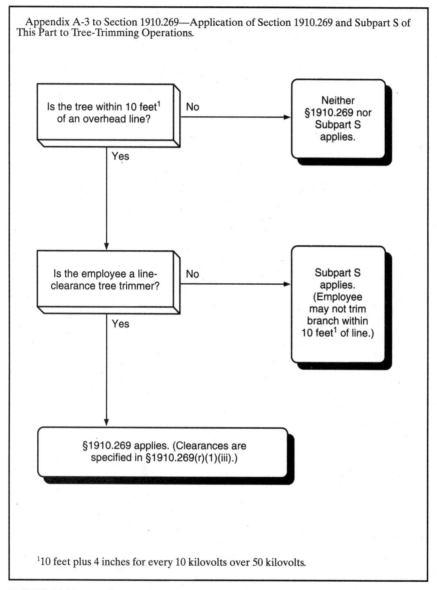

[1]10 feet plus 4 inches for every 10 kilovolts over 50 kilovolts.

FIGURE 4.3 (*Continued*)   Electric Power Generation, Transmission, and Distribution Rule. This rule is reproduced as issued in the Monday, January 31, 1994 issue of the Federal Register. Appendixes are included.

Appendix A-4 to Section 1910.269—Application of Section 1910.147, Section 1910.269 and Section 1910.333 to Hazardous Energy Control Procedures (Lockout/Tagout).

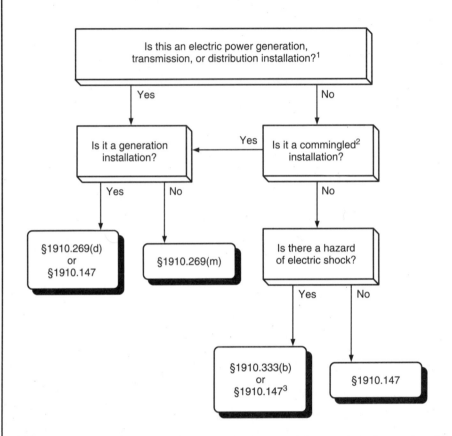

[1]If the installation conforms to §§ 1910.303 through 1910.308 of this part, the lockout and tagging procedures of § 1910.333(b) of this part may be followed for electric shock hazards.
[2]Commingled to the extent that the electric power generation, transmission, or distribution installation poses the greater hazard.
[3]Section 1910.333(b)(2)(iii)(D) and (b)(2)(iv)(B) of this part still apply.

FIGURE 4.3 (*Continued*)   Electric Power Generation, Transmission, and Distribution Rule. This rule is reproduced as issued in the Monday, January 31, 1994 issue of the Federal Register. Appendixes are included.

Appendix A-5 to Section 1910.269—Application of Section 1910.146 and Section 1910.269 to Permit-Required Confined Spaces.

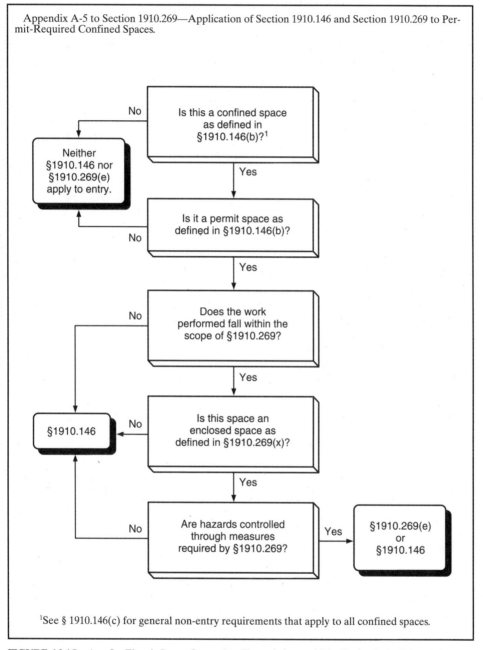

[1]See § 1910.146(c) for general non-entry requirements that apply to all confined spaces.

FIGURE 4.3 (*Continued*) Electric Power Generation, Transmission, and Distribution Rule. This rule is reproduced as issued in the Monday, January 31, 1994 issue of the Federal Register. Appendixes are included.

§ 1910.147 The control of hazardous energy (lockout/tagout).

(a) *Scope, application and purpose—*

(1) *Scope.*

(i) This standard covers the servicing and maintenance of machines and equipment in which the *unexpected* energization or start up of the machines or equipment, or release of stored energy could cause injury to employees. This standard establishes minimum performance requirements for the control of such hazardous energy.

(ii) This standard does not cover the following:

(A) Construction, agriculture and maritime employment;

(B) Installations under the exclusive control of electric utilities for the purpose of power generation, transmission and distribution, including related equipment for communication or metering; and

(C) Exposure to electrical hazards from work on, near, or with conductors or equipment in electric utilization installations, which is covered by Subpart S of this part; and

(D) Oil and gas well drilling and servicing.

(2) *Application.* (i) This standard applies to the control of energy during servicing and/or maintenance of machines and equipment.

(ii) Normal production operations are not covered by this standard (See

Subpart O of this Part). Servicing and/or maintenance which takes place during normal production operations is covered by this standard only if::

(A) An employee is required to remove or bypass a guard or other safety device; or

(B) An employee is required to place any part of his or her body into an area on a machine or piece of equipment where work is actually performed upon the material being processed (point of operation) or where an associated danger zone exists during a machine operating cycle.

Note: *Exception to paragraph (a)(2)(ii):* Minor tool changes and adjustments, and other minor servicing activities, which take place during normal production operations, are not covered by this standard if they are routine, repetitive, and integral to the use of the equipment for production, provided that the work is performed using alternative measures which provide effective protection (See Subpart O of this Part).

(iii) This standard does not apply to the following.

(A) Work on cord and plug connected electric equipment for which exposure to the hazards of unexpected energization or start up of the equipment is controlled by the unplugging of the equipment from the energy source and by the plug being under the exclusive control of the employee performing the servicing or maintenance.

(B) Hot tap operations involving transmission and distribution systems for substances such as gas, steam, water or petroleum products when they are performed on pressurized pipelines, provided that the employer demonstrates that (1) continuity of service is essential; (2) shutdown of the system is impractical; and (3) documented procedures are followed, and special equipment is used which will provide proven effective protection for employees.

(3) *Purpose.* (i) This section requires employers to establish a program and utilize procedures for affixing appropriate lockout devices or tagout devices to energy isolating devices, and to otherwise disable machines or equipment to prevent unexpected energization, start-up or release of stored energy in order to prevent injury to employees.

(ii) When other standards in this part require the use of lockout or tagout, they shall be used and supplemented by the procedural and training requirements of this section.

(b) *Definitions applicable to this section.*

Affected employee. An employee whose job requires him/her to operate or use a machine or equipment on which

servicing or maintenance is being performed under lockout or tagout, or whose job requires him/her to work in an area in which such servicing or maintenance is being performed.

Authorized employee. A person who locks or implements a tagout system procdure on machines or equipment to perform the servicing or maintenance on that machine or equipment. An authorized employee and an affected employee may be the same person when the affected employee's duties also include performing maintenance or service on a machine or equipment which must be locked or a tagout system implemented.

"Capable of being locked out." An energy isolating device will be considered to be capable of being locked out either if it is designed with a hasp or other attachment or integral part to which, or through which, a lock can be affixed, or if it has a locking mechanism built into it. Other energy isolating devices will also be considered to be capable of being locked out, if lockout can be achieved without the need to dismantle, rebuild, or replace the energy isolating device or permanently alter its energy control capability.

Energized. Connected to an energy source or containing residual or stored energy.

Energy isolating device. A mechanical device that physically prevents the transmission or release or energy, including but not limited to the following: A manually operated electrical circuit breaker; a disconnect switch; a manually operated switch by which the conductors of a circuit can be disconnected from all ungrounded supply conuctors and, in addition, no pole can be operated independently; a slide gate; a slip blind; a line valve; a block; and any similar device used to block or isolate energy. The term does not include a push button, selector switch, and other control circuit type devices.

Energy source. Any source of electrical, mechanical, hydraulic, pneumatic, chemical, thermal, or other energy.

Hot tap. A procedure used in the repair, maintenance and services activities which involves welding on a piece of equipment (pipelines, vessels or tanks) under pressure, in order to install connections or appurtenances. It is commonly used to replace or add sections of pipeline without the interruption of service for air, gas, water, steam, and petrochemical distribution systems.

FIGURE 4.4   Control of Hazardous Energy Source (Lockout/Tagout) (OSHA-CFR Title 29, Part 1910, Subpart J, Paragraph 147).

Lockout. The placement of a lockout device on an energy isolating device, in accordance with an established procedure, ensuring that the energy isolating device and the equipment being controlled cannot be operated until the lockout device is removed.

Lockout device. A device that utilizes a positive means such as a lock, either key or combination type, to hold an energy isolating device in the safe position and prevent the energizing of a machine or equipment.

Normal production operations. The utilization of a machine or equipment to perform its intended production function.

Servicing and/or maintenance. Workplace activities such as constructing, installing, setting up, adjusting, inspecting, modifying, and maintaining and/or servicing machines or equipment. These activities include lubrication, cleaning or unjamming of machines or equipment and making adjustments or tool changes, where the employee may be exposed to the unexpected energization or startup of the equipment or release of hazardous energy.

Setting up. Any work performed to prepare a machine or equipment to perform its normal production operation.

Tagout. The placement of a tagout device on an energy isolating device, in accordance with an established procedure, to indicate that the energy isolating device and the equipment being controlled may not be operated until the tagout device is removed.

Tagout device. A prominent warning device, such as a tag and a means of attachment, which can be securely fastened to an energy isolating device in accordance with an established procedure, to indicate that the energy isolating device and the equipment being controlled may not be operated until the tagout device is removed.

(c) *General*—(1) *Energy control program.* The employer shall establish a program consisting of an energy control procedure and employee training to ensure that before any employee performs any servicing or maintenance on a machine or equipment where the unexpected energizing, start up or release of stored energy could occur and cause injury, the machine or equipment shall be isolated, and rendered inoperative, in accordance with paragraph (c)(4) of this section.

(2) *Lockout/tagout.* (i) If an energy isolating device is not capable of being locked out, the employer's energy control program under paragraph (c)(1) of this section shall utilize a tagout system.

(ii) If an energy isolating device is capable of being locked out, the employer's energy control program under paragraph (c)(1) of this section shall utilize lockout, unless the employer can demonstrate that the utilization of a tagout system will provide full employee protection as set forth in paragraph (c)(3) of this section.

(iii) After October 31, 1989, whenever major replacement, repair, renovation or modification of machines or equipment is performed, and whenever new machines or equipment are installed, energy isolating devices for such machines or equipment shall be designed to accept a lockout device.

(3) *Full employee protection.* (i) When a tagout device is used on an energy isolating device which is capable of being locked out, the tagout device shall be attached at the same location that the lockout device would have been attached, and the employer shall demonstrate that the tagout program will provide a level of safety equivalent to that obtained by using a lockout program.

(ii) In demonstrating that a level of safety is achieved in the tagout program which is equivalent to the level of safety obtained by using a lockout program, the employer shall demonstrate full compliance with all tagout-related provisions of this standard together with such additional elements as are necessary to provide the equivalent safety available from the use of a lockout device. Additional means to be considered as part of the demonstration of full employee protection shall include the implementation of additional safety measures such as the removal of an isolating circuit element, blocking of a controlling switch, opening of an extra disconnecting device, or the removal of a valve handle to reduce the likelihood of inadvertent energization.

(4) *Energy control procedure.* (i) Procedures shall be developed, documented and utilized for the control of potentially hazardous energy when employees are engaged in the activities covered by this section.

Note: *Exception:* The employer need not document the required procedure for a particular machine or equipment, when all of the following elements exist: (1) The machine or equipment has no potential for stored or residual energy or reaccumulation of stored energy after shut down which could endanger employees; (2) the machine or equipment has a single energy source which can be readily identified and isolated; (3) the isolation and locking out of that energy source will completely deenergize and deactivate the machine or equipment; (4) the machine or equipment is isolated from that energy source and locked out during servicing or maintenance; (5) a single lockout device will

achieve a locked-out condition; (6) the lockout device is under the exclusive control of the authorized employee performing the servicing or maintenance; (7) the servicing or maintenance does not create hazards for other employees; and (8) the employer, in utilizing this exception, has had no accidents involving the unexpected activation or reenergization of the machine or equipment during servicing or maintenance.

(ii) The procedures shall clearly and specifically outline the scope, purpose, authorization, rules, and techniques to be utilized for the control of hazardous energy, and the means to enforce compliance including, but not limited to, the following:

(A) A specific statement of the intended use of the procedure;

(B) Specific procedural steps for shutting down, isolating, blocking and securing machines or equipment to control hazardous energy;

(C) Specific procedural steps for the placement, removal and transfer of lockout devices or tagout devices and the responsibility for them; and

(D) Specific requirements for testing a machine or equipment to determine and verify the effectiveness of lockout devices, tagout devices, and other energy control measures.

(5) *Protective materials and hardware.* (i) Locks, tags, chains, wedges, key blocks, adapter pins, self-locking fasteners, or other hardware shall be provided by the employer for isolating, securing or blocking of machines or equipment from energy sources.

(ii) Lockout devices and tagout devices shall be singularly identified; shall be the only devices(s) used for controlling energy; shall not be used for other purposes; and shall meet the following requirements:

(A) *Durable.* (1) Lockout and tagout devices shall be capable of withstanding the environment to which they are exposed for the maximum period of time that exposure is expected.

(2) Tagout devices shall be constructed and printed so that exposure to weather conditions or wet and damp locations will not cause the tag to deteriorate or the message on the tag to become illegible.

(3) Tags shall not deteriorate when used in corrosive environments such as areas where acid and alkali chemicals are handled and stored.

(B) *Standardized.* Lockout and tagout devices shall be standardized within the facility in at least one of the following criteria: Color; shape; or size; and additionally, in the case of tagout devices, print and format shall be standardized.

FIGURE 4.4 (*Continued*) Control of Hazardous Energy Source (Lockout/Tagout) (OSHA-CFR Title 29, Part 1910, Subpart J, Paragraph 147).

(C) *Substantial—(1) Lockout devices.* Lockout devices shall be substantial enough to prevent removal without the use of excessive force or unusual techniques, such as with the use of bolt cutters or other metal cutting tools.

(2) *Tagout devices.* Tagout devices, including and their means of attachment, shall be substantial enough to prevent inadvertent or accidental removal. Tagout device attachment means shall be of a non-reusable type, attachable by hand, self-locking, and non-releasable with a minimum unlocking strength of no less than 50 pounds and having the general design and basic characteristics of being at least equivalent to a one-piece, all-environment-tolerant nylon cable tie.

(D) *Identifiable.* Lockout devices and tagout devices shall indicate the identity of the employee applying the device(s).

(iii) Tagout devices shall warn against hazardous conditions if the machine or equipment is energized and shall include a legend such as the following: *Do Not Start, Do Not Open, Do Not Close, Do Not Energize, Do Not Operate.*

(6) *Periodic inspection.* (i) The employer shall conduct a periodic inspection of the energy control procedure at least annually to ensure that the procedure and the requirements of this standard are being followed.

(A) The periodic inspection shall be perfomed by an authorized employee other than the ones(s) utilizing the energy control procedure being inspected.

(B) The periodic inspection shall be designed to correct any deviations or inadequacies observed.

(C) Where lockout is used for energy control, the periodic inspection shall include a review, between the inspector and each authorized employee, of that employee's responsibilities under the energy control procedure being inspected.

(D) Where tagout is used for energy control, the periodic inspection shall include a review, between the inspector and each authorized and affected employee, of that employee's responsibilities under the energy control procedure being inspected, and the elements set forth in paragraph (c)(7)(ii) of this section.

(ii) The employer shall certify that the periodic inspections have been performed. The certification shall identify the machine or equipment on which the energy control procedure was being utilized, the date of the inspection, the employees included in the inspection, and the person performing the inspection.

(7) *Training and communication.* (i) The employer shall provide training to ensure that the purpose and function of the energy control program are understood by employees and that the knowledge and skills required for the safe application, usage, and removal of energy controls are required by employees. The training shall include the following:

(A) Each authorized employee shall receive training in the recognition of applicable hazardous energy sources, the type and magnitude of the energy available in the workplace, and the methods and means necessary for energy isolation and control.

(B) Each affected employee shall be instructed in the purpose and use of the energy control procedure.

(C) All other employees whose work operations are or may be in an area where energy control procedures may be utilized, shall be instructed about the procedure, and about the prohibition relating to attempts to restart or reenergize machines or equipment which are locked out or tagged out.

(ii) When tagout systems are used, employees shall also be trained in the following limitations of tags:

(A) Tags are essentially warning devices affixed to energy isolating devices, and do not provide the physical restraint on those devices that is provided by a lock.

(B) When a tag is attached to an energy isolating means, it is not to be removed without authorization of the authorized person responsible for it, and it is never to be bypassed, ignored, or otherwise defeated.

(C) Tags must be legible and understandable by all authorized employees, affected employees, and all other employees whose work operations are or may be in the area, in order to be effective.

(D) Tags and their means of attachment must be made of materials which will withstand the environmental conditions encountered in the workplace.

(E) Tags may evoke a false sense of security, and their meaning needs to be understood as part of the overall energy control program.

(F) Tags must be securely attached to energy isolating devices so that they cannot be inadvertently or accidentally detached during use.

(iii) Employee retraining.

(A) Retraining shall be provided for all authorized and affected employees whenever there is a change in their job assignments, a change in machines, equipment or processes that present a new hazard, or when there is a change in the energy control procedures.

(B) Additional retraining shall also be conducted whenever a periodic inspection under paragraph (c)(6) of this section reveals, or whenever the employer has reason to believe, that there are deviations from or inadequacies in the employee's knowledge or use of the energy control procedures.

(C) The retraining shall reestablish employee proficiency and introduce new or revised control methods and procedures, as necessary.

(iv) The employer shall certify that employee training has been accomplished and is being kept up to date. The certification shall contain each employee's name and dates of training.

(8) *Energy isolation.* Implementation of lockout or the tagout system shall be performed only by authorized employees.

(9) *Notification of employees.* Affected employees shall be notified by the employer or authorized employee of the application and removal of lockout devices or tagout devices. Notification shall be given before the controls are applied, and after they are removed from the machine or equipment.

(d) *Application of control.* The established procedure for the application of energy control (implementation of lockout or tagout system procedures) shall cover the following elements and actions and shall be done in the following sequence:

(1) *Preparation for shutdown.* Before an authorized or affected employee turns off a machine or equipment, the authorized employee shall have knowledge of the type and magnitude of the energy, the hazards of the energy to be controlled, and the method or means to control the energy.

(2) *Machine or equipment shutdown.* The machine or equipment shall be turned off or shut down using the procedures required by this standard. An orderly shutdown must be utilized to avoid any additional or increased hazard(s) to employees as a result of equipment deenergization.

(3) *Machine or equipment isolation.* All energy isolating devices that are needed to control the energy to the machine or equipment shall be physically located and operated in such a manner as to isolate the machine or equipment from the energy source(s).

(4) *Lockout or tagout device application.* (i) Lockout or tagout devices shall be affixed to each energy isolating device by authorized employees.

(ii) Lockout devices, where used, shall be affixed in a manner to that will hold the energy isolating devices in a "safe" or "off" position.

FIGURE 4.4 (*Continued*) Control of Hazardous Energy Source (Lockout/Tagout) (OSHA-CFR Title 29, Part 1910, Subpart J, Paragraph 147).

(iii) Tagout devices, where used, shall be affixed in such a manner as will clearly indicate that the operation or movement of energy isolating devices from the "safe" or "off" position is prohibited.

(A) Where tagout devices are used with energy isolating devices designed with the capability of being locked, the tag attachment shall be fastened at the same point at which the lock would have been attached.

(B) Where a tag cannot be affixed directly to the energy isolating device, the tag shall be located as close as safely possible to the device, in a position that will be immediately obvious to anyone attempting to operate the device.

(5) *Stored energy.* (i) Following the application of lockout or tagout devices to energy isolating devices, all potentially hazardous stored or residual energy shall be relieved, disconnected, restrained, and otherwise rendered safe.

(ii) If there is a possibility of reaccumulation of stored energy to a hazardous level, verification of isolation shall be continued until the servicing or maintenance is completed, or until the possibility of such accumulation no longer exists.

(6) *Verification of isolation.* Prior to starting work on machines or equipment that have been locked out or tagged out, the authorized employee shall verify that isolation and deenergization of the machine or equipment have been accomplished.

(e) *Release from lockout or tagout.* Before lockout or tagout devices are removed and energy is restored to the machine or equipment, procedures shall be followed and actions taken by the authorized employee(s) to ensure the following:

(1) *The machine or equipment.* The work area shall be inspected to ensure that nonessential items have been removed and to ensure that machine or equipment components are operationally intact.

(2) *Employees.* (i) The work area shall be checked to ensure that all employees have been safely positioned or removed.

(ii) After lockout or tagout devices are removed and before machines or equipment are energized, affected employees shall be notified that the lockout or tagout devices have been removed.

(3) *Lockout or tagout devices removal.* Each lockout or tagout device shall be removed from each energy isolating

device by the employee who applied the device. *Exception to paragraph (e)(3):* When the authorized employee who applied the lockout or tagout device is not available to remove it, that device may be removed under the direction of the employer, provided that specific procedures and training for such removal have been developed, documented and incorporated into the employer's energy control program. The employer shall demonstrate that the specific procedure provides equivalent safety to the removal of the device by the authorized employee who applied it. The specific procedure shall include at least the following elements:

(i) Verfication by the employer that the authorized employee who applied the device is not at the facility;

(ii) Making all reasonable efforts to contact the authorized employee to inform him/her that his/her lockout or tagout device has been removed; and

(iii) Ensuring that the authorized employee has this knowledge before he/she resumes work at that facility.

(f) *Additional requirements.* (1) *Testing or positioning of machines, equipment or components thereof.* In situations in which lockout or tagout devices must be temporarily removed from the energy isolating device and the machine or equipment energized to test or position the machine, equipment or component thereof, the following sequence of actions shall be followed:

(i) Clear the machine or equipment of tools and materials in accordance with paragraph (e)(1) of this section;

(ii) Remove employees from the machine or equipment area in accordance with paragraph (e)(2) of this section;

(iii) Remove the lockout or tagout devices as specified in paragraph (e)(3) of this section;

(iv) Energize and proceed with testing or positioning;

(v) Deenergize all systems and reapply energy control measures in accordance with paragraph (d) of this section to continue the servicing and/or maintenance.

(2) *Outside personnel (contractors, etc.).* (i) Whenever outside servicing personnel are to be engaged in activities covered by the scope and application of this standard, the on-site employer and the outside employer shall inform each other of their respective lockout or tagout procedures.

(ii) The on-side employer shall ensure

that his/her personnel understand and comply with restrictions and prohibitions of the outside employer's energy control procedures.

(3) *Group lockout or tagout.* (i) When servicing and/or maintenance is performed by a crew, craft, department or other group, they shall utilize a procedure which affords the employees a level of protection equivalent to that provided by the implementation of a personal lockout or tagout device.

(ii) Group lockout or tagout devices shall be used in accordance with the procedures required by paragraph (c)(4) of this section including, but not necessarily limited to, the following specific requirements:

(A) Primary responsibility is vested in an authorized employee for a set number of employees working under the protection of a group lockout or tagout device (such as an operations lock);

(B) Provision for the authorized employee to ascertain the exposure status of individual group members with regard to the lockout or tagout of the machine or equipment and

(C) When more than one crew, craft, department, etc. is involved, assignment of overall job-associated lockout or tagout control responsibility to an authorized employee designated to coordinate affected work forces and ensure continuity of protection; and

(D) Each authorized employee shall affix a personal lockout or tagout device to the group lockout device, group lockbox, or comparable mechanism when he or she begins work, and shall remove those devices when he or she stops working on the machine or equipment being serviced or maintained.

(4) *Shift or personnel changes.* Specific procedures shall be utilized during shift or personnel changes to ensure the continuity of lockout or tagout protection, including provision for the orderly transfer of lockout or tagout devices between off-going and oncoming employees, to minimize exposure to hazards from the unexpected energization, start-up of the machine or equipment, or release of stored energy.

Note: The following Appendix to § 1910.147 services as a non-mandatory guideline to assist employers and employees in complying with the requirements of this section, as well as to provide other helpful information. Nothing in the Appendix adds to or detracts from any of the requirements of this section.

BILLING CODE 4610-26-M

FIGURE 4.4 (*Continued*) Control of Hazardous Energy Source (Lockout/Tagout) (OSHA-CFR Title 29, Part 1910, Subpart J, Paragraph 147).

DEFINITIONS

§ 1910.399 Definitions applicable to this subpart.

Acceptable. An installation or equipment is acceptable to the Assistant Secretary of Labor, and approved within the meaning of this Subpart S:

(i) If it is accepted, or certified, or listed, or labeled, or otherwise determined to be safe by a nationally recognized testing laboratory; or

(ii) With respect to an installation or equipment of a kind which no nationally recognized testing laboratory accepts, certifies, lists, labels, or determines to be safe, if it is inspected or tested by another Federal agency, or

by a State, municipal, or other local authority responsible for enforcing occupational safety provisions of the National Electrical Code and found in compliance with the provisions of the National Electrical Code as applied in this Subpart; or

(iii) With respect to custom-made equipment or related installations which are designed, fabricated for, and intended for use by a particular customer, if it is determined to be safe for its intended use by its manufacturer on the basis of test data which the employer keeps and makes available for inspection to the Assistant Secretary and his authorized representatives. Refer to § 1910.7 for definition of nationally recognized testing laboratory.

Accepted. An installation is "accepted" if it has been inspected and found by a nationally recognized testing laboratory to conform to specified plans or to procedures of applicable codes.

Accessible. (As applied to wiring methods.) Capable of being removed or exposed without damaging the building structure or finish, or not permanently closed in by the structure or finish of the building. (See "concealed" and "exposed.")

Accessible. (As applied to equipment.) Admitting close approach; not guarded by locked doors, elevation, or other effective means. (See "Readily accessible.")

Ampacity. Current-carrying capacity of electric conductors expressed in amperes.

Appliances. Utilization equipment, generally other than industrial, normally built in standardized sizes or types, which is installed or connected as a unit to perform one or more functions such as clothes washing, air conditioning, food mixing, deep frying, etc.

Approved. Acceptable to the authority enforcing this subpart. The authority enforcing this subpart is the Assistant Secretary of Labor for Occupational Safety and Health. The definition of "acceptable" indicates what is acceptable to the Assistant Secretary of Labor, and therefore approved within the meaning of this Subpart.

Approved for the purpose. Approved for a specific purpose, environment, or

FIGURE 4.5   Definition Applying to Part 1910, Subpart S (OSHA-CFR Title 29, Part 1910, Subpart S, Paragraph 399).

application described in a particular standard requirement.

Suitability of equipment or materials for a specific purpose, environment or application may be determined by a nationally recognized testing laboratory, inspection agency or other organization concerned with product evaluation as part of its listing and labeling program. (See *"Labeled"* or *"Listed."*)

Armored cable. Type AC armored cable is a fabricated assembly of insulated conductors in a flexible metallic enclosure.

Askarel. A generic term for a group of nonflammable synthetic chlorinated hydrocarbons used as electrical insulating media. Askarels of various compositional types are used. Under arcing conditions the gases produced, while consisting predominantly of noncombustible hydrogen chloride, can include varying amounts of combustible gases depending upon the askarel type.

Attachment plug (Plug cap) (Cap). A device which, by insertion in a receptacle, establishes connection between the conductors of the attached flexible cord and the conductors connected permanently to the receptacle.

Automatic. Self-acting, operating by its own mechanism when actuated by some impersonal influence, as, for example, a change in current strength, pressure, temperature, or mechanical configuration.

Bare conductor. See *"Conductor."*

Bonding. The permanent joining of metallic parts to form an electrically conductive path which will assure electrical continuity and the capacity to conduct safely any current likely to be imposed.

Bonding jumper. A reliable conductor to assure the required electrical conductivity between metal parts required to be electrically connected.

Branch circuit. The circuit conductors between the final overcurrent device protecting the circuit and the outlet(s).

Building. A structure which stands alone or which is cut off from adjoining structures by fire walls with all openings therein protected by approved fire doors.

Cabinet. An enclosure designed either for surface or flush mounting,

and provided with a frame, mat, or trim in which a swinging door or doors are or may be hung.

Cable tray system. A cable tray system is a unit or assembly of units or sections, and associated fittings, made of metal or other noncombustible materials forming a rigid structural system used to support cables. Cable tray systems include ladders, troughs, channels, solid bottom trays, and other similar structures.

Cablebus. Cablebus is an approved assembly of insulated conductors with fittings and conductor terminations in a completely enclosed, ventilated, protective metal housing.

Center pivot irrigation machine. A center pivot irrigation machine is a multi-motored irrigation machine which revolves around a central pivot and employs alignment switches or similar devices to control individual motors.

Certified. Equipment is "certified" if it (a) has been tested and found by a nationally recognized testing laboratory to meet nationally recognized standards or to be safe for use in a specified manner, or (b) is of a kind whose production is periodically inspected by a nationally recognized testing laboratory, and (c) it bears a label, tag, or other record of certification.

Circuit breaker. (i) (600 volts nominal, or less). A device designed to open and close a circuit by nonautomatic means and to open the circuit automatically on a predetermined overcurrent without injury to itself when properly applied within its rating.

(ii) (Over 600 volts, nominal). A switching device capable of making, carrying, and breaking currents under normal circuit conditions, and also making, carrying for a specified time; and breaking currents under specified abnormal circuit conditions, such as those of short circuit.

Class I locations. Class I locations are those in which flammable gases or vapors are or may be present in the air in quantities sufficient to produce explosive or ignitible mixtures. Class I locations include the following:

(i) *Class I, Division 1.* A Class I, Division 1 location is a location: (a) in which hazardous concentrations of

FIGURE 4.5 (*Continued*)   Definition Applying to Part 1910, Subpart S (OSHA-CFR Title 29, Part 1910, Subpart S, Paragraph 399).

flammable gases or vapors may exist under normal operating conditions; or (b) in which hazardous concentrations of such gases or vapors may exist frequently because of repair or maintenance operations or because of leakage; or (c) in which breakdown or faulty operation of equipment or processes might release hazardous concentrations of flammable gases or vapors, and might also cause simultaneous failure of electric equipment.

NOTE: This classification usually includes locations where volatile flammable liquids or liquefied flammable gases are transferred from one container to another; interiors of spray booths and areas in the vicinity of spraying and painting operations where volatile flammable solvents are used; locations containing open tanks or vats of volatile flammable liquids; drying rooms or compartments for the evaporation of flammable solvents; locations containing fat and oil extraction equipment using volatile flammable solvents; portions of cleaning and dyeing plants where flammable liquids are used; gas generator rooms and other portions of gas manufacturing plants where flammable gas may escape; inadequately ventilated pump rooms for flammable gas or for volatile flammable liquids; the interiors of refrigerators and freezers in which volatile flammable materials are stored in open, lightly stoppered, or easily ruptured containers; and all other locations where ignitible concentrations of flammable vapors or gases are likely to occur in the course of normal operations.

(ii) *Class I, Division 2.* A Class I, Division 2 location is a location: (a) in which volatile flammable liquids or flammable gases are handled, processed, or used, but in which the hazardous liquids, vapors, or gases will normally be confined within closed containers or closed systems from which they can escape only in case of accidental rupture or breakdown of such containers or systems, or in case of abnormal operation of equipment; or (b) in which hazardous concentrations of gases or vapors are normally prevented by positive mechanical ventilation, and which might become hazardous through failure or abnormal operations of the ventilating equipment; or (c) that is adjacent to a Class I, Division 1 location, and to which hazardous concentrations of gases or vapors might occasionally be communicated unless such communication is

prevented by adequate positive-pressure ventilation from a source of clean air, and effective safeguards against ventilation failure are provided.

NOTE: This classification usually includes locations where volatile flammable liquids or flammable gases or vapors are used, but which would become hazardous only in case of an accident or of some unusual operating condition. The quantity of flammable material that might escape in case of accident, the adequacy of ventilating equipment, the total area involved, and the record of the industry or business with respect to explosions or fires are all factors that merit consideration in determining the classification and extent of each location.

Piping without valves, checks, meters, and similar devices would not ordinarily introduce a hazardous condition even though used for flammable liquids or gases. Locations used for the storage of flammable liquids or a liquefied or compressed gases in sealed containers would not normally be considered hazardous unless also subject to other hazardous conditions.

Electrical conduits and their associated enclosures separated from process fluids by a single seal or barrier are classed as a Division 2 location if the outside of the conduit and enclosures is a nonhazardous location.

Class II locations. Class II locations are those that are hazardous because of the presence of combustible dust. Class II locations include the following:

(i) *Class II, Division 1.* A Class II, Division 1 location is a location: (a) In which combustible dust is or may be in suspension in the air under normal operating conditions, in quantities sufficient to produce explosive or ignitible mixtures; or (b) where mechanical failure or abnormal operation of machinery or equipment might cause such explosive or ignitible mixtures to be produced, and might also provide a source of ignition through simultaneous failure of electric equipment, operation of protection devices, or from other causes, or (c) in which combustible dusts of an electrically conductive nature may be present.

NOTE: This classification may include areas of grain handling and processing plants, starch plants, sugar-pulverizing plants, malting plants, hay-grinding plants, coal pulverizing plants, areas where metal dusts and powders are produced or processed, and other similar locations which contain dust producing machinery and

FIGURE 4.5 (*Continued*)   Definition Applying to Part 1910, Subpart S (OSHA-CFR Title 29, Part 1910, Subpart S, Paragraph 399).

equipment (except where the equipment is dust-tight or vented to the outside). These areas would have combustible dust in the air, under normal operating conditions, in quantities sufficient to produce explosive or ignitible mixtures. Combustible dusts which are electrically nonconductive include dusts produced in the handling and processing of grain and grain products, pulverized sugar and cocoa, dried egg and milk powders, pulverized spices, starch and pastes, potato and woodflour, oil meal from beans and seed, dried hay, and other organic materials which may produce combustible dusts when processed or handled. Dusts containing magnesium or aluminum are particularly hazardous and the use of extreme caution is necessary to avoid ignition and explosion.

(ii) *Class II, Division 2.* A Class II, Division 2 location is a location in which: (a) combustible dust will not normally be in suspension in the air in quantities sufficient to produce explosive or ignitible mixtures, and dust accumulations are normally insufficient to interfere with the normal operation of electrical equipment or other apparatus; or (b) dust may be in suspension in the air as a result of infrequent malfunctioning of handling or processing equipment, and dust accumulations resulting therefrom may be ignitible by abnormal operation or failure of electrical equipment or other apparatus.

NOTE: This classification includes locations where dangerous concentrations of suspended dust would not be likely but where dust accumulations might form on or in the vicinity of electric equipment. These areas may contain equipment from which appreciable quantities of dust would escape under abnormal operating conditions or be adjacent to a Class II Division 1 location, as described above, into which an explosive or ignitible concentration of dust may be put into suspension under abnormal operating conditions.

Class III locations. Class III locations are those that are hazardous because of the presence of easily ignitible fibers or flyings but in which such fibers or flyings are not likely to be in suspension in the air in quantities sufficient to produce ignitible mixtures. Class III locations include the following:

(i) *Class III, Division 1.* A Class III, Division 1 location is a location in which easily ignitible fibers or materi-

als producing combustible flyings are handled, manufactured, or used.

NOTE: Such locations usually include some parts of rayon, cotton, and other textile mills; combustible fiber manufacturing and processing plants; cotton gins and cottonseed mills; flax-processing plants; clothing manufacturing plants; woodworking plants, and establishments; and industries involving similar hazardous processes or conditions.

Easily ignitible fibers and flyings include rayon, cotton (including cotton linters and cotton waste), sisal or henequen, istle, jute, hemp, tow, cocoa fiber, oakum, baled waste kapok, Spanish moss, excelsior, and other materials of similar nature.

(ii) *Class III, Division 2.* A Class III, Division 2 location is a location in which easily ignitible fibers are stored or handled, except in process of manufacture.

Collector ring. A collector ring is an assembly of slip rings for transferring electrical energy from a stationary to a rotating member.

Concealed. Rendered inaccessible by the structure or finish of the building. Wires in concealed raceways are considered concealed, even though they may become accessible by withdrawing them. [See "Accessible. (As applied to wiring methods.)"]

Conductor. (i) *Bare.* A conductor having no covering or electrical insulation whatsoever.

(ii) *Covered.* A conductor encased within material of composition or thickness that is not recognized as electrical insulation.

(iii) *Insulated.* A conductor encased within material of composition and thickness that is recognized as electrical insulation.

Conduit body. A separate portion of a conduit or tubing system that provides access through a removable cover(s) to the interior of the system at a junction of two or more sections of the system or at a terminal point of the system. Boxes such as FS and FD or larger cast or sheet metal boxes are not classified as conduit bodies.

Controller. A device or group of devices that serves to govern, in some predetermined manner, the electric power delivered to the apparatus to which it is connected.

Cooking unit, counter-mounted. A cooking appliance designed for mount-

---

FIGURE 4.5 (*Continued*) Definition Applying to Part 1910, Subpart S (OSHA-CFR Title 29, Part 1910, Subpart S, Paragraph 399).

ing in or on a counter and consisting of one or more heating elements, internal wiring, and built-in or separately mountable controls. (*See "Oven, wall-mounted."*)

Covered conductor. See "Conductor."

Cutout. (Over 600 volts, nominal.) An assembly of a fuse support with either a fuseholder, fuse carrier, or disconnecting blade. The fuseholder or fuse carrier may include a conducting element (fuse link), or may act as the disconnecting blade by the inclusion of a nonfusible member.

Cutout box. An enclosure designed for surface mounting and having swinging doors or covers secured directly to and telescoping with the walls of the box proper. (*See "Cabinet."*)

Damp location. See "*Location.*"

Dead front. Without live parts exposed to a person on the operating side of the equipment.

Device. A unit of an electrical system which is intended to carry but not utilize electric energy.

Dielectric heating. Dielectric heating is the heating of a nominally insulating material due to its own dielectric losses when the material is placed in a varying electric field.

Disconnecting means. A device, or group of devices, or other means by which the conductors of a circuit can be disconnected from their source of supply.

Disconnecting (or Isolating) switch. (Over 600 volts, nominal.) A mechanical switching device used for isolating a circuit or equipment from a source of power.

Dry location. See "*Location.*"

Electric sign. A fixed, stationary, or portable self-contained, electrically illuminated utilization equipment with words or symbols designed to convey information or attract attention.

Enclosed. Surrounded by a case, housing, fence or walls which will prevent persons from accidentally contacting energized parts.

Enclosure. The case or housing of apparatus, or the fence or walls surrounding an installation to prevent personnel from accidentally contacting energized parts, or to protect the equipment from physical damage.

Equipment. A general term including material, fittings, devices, appliances, fixtures, apparatus, and the like, used as a part of, or in connection with, an electrical installation.

Equipment grounding conductor. See "*Grounding conductor, equipment.*"

Explosion-proof apparatus. Apparatus enclosed in a case that is capable of withstanding an explosion of a specified gas or vapor which may occur within it and of preventing the ignition of a specified gas or vapor surrounding the enclosure by sparks, flashes, or explosion of the gas or vapor within, and which operates at such an external temperature that it will not ignite a surrounding flammable atmosphere.

Exposed. (As applied to live parts.) Capable of being inadvertently touched or approached nearer than a safe distance by a person. It is applied to parts not suitably guarded, isolated, or insulated. (See "*Accessible.*" and "*Concealed.*")

Exposed. (As applied to wiring methods.) On or attached to the surface or behind panels designed to allow access. [See "*Accessible.* (As applied to wiring methods.)"]

Exposed. (For the purposes of § 1910.308(e), *Communications systems.*) Where the circuit is in such a position that in case of failure of supports or insulation, contact with another circuit may result.

Externally operable. Capable of being operated without exposing the operator to contact with live parts.

Feeder. All circuit conductors between the service equipment, or the generator switchboard of an isolated plant, and the final branch-circuit overcurrent device.

Fitting. An accessory such as a locknut, bushing, or other part of a wiring system that is intended primarily to perform a mechanical rather than an electrical function.

Fuse. (Over 600 volts, nominal.) An overcurrent protective device with a circuit opening fusible part that is heated and severed by the passage of overcurrent through it. A fuse comprises all the parts that form a unit capable of performing the prescribed functions. It may or may not be the

FIGURE 4.5 (*Continued*)   Definition Applying to Part 1910, Subpart S (OSHA-CFR Title 29, Part 1910, Subpart S, Paragraph 399).

complete device necessary to connect it into an electrical circuit.

Ground. A conducting connection, whether intentional or accidental, between an electrical circuit or equipment and the earth, or to some conducting body that serves in place of the earth.

Grounded. Connected to earth or to some conducting body that serves in place of the earth.

Grounded, effectively. (Over 600 volts, nominal.) Permanently connected to earth through a ground connection of sufficiently low impedance and having sufficient ampacity that ground fault current which may occur cannot build up to voltages dangerous to personnel.

Grounded conductor. A system or circuit conductor that is intentionally grounded.

Grounding conductor. A conductor used to connect equipment or the grounded circuit of a wiring system to a grounding electrode or electrodes.

Grounding conductor, equipment. The conductor used to connect the non-current-carrying metal parts of equipment, raceways, and other enclosures to the system grounded conductor and/or the grounding electrode conductor at the service equipment or at the source of a separately derived system.

Grounding electrode conductor. The conductor used to connect the grounding electrode to the equipment grounding conductor and/or to the grounded conductor of the circuit at the service equipment or at the source of a separately derived system.

Ground-fault circuit-interrupter. A device whose function is to interrupt the electric circuit to the load when a fault current to ground exceeds some predetermined value that is less than that required to operate the overcurrent protective device of the supply circuit.

Guarded. Covered, shielded, fenced, enclosed, or otherwise protected by means of suitable covers, casings, barriers, rails, screens, mats, or platforms to remove the likelihood of approach to a point of danger or contact by persons or objects.

Health care facilities. Buildings or portions of buildings and mobile homes that contain, but are not limited to, hospitals, nursing homes, extended care facilities, clinics, and medical and dental offices, whether fixed or mobile.

Heating equipment. For the purposes of § 1910.306(g), the term *heating equipment* includes any equipment used for heating purposes if heat is generated by induction or dielectric methods.

Hoistway. Any shaftway, hatchway, well hole, or other vertical opening or space in which an elevator or dumbwaiter is designed to operate.

Identified. Identified, as used in reference to a conductor or its terminal, means that such conductor or terminal can be readily recognized as grounded.

Induction heating. Induction heating is the heating of a nominally conductive material due to its own I^2R losses when the material is placed in a varying electromagnetic field.

Insulated conductor. See *Conductor.*

Interrupter switch. (Over 600 volts, nominal.) A switch capable of making, carrying, and interrupting specified currents.

Irrigation machine. An irrigation machine is an electrically driven or controlled machine, with one or more motors, not hand portable, and used primarily to transport and distribute water for agricultural purposes.

Isolated. Not readily accessible to persons unless special means for access are used.

Isolated power system. A system comprising an isolating transformer or its equivalent, a line isolation monitor, and its ungrounded circuit conductors.

Labeled. Equipment is *labeled* if there is attached to it a label, symbol, or other identifying mark of a nationally recognized testing laboratory which, (a) makes periodic inspections of the production of such equipment, and (b) whose labeling indicates compliance with nationally recognized standards or tests to determine safe use in a specified manner.

Lighting outlet. An outlet intended for the direct connection of a lampholder, a lighting fixture, or a pendant cord terminating in a lampholder.

Line-clearance tree trimming. The pruning, trimming, repairing, main-

FIGURE 4.5 (*Continued*) Definition Applying to Part 1910, Subpart S (OSHA-CFR Title 29, Part 1910, Subpart S, Paragraph 399).

taining, removing, or clearing of trees or cutting of brush that is within 10 feet (305 cm) of electric supply lines and equipment.

Listed. Equipment is *listed* if it is of a kind mentioned in a list which, (a) is published by a nationally recognized laboratory which makes periodic inspection of the production of such equipment, and (b) states such equipment meets nationally recognized standards or has been tested and found safe for use in a specified manner.

Location—(i) *Damp location.* Partially protected locations under canopies, marquees, roofed open porches, and like locations, and interior locations subject to moderate degrees of moisture, such as some basements, some barns, and some cold-storage warehouses.

(ii) *Dry location.* A location not normally subject to dampness or wetness. A location classified as dry may be temporarily subject to dampness or wetness, as in the case of a building under construction.

(iii) *Wet location.* Installations underground or in concrete slabs or masonry in direct contact with the earth, and locations subject to saturation with water or other liquids, such as vehicle-washing areas, and locations exposed to weather and unprotected.

May. If a discretionary right, privilege, or power is conferred, the word "may" is used. If a right, privilege, or power is abridged or if an obligation to abstain from acting is imposed, the word "may" is used with a restrictive "no," "not," or "only." (E.g., no employer may . . . ; an employer may not . . . ; only qualified persons may. . . .)

Medium voltage cable. Type MV medium voltage cable is a single or multiconductor solid dielectric insulated cable rated 2000 volts or higher.

Metal-clad cable. Type MC cable is a factory assembly of one or more conductors, each individually insulated and enclosed in a metallic sheath of interlocking tape, or a smooth or corrugated tube.

Mineral-insulated metal-sheathed cable. Type MI mineral-insulated metal-sheathed cable is a factory assembly of one or more conductors insulated with a highly compressed refractory mineral insulation and enclosed in a liquidtight and gastight continuous copper sheath.

Mobile X-ray. X-ray equipment mounted on a permanent base with wheels and/or casters for moving while completely assembled.

Nonmetallic-sheathed cable. Nonmetallic-sheathed cable is a factory assembly of two or more insulated conductors having an outer sheath of moisture resistant, flame-retardant, nonmetallic material. Nonmetallic sheathed cable is manufactured in the following types:

(i) *Type NM.* The overall covering has a flame-retardant and moisture-resistant finish.

(ii) *Type NMC.* The overall covering is flame-retardant, moisture-resistant, fungus-resistant, and corrosion-resistant.

Oil (filled) cutout. (Over 600 volts, nominal.) A cutout in which all or part of the fuse support and its fuse link or disconnecting blade are mounted in oil with complete immersion of the contacts and the fusible portion of the conducting element (fuse link), so that arc interruption by severing of the fuse link or by opening of the contacts will occur under oil.

Open wiring on insulators. Open wiring on insulators is an exposed wiring method using cleats, knobs, tubes, and flexible tubing for the protection and support of single insulated conductors run in or on buildings, and not concealed by the building structure.

Outlet. A point on the wiring system at which current is taken to supply utilization equipment.

Outline lighting. An arrangement of incandescent lamps or electric discharge tubing to outline or call attention to certain features such as the shape of a building or the decoration of a window.

Oven, wall-mounted. An oven for cooking purposes designed for mounting in or on a wall or other surface and consisting of one of more heating elements, internal wiring, and built-in or separately mountable controls. (See *Cooking unit, counter-mounted.*)

Overcurrent. Any current in excess of the rated current of equipment or the ampacity of a conductor. It may

FIGURE 4.5 (*Continued*) Definition Applying to Part 1910, Subpart S (OSHA-CFR Title 29, Part 1910, Subpart S, Paragraph 399).

Show window. Any window used or designed to be used for the display of goods or advertising material, whether it is fully or partly enclosed or entirely open at the rear and whether or not it has a platform raised higher than the street floor level.

Sign. See *Electric Sign.*

Signaling circuit. Any electric circuit that energizes signaling equipment.

Special permission. The written consent of the authority having jurisdiction.

Storable swimming or wading pool. A pool with a maximum dimension of 15 feet and a maximum wall height of 3 feet and is so constructed that it may be readily disassembled for storage and reassembled to its original integrity.

Switchboard. A large single panel, frame, or assembly of panels which have switches, buses, instruments, overcurrent and other protective devices mounted on the face or back or both. Switchboards are generally accessible from the rear as well as from the front and are not intended to be installed in cabinets. (See *Panelboard.*)

Switches.

(i) *General-use switch.* A switch intended for use in general distribution and branch circuits. It is rated in amperes, and it is capable of interrupting its rated current at its rated voltage.

(ii) *General-use snap switch.* A form of general-use switch so constructed that it can be installed in flush device boxes or on outlet box covers, or otherwise used in conjunction with wiring systems recognized by this subpart.

(iii) *Isolating switch.* A switch intended for isolating an electric circuit from the source of power. It has no interrupting rating, and it is intended to be operated only after the circuit has been opened by some other means.

(iv) *Motor-circuit switch.* A switch, rated in horsepower, capable of interrupting the maximum operating overload current of a motor of the same horsepower rating as the switch at the rated voltage.

Switching devices. (Over 600 volts, nominal.) Devices designed to close and/or open one or more electric circuits. Included in this category are circuit breakers, cutouts, disconnecting

(or isolating) switches, disconnecting means, interrupter switches, and oil (filled) cutouts.

Transportable X-ray. X-ray equipment installed in a vehicle or that may readily be disassembled for transport in a vehicle.

Utilization equipment. Utilization equipment means equipment which utilizes electric energy for mechanical, chemical, heating, lighting, or similar useful purpose.

Utilization system. A utilization system is a system which provides electric power and light for employee workplaces, and includes the premises wiring system and utilization equipment.

Ventilated. Provided with a means to permit circulation of air sufficient to remove an excess of heat, fumes, or vapors.

Volatile flammable liquid. A flammable liquid having a flash point below 38 degrees C (100 degrees F) or whose temperature is above its flash point.

Voltage (of a circuit). The greatest root-mean-square (effective) difference of potential between any two conductors of the circuit concerned.

Voltage, nominal. A nominal value assigned to a circuit or system for the purpose of conveniently designating its voltage class (as 120/240, 480Y/277, 600, etc.). The actual voltage at which a circuit operates can vary from the nominal within a range that permits satisfactory operation of equipment.

Voltage to ground. For grounded circuits, the voltage between the given conductor and that point or conductor of the circuit that is grounded; for ungrounded circuits, the greatest voltage between the given conductor and any other conductor of the circuit.

Watertight. So constructed that moisture will not enter the enclosure.

Weatherproof. So constructed or protected that exposure to the weather will not interfere with successful operation. Rainproof, raintight, or watertight equipment can fulfill the requirements for weatherproof where varying weather conditions other than wetness, such as snow, ice, dust, or temperature extremes, are not a factor.

Wet location. See *Location.*

FIGURE 4.5 (*Continued*)   Definition Applying to Part 1910, Subpart S (OSHA-CFR Title 29, Part 1910, Subpart S, Paragraph 399).

Wireways. Wireways are sheet-metal troughs with hinged or removable covers for housing and protecting electric wires and cable and in which conductors are laid in place after the wireway has been installed as a complete system.

[46 FR 4056, Jan. 16, 1981; 46 FR 40185, Aug. 7, 1981, as amended at 53 FR 12123, Apr. 12, 1988; 55 FR 32020, Aug. 6, 1990; 55 FR 46054, Nov. 1, 1990]

FIGURE 4.5 (*Continued*)   Definition Applying to Part 1910, Subpart S (OSHA-CFR Title 29, Part 1910, Subpart S, Paragraph 399).

INSTALLATION SAFETY REQUIREMENTS

§ 1926.402 Applicability.

(a) *Covered.* Sections 1926.402 through 1926.408 contain installation safety requirements for electrical equipment and installations used to provide electric power and light at the jobsite. These sections apply to installations, both temporary and permanent, used on the jobsite; but these sections do not apply to existing permanent installations that were in place before the construction activity commenced.

NOTE: If the electrical installation is made in accordance with the National Electrical Code ANSI/NFPA 70-1984, exclusive of Formal Interpretations and Tentative Interim Amendments, it will be deemed to be in compliance with §§ 1926.403 through 1926.408, except for §§ 1926.404(b)(1) and 1926.405(a)(2)(ii) (E), (F), (G), and (J).

(b) *Not covered.* Sections 1926.402 through 1926.408 do not cover installations used for the generation, transmission, and distribution of electric energy, including related communica-

---

FIGURE 4.6   Installation Safety Requirements (OSHA-CFR Title 29, Part 1926, Subpart K, Paragraphs 402–408).

provisions of paragraphs (a) through (g) of this section and with the following provisions which supplement or modify those requirements. The provisions of paragraphs (j)(2), (j)(3), and (j)(4) of this section do not apply to equipment on the supply side of the service conductors.

(2) *Enclosure for electrical installations.* Electrical installations in a vault, room, closet or in an area surrounded by a wall, screen, or fence, access to which is controlled by lock and key or other equivalent means, are considered to be accessible to qualified persons only. A wall, screen, or fence less than 8 feet (2.44 m) in height is not considered adequate to prevent access unless it has other features that provide a degree of isolation equivalent to an 8-foot (2.44-m) fence. The entrances to all buildings, rooms or enclosures containing exposed live parts or exposed conductors operating at over 600 volts, nominal, shall be kept locked or shall be under the observation of a qualified person at all times.

(i) *Installations accessible to qualified persons only.* Electrical installations having exposed live parts shall be accessible to qualified persons only and shall comply with the applicable provisions of paragraph (j)(3) of this section.

(ii) *Installations accessible to unqualified persons.* Electrical installations that are open to unqualified persons shall be made with metal-enclosed equipment or shall be enclosed in a vault or in an area, access to which is controlled by a lock. Metal-enclosed switchgear, unit substations, transformers, pull boxes, connection boxes, and other similar associated equipment shall be marked with appropriate caution signs. If equipment is exposed to physical damage from vehicular traffic, guards shall be provided to prevent such damage. Ventilating or similar openings in metal-enclosed equipment shall be designed so that foreign objects inserted through these openings will be deflected from energized parts.

(3) *Workspace about equipment.* Sufficient space shall be provided and maintained about electric equipment to permit ready and safe operation and maintenance of such equipment. Where energized parts are exposed, the minimum clear workspace shall not be less than 6 feet 6 inches (1.98 m) high (measured vertically from the floor or platform), or less than 3 feet (914 mm) wide (measured parallel to the equipment). The depth shall be as required in Table K-2. The workspace shall be adequate to permit at least a 90-degree opening of doors or hinged panels.

(i) *Working space.* The minimum clear working space in front of electric equipment such as switchboards, control panels, switches, circuit breakers, motor controllers, relays, and similar equipment shall not be less than specified in Table K-2 unless otherwise specified in this subpart. Distances shall be measured from the live parts if they are exposed, or from the enclosure front or opening if the live parts are enclosed. However, working space is not required in back of equipment such as deadfront switchboards or control assemblies where there are no renewable or adjustable parts (such as fuses or switches) on the back and where all connections are accessible from locations other than the back. Where rear access is required to work on de-energized parts on the back of enclosed equipment, a minimum working space of 30 inches (762 mm) horizontally shall be provided.

TABLE K-2—MINIMUM DEPTH OF CLEAR WORKING SPACE IN FRONT OF ELECTRIC EQUIPMENT

Nominal voltage to ground	Conditions[1]		
	(a)	(b)	(c)
	Feet[2]	Feet[2]	Feet[2]
601 to 2,500	3	4	5
2,501 to 9,000	4	5	6
9,001 to 25,000	5	6	9
25,001 to 75 kV	6	8	10
Above 75kV	8	10	12

[1]Conditions (a), (b), and (c) are as follows: (a) Exposed live parts on one side and no live or grounded parts on the other side of the working space, or exposed live parts on both sides effectively guarded by insulating materials. Insulated wire or insulated busbars operating at not over 300 volts are not considered live parts. (b) Exposed live parts on one side and grounded parts on the other side. Walls constructed of concrete, brick, or tile are considered to be grounded surfaces. (c) Exposed live parts on both sides of the workspace [not guarded as provided in Condition (a)] with the operator between.
[2] NOTE: For SI units: one foot = 0.3048 m.

FIGURE 4.6 (*Continued*)   Installation Safety Requirements (OSHA-CFR Title 29, Part 1926, Subpart K, Paragraphs 402–408).

(ii) *Lighting outlets and points of control.* The lighting outlets shall be so arranged that persons changing lamps or making repairs on the lighting system will not be endangered by live parts or other equipment. The points of control shall be so located that persons are not likely to come in contact with any live part or moving part of the equipment while turning on the lights.

(iii) *Elevation of unguarded live parts.* Unguarded live parts above working space shall be maintained at elevations not less than specified in Table K-3.

TABLE K-3—ELEVATION OF UNGUARDED ENERGIZED PARTS ABOVE WORKING SPACE

Nominal voltage between phases	Minimum elevation
601–7,500	8 feet 6 inches.[1]
7,501–35,000	9 feet.
Over 35kV	9 feet + 0.37 inches per kV above 35kV.

[1] NOTE: For SI units: one inch = 25.4 mm; one foot = 0.3048 m.

(4) *Entrance and access to workspace.* At least one entrance not less than 24 inches (610 mm) wide and 6 feet 6 inches (1.98 m) high shall be provided to give access to the working space about electric equipment. On switchboard and control panels exceeding 48 inches (1.22 m) in width, there shall be one entrance at each end of such board where practicable. Where bare energized parts at any voltage or insulated energized parts above 600 volts are located adjacent to such entrance, they shall be guarded.

(Information collection requirements contained in paragraphs (g) and (h) were approved by the Office of Management and Budget under control number 1218–0130)

§ 1926.404 **Wiring design and protection.**

(a) *Use and identification of grounded and grounding conductors—(1) Identification of conductors.* A conductor used as a grounded conductor shall be identifiable and distinguishable from all other conductors. A conductor used as an equipment grounding conductor shall be identifiable and distinguishable from all other conductors.

(2) *Polarity of connections.* No grounded conductor shall be attached to any terminal or lead so as to reverse designated polarity.

(3) *Use of grounding terminals and devices.* A grounding terminal or grounding-type device on a receptacle, cord connector, or attachment plug shall not be used for purposes other than grounding.

(b) *Branch circuits—(1) Ground-fault protection—(i) General.* The employer shall use either ground fault circuit interrupters as specified in paragraph (b)(1)(ii) of this section or an assured equipment grounding conductor program as specified in paragraph (b)(1)(iii) of this section to protect employees on construction sites. These requirements are in addition to any other requirements for equipment grounding conductors.

(ii) *Ground-fault circuit interrupters.* All 120-volt, single-phase, 15- and 20-ampere receptacle outlets on construction sites, which are not a part of the permanent wiring of the building or structure and which are in use by employees, shall have approved ground-fault circuit interrupters for personnel protection. Receptacles on a two-wire, single-phase portable or vehicle-mounted generator rated not more than 5kW, where the circuit conductors of the generator are insulated from the generator frame and all other grounded surfaces, need not be protected with ground-fault circuit interrupters.

(iii) *Assured equipment grounding conductor program.* The employer shall establish and implement an assured equipment grounding conductor program on construction sites covering all cord sets, receptacles which are not a part of the building or structure, and equipment connected by cord and plug which are available for use or used by employees. This program shall comply with the following minimum requirements:

(A) A written description of the program, including the specific procedures adopted by the employer, shall be available at the jobsite for inspection and copying by the Assistant Secretary and any affected employee.

(B) The employer shall designate one or more competent persons (as de-

FIGURE 4.6 (*Continued*)   Installation Safety Requirements (OSHA-CFR Title 29, Part 1926, Subpart K, Paragraphs 402–408).

(iii) *Disconnection of fuses and thermal cutouts.* Except for devices provided for current-limiting on the supply side of the service disconnecting means, all cartridge fuses which are accessible to other than qualified persons and all fuses and thermal cutouts on circuits over 150 volts to ground shall be provided with disconnecting means. This disconnecting means shall be installed so that the fuse or thermal cutout can be disconnected from its supply without disrupting service to equipment and circuits unrelated to those protected by the overcurrent device.

(iv) *Location in or on premises.* Overcurrent devices shall be readily accessible. Overcurrent devices shall not be located where they could create an employee safety hazard by being exposed to physical damage or located in the vicinity of easily ignitible material.

(v) *Arcing or suddenly moving parts.* Fuses and circuit breakers shall be so located or shielded that employees will not be burned or otherwise injured by their operation.

(vi) *Circuit breakers*—(A) Circuit breakers shall clearly indicate whether they are in the open (off) or closed (on) position.

(B) Where circuit breaker handles on switchboards are operated vertically rather than horizontally or rotationally, the up position of the handle shall be the closed (on) position.

(C) If used as switches in 120-volt, fluorescent lighting circuits, circuit breakers shall be marked "SWD."

(2) *Over 600 volts, nominal.* Feeders and branch circuits over 600 volts, nominal, shall have short-circuit protection.

(f) *Grounding.* Paragraphs (f)(1) through (f)(11) of this section contain grounding requirements for systems, circuits, and equipment.

(1) *Systems to be grounded.* The following systems which supply premises wiring shall be grounded:

(i) *Three-wire DC systems.* All 3-wire DC systems shall have their neutral conductor grounded.

(ii) *Two-wire DC systems.* Two-wire DC systems operating at over 50 volts through 300 volts between conductors shall be grounded unless they are rec-

tifier-derived from an AC system complying with paragraphs (f)(1)(iii), (f)(1)(iv), and (f)(1)(v) of this section.

(iii) *AC circuits, less than 50 volts.* AC circuits of less than 50 volts shall be grounded if they are installed as overhead conductors outside of buildings or if they are supplied by transformers and the transformer primary supply system is ungrounded or exceeds 150 volts to ground.

(iv) *AC systems, 50 volts to 1000 volts.* AC systems of 50 volts to 1000 volts shall be grounded under any of the following conditions, unless exempted by paragraph (f)(1)(v) of this section:

(A) If the system can be so grounded that the maximum voltage to ground on the ungrounded conductors does not exceed 150 volts;

(B) If the system is nominally rated 480Y/277 volt, 3-phase, 4-wire in which the neutral is used as a circuit conductor;

(C) If the system is nominally rated 240/120 volt, 3-phase, 4-wire in which the midpoint of one phase is used as a circuit conductor; or

(D) If a service conductor is uninsulated.

(v) *Exceptions.* AC systems of 50 volts to 1000 volts are not required to be grounded if the system is separately derived and is supplied by a transformer that has a primary voltage rating less than 1000 volts, provided all of the following conditions are met:

(A) The system is used exclusively for control circuits,

(B) The conditions of maintenance and supervision assure that only qualified persons will service the installation,

(C) Continuity of control power is required, and

(D) Ground detectors are installed on the control system.

(2) *Separately derived systems.* Where paragraph (f)(1) of this section requires grounding of wiring systems whose power is derived from generator, transformer, or converter windings and has no direct electrical connection, including a solidly connected grounded circuit conductor, to supply conductors originating in another system, paragraph (f)(5) of this section shall also apply.

FIGURE 4.6 (*Continued*)   Installation Safety Requirements (OSHA-CFR Title 29, Part 1926, Subpart K, Paragraphs 402–408).

(3) *Portable and vehicle-mounted generators*—(i) *Portable generators.* Under the following conditions, the frame of a portable generator need not be grounded and may serve as the grounding electrode for a system supplied by the generator:

(A) The generator supplies only equipment mounted on the generator and/or cord- and plug-connected equipment through receptacles mounted on the generator, and

(B) The noncurrent-carrying metal parts of equipment and the equipment grounding conductor terminals of the receptacles are bonded to the generator frame.

(ii) *Vehicle-mounted generators.* Under the following conditions the frame of a vehicle may serve as the grounding electrode for a system supplied by a generator located on the vehicle:

(A) The frame of the generator is bonded to the vehicle frame, and

(B) The generator supplies only equipment located on the vehicle and/or cord- and plug-connected equipment through receptacles mounted on the vehicle or on the generator, and

(C) The noncurrent-carrying metal parts of equipment and the equipment grounding conductor terminals of the receptacles are bonded to the generator frame, and

(D) The system complies with all other provisions of this section.

(iii) *Neutral conductor bonding.* A neutral conductor shall be bonded to the generator frame if the generator is a component of a separately derived system. No other conductor need be bonded to the generator frame.

(4) *Conductors to be grounded.* For AC premises wiring systems the identified conductor shall be grounded.

(5) *Grounding connections*—(i) *Grounded system.* For a grounded system, a grounding electrode conductor shall be used to connect both the equipment grounding conductor and the grounded circuit conductor to the grounding electrode. Both the equipment grounding conductor and the grounding electrode conductor shall be connected to the grounded circuit conductor on the supply side of the service disconnecting means, or on the supply side of the system disconnect-ing means or overcurrent devices if the system is separately derived.

(ii) *Ungrounded systems.* For an ungrounded service-supplied system, the equipment grounding conductor shall be connected to the grounding electrode conductor at the service equipment. For an ungrounded separately derived system, the equipment grounding conductor shall be connected to the grounding electrode conductor at, or ahead of, the system disconnecting means or overcurrent devices.

(6) *Grounding path.* The path to ground from circuits, equipment, and enclosures shall be permanent and continuous.

(7) *Supports, enclosures, and equipment to be grounded*—(i) *Supports and enclosures for conductors.* Metal cable trays, metal raceways, and metal enclosures for conductors shall be grounded, except that:

(A) Metal enclosures such as sleeves that are used to protect cable assemblies from physical damage need not be grounded; and

(B) Metal enclosures for conductors added to existing installations of open wire, knob-and-tube wiring, and nonmetallic-sheathed cable need not be grounded if all of the following conditions are met:

(1) Runs are less than 25 feet (7.62 m);

(2) Enclosures are free from probable contact with ground, grounded metal, metal laths, or other conductive materials; and

(3) Enclosures are guarded against employee contact.

(ii) *Service equipment enclosures.* Metal enclosures for service equipment shall be grounded.

(iii) *Fixed equipment.* Exposed noncurrent-carrying metal parts of fixed equipment which may become energized shall be grounded under any of the following conditions:

(A) If within 8 feet (2.44 m) vertically or 5 feet (1.52 m) horizontally of ground or grounded metal objects and subject to employee contact.

(B) If located in a wet or damp location and subject to employee contact.

(C) If in electrical contact with metal.

(D) If in a hazardous (classified) location.

FIGURE 4.6 (*Continued*)   Installation Safety Requirements (OSHA-CFR Title 29, Part 1926, Subpart K, Paragraphs 402–408).

(E) If supplied by a metal-clad, metal-sheathed, or grounded metal raceway wiring method.

(F) If equipment operates with any terminal at over 150 volts to ground; however, the following need not be grounded:

(1) Enclosures for switches or circuit breakers used for other than service equipment and accessible to qualified persons only;

(2) Metal frames of electrically heated appliances which are permanently and effectively insulated from ground; and

(3) The cases of distribution apparatus such as transformers and capacitors mounted on wooden poles at a height exceeding 8 feet (2.44 m) above ground or grade level.

(iv) *Equipment connected by cord and plug.* Under any of the conditions described in paragraphs (f)(7)(iv)(A) through (f)(7)(iv)(C) of this section, exposed noncurrent-carrying metal parts of cord- and plug-connected equipment which may become energized shall be grounded:

(A) If in a hazardous (classified) location (see § 1926.407).

(B) If operated at over 150 volts to ground, except for guarded motors and metal frames of electrically heated appliances if the appliance frames are permanently and effectively insulated from ground.

(C) If the equipment is one of the types listed in paragraphs (f)(7)(iv)(C)(1) through (f)(7)(iv)(C)(5) of this section. However, even though the equipment may be one of these types, it need not be grounded if it is exempted by paragraph (f)(7)(iv)(C)(6).

(1) Hand held motor-operated tools;

(2) Cord- and plug-connected equipment used in damp or wet locations or by employees standing on the ground or on metal floors or working inside of metal tanks or boilers;

(3) Portable and mobile X-ray and associated equipment;

(4) Tools likely to be used in wet and/or conductive locations; and

(5) Portable hand lamps.

(6) Tools likely to be used in wet and/or conductive locations need not be grounded if supplied through an isolating transformer with an un-grounded secondary of not over 50 volts. Listed or labeled portable tools and appliances protected by a system of double insulation, or its equivalent, need not be grounded. If such a system is employed, the equipment shall be distinctively marked to indicate that the tool or appliance utilizes a system of double insulation.

(v) *Nonelectrical equipment.* The metal parts of the following nonelectrical equipment shall be grounded: Frames and tracks of electrically operated cranes; frames of nonelectrically driven elevator cars to which electric conductors are attached; hand-operated metal shifting ropes or cables of electric elevators, and metal partitions, grill work, and similar metal enclosures around equipment of over IkV between conductors.

(8) *Methods of grounding equipment*—(i) *With circuit conductors.* Noncurrent-carrying metal parts of fixed equipment, if required to be grounded by this subpart, shall be grounded by an equipment grounding conductor which is contained within the same raceway, cable, or cord, or runs with or encloses the circuit conductors. For DC circuits only, the equipment grounding conductor may be run separately from the circuit conductors.

(ii) *Grounding conductor.* A conductor used for grounding fixed or movable equipment shall have capacity to conduct safely any fault current which may be imposed on it.

(iii) *Equipment considered effectively grounded.* Electric equipment is considered to be effectively grounded if it is secured to, and in electrical contact with, a metal rack or structure that is provided for its support and the metal rack or structure is grounded by the method specified for the noncurrent-carrying metal parts of fixed equipment in paragraph (f)(8)(i) of this section. Metal car frames supported by metal hoisting cables attached to or running over metal sheaves or drums of grounded elevator machines are also considered to be effectively grounded.

(9) *Bonding.* If bonding conductors are used to assure electrical continuity, they shall have the capacity to con-

FIGURE 4.6 (*Continued*) Installation Safety Requirements (OSHA-CFR Title 29, Part 1926, Subpart K, Paragraphs 402–408).

duct any fault current which may be imposed.

(10) *Made electrodes.* If made electrodes are used, they shall be free from nonconductive coatings, such as paint or enamel; and, if practicable, they shall be embedded below permanent moisture level. A single electrode consisting of a rod, pipe or plate which has a resistance to ground greater than 25 ohms shall be augmented by one additional electrode installed no closer than 6 feet (1.83 m) to the first electrode.

(11) *Grounding of systems and circuits of 1000 volts and over (high voltage)—(i) General.* If high voltage systems are grounded, they shall comply with all applicable provisions of paragraphs (f)(1) through (f)(10) of this section as supplemented and modified by this paragraph (f)(11).

(ii) *Grounding of systems supplying portable or mobile equipment.* Systems supplying portable or mobile high voltage equipment, other than substations installed on a temporary basis, shall comply with the following:

(A) Portable and mobile high voltage equipment shall be supplied from a system having its neutral grounded through an impedance. If a delta-connected high voltage system is used to supply the equipment, a system neutral shall be derived.

(B) Exposed noncurrent-carrying metal parts of portable and mobile equipment shall be connected by an equipment grounding conductor to the point at which the system neutral impedance is grounded.

(C) Ground-fault detection and relaying shall be provided to automatically de-energize any high voltage system component which has developed a ground fault. The continuity of the equipment grounding conductor shall be continuously monitored so as to de-energize automatically the high voltage feeder to the portable equipment upon loss of continuity of the equipment grounding conductor.

(D) The grounding electrode to which the portable or mobile equipment system neutral impedance is connected shall be isolated from and separated in the ground by at least 20 feet (6.1 m) from any other system or equipment grounding electrode, and

there shall be no direct connection between the grounding electrodes, such as buried pipe, fence or like objects.

(iii) *Grounding of equipment.* All noncurrent-carrying metal parts of portable equipment and fixed equipment including their associated fences, housings, enclosures, and supporting structures shall be grounded. However, equipment which is guarded by location and isolated from ground need not be grounded. Additionally, pole-mounted distribution apparatus at a height exceeding 8 feet (2.44 m) above ground or grade level need not be grounded.

(Approved by the Office of Management and Budget under control number 1218-0130)

[51 FR 25318, July 11, 1986, as amended at 54 FR 24334, June 7, 1989]

§ 1926.405 Wiring methods, components, and equipment for general use.

(a) *Wiring methods.* The provisions of this paragraph do not apply to conductors which form an integral part of equipment such as motors, controllers, motor control centers and like equipment.

(1) *General requirements—(i) Electrical continuity of metal raceways and enclosures.* Metal raceways, cable armor, and other metal enclosures for conductors shall be metallically joined together into a continuous electric conductor and shall be so connected to all boxes, fittings, and cabinets as to provide effective electrical continuity.

(ii) *Wiring in ducts.* No wiring systems of any type shall be installed in ducts used to transport dust, loose stock or flammable vapors. No wiring system of any type shall be installed in any duct used for vapor removal or in any shaft containing only such ducts.

(2) *Temporary wiring—(i) Scope.* The provisions of paragraph (a)(2) of this section apply to temporary electrical power and lighting wiring methods which may be of a class less than would be required for a permanent installation. Except as specifically modified in paragraph (a)(2) of this section, all other requirements of this subpart for permanent wiring shall apply to temporary wiring installations. Tem-

FIGURE 4.6 (*Continued*) Installation Safety Requirements (OSHA-CFR Title 29, Part 1926, Subpart K, Paragraphs 402–408).

porary wiring shall be removed immediately upon completion of construction or the purpose for which the wiring was installed.

(ii) *General requirements for temporary wiring*—(A) Feeders shall originate in a distribution center. The conductors shall be run as multiconductor cord or cable assemblies or within raceways; or, where not subject to physical damage, they may be run as open conductors on insulators not more than 10 feet (3.05 m).

(B) Branch circuits shall originate in a power outlet or panelboard. Conductors shall be run as multiconductor cord or cable assemblies or open conductors, or shall be run in raceways. All conductors shall be protected by overcurrent devices at their ampacity. Runs of open conductors shall be located where the conductors will not be subject to physical damage, and the conductors shall be fastened at intervals not exceeding 10 feet (3.05 m). No branch-circuit conductors shall be laid on the floor. Each branch circuit that supplies receptacles or fixed equipment shall contain a separate equipment grounding conductor if the branch circuit is run as open conductors.

(C) Receptacles shall be of the grounding type. Unless installed in a complete metallic raceway, each branch circuit shall contain a separate equipment grounding conductor, and all receptacles shall be electrically connected to the grounding conductor. Receptacles for uses other than temporary lighting shall not be installed on branch circuits which supply temporary lighting. Receptacles shall not be connected to the ungrounded conductor of multiwire circuits which supply temporary lighting.

(D) Disconnecting switches or plug connectors shall be installed to permit the disconnection of all ungrounded conductors of each temporary circuit.

(E) All lamps for general illumination shall be protected from accidental contact or breakage. Metal-case sockets shall be grounded.

(F) Temporary lights shall not be suspended by their electric cords unless cords and lights are designed for this means of suspension.

(G) Portable electric lighting used in wet and/or other conductive locations, as for example, drums, tanks, and vessels, shall be operated at 12 volts or less. However, 120-volt lights may be used if protected by a ground-fault circuit interrupter.

(H) A box shall be used wherever a change is made to a raceway system or a cable system which is metal clad or metal sheathed.

(I) Flexible cords and cables shall be protected from damage. Sharp corners and projections shall be avoided. Flexible cords and cables may pass through doorways or other pinch points, if protection is provided to avoid damage.

(J) Extension cord sets used with portable electric tools and appliances shall be of three-wire type and shall be designed for hard or extra-hard usage. Flexible cords used with temporary and portable lights shall be designed for hard or extra-hard usage.

NOTE: The National Electrical Code, ANSI/NFPA 70, in Article 400, Table 400-4, lists various types of flexible cords, some of which are noted as being designed for hard or extra-hard usage. Examples of these types of flexible cords include hard service cord (types S, ST, SO, STO) and junior hard service cord (types SJ, SJO, SJT, SJTO).

(iii) *Guarding.* For temporary wiring over 600 volts, nominal, fencing, barriers, or other effective means shall be provided to prevent access of other than authorized and qualified personnel.

(b) *Cabinets, boxes, and fittings.* (1) *Conductors entering boxes, cabinets, or fittings.* Conductors entering boxes, cabinets, or fittings shall be protected from abrasion, and openings through which conductors enter shall be effectively closed. Unused openings in cabinets, boxes, and fittings shall also be effectively closed.

(2) *Covers and canopies.* All pull boxes, junction boxes, and fittings shall be provided with covers. If metal covers are used, they shall be grounded. In energized installations each outlet box shall have a cover, faceplate, or fixture canopy. Covers of outlet boxes having holes through which flexible cord pendants pass shall be provided with bushings de-

FIGURE 4.6 (*Continued*)   Installation Safety Requirements (OSHA-CFR Title 29, Part 1926, Subpart K, Paragraphs 402–408).

signed for the purpose or shall have smooth, well-rounded surfaces on which the cords may bear.

(3) *Pull and junction boxes for systems over 600 volts, nominal.* In addition to other requirements in this section for pull and junction boxes, the following shall apply to these boxes for systems over 600 volts, nominal:

(i) *Complete enclosure.* Boxes shall provide a complete enclosure for the contained conductors or cables.

(ii) *Covers.* Boxes shall be closed by covers securely fastened in place. Underground box covers that weigh over 100 pounds (43.6 kg) meet this requirement. Covers for boxes shall be permanently marked "HIGH VOLTAGE." The marking shall be on the outside of the box cover and shall be readily visible and legible.

(c) *Knife switches.* Single-throw knife switches shall be so connected that the blades are dead when the switch is in the open position. Single-throw knife switches shall be so placed that gravity will not tend to close them. Single-throw knife switches approved for use in the inverted position shall be provided with a locking device that will ensure that the blades remain in the open position when so set. Double-throw knife switches may be mounted so that the throw will be either vertical or horizontal. However, if the throw is vertical, a locking device shall be provided to ensure that the blades remain in the open position when so set.

(d) *Switchboards and panelboards.* Switchboards that have any exposed live parts shall be located in permanently dry locations and accessible only to qualified persons. Panelboards shall be mounted in cabinets, cutout boxes, or enclosures designed for the purpose and shall be dead front. However, panelboards other than the dead front externally-operable type are permitted where accessible only to qualified persons. Exposed blades of knife switches shall be dead when open.

(e) *Enclosures for damp or wet locations* (1) *Cabinets, fittings, and boxes.* Cabinets, cutout boxes, fittings, boxes, and panelboard enclosures in damp or wet locations shall be installed so as to prevent moisture or water from entering and accumulating within the en-

closures. In wet locations the enclosures shall be weatherproof.

(2) *Switches and circuit breakers.* Switches, circuit breakers, and switchboards installed in wet locations shall be enclosed in weatherproof enclosures.

(f) *Conductors for general wiring.* All conductors used for general wiring shall be insulated unless otherwise permitted in this Subpart. The conductor insulation shall be of a type that is suitable for the voltage, operating temperature, and location of use. Insulated conductors shall be distinguishable by appropriate color or other means as being grounded conductors, ungrounded conductors, or equipment grounding conductors.

(g) *Flexible cords and cables*—(1) *Use of flexible cords and cables*—(i) *Permitted uses.* Flexible cords and cables shall be suitable for conditions of use and location. Flexible cords and cables shall be used only for:

(A) Pendants;

(B) Wiring of fixtures;

(C) Connection of portable lamps or appliances;

(D) Elevator cables;

(E) Wiring of cranes and hoists;

(F) Connection of stationary equipment to facilitate their frequent interchange;

(G) Prevention of the transmission of noise or vibration; or

(H) Appliances where the fastening means and mechanical connections are designed to permit removal for maintenance and repair.

(ii) *Attachment plugs for cords.* If used as permitted in paragraphs (g)(1)(i)(C), (g)(1)(i)(F), or (g)(1)(i)(H) of this section, the flexible cord shall be equipped with an attachment plug and shall be energized from a receptacle outlet.

(iii) *Prohibited uses.* Unless necessary for a use permitted in paragraph (g)(1)(i) of this section, flexible cords and cables shall not be used:

(A) As a substitute for the fixed wiring of a structure;

(B) Where run through holes in walls, ceilings, or floors;

(C) Where run through doorways, windows, or similar openings, except as permitted in paragraph (a)(2)(ii)(1) of this section;

FIGURE 4.6 (*Continued*) Installation Safety Requirements (OSHA-CFR Title 29, Part 1926, Subpart K, Paragraphs 402–408).

(D) Where attached to building surfaces; or

(E) Where concealed behind building walls, ceilings, or floors.

(2) *Identification, splices, and terminations—(i) Identification.* A conductor of a flexible cord or cable that is used as a grounded conductor or an equipment grounding conductor shall be distinguishable from other conductors.

(ii) *Marking.* Type SJ, SJO, SJT, SJTO, S, SO, ST, and STO cords shall not be used unless durably marked on the surface with the type designation, size, and number of conductors.

(iii) *Splices.* Flexible cords shall be used only in continuous lengths without splice or tap. Hard service flexible cords No. 12 or larger may be repaired if spliced so that the splice retains the insulation, outer sheath properties, and usage characteristics of the cord being spliced.

(iv) *Strain relief.* Flexible cords shall be connected to devices and fittings so that strain relief is provided which will prevent pull from being directly transmitted to joints or terminal screws.

(v) *Cords passing through holes.* Flexible cords and cables shall be protected by bushings or fittings where passing through holes in covers, outlet boxes, or similar enclosures.

(h) *Portable cables over 600 volts, nominal.* Multiconductor portable cable for use in supplying power to portable or mobile equipment at over 600 volts, nominal, shall consist of No. 8 or larger conductors employing flexible stranding. Cables operated at over 2000 volts shall be shielded for the purpose of confining the voltage stresses to the insulation. Grounding conductors shall be provided. Connectors for these cables shall be of a locking type with provisions to prevent their opening or closing while energized. Strain relief shall be provided at connections and terminations. Portable cables shall not be operated with splices unless the splices are of the permanent molded, vulcanized, or other equivalent type. Termination enclosures shall be marked with a high voltage hazard warning, and terminations shall be accessible only to authorized and qualified personnel.

(i) *Fixture wires—(1) General.* Fixture wires shall be suitable for the voltage, temperature, and location of use. A fixture wire which is used as a grounded conductor shall be identified.

(2) *Uses permitted.* Fixture wires may be used:

(i) For installation in lighting, fixtures and in similar equipment where enclosed or protected and not subject to bending or twisting in use; or

(ii) For connecting lighting fixtures to the branch-circuit conductors supplying the fixtures.

(3) *Uses not permitted.* Fixture wires shall not be used as branch-circuit conductors except as permitted for Class 1 power-limited circuits.

(j) *Equipment for general use—(1) Lighting fixtures, lampholders, lamps, and receptacles—(i) Live parts.* Fixtures, lampholders, lamps, rosettes, and receptacles shall have no live parts normally exposed to employee contact. However, rosettes and cleat-type lampholders and receptacles located at least 8 feet (2.44 m) above the floor may have exposed parts.

(ii) *Support.* Fixtures, lampholders, rosettes, and receptacles shall be securely supported. A fixture that weighs more than 6 pounds (2.72 kg) or exceeds 16 inches (406 mm) in any dimension shall not be supported by the screw shell of a lampholder.

(iii) *Portable lamps.* Portable lamps shall be wired with flexible cord and an attachment plug of the polarized or grounding type. If the portable lamp uses an Edison-based lampholder, the grounded conductor shall be identified and attached to the screw shell and the identified blade of the attachment plug. In addition, portable handlamps shall comply with the following:

(A) Metal shell, paperlined lampholders shall not be used;

(B) Handlamps shall be equipped with a handle of molded composition or other insulating material;

(C) Handlamps shall be equipped with a substantial guard attached to the lampholder or handle;

(D) Metallic guards shall be grounded by the means of an equipment grounding conductor run within the power supply cord.

FIGURE 4.6 (*Continued*) Installation Safety Requirements (OSHA-CFR Title 29, Part 1926, Subpart K, Paragraphs 402–408).

(iv) *Lampholders.* Lampholders of the screw-shell type shall be installed for use as lampholders only. Lampholders installed in wet or damp locations shall be of the weatherproof type.

(v) *Fixtures.* Fixtures installed in wet or damp locations shall be identified for the purpose and shall be installed so that water cannot enter or accumulate in wireways, lampholders, or other electrical parts.

(2) *Receptacles, cord connectors, and attachment plugs (caps)—(i) Configuration.* Receptacles, cord connectors, and attachment plugs shall be constructed so that no receptacle or cord connector will accept an attachment plug with a different voltage or current rating than that for which the device is intended. However, a 20-ampere T-slot receptacle or cord connector may accept a 15-ampere attachment plug of the same voltage rating. Receptacles connected to circuits having different voltages, frequencies, or types of current (ac or dc) on the same premises shall be of such design that the attachment plugs used on these circuits are not interchangeable.

(ii) *Damp and wet locations.* A receptacle installed in a wet or damp location shall be designed for the location.

(3) *Appliances—(i) Live parts.* Appliances, other than those in which the current-carrying parts at high temperatures are necessarily exposed, shall have no live parts normally exposed to employee contact.

(ii) *Disconnecting means.* A means shall be provided to disconnect each appliance.

(iii) *Rating.* Each appliance shall be marked with its rating in volts and amperes or volts and watts.

(4) *Motors.* This paragraph applies to motors, motor circuits, and controllers.

(i) *In sight from.* If specified that one piece of equipment shall be "in sight from" another piece of equipment, one shall be visible and not more than 50 feet (15.2 m) from the other.

(ii) *Disconnecting means—(A)* A disconnecting means shall be located in sight from the controller location. The controller disconnecting means for motor branch circuits over 600 volts, nominal, may be out of sight of the controller, if the controller is marked with a warning label giving the location and identification of the disconnecting means which is to be locked in the open position.

(B) The disconnecting means shall disconnect the motor and the controller from all ungrounded supply conductors and shall be so designed that no pole can be operated independently.

(C) If a motor and the driven machinery are not in sight from the controller location, the installation shall comply with one of the following conditions:

(1) The controller disconnecting means shall be capable of being locked in the open position.

(2) A manually operable switch that will disconnect the motor from its source of supply shall be placed in sight from the motor location.

(D) The disconnecting means shall plainly indicate whether it is in the open (off) or closed (on) position.

(E) The disconnecting means shall be readily accessible. If more than one disconnect is provided for the same equipment, only one need be readily accessible.

(F) An individual disconnecting means shall be provided for each motor, but a single disconnecting means may be used for a group of motors under any one of the following conditions:

(1) If a number of motors drive special parts of a single machine or piece of apparatus, such as a metal or woodworking machine, crane, or hoist;

(2) If a group of motors is under the protection of one set of branch-circuit protective devices; or

(3) If a group of motors is in a single room in sight from the location of the disconnecting means.

(iii) *Motor overload, short-circuit, and ground-fault protection.* Motors, motor-control apparatus, and motor branch-circuit conductors shall be protected against overheating due to motor overloads or failure to start, and against short-circuits or ground faults. These provisions do not require overload protection that will stop a motor where a shutdown is likely to

FIGURE 4.6 (*Continued*)   Installation Safety Requirements (OSHA-CFR Title 29, Part 1926, Subpart K, Paragraphs 402–408).

introduce additional or increased hazards, as in the case of fire pumps, or where continued operation of a motor is necessary for a safe shutdown of equipment or process and motor overload sensing devices are connected to a supervised alarm.

(iv) *Protection of live parts—all voltages—*(A) Stationary motors having commutators, collectors, and brush rigging located inside of motor end brackets and not conductively connected to supply circuits operating at more than 150 volts to ground need not have such parts guarded. Exposed live parts of motors and controllers operating at 50 volts or more between terminals shall be guarded against accidental contact by any of the following:

(*1*) By installation in a room or enclosure that is accessible only to qualified persons;

(*2*) By installation on a balcony, gallery, or platform, so elevated and arranged as to exclude unqualified persons; or

(*3*) By elevation 8 feet (2.44 m) or more above the floor.

(B) Where live parts of motors and controllers operating at over 150 volts to ground are guarded against accidental contact only by location, and where adjustment or other attendance may be necessary during the operation of the apparatus, insulating mats or platforms shall be provided so that the attendant cannot readily touch live parts unless standing on the mats or platforms.

(5) *Transformers—*(i) *Application.* The following paragraphs cover the installation of all transformers, except:

(A) Current transformers;

(B) Dry-type transformers installed as a component part of other apparatus;

(C) Transformers which are an integral part of an X-ray, high frequency, or electrostatic-coating apparatus;

(D) Transformers used with Class 2 and Class 3 circuits, sign and outline lighting, electric discharge lighting, and power-limited fire-protective signaling circuits.

(ii) *Operating voltage.* The operating voltage of exposed live parts of transformer installations shall be indicated

by warning signs or visible markings on the equipment or structure.

(iii) *Transformers over 35 kV.* Dry-type, high fire point liquid-insulated, and askarel-insulated transformers installed indoors and rated over 35 kV shall be in a vault.

(iv) *Oil-insulated transformers.* If they present a fire hazard to employees, oil-insulated transformers installed indoors shall be in a vault.

(v) *Fire protection.* Combustible material, combustible buildings and parts of buildings, fire escapes, and door and window openings shall be safeguarded from fires which may originate in oil-insulated transformers attached to or adjacent to a building or combustible material.

(vi) *Transformer vaults.* Transformer vaults shall be constructed so as to contain fire and combustible liquids within the vault and to prevent unauthorized access. Locks and latches shall be so arranged that a vault door can be readily opened from the inside.

(vii) *Pipes and ducts.* Any pipe or duct system foreign to the vault installation shall not enter or pass through a transformer vault.

(viii) *Material storage.* Materials shall not be stored in transformer vaults.

(6) *Capacitors—*(i) *Drainage of stored charge.* All capacitors, except surge capacitors or capacitors included as a component part of other apparatus, shall be provided with an automatic means of draining the stored charge and maintaining the discharged state after the capacitor is disconnected from its source of supply.

(ii) *Over 600 volts.* Capacitors rated over 600 volts, nominal, shall comply with the following additional requirements:

(A) Isolating or disconnecting switches (with no interrupting rating) shall be interlocked with the load interrupting device or shall be provided with prominently displayed caution signs to prevent switching load current.

(B) For series capacitors the proper switching shall be assured by use of at least one of the following:

(*1*) Mechanically sequenced isolating and bypass switches,

(*2*) Interlocks, or

FIGURE 4.6 (*Continued*) Installation Safety Requirements (OSHA-CFR Title 29, Part 1926, Subpart K, Paragraphs 402–408).

(*3*) Switching procedure prominently displayed at the switching location.

(Information collection requirements contained in paragraphs (g)(2)(ii), (j)(3)(iii), (j)(4)(ii)(A), (j)(5)(ii), and (j)(6)(ii)(B)(*3*) were approved by the Office of Management and Budget under control number 1218-0130)

§ 1926.406 Specific purpose equipment and installations.

(a) *Cranes and hoists.* This paragraph applies to the installation of electric equipment and wiring used in connection with cranes, monorail hoists, hoists, and all runways.

(1) *Disconnecting means*—(i) *Runway conductor disconnecting means.* A readily accessible disconnecting means shall be provided between the runway contact conductors and the power supply.

(ii) *Disconnecting means for cranes and monorail hoists.* A disconnecting means, capable of being locked in the open position, shall be provided in the leads from the runway contact conductors or other power supply on any crane or monorail hoist.

(A) If this additional disconnecting means is not readily accessible from the crane or monorail hoist operating station, means shall be provided at the operating station to open the power circuit to all motors of the crane or monorail hoist.

(B) The additional disconnect may be omitted if a monorail hoist or hand-propelled crane bridge installation meets all of the following:

(*1*) The unit is floor controlled;

(*2*) The unit is within view of the power supply disconnecting means; and

(*3*) No fixed work platform has been provided for servicing the unit.

(2) *Control.* A limit switch or other device shall be provided to prevent the load block from passing the safe upper limit of travel of any hoisting mechanism.

(3) *Clearance.* The dimension of the working space in the direction of access to live parts which may require examination, adjustment, servicing, or maintenance while alive shall be a minimum of 2 feet 6 inches (762 mm). Where controls are enclosed in cabinets, the door(s) shall open at least 90

degrees or be removable, or the installation shall provide equivalent access.

(4) *Grounding.* All exposed metal parts of cranes, monorail hoists, hoists and accessories including pendant controls shall be metallically joined together into a continuous electrical conductor so that the entire crane or hoist will be grounded in accordance with § 1926.404(f). Moving parts, other than removable accessories or attachments, having metal-to-metal bearing surfaces shall be considered to be electrically connected to each other through the bearing surfaces for grounding purposes. The trolley frame and bridge frame shall be considered as electrically grounded through the bridge and trolley wheels and its respective tracks unless conditions such as paint or other insulating materials prevent reliable metal-to-metal contact. In this case a separate bonding conductor shall be provided.

(b) *Elevators, escalators, and moving walks*—(1) *Disconnecting means.* Elevators, escalators, and moving walks shall have a single means for disconnecting all ungrounded main power supply conductors for each unit.

(2) *Control panels.* If control panels are not located in the same space as the drive machine, they shall be located in cabinets with doors or panels capable of being locked closed.

(c) *Electric welders—disconnecting means*—(1) *Motor-generator, AC transformer, and DC rectifier arc welders.* A disconnecting means shall be provided in the supply circuit for each motor-generator arc welder, and for each AC transformer and DC rectifier arc welder which is not equipped with a disconnect mounted as an integral part of the welder.

(2) *Resistance welders.* A switch or circuit breaker shall be provided by which each resistance welder and its control equipment can be isolated from the supply circuit. The ampere rating of this disconnecting means shall not be less than the supply conductor ampacity.

(d) *X-Ray equipment*—(1) *Disconnecting means*—(i) *General.* A disconnecting means shall be provided in the supply circuit. The disconnecting means shall be operable from a location readily accessible from the X-ray

FIGURE 4.6 (*Continued*)   Installation Safety Requirements (OSHA-CFR Title 29, Part 1926, Subpart K, Paragraphs 402–408).

control. For equipment connected to a 120-volt branch circuit of 30 amperes or less, a grounding-type attachment plug cap and receptacle of proper rating may serve as a disconnecting means.

(ii) *More than one piece of equipment.* If more than one piece of equipment is operated from the same high-voltage circuit, each piece or each group of equipment as a unit shall be provided with a high-voltage switch or equivalent disconnecting means. This disconnecting means shall be constructed, enclosed, or located so as to avoid contact by employees with its live parts.

(2) *Control—Radiographic and fluoroscopic types.* Radiographic and fluoroscopic-type equipment shall be effectively enclosed or shall have interlocks that deenergize the equipment automatically to prevent ready access to live current-carrying parts.

§ 1926.407 **Hazardous (classified) locations.**

(a) *Scope.* This section sets forth requirements for electric equipment and wiring in locations which are classified depending on the properties of the flammable vapors, liquids or gases, or combustible dusts or fibers which may be present therein and the likelihood that a flammable or combustible concentration or quantity is present. Each room, section or area shall be considered individually in determining its classification. These hazardous (classified) locations are assigned six designations as follows:

Class I, Division 1
Class I, Division 2
Class II, Division 1
Class II, Division 2
Class III, Division 1
Class III, Division 2

For definitions of these locations see § 1926.449. All applicable requirements in this subpart apply to all hazardous (classified) locations, unless modified by provisions of this section.

(b) *Electrical installations.* Equipment, wiring methods, and installations of equipment in hazardous (classified) locations shall be approved as intrinsically safe or approved for the hazardous (classified) location or safe for the hazardous (classified) location.

Requirements for each of these options are as follows:

(1) *Intrinsically safe.* Equipment and associated wiring approved as intrinsically safe is permitted in any hazardous (classified) location included in its listing or labeling.

(2) *Approved for the hazardous (classified) location—(i) General.* Equipment shall be approved not only for the class of location but also for the ignitible or combustible properties of the specific gas, vapor, dust, or fiber that will be present.

NOTE: NFPA 70, the National Electrical Code, lists or defines hazardous gases, vapors, and dusts by "Groups" characterized by their ignitible or combustible properties.

(ii) *Marking.* Equipment shall not be used unless it is marked to show the class, group, and operating temperature or temperature range, based on operation in a 40-degree C ambient, for which it is approved. The temperature marking shall not exceed the ignition temperature of the specific gas, vapor, or dust to be encountered. However, the following provisions modify this marking requirement for specific equipment:

(A) Equipment of the non-heat-producing type (such as junction boxes, conduit, and fitting) and equipment of the heat-producing type having a maximum temperature of not more than 100 degrees C (212 degrees F) need not have a marked operating temperature or temperature range.

(B) Fixed lighting fixtures marked for use only in Class I, Division 2 locations need not be marked to indicate the group.

(C) Fixed general-purpose equipment in Class I locations, other than lighting fixtures, which is acceptable for use in Class I, Division 2 locations need not be marked with the class, group, division, or operating temperature.

(D) Fixed dust-tight equipment, other than lighting fixtures, which is acceptable for use in Class II, Division 2 and Class III locations need not be marked with the class, group, division, or operating temperature.

(3) *Safe for the hazardous (classified) location.* Equipment which is

FIGURE 4.6 (*Continued*)   Installation Safety Requirements (OSHA-CFR Title 29, Part 1926, Subpart K, Paragraphs 402–408).

safe for the location shall be of a type and design which the employer demonstrates will provide protection from the hazards arising from the combustibility and flammability of vapors, liquids, gases, dusts, or fibers.

NOTE: The National Electrical Code, NFPA 70, contains guidelines for determining the type and design of equipment and installations which will meet this requirement. The guidelines of this document address electric wiring, equipment, and systems installed in hazardous (classified) locations and contain specific provisions for the following: wiring methods, wiring connections, conductor insulation, flexible cords, sealing and drainage, transformers, capacitors, switches, circuit breakers, fuses, motor controllers, receptacles, attachment plugs, meters, relays, instruments, resistors, generators, motors, lighting fixtures, storage battery charging equipment, electric cranes, electric hoists and similar equipment, utilization equipment, signaling systems, alarm systems, remote control systems, local loud speaker and communication systems, ventilation piping, live parts, lightning surge protection, and grounding. Compliance with these guidelines will constitute one means, but not the only means, of compliance with this paragraph.

(c) *Conduits.* All conduits shall be threaded and shall be made wrench-tight. Where it is impractical to make a threaded joint tight, a bonding jumper shall be utilized.

(Information collection requirements contained in paragraph (b)(2)(ii) were approved by the Office of Management and Budget under control number 1218-0130)

§ 1926.408 Special systems.

(a) *Systems over 600 volts, nominal.* Paragraphs (a)(1) through (a)(4) of this section contain general requirements for all circuits and equipment operated at over 600 volts.

(1) *Wiring methods for fixed installations—(i) Above ground.* Above-ground conductors shall be installed in rigid metal conduit, in intermediate metal conduit, in cable trays, in cable-bus, in other suitable raceways, or as open runs of metal-clad cable designed for the use and purpose. However, open runs of non-metallic-sheathed cable or of bare conductors or busbars may be installed in locations which are accessible only to qualified persons. Metallic shielding components, such as tapes, wires, or braids for conductors,

shall be grounded. Open runs of insulated wires and cables having a bare lead sheath or a braided outer covering shall be supported in a manner designed to prevent physical damage to the braid or sheath.

(ii) *Installations emerging from the ground.* Conductors emerging from the ground shall be enclosed in raceways. Raceways installed on poles shall be of rigid metal conduit, intermediate metal conduit, PVC schedule 80 or equivalent extending from the ground line up to a point 8 feet (2.44 m) above finished grade. Conductors entering a building shall be protected by an enclosure from the ground line to the point of entrance. Metallic enclosures shall be grounded.

(2) *Interrupting and isolating devices—(i) Circuit breakers.* Circuit breakers located indoors shall consist of metal-enclosed or fire-resistant, cell-mounted units. In locations accessible only to qualified personnel, open mounting of circuit breakers is permitted. A means of indicating the open and closed position of circuit breakers shall be provided.

(ii) *Fused cutouts.* Fused cutouts installed in buildings or transformer vaults shall be of a type identified for the purpose. They shall be readily accessible for fuse replacement.

(iii) *Equipment isolating means.* A means shall be provided to completely isolate equipment for inspection and repairs. Isolating means which are not designed to interrupt the load current of the circuit shall be either inter-locked with a circuit interrupter or provided with a sign warning against opening them under load.

(3) *Mobile and portable equipment—(i) Power cable connections to mobile machines.* A metallic enclosure shall be provided on the mobile machine for enclosing the terminals of the power cable. The enclosure shall include provisions for a solid connection for the ground wire(s) terminal to ground effectively the machine frame. The method of cable termination used shall prevent any strain or pull on the cable from stressing the electrical connections. The enclosure shall have provision for locking so only authorized qualified persons may open it and

FIGURE 4.6 (*Continued*)   Installation Safety Requirements (OSHA-CFR Title 29, Part 1926, Subpart K, Paragraphs 402–408).

shall be marked with a sign warning of the presence of energized parts.

(ii) *Guarding live parts.* All energized switching and control parts shall be enclosed in effectively grounded metal cabinets or enclosures. Circuit breakers and protective equipment shall have the operating means projecting through the metal cabinet or enclosure so these units can be reset without locked doors being opened. Enclosures and metal cabinets shall be locked so that only authorized qualified persons have access and shall be marked with a sign warning of the presence of energized parts. Collector ring assemblies on revolving-type machines (shovels, draglines, etc.) shall be guarded.

(4) *Tunnel installations*—(i) *Application.* The provisions of this paragraph apply to installation and use of high-voltage power distribution and utilization equipment which is associated with tunnels and which is portable and/or mobile, such as substations, trailers, cars, mobile shovels, draglines, hoists, drills, dredges, compressors, pumps, conveyors, and underground excavators.

(ii) *Conductors.* Conductors in tunnels shall be installed in one or more of the following:

(A) Metal conduit or other metal raceway,

(B) Type MC cable, or

(C) Other suitable multiconductor cable.

Conductors shall also be so located or guarded as to protect them from physical damage. Multiconductor portable cable may supply mobile equipment. An equipment grounding conductor shall be run with circuit conductors inside the metal raceway or inside the multiconductor cable jacket. The equipment grounding conductor may be insulated or bare.

(iii) *Guarding live parts.* Bare terminals of transformers, switches, motor controllers, and other equipment shall be enclosed to prevent accidental contact with energized parts. Enclosures for use in tunnels shall be drip-proof, weatherproof, or submersible as required by the environmental conditions.

(iv) *Disconnecting means.* A disconnecting means that simultaneously opens all ungrounded conductors shall be installed at each transformer or motor location.

(v) *Grounding and bonding.* All non-energized metal parts of electric equipment and metal raceways and cable sheaths shall be grounded and bonded to all metal pipes and rails at the portal and at intervals not exceeding 1000 feet (305 m) throughout the tunnel.

(b) *Class 1, Class 2, and Class 3 remote control, signaling, and power-limited circuits*— (1) *Classification.* Class 1, Class 2, or Class 3 remote control, signaling, or power-limited circuits are characterized by their usage and electrical power limitation which differentiates them from light and power circuits. These circuits are classified in accordance with their respective voltage and power limitations as summarized in paragraphs (b)(1)(i) through (b)(1)(iii) of this section.

(i) *Class 1 circuits*—(A) A Class 1 power-limited circuit is supplied from a source having a rated output of not more than 30 volts and 1000 volt-amperes.

(B) A Class 1 remote control circuit or a Class 1 signaling circuit has a voltage which does not exceed 600 volts; however, the power output of the source need not be limited.

(ii) *Class 2 and Class 3 circuits*—(A) Power for Class 2 and Class 3 circuits is limited either inherently (in which no overcurrent protection is required) or by a combination of a power source and overcurrent protection.

(B) The maximum circuit voltage is 150 volts AC or DC for a Class 2 inherently limited power source, and 100 volts AC or DC for a Class 3 inherently limited power source.

(C) The maximum circuit voltage is 30 volts AC and 60 volts DC for a Class 2 power source limited by overcurrent protection, and 150 volts AC or DC for a Class 3 power source limited by overcurrent protection.

(iii) *Application.* The maximum circuit voltages in paragraphs (b)(1)(i) and (b)(1)(ii) of this section apply to sinusoidal AC or continuous DC power sources, and where wet contact occurrence is not likely.

(2) *Marking.* A Class 2 or Class 3 power supply unit shall not be used

FIGURE 4.6 (*Continued*) Installation Safety Requirements (OSHA-CFR Title 29, Part 1926, Subpart K, Paragraphs 402–408).

unless it is durably marked where plainly visible to indicate the class of supply and its electrical rating.

(c) *Communications systems*—(1) *Scope.* These provisions for communication systems apply to such systems as central-station-connected and non-central-station-connected telephone circuits, radio receiving and transmitting equipment, and outside wiring for fire and burglar alarm, and similar central station systems. These installations need not comply with the provisions of §§ 1926.403 through 1926.408(b), except § 1926.404(c)(1)(ii) and § 1926.407.

(2) *Protective devices*—(i) *Circuits exposed to power conductors.* Communication circuits so located as to be exposed to accidental contact with light or power conductors operating at over 300 volts shall have each circuit so exposed provided with an approved protector.

(ii) *Antenna lead-ins.* Each conductor of a lead-in from an outdoor antenna shall be provided with an antenna discharge unit or other means that will drain static charges from the antenna system.

(3) *Conductor location*—(i) *Outside of buildings*—(A) Receiving distribution lead-in or aerial-drop cables attached to buildings and lead-in conductors to radio transmitters shall be so installed as to avoid the possibility of accidental contact with electric light or power conductors.

(B) The clearance between lead-in conductors and any lightning protection conductors shall not be less than 6 feet (1.83 m).

(ii) *On poles.* Where practicable, communication conductors on poles shall be located below the light or power conductors. Communications conductors shall not be attached to a crossarm that carries light or power conductors.

(iii) *Inside of buildings.* Indoor antennas, lead-ins, and other communication conductors attached as open conductors to the inside of buildings shall be located at least 2 inches (50.8 mm) from conductors of any light or power or Class 1 circuits unless a special and equally protective method of conductor separation is employed.

(4) *Equipment location.* Outdoor metal structures supporting antennas, as well as self-supporting antennas such as vertical rods or dipole structures, shall be located as far away from overhead conductors of electric light and power circuits of over 150 volts to ground as necessary to avoid the possibility of the antenna or structure falling into or making accidental contact with such circuits.

(5) *Grounding*—(i) *Lead-in conductors.* If exposed to contact with electric light or power conductors, metal sheath of aerial cables entering buildings shall be grounded or shall be interrupted close to the entrance to the building by an insulating joint or equivalent device. Where protective devices are used, they shall be grounded.

(ii) *Antenna structures.* Masts and metal structures supporting antennas shall be permanently and effectively grounded without splice or connection in the grounding conductor.

(iii) *Equipment enclosures.* Transmitters shall be enclosed in a metal frame or grill or separated from the operating space by a barrier, all metallic parts of which are effectively connected to ground. All external metal handles and controls accessible to the operating personnel shall be effectively grounded. Unpowered equipment and enclosures shall be considered grounded where connected to an attached coaxial cable with an effectively grounded metallic shield.

(Information collection requirements contained in paragraph (b)(2) were approved by the Office of Management and Budget under control number 1218-0130)

FIGURE 4.6 (*Continued*) Installation Safety Requirements (OSHA-CFR Title 29, Part 1926, Subpart K, Paragraphs 402–408).

SAFETY-RELATED WORK PRACTICES

§ 1926.416 General requirements.

(a) *Protection of employees*—(1) No employer shall permit an employee to work in such proximity to any part of an electric power circuit that the employee could contact the electric power circuit in the course of work, unless the employee is protected against electric shock by deenergizing the circuit and grounding it or by guarding it effectively by insulation or other means.

(2) In work areas where the exact location of underground electric power-lines is unknown, employees using jack-hammers, bars, or other hand tools which may contact a line shall be provided with insulated protective gloves.

(3) Before work is begun the employer shall ascertain by inquiry or direct observation, or by instruments, whether any part of an energized electric power circuit, exposed or concealed, is so located that the performance of the work may bring any person, tool, or machine into physical or electrical contact with the electric power circuit. The employer shall post and maintain proper warning signs where such a circuit exists. The employer shall advise employees of the location of such lines, the hazards involved, and the protective measures to be taken.

(b) *Passageways and open spaces*— (1) Barriers or other means of guarding shall be provided to ensure that workspace for electrical equipment will not be used as a passageway during periods when energized parts of electrical equipment are exposed.

(2) Working spaces, walkways, and similar locations shall be kept clear of cords so as not to create a hazard to employees.

(c) *Load ratings.* In existing installations, no changes in circuit protection shall be made to increase the load in excess of the load rating of the circuit wiring.

(d) *Fuses.* When fuses are installed or removed with one or both terminals energized, special tools insulated for the voltage shall be used.

(e) *Cords and cables.* (1) Worn or frayed electric cords or cables shall not be used.

(2) Extension cords shall not be fastened with staples, hung from nails, or suspended by wire.

§ 1926.417 Lockout and tagging of circuits.

(a) *Controls.* Controls that are to be deactivated during the course of work on energized or deenergized equipment or circuits shall be tagged.

(b) *Equipment and circuits.* Equipment or circuits that are deenergized shall be rendered inoperative and shall have tags attached at all points where such equipment or circuits can be energized.

(c) *Tags.* Tags shall be placed to identify plainly the equipment or circuits being worked on.

FIGURE 4.7 Safety-Related Work Practices for Construction Workers (OSHA-CFR Title 29, Part 1926, Subpart K, Paragraphs 416–417).

SAFETY-RELATED MAINTENANCE AND
ENVIRONMENTAL CONSIDERATIONS

§1926.431 Maintenance of equipment.

The employer shall ensure that all wiring components and utilization equipment in hazardous locations are maintained in a dust-tight, dust-ignition-proof, or explosion-proof condition, as appropriate. There shall be no loose or missing screws, gaskets, threaded connections, seals, or other impairments to a tight condition.

§1926.432 Environmental deterioration of equipment.

(a) *Deteriorating agents*—(1) Unless identified for use in the operating environment, no conductors or equipment shall be located:

(i) In damp or wet locations;

(ii) Where exposed to gases, fumes, vapors, liquids, or other agents having a deteriorating effect on the conductors or equipment; or

(iii) Where exposed to excessive temperatures.

(2) Control equipment, utilization equipment, and busways approved for use in dry locations only shall be protected against damage from the weather during building construction.

(b) *Protection against corrosion.* Metal raceways, cable armor, boxes, cable sheathing, cabinets, elbows, couplings, fittings, supports, and support hardware shall be of materials appropriate for the environment in which they are to be installed.

FIGURE 4.8 Safety-Related Maintenance and Environmental Considerations (OSHA-CFR Title 29, Part 1926, Subpart K, Paragraphs 431–432).

SAFETY REQUIREMENTS FOR SPECIAL EQUIPMENT

§ 1926.441 Batteries and battery charging.

(a) *General requirements*—(1) Batteries of the unsealed type shall be located in enclosures with outside vents or in well ventilated rooms and shall be arranged so as to prevent the escape of fumes, gases, or electrolyte spray into other areas.

(2) Ventilation shall be provided to ensure diffusion of the gases from the battery and to prevent the accumulation of an explosive mixture.

(3) Racks and trays shall be substantial and shall be treated to make them resistant to the electrolyte.

(4) Floors shall be of acid resistant construction unless protected from acid accumulations.

(5) Face shields, aprons, and rubber gloves shall be provided for workers handling acids or batteries.

(6) Facilities for quick drenching of the eyes and body shall be provided within 25 feet (7.62 m) of battery handling areas.

(7) Facilities shall be provided for flushing and neutralizing spilled electrolyte and for fire protection.

(b) *Charging*—(1) Battery charging installations shall be located in areas designated for that purpose.

(2) Charging apparatus shall be protected from damage by trucks.

(3) When batteries are being charged, the vent caps shall be kept in place to avoid electrolyte spray. Vent caps shall be maintained in functioning condition.

FIGURE 4.9 Safety Requirements for Special Equipment (OSHA-CFR Title 29, Part 1926, Subpart K, Paragraph 441).

fied testing laboratory accepts, certifies, lists, labels, or determines to be safe, if it is inspected or tested by another Federal agency, or by a State, municipal, or other local authority responsible for enforcing occupational safety provisions of the National Electrical Code, and found in compliance with those provisions; or

(c) With respect to custom-made equipment or related installations which are designed, fabricated for, and intended for use by a particular customer, if it is determined to be safe for its intended use by its manufacturer on the basis of test data which the employer keeps and makes available for inspection to the Assistant Secretary and his authorized representatives.

Accepted. An installation is "accepted" if it has been inspected and found to be safe by a qualified testing laboratory.

Accessible. (As applied to wiring methods.) Capable of being removed or exposed without damaging the building structure or finish, or not permanently closed in by the structure or finish of the building. (See *"concealed"* and *"exposed."*)

Accessible. (As applied to equipment.) Admitting close approach; not guarded by locked doors, elevation, or other effective means. (See *"Readily accessible."*)

Ampacity. The current in amperes a conductor can carry continuously under the conditions of use without exceeding its temperature rating.

Appliances. Utilization equipment, generally other than industrial, normally built in standardized sizes or types, which is installed or conneceted as a unit to perform one or more functions.

Approved. Acceptable to the authority enforcing this Subpart. The authority enforcing this Subpart is the Assistant Secretary of Labor for Occupational Safety and Health. The definition of "acceptable" indicates what is acceptable to the Assistant Secretary of Labor, and therefore approved within the meaning of this Subpart.

Askarel. A generic term for a group of nonflammable synthetic chlorinated hydrocarbons used as electrical insulating media. Askarels of various compositional types are used. Under

DEFINITIONS

§ 1926.449 Definitions applicable to this subpart.

The definitions given in this section apply to the terms used in Subpart K. The definitions given here for "approved" and "qualified person" apply, instead of the definitions given in § 1926.32, to the use of these terms in Subpart K.

Acceptable. An installation or equipment is acceptable to the Assistant Secretary of Labor, and approved within the meaning of this Subpart K:

(a) If it is accepted, or certified, or listed, or labeled, or otherwise determined to be safe by a qualified testing laboratory capable of determining the suitability of materials and equipment for installation and use in accordance with this standard; or

(b) With respect to an installation or equipment of a kind which no quali-

FIGURE 4.10   Definitions Applying to Part 1926, Subpart K (OSHA-CFR Title 29, Part 1926, Subpart K, Paragraph 449).

arcing conditions the gases produced, while consisting predominantly of noncombustible hydrogen chloride, can include varying amounts of combustible gases depending upon the askarel type.

Attachment plug (Plug cap)(Cap). A device which, by insertion in a receptacle, establishes connection between the conductors of the attached flexible cord and the conductors connected permanently to the receptacle.

Automatic. Self-acting, operating by its own mechanism when actuated by some impersonal influence, as for example, a change in current strength, pressure, temperature, or mechanical configuration.

Bare conductor. See "Conductor."

Bonding. The permanent joining of metallic parts to form an electrically conductive path which will assure electrical continuity and the capacity to conduct safely any current likely to be imposed.

Bonding jumper. A reliable conductor to assure the required electrical conductivity between metal parts required to be electrically connected.

Branch circuit. The circuit conductors between the final overcurrent device protecting the circuit and the outlet(s).

Building. A structure which stands alone or which is cut off from adjoining structures by fire walls with all openings therein protected by approved fire doors.

Cabinet. An enclosure designed either for surface or flush mounting, and provided with a frame, mat, or trim in which a swinging door or doors are or may be hung.

Certified. Equipment is "certified" if it:

(a) Has been tested and found by a qualified testing laboratory to meet applicable test standards or to be safe for use in a specified manner, and

(b) Is of a kind whose production is periodically inspected by a qualified testing laboratory. Certified equipment must bear a label, tag, or other record of certification.

Circuit breaker—(a) (600 volts nominal, or less.) A device designed to open and close a circuit by nonautomatic means and to open the circuit automatically on a predetermined overcur-

rent without injury to itself when properly applied within its rating.

(b) (Over 600 volts, nominal.) A switching device capable of making, carrying, and breaking currents under normal circuit conditions, and also making, carrying for a specified time, and breaking currents under specified abnormal circuit conditions, such as those of short circuit.

Class I locations. Class I locations are those in which flammable gases or vapors are or may be present in the air in quantities sufficient to produce explosive or ignitible mixtures. Class I locations include the following:

(a) *Class I, Division 1.* A Class I, Division 1 location is a location:

(1) In which ignitible concentrations of flammable gases or vapors may exist under normal operating conditions; or

(2) In which ignitible concentrations of such gases or vapors may exist frequently because of repair or maintenance operations or because of leakage; or

(3) In which breakdown or faulty operation of equipment or processes might release ignitible concentrations of flammable gases or vapors, and might also cause simultaneous failure of electric equipment.

NOTE: This classification usually includes locations where volatile flammable liquids or liquefied flammable gases are transferred from one container to another; interiors of spray booths and areas in the vicinity of spraying and painting operations where volatile flammable solvents are used; locations containing open tanks or vats of volatile flammable liquids; drying rooms or compartments for the evaporation of flammable solvents; inadequately ventilated pump rooms for flammable gas or for volatile flammable liquids; and all other locations where ignitible concentrations of flammable vapors or gases are likely to occur in the course of normal operations.

(b) *Class I, Division 2.* A Class I, Division 2 location is a location:

(1) In which volatile flammable liquids or flammable gases are handled, processed, or used, but in which the hazardous liquids, vapors, or gases will normally be confined within closed containers or closed systems from which they can escape only in case of accidental rupture or breakdown of

FIGURE 4.10 (*Continued*) Definitions Applying to Part 1926, Subpart K (OSHA-CFR Title 29, Part 1926, Subpart K, Paragraph 449).

such containers or systems, or in case of abnormal operation of equipment; or

(2) In which ignitible concentrations of gases or vapors are normally prevented by positive mechanical ventilation, and which might become hazardous through failure or abnormal operations of the ventilating equipment; or

(3) That is adjacent to a Class I, Division 1 location, and to which ignitible concentrations of gases or vapors might occasionally be communicated unless such communication is prevented by adequate positive-pressure ventilation from a source of clean air, and effective safeguards against ventilation failure are provided.

NOTE: This classification usually includes locations where volatile flammable liquids or flammable gases or vapors are used, but which would become hazardous only in case of an accident or of some unusual operating condition. The quantity of flammable material that might escape in case of accident, the adequacy of ventilating equipment, the total area involved, and the record of the industry or business with respect to explosions or fires are all factors that merit consideration in determining the classification and extent of each location.

Piping without valves, checks, meters, and similar devices would not ordinarily introduce a hazardous condition even though used for flammable liquids or gases. Locations used for the storage of flammable liquids or of liquefied or compressed gases in sealed containers would not normally be considered hazardous unless also subject to other hazardous conditions.

Electrical conduits and their associated enclosures separated from process fluids by a single seal or barrier are classed as a Division 2 location if the outside of the conduit and enclosures is a nonhazardous location.

Class II locations. Class II locations are those that are hazardous because of the presence of combustible dust. Class II locations include the following:

(a) *Class II, Division 1.* A Class II, Division 1 location is a location:

(1) In which combustible dust is or may be in suspension in the air under normal operating conditions, in quantities sufficient to produce explosive or ignitible mixtures; or

(2) Where mechanical failure or abnormal operation of machinery or equipment might cause such explosive or ignitible mixtures to be produced,

and might also provide a source of ignition through simultaneous failure of electric equipment, operation of protection devices, or from other causes, or

(3) In which combustible dusts of an electrically conductive nature may be present.

NOTE: Combustible dusts which are electrically nonconductive include dusts produced in the handling and processing of grain and grain products, pulverized sugar and cocoa, dried egg and milk powders, pulverized spices, starch and pastes, potato and wood-flour, oil meal from beans and seed, dried hay, and other organic materials which may produce combustible dusts when processed or handled. Dusts containing magnesium or aluminum are particularly hazardous and the use of extreme caution is necessary to avoid ignition and explosion.

(b) *Class II, Division 2.* A Class II, Division 2 location is a location in which:

(1) Combustible dust will not normally be in suspension in the air in quantities sufficient to produce explosive or ignitible mixtures, and dust accumulations are normally insufficient to interfere with the normal operation of electrical equipment or other apparatus; or

(2) Dust may be in suspension in the air as a result of infrequent malfunctioning of handling or processing equipment, and dust accumulations resulting therefrom may be ignitible by abnormal operation or failure of electrical equipment or other apparatus.

NOTE: This classification includes locations where dangerous concentrations of suspended dust would not be likely but where dust accumulations might form on or in the vicinity of electric equipment. These areas may contain equipment from which appreciable quantities of dust would escape under abnormal operating conditions or be adjacent to a Class II Division 1 location, as described above, into which an explosive or ignitible concentration of dust may be put into suspension under abnormal operating conditions.

Class III locations. Class III locations are those that are hazardous because of the presence of easily ignitible fibers or flyings but in which such fibers or flyings are not likely to be in suspension in the air in quantities sufficient to produce ignitible mixtures.

FIGURE 4.10 (*Continued*) Definitions Applying to Part 1926, Subpart K (OSHA-CFR Title 29, Part 1926, Subpart K, Paragraph 449).

Class 111 locations include the following:

(a) *Class III, Division 1.* A Class III, Division 1 location is a location in which easily ignitible fibers or materials producing combustible flyings are handled, manufactured, or used.

NOTE: Easily ignitible fibers and flyings include rayon, cotton (including cotton linters and cotton waste), sisal or henequen, istle, jute, hemp, tow, cocoa fiber, oakum, baled waste kapok, Spanish moss, excelsior, sawdust, woodchips, and other material of similar nature.

(b) *Class III, Division 2.* A Class III, Division 2 location is a location in which easily ignitible fibers are stored or handled, except in process of manufacture.

Collector ring. A collector ring is an assembly of slip rings for transferring electrical energy from a stationary to a rotating member.

Concealed. Rendered inaccessible by the structure or finish of the building. Wires in concealed raceways are considered concealed, even though they may become accessible by withdrawing them. [See *"Accessible."* (As applied to wiring methods.)"]

Conductor—(a) *Bare.* A conductor having no covering or electrical insulation whatsoever.

(b) *Covered.* A conductor encased within material of composition or thickness that is not recognized as electrical insulation.

(c) *Insulated.* A conductor encased within material of composition and thickness that is recognized as electrical insulation.

Controller. A device or group of devices that serves to govern, in some predetermined manner, the electric power delivered to the apparatus to which it is connected.

Covered conductor. See *"Conductor."*

Cutout. (Over 600 volts, nominal.) An assembly of a fuse support with either a fuseholder, fuse carrier, or disconnecting blade. The fuseholder or fuse carrier may include a conducting element (fuse link), or may act as the disconnecting blade by the inclusion of a nonfusible member.

Cutout box. An enclosure designed for surface mounting and having swinging doors or covers secured directly to and telescoping with the walls of the box proper. (See *"Cabinet."*)

Damp location. See *"Location."*

Dead front. Without live parts exposed to a person on the operating side of the equipment.

Device. A unit of an electrical system which is intended to carry but not utilize electric energy.

Disconnecting means. A device, or group of devices, or other means by which the conductors of a circuit can be disconnected from their source of supply.

Disconnecting (or Isolating) switch. (Over 600 volts, nominal.) A mechanical switching device used for isolating a circuit or equipment from a source of power.

Dry location. See *"Location."*

Enclosed. Surrounded by a case, housing, fence or walls which will prevent persons from accidentally contacting energized parts.

Enclosure. The case or housing of apparatus, or the fence or walls surrounding an installation to prevent personnel from accidentally contacting energized parts, or to protect the equipment from physical damage.

Equipment. A general term including material, fittings, devices, appliances, fixtures, apparatus, and the like, used as a part of, or in connection with, an electrical installation.

Equipment grounding conductor. See *"Grounding conductor, equipment."*

Explosion-proof apparatus. Apparatus enclosed in a case that is capable of withstanding an explosion of a specified gas or vapor which may occur within it and of preventing the ignition of a specified gas or vapor surrounding the enclosure by sparks, flashes, or explosion of the gas or vapor within, and which operates at such an external temperature that it will not ignite a surrounding flammable atmosphere.

Exposed. (As applied to live parts.) Capable of being inadvertently touched or approached nearer than a safe distance by a person. It is applied to parts not suitably guarded, isolated, or insulated. (See *"Accessible"* and *"Concealed."*)

FIGURE 4.10 (*Continued*)   Definitions Applying to Part 1926, Subpart K (OSHA-CFR Title 29, Part 1926, Subpart K, Paragraph 449).

Exposed. (As applied to wiring methods.) On or attached to the surface or behind panels designed to allow access. [See *"Accessible.* (As applied to wiring methods.)"]

Exposed. (For the purposes of § 1926.408(d), Communications systems.) Where the circuit is in such a position that in case of failure of supports or insulation, contact with another circuit may result.

Externally operable. Capable of being operated without exposing the operator to contact with live parts.

Feeder. All circuit conductors between the service equipment, or the generator switchboard of an isolated plant, and the final branch-circuit overcurrent device.

Festoon lighting. A string of outdoor lights suspended between two points more than 15 feet (4.57 m) apart.

Fitting. An accessory such as a locknut, bushing, or other part of a wiring system that is intended primarily to perform a mechanical rather than an electrical function.

Fuse. (Over 600 volts, nominal.) An overcurrent protective device with a circuit opening fusible part that is heated and severed by the passage of overcurrent through it. A fuse comprises all the parts that form a unit capable of performing the prescribed functions. It may or may not be the complete device necessary to connect it into an electrical circuit.

Ground. A conducting connection, whether intentional or accidental, between an electrical circuit or equipment and the earth, or to some conducting body that serves in place of the earth.

Grounded. Connected to earth or to some conducting body that serves in place of the earth.

Grounded, effectively (Over 600 volts, nominal.) Permanently connected to earth through a ground connection of sufficiently low impedance and having sufficient ampacity that ground fault current which may occur cannot build up to voltages dangerous to personnel.

Grounded conductor. A system or circuit conductor that is intentionally grounded.

Grounding conductor. A conductor used to connect equipment or the grounded circuit of a wiring system to a grounding electrode or electrodes.

Grounding conductor, equipment. The conductor used to connect the noncurrent-carrying metal parts of equipment, raceways, and other enclosures to the system grounded conductor and/or the grounding electrode conductor at the service equipment or at the source of a separately derived system.

Grounding electrode conductor. The conductor used to connect the grounding electrode to the equipment grounding conductor and/or to the grounded conductor of the circuit at the service equipment or at the source of a separately derived system.

Ground-fault circuit interrupter. A device for the protection of personnel that functions to deenergize a circuit or portion thereof within an established period of time when a current to ground exceeds some predetermined value that is less than that required to operate the overcurrent protective device of the supply circuit.

Guarded. Covered, shielded, fenced, enclosed, or otherwise protected by means of suitable covers, casings, barriers, rails, screens, mats, or platforms to remove the likelihood of approach to a point of danger or contact by persons or objects.

Hoistway. Any shaftway, hatchway, well hole, or other vertical opening or space in which an elevator or dumbwaiter is designed to operate.

Identified (conductors or terminals). Identified, as used in reference to a conductor or its terminal, means that such conductor or terminal can be recognized as grounded.

Identified (for the use). Recognized as suitable for the specific purpose, function, use, environment, application, etc. where described as a requirement in this standard. Suitability of equipment for a specific purpose, environment, or application is determined by a qualified testing laboratory where such identification includes labeling or listing.

Insulated conductor. See *"Conductor."*

Interrupter switch. (Over 600 volts, nominal.) A switch capable of making, carrying, and interrupting specified currents.

FIGURE 4.10 (*Continued*) Definitions Applying to Part 1926, Subpart K (OSHA-CFR Title 29, Part 1926, Subpart K, Paragraph 449).

Intrinsically safe equipment and associated wiring. Equipment and associated wiring in which any spark or thermal effect, produced either normally or in specified fault conditions, is incapable, under certain prescribed test conditions, of causing ignition of a mixture of flammable or combustible material in air in its most easily ignitible concentration.

Isolated. Not readily accessible to persons unless special means for access are used.

Isolated power system. A system comprising an isolating transformer or its equivalent, a line isolation monitor, and its ungrounded circuit conductors.

Labeled. Equipment or materials to which has been attached a label, symbol or other identifying mark of a qualified testing laboratory which indicates compliance with appropriate standards or performance in a specified manner.

Lighting outlet. An outlet intended for the direct connection of a lampholder, a lighting fixture, or a pendant cord terminating in a lampholder.

Listed. Equipment or materials included in a list published by a qualified testing laboratory whose listing states either that the equipment or material meets appropriate standards or has been tested and found suitable for use in a specified manner.

Location—(a) *Damp location.* Partially protected locations under canopies, marquees, roofed open porches, and like locations, and interior locations subject to moderate degrees of moisture, such as some basements.

(b) *Dry location.* A location not normally subject to dampness or wetness. A location classified as dry may be temporarily subject to dampness or wetness, as in the case of a building under construction.

(c) *Wet location.* Installations underground or in concrete slabs or masonry in direct contact with the earth, and locations subject to saturation with water or other liquids, such as locations exposed to weather and unprotected.

Mobile X-ray. X-ray equipment mounted on a permanent base with wheels and/or casters for moving while completely assembled.

Motor control center. An assembly of one or more enclosed sections having a common power bus and principally containing motor control units.

Outlet. A point on the wiring system at which current is taken to supply utilization equipment.

Overcurrent. Any current in excess of the rated current of equipment or the ampacity of a conductor. It may result from overload (see definition), short circuit, or ground fault. A current in excess of rating may be accommodated by certain equipment and conductors for a given set of conditions. Hence the rules for overcurrent protection are specific for particular situations.

Overload. Operation of equipment in excess of normal, full load rating, or of a conductor in excess of rated ampacity which, when it persists for a sufficient length of time, would cause damage or dangerous overheating. A fault, such as a short circuit or ground fault, is not an overload. (See"*Overcurrent.*")

Panelboard. A single panel or group of panel units designed for assembly in the form of a single panel; including buses, automatic overcurrent devices, and with or without switches for the control of light, heat, or power circuits; designed to be placed in a cabinet or cutout box placed in or against a wall or partition and accessible only from the front. (See "*Switchboard.*")

Portable X-ray. X-ray equipment designed to be hand-carried.

Power fuse. (Over 600 volts, nominal.) See "*Fuse.*"

Power outlet. An enclosed assembly which may include receptacles, circuit breakers, fuseholders, fused switches, buses and watt-hour meter mounting means; intended to serve as a means for distributing power required to operate mobile or temporarily installed equipment.

Premises wiring system. That interior and exterior wiring, including power, lighting, control, and signal circuit wiring together with all of its associated hardware, fittings, and wiring devices, both permanently and temporarily installed, which extends from the load end of the service drop, or load end of the service lateral conductors to the outlet(s). Such wiring does

FIGURE 4.10 (*Continued*) Definitions Applying to Part 1926, Subpart K (OSHA-CFR Title 29, Part 1926, Subpart K, Paragraph 449).

not include wiring internal to appliances, fixtures, motors, controllers, motor control centers, and similar equipment.

Qualified person. One familiar with the construction and operation of the equipment and the hazards involved.

Qualified testing laboratory. A properly equipped and staffed testing laboratory which has capabilities for and which provides the following services:

(a) Experimental testing for safety of specified items of equipment and materials referred to in this standard to determine compliance with appropriate test standards or performance in a specified manner;

(b) Inspecting the run of such items of equipment and materials at factories for product evaluation to assure compliance with the test standards;

(c) Service-value determinations through field inspections to monitor the proper use of labels on products and with authority for recall of the label in the event a hazardous product is installed;

(d) Employing a controlled procedure for identifying the listed and/or labeled equipment or materials tested; and

(e) Rendering creditable reports and findings that are objective and without bias of the tests and test methods employed.

Raceway. A channel designed expressly for holding wires, cables, or busbars, with additional functions as permitted in this subpart. Raceways may be of metal or insulating material, and the term includes rigid metal conduit, rigid nonmetallic conduit, intermediate metal conduit, liquidtight flexible metal conduit, flexible metallic tubing, flexible metal conduit, electrical metallic tubing, underfloor raceways, cellular concrete floor raceways, cellular metal floor raceways, surface raceways, wireways, and busways.

Readily accessible. Capable of being reached quickly for operation, renewal, or inspections, without requiring those to whom ready access is requisite to climb over or remove obstacles or to resort to portable ladders, chairs, etc. (See *"Accessible."*)

Receptacle. A receptacle is a contact device installed at the outlet for the connection of a single attachment plug. A single receptacle is a single contact device with no other contact device on the same yoke. A multiple receptacle is a single device containing two or more receptacles.

Receptacle outlet. An outlet where one or more receptacles are installed.

Remote-control circuit. Any electric circuit that controls any other circuit through a relay or an equivalent device.

Sealable equipment. Equipment enclosed in a case or cabinet that is provided with a means of sealing or locking so that live parts cannot be made accessible without opening the enclosure. The equipment may or may not be operable without opening the enclosure.

Separately derived system. A premises wiring system whose power is derived from generator, transformer, or converter windings and has no direct electrical connection, including a solidly connected grounded circuit conductor, to supply conductors originating in another system.

Service. The conductors and equipment for delivering energy from the electricity supply system to the wiring system of the premises served.

Service conductors. The supply conductors that extend from the street main or from transformers to the service equipment of the premises supplied.

Service drop. The overhead service conductors from the last pole or other aerial support to and including the splices, if any, connecting to the service-entrance conductors at the building or other structure.

Service-entrance conductors, overhead system. The service conductors between the terminals of the service equipment and a point usually outside the building, clear of building walls, where joined by tap or splice to the service drop.

Service-entrance conductors, underground system. The service conductors between the terminals of the service equipment and the point of connection to the service lateral. Where service equipment is located outside the building walls, there may be no service-entrance conductors, or they may be entirely outside the building.

FIGURE 4.10 (*Continued*)   Definitions Applying to Part 1926, Subpart K (OSHA-CFR Title 29, Part 1926, Subpart K, Paragraph 449).

Service equipment. The necessary equipment, usually consisting of a circuit breaker or switch and fuses, and their accessories, located near the point of entrance of supply conductors to a building or other structure, or an otherwise defined area, and intended to constitute the main control and means of cutoff of the supply.

Service raceway. The raceway that encloses the service-entrance conductors.

Signaling circuit. Any electric circuit that energizes signaling equipment.

Switchboard. A large single panel, frame, or assembly of panels which have switches, instruments, overcurrent and other protective devices mounted on the face or back or both. Switchboards are generally accessible from the rear as well as from the front and are not intended to be installed in cabinets. (See "Panelboard.")

Switches—(a) *General-use switch.* A switch intended for use in general distribution and branch circuits. It is rated in amperes, and it is capable of interrupting its rated current at its rated voltage.

(b) *General-use snap switch.* A form of general-use switch so constructed that it can be installed in flush device boxes or on outlet box covers, or otherwise used in conjunction with wiring systems recognized by this subpart.

(c) *Isolating switch.* A switch intended for isolating an electric circuit from the source of power. It has no interrupting rating, and it is intended to be operated only after the circuit has been opened by some other means.

(d) *Motor-circuit switch.* A switch, rated in horsepower, capable of interrupting the maximum operating overload current of a motor of the same horsepower rating as the switch at the rated voltage.

Switching devices. (Over 600 volts, nominal.) Devices designed to close and/or open one or more electric circuits. Included in this category are circuit breakers, cutouts, disconnecting (or isolating) switches, disconnecting means, and interrupter switches.

Transportable X-ray. X-ray equipment installed in a vehicle or that may readily be disassembled for transport in a vehicle.

Utilization equipment. Utilization equipment means equipment which utilizes electric energy for mechanical, chemical, heating, lighting, or similar useful purpose.

Utilization system. A utilization system is a system which provides electric power and light for employee workplaces, and includes the premises wiring system and utilization equipment.

Ventilated. Provided with a means to permit circulation of air sufficient to remove an excess of heat, fumes, or vapors.

Volatile flammable liquid. A flammable liquid having a flash point below 38 degrees C (100 degrees F) or whose temperature is above its flash point, or a Class II combustible liquid having a vapor pressure not exceeding 40 psia (276 kPa) at 38° C (100° F) whose temperature is above its flash point.

Voltage. (Of a circuit.) The greatest root-mean-square (effective) difference of potential between any two conductors of the circuit concerned.

Voltage, nominal. A nominal value assigned to a circuit or system for the purpose of conveniently designating its voltage class (as 120/240, 480Y/277, 600, etc.). The actual voltage at which a circuit operates can vary from the nominal within a range that permits satisfactory operation of equipment.

Voltage to ground. For grounded circuits, the voltage between the given conductor and that point or conductor of the circuit that is grounded; for ungrounded circuits, the greatest voltage between the given conductor and any other conductor of the circuit.

Watertight. So constructed that moisture will not enter the enclosure.

Weatherproof. So constructed or protected that exposure to the weather will not interfere with successful operation. Rainproof, raintight, or watertight equipment can fulfill the requirements for weatherproof where varying weather conditions other than wetness, such as snow, ice, dust, or temperature extremes, are not a factor.

Wet location. See "Location."

FIGURE 4.10 (*Continued*) Definitions Applying to Part 1926, Subpart K (OSHA-CFR Title 29, Part 1926, Subpart K, Paragraph 449).

CHAPTER 5
ACCIDENT PREVENTION, ACCIDENT INVESTIGATION, RESCUE, AND FIRST AID

ACCIDENT PREVENTION

No matter how carefully a system is engineered, no matter how carefully employees perform their tasks, and no matter how well trained employees are in the recognition and avoidance of hazards, accidents still happen. This section provides a general approach that may be employed to reduce the number and severity of accidents. Four basic steps—employee responsibility, safe installations, safe work practices, and employee training–combine to create the type of safe work environment that should be the goal of every facility.

Individual Responsibility

The person most responsible for your own personal safety is you. No set of regulations, rules, or procedures can ever replace common sense in the workplace. This statement should not be construed to mean an employer has no responsibility to the safest practical work environment, nor does it mean that the injured person is "at fault" in a legal sense. Determining responsibility for accidents is, in part, a legal problem and is beyond the scope of this handbook.

Time after time, accident investigations reveal that the injured person was the last link in the chain. If the injured person had only been wearing their safety equipment or following proper procedures, or if they had only checked one last time, the accident never would have occurred.

Table 5.1 lists five behavioral approaches that will help to improve the safety of all employees. To make certain employees have both the responsibility and the authority to carry out the five steps listed in Table 5.1, employers should adopt a policy similar to the one listed in Table 5.2. Simply putting such a statement in a safety handbook is not sufficient. An employer must believe in this principle and must "put teeth into it." Such a credo provides the absolute maximum in individual employee responsibility and authority and will maximize the safety performance of the organization.

TABLE 5.1   Employee Safety Behavior

• Determine the nature and extent of hazards before starting a job
• Each employee should be satisfied that conditions are safe before beginning work on any job or any part of a job
• All employees should be thoroughly familiar with and should consistently use the work procedures and the safety equipment that will be employed in the performance of the job at hand
• While working, each employee should consider the effects of each step and do nothing which might endanger themselves or others
• Each employee should be thoroughly familiar with emergency procedures

---

TABLE 5.2   Recommended Safety Credo

If it cannot be done safely, it need not be done!

Installation Safety

Design.   Proper design of electrical systems is composed of three parts—selection, installation, and calibration.

• *Selection.*   Electric equipment should be selected and applied conservatively. That is, maximum ratings must be well in excess of the quantities in which they will be exposed to in the system they are employed in. To help with this, manufacturing organizations such as the National Electrical Manufacturer's Association (NEMA) have established ratings for equipment which ensure that member companies only manufacture the highest-quality equipment. Equipment is tested per manufacturer's procedures by independent laboratories such as the Underwriter's Laboratory (UL). Equipment that is rated and labeled by such organizations should be used in electrical systems to help ensure safety. OSHA, NEC,* and NESC requirements should be considered as minimum criteria for safe selection.

• *Installation.*   Equipment should be installed in a safe and credible manner. Adequate work spaces for safety clearance should be allowed, safety barriers should be provided when necessary, and electrical installations should never be mixed with areas which are used for general public access.

• *Calibration.*   Equipment always should be properly calibrated. For example, protective devices should be calibrated so that they will operate for the minimum abnormal system condition. Equipment that is improperly calibrated can result in accidents as though the equipment had been improperly selected to begin with.

Electrical Protective Devices.   Protective devices such as circuit breakers, fuses, and switches must be capable of interrupting the currents to which they will be subjected. The National Electrical Code has numerous passages which require proper sizing of protective devices.

Maintenance.   Improperly maintained equipment is hazardous. For example, circuit breakers can explode violently if not properly maintained. Equipment should

---

* National Electric Code and NEC are registered trademarks of the National Fire Protection Association.

be periodically inspected and tested. If deficiencies are observed, the equipment must be repaired, adjusted, or replaced as required.

Power System Studies.   The following information appeared in the winter 1992–1993 issue of *NETA World* magazine.

A short-circuit study determines the magnitude of the currents that flow for faults placed at various buses throughout the power system. This information is used to determine interrupting requirements for fuses and circuit breakers and to set trip points for the overcurrent devices.

A coordination study is performed to make certain the overcurrent devices in a system will trip selectively. Selective tripping means that only the nearest upstream device to the short circuit trips to clear the circuit.

The two studies, taken together, are used to properly select and calibrate the protective devices used in the power system. The information which they provide is used for the following purposes:

- Fuses and circuit breakers are selected so that they are capable of interrupting the maximum fault current which will flow through them.

- Instantaneous elements are selected so that they will respond (or in some cases not respond) to the short-circuit currents which will flow through them.

- Time curves and instantaneous settings are selected so that the nearest upstream device to the short circuit is the one which operates to clear the fault.

- Protective devices are selected so that the short circuit is cleared in a minimum amount of time with as little collateral damage as possible.

- Protective devices are selected so that fault currents which flow through cables and transformers will not cause thermal or mechanical damage to those pieces of equipment.

Each of these points is critical to the safe and economical operation of a power system. For example, if circuit breakers or fuses are incapable of interrupting fault currents, they may explode violently, injuring personnel in the area. If the wrong protective device operates, a "small" outage may expand to include an entire plant. If a transformer overload relay is too slow, the transformer may be damaged by excessive temperature rise. The only way that such misoperations can be avoided is to perform a short-circuit analysis and a coordination study and then to select and set protective devices according to their results.

The NEC is the principal source of regulation in the area of electrical installation and design requirements for industrial and commercial facilities. The 1993 NEC has several sections which are pertinent. Table 5.3 reproduces a few of these sections.

In addition, the 1990 edition of ANSI/NFPA 70B, Electrical Equipment Maintenance, also has a section which applies. This is reproduced in Table 5.4. The only way to comply with these requirements is to ensure that a short-circuit analysis and a coordination study are performed for the power system.

Few would deny that such studies should be performed during the design phase of an electrical power system. But how about later, as the system ages? Several things happen to require the performance and/or reevaluation of these studies for an existing system:

- Electric utilities constantly add capacity. Your utility may have had a 200,000-kilovoltampere (kVA) fault capacity when the plant was new 20 years ago. Now, however, the utility's capacity may have doubled or even tripled. Such changes can cause fault duties to rise above the ratings of marginal interrupting equipment.

TABLE 5.3 NEC Requirements for Short-Circuit Analyses and Coordination Studies

Location in 1993 NEC	Item
Definitions	Interrupting Rating. The highest current at rated voltage that a device is intended to interrupt under standard test conditions.
Article 110	110-9. Interrupting Rating. Equipment intended to break current at fault levels shall have an interrupting rating sufficient for the nominal circuit voltage and the current that is available at the line terminals of the equipment.
	Equipment intended to break current at other than fault levels shall have an interrupting rating at nominal circuit voltage sufficient for the current that must be interrupted.
	110-10. Circuit Impedance and Other Characteristics. The overcurrent protective devices, the total impedance, the component short-circuit withstand ratings, and other characteristics of the circuit to be protected shall be so selected and coordinated as to permit the circuit protective devices that are used to clear a fault without the occurrence of extensive damage to the electrical components of the circuit. This fault shall be assumed to be either between two or more of the circuit conductors, or between any circuit conductor and the grounding conductor or enclosing metal raceway.
Article 240	240-12. Electrical System Coordination. Where an orderly shutdown is required to minimize hazard(s) to personnel and equipment, a system of coordination based on the following two conditions shall be permitted:
	(1) Coordinated short-circuit protection
	(2) Overload indication based on monitoring systems or devices.

- Many plants are beginning to internally generate electricity. This generation adds to the fault capacity of the system.
- Operating procedures may have changed. A bus tie circuit breaker that was normally open may now be normally closed. Such a change can greatly increase fault capacity.
- Technical standards can change. For example, in 1985 the protection requirements for liquid-filled transformers changed. Studies showed that many transformers

TABLE 5.4 ANSI/NFPA 70B Requirements for Short-Circuit Analyses and Coordination Studies

Location in 1990 ANSI/NFPA 70B	Item
Paragraph 5-4.3	An up-to-date short circuit and coordination study is essential for safety of personnel and equipment. It is necessary to analyze the momentary and interrupting rating requirements of the protective devices. That is, will the circuit breaker or fuse safely interrupt the fault or explode in attempting to perform this function?
	Another phase of the study is that of developing the application of the protective devices to realize minimum equipment damage and the least disturbance to the system in the event of a fault.

were being mechanically damaged by high current through faults. The protection requirements became more stringent for such installations. Although the standards do not require existing systems to be changed, would it not make sense to at least review your system? The protection changes might be minimal.

- New installations or plant modernization may add capacity and other coordination streams to the system. For example, coordination studies require that the main breaker coordinate with the largest feeder device. If a larger feeder device is added later, the coordination study must be reviewed.

In general, short-circuit analyses and coordination studies should be reviewed at least every 5 years. These studies should be performed by a registered professional engineer. Many consulting firms have the ability and the experience to perform them; however, since short-circuit analyses and coordination studies are specialized types of engineering services, not all architect and engineering firms have the experience to do them. Closely review the qualifications of the firm which you retain.

ANSI/IEEE standard Std-399, Power Systems Analysis, is the standard which covers most of the engineering studies that are key to the proper design and performance of an electrical power system. The *Brown Book* is part of the IEEE color book series and should be referenced when you are deciding what studies to perform and how to perform them.

The *Brown Book* lists ten studies including load flow, short-circuit analysis, stability, motor starting, harmonic analysis, switching transients, reliability, cable ampacity, ground mat, and coordination. Whether any of these studies, besides the short-circuit analysis and coordination study, are performed will be determined by the specifics of the power system under consideration.

Proper selection, sizing, and calibration of the protective devices in a power system directly affect safety, efficiency, and economics. Common sense and regulatory requirements dictate that a short-circuit analysis and coordination study should be performed.

FIRST AID

This handbook provides general coverage of the subject with expanded information on handling electrical injuries. Potential first aid givers should remember four very important points. Before an accident happens:

- Obtain hands-on first aid training for yourself and all employees. Such training may be obtained from the American Heart Association, the American Red Cross, or local sources such as fire departments or police departments.

If an accident does happen:

- Act quickly!!! You may be the only person that can prevent a death.
- Do not administer first aid that you are not qualified to administer. Injuries can be aggravated by improperly administered first aid.
- Get qualified medical help quickly. Paramedics and emergency medical technicians are trained to provide emergency first aid and should be summoned as soon as possible.

This handbook is not intended to be used as a first aid training manual. Table 5.5 summarizes the first aid steps that are discussed in the following sections.

TABLE 5.5   General First Aid Procedure

- Act quickly
- Survey the situation
- Develop a plan
- Assess the victim's condition
- Summon help if needed
- Move the victim if danger is imminent
- Administer required first aid:
  Shock
  Electrical Burns

General First Aid

Act Quickly.   *Remember—you may be the only person between the victim and death.* Whatever you do, do it quickly. This does not imply that you should act impetuously. Your actions should be planned and methodical, but you should not waste any time. Do not attempt to perform procedures for which you have no training or experience. Improperly applied procedures can be deadly.

Survey the Situation.   Remember that your purpose as a first aid giver is to help the problem, not contribute to it. If you are injured in the process of administering first aid, you cannot help the victim. If your preliminary assessment indicates that you need to wear safety clothing, put it on first, then administer aid. Table 5.6 lists key points that should be checked before you rush in.

TABLE 5.6   First Aid Checklist

- Is the circuit still energized?
- Is the victim contacting the circuit?
- Are noxious gases or materials present that may cause injury?
- Is fire present or possible?

Develop a Plan.   After the initial survey of the situation, develop the plan of attack. The specifics of any given situation will vary; however, the following guidelines should be used:

- If the victim is in immediate danger he or she should be moved to a safe position. (See the next section on moving the victim and later sections on rescue techniques.)
- If the victim is non-responsive assess his or her condition and respond accordingly. (See the later section on assessing the victim's condition.)
- If the victim is responsive, make him or her as comfortable as possible and summon aid. Do not abandon the victim until aid has arrived.
- Constantly monitor the condition of the victim. Electric shock can cause delayed failures and irregularities of heart rhythm.

Assess the Victim's Condition.   The procedures to be used in administering first aid depend on the condition of the victim. If the victim is responsive, no action may be required. Table 5.7 lists the procedures to perform if the victim is awake and responsive.

TABLE 5.7   What to Do if the Victim Is Responsive

- Ask the victim what is wrong
- Assess the victim's condition and treat the injuries as best as possible
- Treat the worst injuries first
- When the victim is out of immediate danger, or if you are unable to help because the injuries are beyond your abilities, summon help
- Attend to the victim(s) and keep them safe until help arrives
- When help arrives, give the first aid workers your assessment of the situation and stand by to help

If the victim is not responsive, you must perform a "hands-on" assessment of his or her condition. Table 5.8 lists the ABCs of first aid. This memory device can help the first aid giver to remember the proper procedure when examining a nonresponsive victim.

TABLE 5.8   The ABCs of First Aid

Airway
Breathing
Circulation
Doctor

One of the biggest surprises to those who have not worked with accident victims is that the trauma of the accident can induce severe bleeding through the mouth and/or vomiting. Be prepared for these conditions before working with an injured person. When you have prepared yourself for this situation, begin the ABCs.

- **A**—Check the victim's **Airway**. Figure 5.1 illustrates the correct way to clear an injured persons airway. Remember to avoid moving the victim and to keep the victim's spine straight to avoid aggravating an injury. *Caution: An accident victim may suffer from involuntary muscular reflexes and other such spasms. The strongest muscle in the human body is the jaw. Because of this, rescue workers should put their fingers into the victim's mouth only when absolutely necessary.*

  Start by opening the victim's mouth as shown in Fig. 5.1. Search the mouth for foreign matter or other objects which may be blocking the air passage. Many times the victim's tongue may be blocking the air passage. To fix this problem, put your hand behind the victim's neck, gently pull the jaw forward, and, if required, carefully tilt the head back. If the air passage is clear and the victim is still not breathing, you should perform resuscitation.

- **B**—Check the victim's **Breathing**. First check to see if the victim is breathing. This can be done by observing his or her chest to see if it is moving. Then place your ear close to the victim's mouth and nose and listen carefully. If the victim is breathing but choking or gurgling sounds are heard, proceed to the next step which is clearing the airway.

- **C**—Check the victim's **Circulation**. Circulation should be checked by feeling for the victim's pulse at the carotid artery as shown in Fig. 5.2. To find the carotid artery, place your fingertips gently on the victim's larynx. Gently slide the fingers down into the groove between the windpipe and the muscle at the back of the neck.

TO OPEN AIRWAY

CLEAR MOUTH

TILT HEAD BACK

OBSTRUCTED   OPENED

FIGURE 5.1   Clearing the airway of an injured worker.

FIGURE 5.2   Checking the circulation.

The carotid artery is located in this area. Gently feel for the pulse. Table 5.9 shows the steps to take for the various combinations of problems that may be found.

• **D**—Summon the **D**octor. After the victim's condition has been stabilized, summon help. If the resuscitation efforts are proving unsuccessful, the first aid giver may want to summon more qualified assistance even though the victim is not yet stabilized.

Summon Help if Needed.   One of the most difficult decisions is to determine when to summon help. If help is not sum-

TABLE 5.9   How to Handle Unresponsive Victims

Breathing—pulse normal	Make victim comfortable. If help has not been summoned, do so and stand by until it arrives
No breathing—pulse normal	Perform mouth-to-mouth resuscitation until breathing is restored or until help arrives and takes over
Breathing normal—no pulse	Perform heart-lung resuscitation (CPR) until pulse is restored or until help arrives and takes over
No breathing—no pulse	Perform heart-lung resuscitation (CPR) until pulse is restored or until help arrives and takes over

moned soon enough, the victim may die. On the other hand, if the first aid giver leaves to summon help, the victim may die. No concrete rules can be given here; however, the following guidelines may help:

- Relieve any immediate danger to the victim before summoning help.
- Perform the ABCs before summoning help.
- If the victim is not breathing or has no pulse, perform resuscitation before summoning help.
- If anyone else is in the area, yell or call for help while performing the preliminary accident assessment.

Remember that the first aid giver is in charge of the victim until more qualified help arrives. Do not abandon the victim if immediate aid is required.

Move the Victim if Danger is Imminent. Unless they are in imminent danger, accident victims should be moved only when necessary and only by personnel who are qualified to move them. A victim of violent injury, such as a fall, may have spinal or other internal injuries. Moving such a victim could cause increased problems including paralysis or even death. Moving an injury victim is discussed in detail in the Rescue Techniques section of this handbook.

First Aid for Electric Shock. Electric shock is one of the most difficult of all injuries to diagnose. In some cases, even if the injury is fatal, no external signs may be visible. Table 5.10 lists some of the clues and symptoms which may be present when a victim has received an electric shock.

TABLE 5.10 Typical Symptoms of Electric Shock

• Victim may lose consciousness. This may occur at the moment of contact; however, it can also occur later
• Victim has a weak or irregular pulse
• Victim has trouble breathing or has stopped breathing
• Small burns may appear at the entry and exit points of the electric current

Many prospective first aid givers are themselves injured when they contact an energized wire or a victim who is still in contact with an energized wire. Table 5.11 lists the precautions for working on or around accident victims who may be in con-

TABLE 5.11 Precautions for Performing First Aid on an Electric Shock Victim

• Do not touch any energized wires with any part of your body or with any conductive tools or equipment
• Do not touch a victim who is still in contact with an energized wire with any part of your body or with conductive tools or equipment
• Do not try to move any energized wires unless you are qualified to do so. Qualified in this instance means that you are trained in the performance of such a procedure and are able to avoid electrical hazards

tact with live wires. After cutting the power to the circuits or removing the victim from contact, if the victim is responsive and shows no signs of breathing or heart problems, the procedures listed in Table 5.12 should be followed. After cutting the power to the circuits or removing the victim from contact, if the victim is nonresponsive, the procedures listed in Table 5.13 should be followed.

TABLE 5.12   First Aid Procedures for Conscious Electric Shock Victims Who Exhibit No Symptoms

- Keep the victim still and quiet. Remember that heart and respiratory problems can be delayed in electric shock victims
- Monitor the victim's condition for at least $\frac{1}{2}$ h
- If the victim continues to show no symptoms, take them to a doctor for a thorough examination

TABLE 5.13   First Aid Procedures for Unconscious Electric Shock Victims with Symptoms

- Check the ABCs. If the victim is not breathing or has heart irregularities, perform resuscitation as described later in this handbook
- If wounds are evident or burns are evident, cover them with sterile dressings
- Try to cool burns with sterile compresses
- Immediately seek medical aid

First Aid for Electrical Burns.   Electrical burns may be internal and/or external. External burns are caused by the intense heat of the electric arc coupled with the current flow, while internal burns are caused by the current flow heating the tissue. Internal burns are virtually impossible to diagnose in the field. The symptoms of internal electrical burns are identical to the symptoms caused by severe electric shock. In addition to the symptoms described in Table 5.10, the victim may also experience significant pain caused by the damaged tissue. External burns are similar to thermally induced burns caused by fire or other heat sources.

For both internal and external burns, the first aid techniques are identical to those given in Tables 5.12 and 5.13. The treatment of burns is a very specialized medical procedure. Be certain to seek specialized help as quickly as possible.

Resuscitation (Artificial Respiration)

Breathing trauma is one of the two very serious symptoms that result from severe electric shock or internal burns. When breathing is stopped or made irregular by electricity, it must be restored by resuscitation. Over the years many different types of resuscitation have been developed. Mouth to mouth resuscitation is the current preferred technique.

In order to be most effective, resuscitation must be started as soon as possible after breathing has ceased. Figure 5.3 shows a curve which approximates the possibility of success plotted against elapsed time before the start of resuscitation. Figure

5.4 illustrates a currently accepted procedure for the performance of artificial respiration. *Caution:* With the proliferation of communicable diseases such as acquired immunodeficiency syndrome (AIDS) and hepatitis, the decision of whether to perform live-saving mouth-to-mouth resuscitation has become much more difficult. Instruments such as breathing tubes can be used to protect the victim and the rescuer.

FIGURE 5.3   Elapsed time versus possibility of success for artificial respiration.

AIR DELIVERY COMPARISONS

THE MOUTH-TO-MOUTH (M-M) OR (MOUTH-TO-NOSE) (M-N) METHOD OF ARTIFICIAL RESPIRATION

PREFERRED METHOD

ENDORSED BY

American Heart Association – American Medical Association
American Red Cross – U.S. Public Health Service
Industrial Medical Association – Edison Electric Institute

FIGURE 5.4   The preferred method of artificial respiration—mouth-to-mouth resuscitation.

In An EMERGENCY

- ✓ OBSERVE HAZARDS
- ✓ PROTECT YOURSELF
- ✓ THINK

Then

IF NECESSARY...
REMOVE THE INJURED
FROM HAZARDOUS
AREA

IF THE INJURED IS NOT BREATHING

- ✓ OPEN AIRWAY
- ✓ RESTORE BREATHING

ACT QUICKLY
SECONDS COUNT

A

TO OPEN AIRWAY

CLEAR MOUTH

TILT HEAD BACK

OBSTRUCTED   OPENED

B

TO RESTORE BREATHING

1 KEEP INJURED'S HEAD TILTED

2 PINCH NOSTRILS CLOSED
OR CLOSE MOUTH

3 TAKE A DEEP BREATH

4 PLACE YOUR MOUTH OVER
HIS MOUTH (OR NOSE)

5 BLOW FORCEFULLY

6 REMOVE YOUR MOUTH AND
ALLOW HIM TO EXHALE

Repeat CYCLE 12 TIMES PER MINUTE

1

KEEP INJURED'S HEAD TILTED

MOUTH-TO-MOUTH   MOUTH-TO-NOSE

ONE HAND ON
FOREHEAD

OTHER HAND BEHIND
NECK

ONE HAND ON
FOREHEAD

OTHER HAND HOLDS
MOUTH CLOSED

Note
A BABY'S NECK IS VERY PLIABLE...
DON'T EXAGGERATE HEAD TILT

2

PINCH NOSTRILS CLOSED OR CLOSE MOUTH

MOUTH-TO-MOUTH | MOUTH-TO-NOSE

USE THUMB &
FOREFINGER OF
THE HAND YOU HAVE
ON HIS FOREHEAD

MAKE SURE LIPS
ARE SEALED

THIS IS THE BASIC
DIFFERENCE BETWEEN
MOUTH-TO-MOUTH & MOUTH-TO-NOSE

FIGURE 5.4 (*Continued*) The preferred method of artificial respiration—mouth-to-mouth resuscitation.

POSSIBLE NECK FRACTURE

Note: If the victim has lacerations (cuts) of the face and forehead from an accident, the victim's neck may be fractured, and all forward, backward, lateral (sideways), or turning movements should be avoided. Use the modified jaw thrust maneuver. Place your hands on either side of the victim's head to maintain it in a fixed, neutral position without the neck's being extended. Use index fingers to move the lower jaw forward without tilting the head backward or turning it. Perform mouth-to-nose resuscitation.

MODIFIED JAW THRUST

(Illustration reprinted with express permission of the American National Red Cross, from Cardiopulmonary Resuscitation, Copyright 1981.)

3
TAKE A DEEP BREATH
- ENOUGH AIR FOR YOURSELF AND THE INJURED

4
PLACE MOUTH COMPLETELY OVER HIS MOUTH (OR NOSE)
- OPEN YOUR MOUTH WIDELY
- MAKE AIRTIGHT SEAL

Note ON A BABY PLACE MOUTH OVER BOTH MOUTH & NOSE

6
REMOVE YOUR MOUTH AND ALLOW HIM TO EXHALE

- WATCH HIS CHEST FALL
- LISTEN FOR AIR ESCAPING FROM HIS LUNGS

Note
IN MOUTH-TO-NOSE YOU MAY HAVE TO OPEN HIS MOUTH TO ALLOW AIR TO ESCAPE

5
BLOW FORCEFULLY

UNTIL YOU SEE HIS CHEST RISE

ABOUT TWICE HIS NORMAL BREATH

Note BABIES REQUIRE ONLY SMALL PUFFS OF AIR

Caution YOUR FIRST BLOWING EFFORT MAY REVEAL AN OBSTRUCTION—IF SO...

ADULT
ROLL HIM ON HIS SIDE AND SLAP HIM ON THE BACK

BABY
PICK HIM UP AND LAY HIM OVER YOUR ARM—SLAP HIM ON THE BACK

REPEAT CYCLE 12 TIMES PER MINUTE

RATE FOR BABIES 20 PUFFS PER MINUTE

Check EVERY BREATH BY...

1 SEEING CHEST RISE & FALL

2 FEELING RESISTANCE OF LUNGS AS THEY EXPAND

3 HEARING AIR ESCAPE DURING EXHALATION

FIGURE 5.4 (*Continued*) The preferred method of artificial respiration—mouth-to-mouth resuscitation.

Continue

UNTIL...HE IS BREATHING
NORMALLY OR...

HE REACHES A HOSPITAL
OR...

A DOCTOR TAKES OVER

DON'T GIVE UP

Remember

1 KEEP HEAD TILTED

2 PINCH NOSTRILS (OR
   CLOSE MOUTH)

3 TAKE A DEEP BREATH

4 SEAL MOUTH COMPLETELY

5 BLOW FORCEFULLY

6 REMOVE YOUR MOUTH

Repeat 12 TIMES A MINUTE

FIGURE 5.4 (*Continued*) The preferred method of artificial respiration—mouth-to-mouth resuscitation.

Heart-Lung Resuscitation

Heart-lung resuscitation is also called cardiopulmonary resuscitation (CPR). This technique should be applied when the victim has no pulse and no respiration. The procedure should be started as soon as possible to maximize the probability of successfully restoring full function to the victim.

Remember that while CPR is being performed, the first aid giver is actually pumping blood and breathing for the victim. Do not give up until qualified medical personnel say to. Figure 5.5 is a graphic representation of the proper procedure for performing heart-lung resuscitation.

HEART-LUNG
RESUSCITATION
IS
ARTIFICIAL RESPIRATION
(MOUTH-TO-MOUTH OR MOUTH-TO-NOSE)
PLUS
ARTIFICIAL CIRCULATION
(EXTERNAL CARDIAC COMPRESSION)

HEART-LUNG
RESUSCITATION
HAS BEEN

ENDORSED BY:
American Heart Association – American Medical Association
American Red Cross – U.S. Public Health Service
Industrial Medical Association – Edison Electric Institute

FIGURE 5.5 Heart-lung resuscitation procedure.

WE SOMETIMES FACE EMERGENCIES SUCH AS —

- ELECTRIC SHOCK
- HEART ATTACK
- DROWNING
- SUFFOCATION
- PHYSICAL SHOCK

WHERE DEATH MAY RESULT FROM

CARDIAC ARREST
AND/OR
LACK OF BREATHING

Note

THE SYMPTOMS OF CARDIAC ARREST AND VENTRICULAR FIBRILLATION ARE THE SAME

TO RESTORE CIRCULATION USE

- EXTERNAL
- CARDIAC
- COMPRESSION

SIGNS THAT CIRCULATION HAS STOPPED

[HEART STANDSTILL OR VENTRICULAR FIBRILLATION] ARE -

1. NO CAROTID PULSE
2. WIDELY DILATED PUPILS
3. ASHEN-GRAY SKIN COLOR

Pupils

CHECK BY LIFTING EYELID TO SEE IF PUPIL CONTRACTS WHEN EXPOSED TO LIGHT

NORMAL PUPIL   DILATED PUPIL

PUPILS THAT REMAIN WIDELY DILATED INDICATE LACK OF CIRCULATION

Color

ASHEN-GRAY SKIN COLOR INDICATES LACK OF OXYGENATED BLOOD

IF THE INJURED IS NOT BREATHING

Open AIRWAY

IF THIS DOES NOT HELP

Restore BREATHING

IF HIS HEART HAS STOPPED

Restore CIRCULATION

ACT QUICKLY SECONDS COUNT

Pulse

CHECK CAROTID ARTERY

- LOCATED IN NECK ON EITHER SIDE OF WINDPIPE

- USE INDEX AND MIDDLE FINGERS OF ONE HAND
- PULSE SHOULD BE "FELT" NOT "COMPRESSED"

NO PULSE MEANS NO CIRCULATION

BASIC STEPS IN EXTERNAL CARDIAC COMPRESSION

1. LAY INJURED ON HIS BACK ON A FIRM SURFACE
2. KNEEL AT HIS SIDE
3. PLACE THE HEEL OF ONE HAND ON LOWER HALF OF HIS STERNUM (BREASTBONE)
4. PLACE YOUR OTHER HAND ON TOP OF THE FIRST
5. EXERT DOWNWARD PRESSURE
6. RELEASE PRESSURE

Repeat COMPRESSIONS 60 TIMES A MINUTE

FIGURE 5.5 (*Continued*) Heart-lung resuscitation procedure.

1. LAY INJURED ON HIS BACK ON A FIRM SURFACE

- FOR EFFECTIVE ARTIFICIAL CIRCULATION OF BLOOD - THE HEART MUST BE COMPRESSED BETWEEN STERNUM (BREASTBONE) AND SPINE

2. KNEEL AT HIS SIDE

- IN LINE WITH LOWER HALF OF HIS CHEST

3. PLACE THE HEEL OF ONE HAND ON THE LOWER HALF OF HIS STERNUM

- FEEL FOR LOWER END OF STERNUM
- PLACE ONLY THE HEEL OF YOUR HAND ON HIS STERNUM
- KEEP YOUR FINGERS ELEVATED DO NOT TOUCH HIS RIBS

INCORRECT HAND POSITION CAN CAUSE INTERNAL INJURIES

Note | ONLY TWO FINGERS ARE REQUIRED TO COMPRESS THE BREASTBONE OF A BABY

4. PLACE YOUR OTHER HAND ON TOP OF THE FIRST

- THIS WILL HELP MAINTAIN HAND POSITION
- IT WILL ALSO BE EASIER TO EXERT PROPER PRESSURE

Note
- THE HEEL OF ONLY ONE HAND WILL PROVIDE ENOUGH PRESSURE TO COMPRESS THE BREASTBONE OF CHILDREN

5. EXERT DOWNWARD PRESSURE

- ROCK FORWARD UNTIL YOUR SHOULDERS ARE ALMOST DIRECTLY ABOVE INJURED'S CHEST
- KEEP YOUR ARMS STRAIGHT
- APPLY ENOUGH PRESSURE (80 TO 100 POUNDS) TO DEPRESS THE STERNUM 1½ TO 2 INCHES
- USE THE WEIGHT OF YOUR UPPER BODY

COMPRESSION FORCES BLOOD OUT OF THE HEART

6. RELEASE PRESSURE

- ROCK BACK
- MAINTAIN HAND POSITION - DO NOT LIFT HANDS OFF STERNUM

RELEASE OF PRESSURE ALLOWS HEART TO REFILL WITH BLOOD

Repeat COMPRESSIONS 60 TIMES PER MINUTE (ONCE A SECOND)

Note
THE RATE FOR BABIES AND CHILDREN IS 80 TO 100 COMPRESSIONS PER MINUTE

In An EMERGERGENCY

✓ OBSERVE HAZARDS

✓ PROTECT YOURSELF

✓ THINK BEFORE YOU ACT

Then
IF NECESSARY
REMOVE THE INJURED
FROM HAZARDOUS AREA

FIGURE 5.5 (*Continued*) Heart-lung resuscitation procedure.

IF THE INJURED IS UNCONSCIOUS AND NOT BREATHING

A PROVIDE AN OPEN AIRWAY

IF THIS DOES NOT RESTORE BREATHING

B GIVE 5 OR 6 QUICK BREATHS BY MOUTH-TO-MOUTH

IF HE RESPONDS, CONTINUE MOUTH-TO-MOUTH RESPIRATION UNTIL HE IS BREATHING WITHOUT HELP

Then

- WATCH HIM CLOSELY - HIS BREATHING MAY STOP AGAIN
- GIVE ANY ADDITIONAL FIRST AID NEEDED
- CALL FOR HELP

IF HE DOES NOT SEEM TO RESPOND TO THE FIRST 5 OR 6 QUICK BREATHS

✓ CHECK FOR PULSE

✓ CHECK PUPIL FOR DILATION

✓ NOTE SKIN COLOR

IF A PULSE IS FELT, PUPIL CONTRACTS AND COLOR IMPROVES -

CONTINUE MOUTH-TO-MOUTH UNTIL HE IS BREATHING WITHOUT HELP

Then

- WATCH HIM CLOSELY - HIS BREATHING MAY STOP AGAIN
- GIVE ANY ADDITIONAL FIRST AID NEEDED
- CALL FOR HELP

IF NO PULSE IS PRESENT, PUPIL DOES NOT CONTRACT AND SKIN COLOR IS NOT NORMAL, HIS HEART HAS STOPPED

RESTORE **CIRCULATION**

USE HEART- LUNG RESUSCITATION

MOUTH-TO-MOUTH RESPIRATION
+
EXTERNAL CARDIAC COMPRESSION
=
HEART-LUNG RESUSCITATION

ONE RESCUER | AFTER EVERY 15 COMPRESSIONS GIVE 2 QUICK BREATHS RATIO 15 TO 2

TWO RESCUERS | AFTER EVERY FIFTH COMPRESSION INTERPOSE ONE BREATH RATIO 5 TO 1

CONTINUE HEART-LUNG RESUSCITATION UNTIL HE RECOVERS OR HE REACHES A HOSPITAL OR A DOCTOR TAKES OVER

Important

- CONTINUE H-L-R ON WAY TO HOSPITAL
- DO NOT ALLOW ANY PRESSURE-CYCLING MECHANICAL RESUSCITATOR TO BE USED WITH CARDIAC COMPRESSION
- DO NOT ALLOW ANYONE (POLICE, FIREMEN OR AMBULANCE CREW) TO TAKE OVER - UNLESS THEY ARE EXPERT IN H-L-R

REMEMBER YOUR **A,B,C'**s
HEART-LUNG RESUSCITATION INVOLVES

AIRWAY OPENED

BREATHING RESTORED

CIRCULATION RESTORED

DOCTOR

PRACTICE AND COMMON SENSE ARE ESSENTIAL TO SUCCESSFUL HEART-LUNG RESUSCITATION

FIGURE 5.5 (*Continued*) Heart-lung resuscitation procedure.

RESCUE TECHNIQUES

General Rescue Procedures

The first priority in any emergency is to remove living victims from the danger area if they cannot escape themselves. This procedure is called *rescue*. In some instances the rescuer will be risking his or her life in order to rescue a victim. The decision to risk one's life is a personal one and cannot be regulated by any sort of standard procedures. In any case, good judgment must be exercised by the rescuer. Remember that becoming a second victim does not help anyone.

The American Red Cross method of rescue is shown in Table 5.14. Notice that the steps are virtually identical to those employed in preparing for first aid procedures. Rescue is, in fact, one of the preliminary steps in the performance of first aid.

After the victim has been removed from the hazardous area (in the case of an electrical accident, *do not touch the victim* until electric circuits have been de-energized and/or the victim has been removed from contact of the energized circuits) and after first aid has been administered, the accident area should be secured and made safe for other persons. *Do not disturb* the accident area beyond what is necessary to protect other persons. An accident investigation should be carried out by qualified personnel to determine the nature and cause of the accident and what corrective actions need to be taken to prevent the accident from occurring again.

The following outline details the generalized procedures defined by Table 5.14. This outline was taken from the AVO Multi-Amp Institute textbook entitled *High Voltage Rescue Techniques.*

1. Survey the scene. A quick survey (1 min or less—time is critical) to enable the rescuer to develop a mental plan. Consider the following:
   a. Anticipating conditions
      (1) Probable life-threatening hazards
      (2) Observed location of victim
      (3) Observed condition of victim
   b. Facts of the situation
      (1) Time and conditions
      (2) Situations—What happened?
      (3) Contributing factors

TABLE 5.14   Primary Rescue Steps

---

1. Survey the scene
   a. Develop an action plan
2. Primary survey
   a. Locate the victim
   b. Assess the victim's condition
   c. Try to arouse the victim
   d. Move the victim to a safe place. *Caution*—do not jostle the victim any more than is necessary when moving. See later sections for a discussion of proper movement techniques
   e. Apply first aid as soon as the victim is in a safe location
3. Call for emergency medical assistance

---

c. Weighing facts
  (1) Rescue requirements
  (2) Accomplish rescue alone?
  (3) Equipment and manpower needed/available
  (4) Additional assistance now or later
  (5) If electrical contact, get de-energized
d. Determining procedures
  (1) Immediate action
  (2) Course of action
e. Initial action decision. May be made before a complete survey. May determine a future course of action.
2. Primary survey plan activated. From the initial decision and action until the victim is being transported to medical facilities, the following would be considered.
  a. Victim location
    (1) Accessibility of victim
    (2) Electric circuit contact
    (3) Remove circuit contacts
    (4) Try to arouse victim
    (5) Help needed/called
    (6) Assess condition of victim (ABCs plus broken bones, burns, twisted torso, etc.)
  b. Emergency aid required
    (1) What and where to give emergency aid?
    (2) How to move victim to safety
    (3) Emergency aid given
3. Call emergency medical service
  a. How to move victim to medical aid
  b. Continue emergency aid as required
4. Secondary survey
  a. Secure the area
    (1) Do not damage or disturb physical evidence
    (2) Isolate hazards
    (3) Keep untrained personnel away
  b. What happened
    (1) Ask victim
    (2) Ask witnesses
    (3) Examine physical evidence
    (4) Photographs, sketches
    (5) Preserve physical evidence
  c. Reports
    (1) Written records
    (2) Notification
  d. Follow up
    (1) Reports distributed
    (2) Action taken to prevent future similar accidents

Note: The action taken during the actual physical rescue must be started and accomplished very rapidly so that the victim is out of further danger and emergency aid may begin quickly. See Fig. 5.3. Accident investigation techniques are discussed later in this chapter.

Elevated Rescue

The physical techniques that are used for any type of rescue should be learned and practiced in a controlled environment under the direction of experienced, qualified training personnel.

Figure 5.6 graphically depicts a generally accepted method for performing an elevated, pole-top rescue. Note that this rescue technique requires a skilled line person with climbing ability. Do not attempt such a rescue unless you have had the requisite training. All rescue techniques should be accomplished using the basic rescue approach outline which is illustrated in the previous section.

YOU MAY HAVE TO HELP A MAN ON A POLE REACH THE GROUND SAFELY WHEN HE—

- BECOMES ILL
- IS INJURED
- LOSES CONSCIOUSNESS

YOU MUST KNOW—

- WHEN HE NEEDS HELP
- WHEN AND WHY TIME IS CRITICAL
- THE APPROVED METHOD OF LOWERING

BASIC STEPS IN

POLE TOP RESCUE

Evaluate THE SITUATION

Provide FOR YOUR PROTECTION

Climb TO RESCUE POSITION

Determine INJURED'S CONDITION

Then
IF NECESSARY—

- GIVE FIRST AID
- LOWER INJURED
- GIVE FOLLOW-UP CARE
- CALL FOR HELP

Evaluate THE SITUATION

CALL TO MAN ON POLE

IF HE DOES NOT ANSWER OR APPEARS STUNNED OR DAZED

- PREPARE TO GO TO HIS AID

TIME IS EXTREMELY IMPORTANT

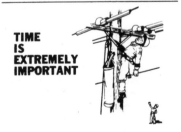

Provide
**FOR YOUR PROTECTION
YOUR SAFETY IS VITAL
TO THE RESCUE**

—PERSONAL TOOLS AND RUBBER GLOVES
(RUBBER SLEEVES, IF REQUIRED)

Check
- ✔ EXTRA RUBBER GOODS?
- ✔ LIVE LINE TOOLS?
- ✔ PHYSICAL CONDITION OF POLE?
  - ✔ DAMAGED CONDUCTORS, EQUIPMENT?
  - ✔ FIRE ON POLE?
  - ✔ BROKEN POLE?
- ✔ HAND LINE ON POLE AND IN GOOD CONDITION?

FIGURE 5.6 Illustrated method for elevated, pole-top rescue.

Climb TO RESCUE POSITION
- CLIMB CAREFULLY

POSITION YOURSELF —
- TO INSURE YOUR SAFETY
- TO CLEAR THE INJURED FROM HAZARD
- TO DETERMINE THE INJURED'S CONDITION
- TO RENDER AID AS REQUIRED
- TO START MOUTH-TO-MOUTH, IF REQUIRED
- TO LOWER INJURED, IF NECESSARY

THE BEST POSITION WILL USUALLY BE — SLIGHTLY ABOVE THE INJURED

IF THE INJURED IS
CONSCIOUS
- TIME MAY NO LONGER BE CRITICAL
- GIVE NECESSARY FIRST AID ON POLE
- REASSURE THE INJURED
- HELP HIM DESCEND POLE
- GIVE FIRST AID ON GROUND
- CALL FOR HELP, IF NECESSARY

Determine
THE INJURED'S CONDITION

HE MAY BE . . .
- CONSCIOUS

- UNCONSCIOUS BUT BREATHING

- UNCONSCIOUS NOT BREATHING

- UNCONSCIOUS NOT BREATHING AND HEART STOPPED

IF THE INJURED IS
UNCONSCIOUS BUT BREATHING
- WATCH HIM CLOSELY IN CASE BREATHING STOPS
- LOWER HIM TO GROUND
- GIVE FIRST AID ON GROUND
- CALL FOR HELP

FIGURE 5.6   (*Continued*) Illustrated method for elevated, pole-top rescue.

IF THE INJURED IS

UNCONSCIOUS
AND NOT BREATHING

- PROVIDE AN OPEN AIRWAY

- GIVE HIM 5 OR 6 QUICK BREATHS

- IF HE RESPONDS . . .

CONTINUE MOUTH-TO-MOUTH UNTIL HE IS BREATHING WITHOUT HELP

IF HE DOES NOT RESPOND TO THE FIRST 5 OR 6 QUICK BREATHS

✔ CHECK SKIN COLOR

✔ CHECK FOR PUPIL DILATION

NORMAL PUPIL   DILATED PUPIL

IF PUPIL CONTRACTS AND COLOR IS GOOD

CONTINUE MOUTH-TO-MOUTH UNTIL HE IS BREATHING WITHOUT HELP

Then

- HELP HIM DESCEND POLE

- WATCH HIM CLOSELY—HIS BREATHING MAY STOP AGAIN

- GIVE ANY ADDITIONAL FIRST AID NEEDED

- CALL FOR HELP

IF PUPIL DOES NOT CONTRACT AND SKIN COLOR IS BAD

HEART HAS STOPPED

- PREPARE TO LOWER HIM IMMEDIATELY

- GIVE 5 OR 6 MORE QUICK BREATHS JUST BEFORE LOWERING

- LOWER HIM TO THE GROUND

- START HEART-LUNG RESUSCITATION

- CALL FOR HELP

THE
METHOD
OF
LOWERING AN
INJURED MAN
IS

* SAFE
* SIMPLE
* AVAILABLE

FIGURE 5.6 (*Continued*) Illustrated method for elevated, pole-top rescue.

RESCUER

EQUIPMENT NEEDED

Position HAND LINE

OVER ARM OR OTHER PART OF STRUCTURE

- 1/2 INCH HAND LINE

PROCEDURE . . .

- *Position* HAND LINE
- *Tie* INJURED
- *Remove* SLACK IN HAND LINE
- *Take* FIRM GRIP ON FALL LINE
- *Cut* INJURED'S SAFETY STRAP
  Lower INJURED

VICTIM / FALL LINE

- POSITION LINE FOR CLEAR PATH TO GROUND

Note USUALLY BEST 2 OR 3 FEET FROM POLE

SHORT END OF LINE IS WRAPPED AROUND FALL LINE TWICE. (TWO WRAPS AROUND FALL LINE.)

FIGURE 5.6   (*Continued*) Illustrated method for elevated, pole-top rescue.

RESCUER TIES HAND LINE AROUND VICTIM'S CHEST USING THREE HALF HITCHES.

Tie INJURED—

PASS LINE AROUND INJURED'S CHEST

TIE THREE HALF-HITCHES

- **KNOT IN FRONT**
- **NEAR ONE ARM PIT**
- **HIGH ON CHEST**
- **SNUG KNOT**

Remove SLACK IN HAND-LINE

- **ONE RESCUER**—REMOVES SLACK ON POLE

- **TWO RESCUERS**—MAN ON GROUND REMOVES SLACK

IMPORTANT
GIVE 5 OR 6 QUICK BREATHS
... IF NECESSARY ...

THEN

Take FIRM GRIP ON FALL LINE

ONE RESCUER—HOLDS FALL LINE WITH ONE HAND

TWO RESCUERS—MAN ON GROUND HOLDS FALL LINE

FIGURE 5.6 (*Continued*) Illustrated method for elevated, pole-top rescue.

Cut INJURED'S SAFETY STRAP

**CUT STRAP ON SIDE
OPPOSITE DESIRED SWING**

Caution

**DO NOT CUT YOUR OWN SAFETY
STRAP OR THE HAND LINE**

RIGHT   WRONG

Lower INJURED

ONE RESCUER

- **GUIDE LOAD LINE WITH
  ONE HAND**
- **CONTROL RATE OF DESCENT
  WITH THE OTHER HAND**

TWO RESCUERS

- **MAN ON THE POLE GUIDES
  THE LOAD LINE**
- **MAN ON THE GROUND
  CONTROLS RATE OF DESCENT**

IF A CONSCIOUS MAN IS BEING ASSISTED
IN CLIMBING DOWN . . .
THE ONLY DIFFERENCE IS
THAT ENOUGH SLACK IS FED INTO THE
LINE TO PERMIT HIM CLIMBING FREEDOM

**ONE MAN
RESCUE**   **TWO OR MORE
MAN RESCUE**

RESCUES DIFFER ONLY IN
CONTROL OF THE FALL LINE

Remember

**THE APPROVED METHOD OF
LOWERING AN INJURED
MAN IS . . .**

- *Position* **HAND LINE**
- *Tie* **INJURED**
- *Remove* **SLACK IN HAND LINE**
- *Take* **FIRM GRIP ON FALL LINE**
- *Cut* **INJURED'S SAFETY STRAP**
- *Lower* **INJURED**

FIGURE 5.6 (*Continued*) Illustrated method for elevated, pole-top rescue.

IF POLE DOES NOT HAVE CROSSARM, RESCUER PLACES HAND-LINE OVER FIBERGLASS BRACKET INSULATOR SUPPORT, OR OTHER SUBSTANTIAL PIECE OF EQUIPMENT SUCH AS A SECONDARY RACK, NEUTRAL BRACKET, OR GUY WIRE ATTACHMENT, STRONG ENOUGH TO SUPPORT THE WEIGHT OF THE INJURED. SHORT END OF LINE IS WRAPPED AROUND FALL LINE TWICE AND TIED AROUND VICTIM'S CHEST USING THREE HALF HITCHES. INJURED'S SAFETY STRAP IS CUT AND RESCUER LOWERS INJURED TO THE GROUND.

LINE MUST BE REMOVED AND
VICTIM EASED ON
TO GROUND

LAY VICTIM ON HIS BACK AND OBSERVE IF VICTIM IS CONSCIOUS. IF VICTIM IS CONSCIOUS, TIME MAY NO LONGER BE CRITICAL. GIVE NECESSARY FIRST AID. CALL FOR HELP.

FIGURE 5.6   (*Continued*) Illustrated method for elevated, pole-top rescue.

IF THE INJURED IS UNCONSCIOUS AND
NOT BREATHING, PROVIDE AN OPEN
AIRWAY. GIVE HIM FIVE OR SIX QUICK
BREATHS. IF HE RESPONDS, CONTINUE
MOUTH-TO-MOUTH RESUSCITATION
UNTIL HE IS BREATHING WITHOUT
HELP. IF NO PULSE IS PRESENT, PUPIL
DOES NOT CONTRACT, AND SKIN
COLOR IS NOT NORMAL, HIS HEART
HAS STOPPED. RESTORE CIRCULATION.
USE HEART-LUNG RESUSCITATION.

BUCKET TRUCK
RESCUE
TIME
IS
CRITICAL

EQUIP PORTION OF INSULATED BOOM
OF TRUCK WITH ROPE BLOCKS
DESIGNED FOR HOT-LINE WORK.

FIGURE 5.6 (*Continued*) Illustrated method for elevated, pole-top rescue.

STRAP IS PLACED AROUND INSULATED BOOM APPROXIMATELY TEN FEET FROM BUCKET TO SUPPORT ROPE BLOCKS. BLOCKS ARE HELD TAUT ON BOOM FROM STRAP TO TOP OF BOOM.

RESCUER ON THE GROUND EVALUATES THE CONDITIONS WHEN AN EMERGENCY ARISES. THE BUCKET IS LOWERED USING THE LOWER CONTROLS. OBSTACLES IN THE PATH OF THE BUCKET MUST BE AVOIDED.

FIGURE 5.6   (*Continued*) Illustrated method for elevated, pole-top rescue.

HOOK ON ROPE BLOCKS IS ENGAGED IN A RING ON THE LINEMAN'S SAFETY STRAP. SAFETY STRAP IS RELEASED FROM BOOM OF TRUCK.

ROPE BLOCKS ARE DRAWN TAUT BY RESCUER ON THE GROUND. UNCONSCIOUS VICTIM IS RAISED OUT OF BUCKET WITH ROPE BLOCKS.

FIGURE 5.6   (*Continued*) Illustrated method for elevated, pole-top rescue.

RESCUER EASES VICTIM ON TO THE GROUND. CARE SHOULD BE TAKEN TO PROTECT THE INJURED VICTIM FROM FURTHER INJURY.

RELEASE ROPE BLOCKS FROM VICTIM.

FIGURE 5.6 (*Continued*) Illustrated method for elevated, pole-top rescue.

BASKET OR BUCKET ON AERIAL
DEVICE MAY BE CONSTRUCTED
TO TILT AFTER BEING RELEASED,
ELIMINATING THE NEED FOR
SPECIAL RIGGING TO REMOVE AN
INJURED PERSON FROM THE BASKET
OR BUCKET.

LAY VICTIM ON HIS BACK AND
OBSERVE IF VICTIM IS CONSCIOUS.
IF VICTIM IS CONSCIOUS, TIME MAY
NO LONGER BE CRITICAL. GIVE
NECESSARY FIRST AID. CALL
FOR HELP.

IF THE INJURED IS UNCONSCIOUS
AND NOT BREATHING, PROVIDE AN
OPEN AIRWAY. GIVE HIM FIVE OR
SIX QUICK BREATHS. IF HE RESPONDS,
CONTINUE MOUTH-TO-MOUTH
RESUSCITATION UNTIL HE IS
BREATHING WITHOUT HELP.

FIGURE 5.6 (*Continued*) Illustrated method for elevated, pole-top rescue.

Confined-Space Rescue

Confined-space rescue is made more complex by two basic problems. First, the confined space may become filled with gases which are not breathable or, worse, are toxic and therefore hazardous to human life. Second, the confined space does not allow for free motion of rescue personnel. This means that rescue workers may not be able to easily get a grip on the victim.

Atmosphere Checking in Confined-Space Rescues. Before the rescue is attempted, the atmosphere must be tested for the presence of adequate supplies of oxygen, excessive quantities of toxic gases, and excessive quantities of combustible gases. Figure 5.7 shows a typical monitoring setup for an underground confined-space area. If the rescuer must descend into a confined space that does not have adequate oxygen concentrations or has excessive quantities of toxic or combustible gases, the rescuer must wear respiration gear.

FIGURE 5.7   Vault atmosphere monitoring.

Oxygen levels must be no less than 19.5 percent and no more than 23.5 percent. Table 5.15 lists the potential effects of insufficient oxygen. The permissible levels of toxic gas vary depending on the type of gas and the individual. Generally toxic gases should be kept to levels that are less than 50 parts per million (ppm) by volume. Tables 5.16 and 5.17 list the potential effects that carbon monoxide CO and hydrogen sulfide H_2S will have.

Securing the Victim to the Rescue Line. The method used to secure a victim to the line depends upon the logistics of the given rescue. The nature of the injuries and the space available for the rescue both affect the method used. The simplest way is to tie a hand line around the victim using three half hitches as shown in Fig. 5.8. Figure 5.9 shows a preferred method using a padded harness designed specifically for such rescue efforts. If space allows or if the victim's injuries require it, a full rope body harness may be rigged as shown in Fig. 5.10. Figure 5.11 shows a victim being lifted using the rope body harness. Sometimes a victim's injuries may be so severe that they must be securely immobilized before being removed from the accident area. Both of the devices shown in Fig. 5.12 may be used.

Retrieving the Victim. After the victim has been secured to the rescue line, he or she must be raised from the confined space to an open area where treatment may be administered. A variety of different methods have been developed to raise victims. Figures 5. through 5.17 show various types of rigs that may be used as pulley points to retrieve victims.

The key to a successful victim retrieval is teamwork and adequate planning. Remember that human beings can weigh as much as 300 or 400 lb. Also remember

TABLE 5.15   Potential Effects of an Oxygen-Deficient Atmosphere

Oxygen content (% by volume)	Effects and symptoms* (at atmosphere pressure)
19.5	Minimum permissible oxygen level for normal functioning
15–19	Decreased ability to work strenuously. May impair coordination and may induce early symptoms in persons with coronary, pulmonary, or circulatory problems
12–14	Respiration increases in exertion; pulse increases, impaired coordination, perception, judgment
10–12	Respiration further increases in rate and depth, poor judgment, lips blue
8–10	Mental failure, fainting, unconsciousness, ashen face, blueness of lips, nausea, and vomiting
6–8	Eight min, 100% fatal; 6 min, 50% fatal; 4–5 min, recovery with treatment
4–6	Coma in 40 s, convulsions, respiration ceases, death

* The effects and symptoms at a given oxygen content are guidelines and will vary with the individual's state of health and physical activity.

TABLE 5.16   Potential Effects of Carbon Monoxide Exposure

PPM*	Effects and symptoms[†]	Time
35	Permissible exposure level limit	8 h
200	Slight headache	3 h
400	Headache, discomfort	2 h
600	Headache, discomfort	1 h
1000–2000	Confusion, headache, nausea	2 h
1000–2000	Tendency to stagger	$1\frac{1}{4}$ h
1000–2000	Slight palpitation of heart	30 min
2000–2500	Unconsciousness	30 min
4000	Fatal	Less than 1 h

* PPM—parts per million; volume measurement of gas concentration.
[†] The effects and symptoms at a given are guidelines and will vary with the individual's state of health and physical activity.

TABLE 5.17   Potential Effects of Hydrogen Sulfide Exposure

PPM	Effects and symptoms	Time
10	Permissible exposure level limit	8 h
50–100	Mild eye irritation, mild respiratory irritation	1 h
200–300	Marked eye irritation, marked respiratory irritation	1 h
500–700	Unconsciousness, death	$\frac{1}{4}$–1 h
1000 or more	Unconsciousness, death	Minutes

PASS LINE AROUND INJURED'S CHEST

TIE THREE HALF-HITCHES

- KNOT IN FRONT
- NEAR ONE ARM PIT
- HIGH ON CHEST
- SNUG KNOT

FIGURE 5.8 Securing the victim using a hand line.

FIGURE 5.9 Using a padded safety harness to secure the rescue line to the victim. (*Courtesy AVO, International.*)

FIGURE 5.10 Full body rope harness. (*Courtesy AVO, International.*)

FIGURE 5.11 Full body rope harness being used to lift the victim. (*Courtesy AVO, International.*)

STOKES NAVY STRETCHER

SKED SYSTEM MODEL SK-200

FIGURE 5.12 (*a*) Stokes navy stretcher. (*b*) SKED system model SK-200. (*Courtesy AVO, International.*)

FIGURE 5.13 Tripod hoist operation. (*Courtesy AVO, International.*)

FIGURE 5.14 Quad pod retractable lifeline. (*Courtesy AVO, International.*)

FIGURE 5.15 Gin pole hoist. (*Courtesy AVO, International.*)

FIGURE 5.16 Rope-tied A-frame and tripod hoists. (*Courtesy AVO, International.*)

GIN POLE

LADDER GIN POLE

FIGURE 5.17   Gin pole hoists. (*Courtesy AVO, International.*)

that unconscious victims cannot assist in their own retrieval. Always be certain that the rigging is strong enough.

Ground-Level Rescue

The Problem.   Ground-level victims do not require rescue as often as elevated or confined-space victims. Occasionally, however, victims do need retrieval, especially from metal-clad switchgear assemblies. Walk-in metal-clad switchgear has circuit breaker cubicles which represent a confined-space problem. They also have doorways which must be traversed. In addition to metal-clad gear problems, victims may be endangered by fire, chemical release, or any number of other similar hazards. Regardless of where the rescue is taking place, the general rescue procedures should be the starting point for all rescues.

Retrieving the Victim.   Since moving a victim can induce additional injuries or aggravate existing injuries, always make certain that moving the victim is absolutely necessary. If the victim must be moved, immobilizing him or her using a stretcher or other technique is preferred. However, if time is critical, one of the following carries may be employed.

The method used to move the victim depends on the nature and severity of the hazard to which he or she is exposed. For example, Figs. 5.18 and 5.19 illustrate two methods that may be used to remove a victim from a fire area. In these types of situations, smoke and heat may require that the rescuer stay low to the ground.

FIGURE 5.18   Clothes drag. (*Courtesy AVO, International.*)

FIGURE 5.19   Blanket drag. (*Courtesy AVO, International.*)

If only one person is available for the rescue, and the victim is conscious and mobile, the pack-strap carry (Fig. 5.20) may be employed. The fire-fighter's carry (Fig. 5.21) may be used if the victim is not conscious.

If two people are available for the rescue, any of the carries shown in Figs. 5.22 through 5.24 may be used. The carry shown in Fig. 5.23 generally requires that the victim be conscious.

FIGURE 5.20   Pack-strap carry (conscious victim). (*Courtesy AVO, International.*)

FIGURE 5.21   Fire-fighter's carry. (*Courtesy AVO, International.*)

FIGURE 5.22 Carry by extremities. (*Courtesy AVO, International.*)

ACCIDENT INVESTIGATION

Purpose

When accidents occur, they must be investigated thoroughly. An investigation serves two major purposes as shown in Table 5.18. Note that accident investigations should be performed only by qualified professionals who are experienced in such matters. Litigation can often ensue and result in corporate, personal, or product liability; errors and omissions; insurance subrogation; or other claims.

Accident Prevention. Accidents occur for a reason, and sometimes the reason is not obvious. A thorough investigation can reveal underlying causes. Employers must then act to eliminate those causes so such accidents will not occur again.

Litigation. Modern society is becoming increasingly litigious. Evidence gathered during an accident investigation can be used in court to either defend or prosecute a lawsuit.

General Rules

Several general rules for carrying out accident investigations are listed in Table 5.19. Many investigations have been hampered by well-meaning, inexperienced individuals

FIGURE 5.23 Two-person seat carry. (*Courtesy AVO, International.*)

FIGURE 5.24 Chair carry. (*Courtesy AVO, International.*)

who remove or alter evidence in the interests of cleaning up the area. Remember that only absolutely necessary modifications must be made at the accident scene, and even these should be documented, preferably with photographs and/or videotapes.

One of the major mistakes made by employers is to wait for the lawsuit before an accident investigation begins. Employers owe it to themselves and their employees to investigate accidents completely and thoroughly, as soon after the accident as possible. This is especially true of witness interviews. Time quickly alters or destroys memories of traumatic events; therefore, people must be interviewed immediately.

Whenever possible, *retain an expert.* Forensic engineering firms specialize in the investigation and analysis of accidents. Such organizations have a wealth of factual information available to them. They can determine causes in cases where inexperienced investigators can only guess. For information on forensic consultants contact the American Academy of Forensic Sciences, the Canadian Society of Forensic Sciences, or the International Society of Forensic Sciences.

Data Gathering

Site Survey. The gathering of data should start with a survey of the accident scene. If the basic rules have been followed, the scene will be virtually unchanged. The investigator should follow the steps outlined in Table 5.20.

TABLE 5.18 Reasons for Performing Accident Investigations

* Future accidents may be prevented by elimination of accident causes
* Evidence gathered during the investigation may be required in litigation

TABLE 5.19 General Rules for Performance of an Accident Investigation

* Investigations should be performed only by qualified, experienced personnel
* Until the investigation is complete, the accident scene should be modified only to the extent necessary to eliminate immediate hazards to personnel
* No evidence should be destroyed or thrown away for at least 5 to 10 years after the accident
* Photograph everything from many different angles
* Document everything that is observed or taken in interviews
* Perform the investigation as soon as possible. Remember that human memory is volatile

TABLE 5.20 Steps for an Accident Site Survey

- Visually inspect the area, making notes about general observations
- Photograph or videotape the scene
- Make a detailed inspection and develop a sketch of the entire scene

The first visual inspection can produce amazing insights into the nature and causes of the accident. Things to look for include

- Scorch and burn marks
- Damaged equipment
- Evidence of safety equipment
- Position of victim and or objects

The photographs or videotape, preferably both, can permanently store vital evidence. Because of the two-dimensional nature of photography, shots should be taken from all angles including from above to get a complete perspective. A scale reference can be included in the scene. An audio or written record should be made to clearly define the nature of each photograph, where it was taken, and any specific information that should be noted.

The final detailed inspection and sketch can be hand-done, clearly labeled, and dimensioned. Dimensions are particularly important since they may prove or disprove the possibility of any given event during the accident. The sketch should also reference photographs or videotape evidence that was taken.

Witness Interviews. Witness interviews help to establish what, how, where, and when. However, the investigator must remember that of all the evidence he or she will gather, eyewitness accounts are the least reliable. Human beings tend to be influenced by their own personal backgrounds and prejudices. Within a few hours, or even minutes, of the accident, eye witnesses' memories start to modify. Witnesses should be interviewed as soon as possible and on audiotape if appropriate.

The cautions in the previous paragraph are especially true of the accident victim. The human mind will literally shut off to prevent the agony associated with an accident. In case after case, victims remember nothing for several hours or even days before and after the accident. Information supplied by a victim should always be viewed with skepticism. The more traumatic the injury, the less credible will be the victim's statement.

When interviewing witnesses, the following points should be followed:

- When possible, conduct the interview at the accident site. The familiar surroundings may help to arouse memories that would be lost.
- Prepare a series of questions to be asked before the interview, and start with these questions. If the witness seems more comfortable with a freewheeling statement, allow it; however, avoid rambling and nonrelevant statements since these will only cloud the results.
- Try to keep the witness focused on the facts of the case. Blame, fault, and other such subjective conclusions should be left to the analysis stage of the investigation.

- When the interview is completed, the interview notes should be carefully stored and dated. If you make a summary of the interview, it should be stored with the notes; however, it should not replace the interview notes.
- Arrange for a follow-up interview to deal with questionable or conflicting accounts.

Physical Evidence. One of the most frequent mistakes made by inexperienced investigators is the alteration, destruction, or loss of physical evidence. A scorched or melted wire, a bit of flaked insulation, a piece of torn cloth, or a damaged circuit breaker can all be extremely important evidence.

Physical evidence should be documented in the preliminary stages of the investigation by the use of photographs, sketches, and written notes. After it has been documented, it should be carefully marked and stored. Physical evidence should be kept for a minimum of 5 years and possibly as long as 10 years depending upon the circumstances of the accident.

Accident Analysis

After the evidence has been gathered and the interviews have been taken, the analysis phase begins. The actual steps taken in this portion depend to a large extent on the specifics of the accident itself. However, at least two major steps may be involved.

Experimentation. Actual experimentation includes tests that are performed to evaluate or simulate certain conditions during an accident. For example, pork can be subjected to electric currents to evaluate the degree of burning that occurs for various currents, electric arcs can be staged with manikins to determine the degree of thermal burning that may occur, and air gaps can be checked to see how far an arc will jump in given circumstances. Experimentation is a detailed and sophisticated procedure and should be performed only by organizations with the necessary expertise.

Report. A report is developed based on a comprehensive analysis of all the evidence and experimental data that has been gathered. The report should contain, at a minimum, the sections listed in Table 5.21.

TABLE 5.21 Major Elements of the Final Report of an Accident Investigation

- Overview
- Step-by-step description of the accident
- Conclusion
- Appendices

- *Overview.* This section should include an executive summary type of description of the events leading up to the accident, the accident itself, and the accident aftermath. Only very general information should be included, such as the number of injured persons, the basic cause of the injuries, and the generalized suggestions for preventing such a problem in the future.

- *Step-by-step description of the accident.* Here the investigator takes the reader through each step of the accident from beginning to end. All the physical evidence is discussed, and eyewitness accounts are integrated into this portion of the report. All relevant information should be included, such as the activities of the victim prior to the accident that may have affected his or her behavior, the specific actions of the victim during the accident, the safety equipment that was in use at the time, the actions of witnesses, the duration of the electrical contact, the points on the body which were contacted, and other such details.

- *Conclusion.* The investigator should provide an evaluation of the accident including such information as the steps that could be taken to prevent similar accidents in the future, changes in safety equipment or rules which may be indicated, changes in employee training that may be required, and/or changes in work procedures which may be indicated. Since this is an engineering report, the investigator should avoid comments about who may be responsible for the accident. Such issues are better left to the legal system.

- *Appendices.* All the collected data can be included for reference. Remember that others may draw different conclusions than that of the investigator and should, therefore, be given the advantage of being able to examine all the evidence that has been collected. In addition, the evidence must be present to support the conclusions drawn. *Do not* include the originals of photographs and videotapes. Only copies should be included. The originals should be kept in a secure location such as a locked file cabinet or a safe-deposit box. Of course, physical evidence should not be included except at a formal presentation of the report. However, photographs of physical evidence can be included.

Please note that any and all content of such a report will be subject to insurance contract directives; insurance adjusters instructions; attorney-client privilege; powers granted to worker's compensation investigators; and powers granted to federal, state and provincial agencies that have jurisdiction in the investigations.

CHAPTER 6
LOW-VOLTAGE
SAFETY SYNOPSIS

INTRODUCTION

Each year 120-V circuits cause more death and injury than circuits of all other voltage levels combined. Such low-voltage circuits are extremely hazardous for two reasons. First, low-voltage circuits are the most common. Because they are the final distribution voltage, 240-v and 120-v circuits are used throughout residential, commercial, industrial, and utility systems.

The second reason for the extreme danger of low-voltage circuits is user apathy. Comments such as "It can't hurt you, it's only 120 volts," are heard all too often. Reference to Table 1.1 shows that 120-V circuits can produce currents through the human body which can easily reach fibrillation levels. Consider a perspiring worker using a metal electric drill with one foot immersed in water. Table 6.1 clearly shows that under such conditions, a worker can be subjected to a lethal shock. Furthermore, if sustained for a sufficient period, 120-V contact can create severe burns.

TABLE 6.1 Possible Current Flow in 120-V Circuit

Body part	Resistance, Ω
Wet hand around drill handle	500
Foot immersed in water	100
Internal resistance of body	200
Total resistance	800

Total current flow possible in 120-v circuit = I = (120/800) = 150 mA

A 480-V circuit is more than 4 times as lethal as a 120-V circuit. A 480-V circuit has sufficient energy to sustain arcing faults and to create severe blast conditions. This chapter summarizes some of the safety-related concerns that apply to low-voltage circuits—that is, circuits of 1000 V ac and less and 250-V dc and less. Generally, workers should treat low-voltage circuits with the same degree of respect afforded medium- and high-voltage circuits. Refer to Chaps. 2 and 3 for detailed information. Note that some of the safety-related information covered in this chapter also applies to medium- and high-voltage systems. Where necessary, the information is repeated in Chap. 7.

LOW-VOLTAGE EQUIPMENT

Hand tools and extension cords are the most commonly used pieces of low-voltage equipment. Each of these items is responsible for hundreds of injuries and deaths each year. The following sections summarize the types of usage procedures that should be employed with such equipment.

Extension Cords

Flexible cord sets (extension cords) are used to extend the reach of the power cord for low-voltage operated tools and equipment. They typically have a male plug at one end and a female receptacle at the other. The tool's power plug is inserted into the female receptacle, and the extension cord's male plug is inserted into the power source or into yet another extension cord's female receptacle. Extension cords can be used to supply power to tools that are located many feet or yards away from the source of power.

Extension cords can be extremely hazardous if not used properly. The following precautions should always be observed when using extension cords:

- Closely inspect extension cords before each use. Table 6.2 lists the types of items that should be looked for during the inspection. (Note that Table 6.2 applies to both extension cords and portable tools.)

TABLE 6.2 Visual Inspection Points for Extension Cords and Cord-Connected Tools

- Missing, corroded, or damaged prongs on connecting plugs
- Frayed, worn, or missing insulation
- Improperly exposed conductors
- Loose screws or other poorly made electrical connections
- Missing or incorrectly sized fuses
- Damaged or cracked cases
- Burns or scorch marks

- Never use an extension cord to lift or support a tool.
- Make certain the ground connection is complete from one end of the cord to the other.
- Never alter the plug or receptacle on an extension cord. This applies especially to altering the ground connection.
- If the extension cord is of the locking or twist-locking type, the plugs should be securely locked before using the cord.
- Do not use an extension cord in wet or hazardous environments unless it is rated for such service by the manufacturer. If extension cords are used in wet or hazardous environments, insulating safety equipment such as rubber gloves with appropriate leather protectors should be used.

TABLE 6.3 Recommended Periodic Tests and Test Results for Extension Cords

Test	Description	Pass/fail criteria
Ground continuity test	25 A minimum is passed through the cord's ground circuit	Voltage drop across the cord should not exceed 2.5 V
Insulation breakdown	High voltage is applied to the cord's insulation system and the leakage current or insulation resistance is measured (3000 V maximum direct current applied)	Leakage current no more than 6 μA @ 3000 V (500 MΩ)

- Only personnel who are authorized and trained in the use of extension cords should be allowed to use them.
- Extension cords should be subjected to the electrical tests outlined in Table 6.3. If the cord fails any of the listed tests, it should be replaced or repaired.
- When not in use, extension cords should be carefully rolled and stored in such a way that they cannot be damaged.

An extension cord which exhibits any of the visual inspection problems listed in Table 6.2 or which does not pass the tests listed in Table 6.3 should be removed from service until it can be repaired or replaced.

Plug- and Cord-Connected Equipment

Drills, circular saws, sanders, and other such electrically operated equipment fall into this category. These types of devices are powered via a male plug located at the end of a flexible cord. The flexible cord, in turn, connects to the operating circuits of the tool.

Hand tools generally fall into one of two categories—the standard metal tools with ground, and the double-insulated type of tool. The metallic tool power cord is a standard three-conductor type with a hot wire, neutral wire, and the safety ground. The hot wire and the neutral wire form the actual power circuit of the tool. The safety ground is connected to the metallic frame of the tool. In the event that the hot wire is short-circuited to the case of the tool, the safety ground wire forms a continuous, low-impedance path back to the service box. Figure 6.1 is a pictorial diagram of such an assembly.

Even the relatively low impedance path provided by the safety ground wire can create lethal voltages from the hand to the feet under some circumstances. The double-insulated tool does not employ a metallic case. Rather, its case is made of a high-strength, nonconductive plastic or composite material. The power supply for such tools is a two-conductor power cord with no safety ground. Since the tool case is nonconductive, the user is protected by both the case and the normal insulation of the electric circuit.

Power tools should be subject to the same precautions as those outlined for extension cords in the previous section. Specifically the following should be observed:

FIGURE 6.1 Typical metallic case hand tool.

- Closely inspect tools before each use. Table 6.2 lists the types of items that should be looked for during the inspection. (Note that Table 6.2 applies to both extension cords and portable tools.)
- Never use the tool power cord to lift the tool. If the tool must be lifted, tie a hand line or rope to the tool.
- Make certain the tool's ground connection is complete. For metal-cased tools, the safety ground connection is the difference between life and death when an internal short circuit occurs.
- Never alter the plug or receptacle on a tool. This applies especially to altering the ground connection.
- If a tool employs a twist-lock or locking type of plug, it should be securely fastened before the tool is used.
- Do not use a tool in wet or hazardous environments unless it is rated for such service by the manufacturer.
- If tools are used in wet or hazardous environments, insulating safety equipment such as rubber gloves with appropriate leather protectors should be worn.
- Only personnel who are authorized and trained in the use of power tools should be allowed to use them.
- Cord-connected tools should be subjected to the electrical tests outlined in Table 6.4. If the tool fails any of the listed tests, it should be replaced or repaired.
- When not in use, tools should be carefully stored in such a way that they cannot be damaged.

Any tool which does not meet the pass/fail criteria listed in Table 6.4 should be removed from service until it can be repaired or replaced.

TABLE 6.4 Recommended Periodic Tests and Recommended Results for Cord-Powered Tools

Test	Description	Pass/fail criteria
Ground continuity test	25 A minimum is passed through the cord's ground circuit	Voltage drop across the cord should not exceed 2.5 V
Insulation breakdown	High voltage is applied to the cord's insulation system and the leakage current or insulation resistance is measured (3000 V maximum direct current applied)*	Leakage current not more than 6 microamperes @ 3000 V (500 MΩ)
Leakage test	Measures the current (0 to 10 mA) that would flow through the operator if he or she were to provide a path to ground at normal operating voltage	
Operational check	Operates the tool to verify proper operation and to indicate operating current	Operating current should be within nominal nameplate values

* Refer to tool manufacturer's directions for allowed maximum test voltages.

Current Transformers

The safety hazards of current transformers is identical for both low-, medium-, and high-voltage circuits. Refer to Chap. 7 for a detailed coverage of the nature of current transformer hazards and methods for protecting workers from those hazards.

GROUNDING LOW-VOLTAGE SYSTEMS

The subject of electrical grounding is a complex one. The following sections focus on the grounding concepts and requirements of low-voltage systems as they relate to safety. For more complete coverage of electrical grounding refer to the various ANSI/IEEE standards including IEEE Guide for Safety in AC Substation Grounding—ANSI/IEEE standard 80 and IEEE Recommended Practice for Grounding of Industrial and Commercial Power Systems—ANSI/IEEE standard 142.

What Is a Ground?

A *ground* is an electrically conducting connection between equipment or an electric circuit and the earth, or to some conducting body that serves in place of the earth. If a ground is properly made, the earth or conducting body and the circuit or system will all maintain the same relative voltage.

Figure 6.2*a* shows an electrical system that is not grounded. In such a situation, a voltage will exist between the ground and some of the metallic components of the power system. In Fig. 6.2*b*, the earth connection has been made. When the system is grounded, the voltage is reduced to zero between the previously energized sections of the system.

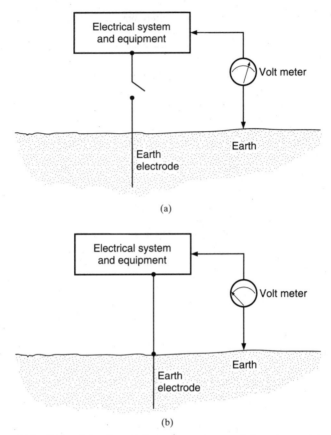

FIGURE 6.2 Grounding. (*a*) Before system is grounded, a voltage exists between the system and the earth. (*b*) When ground connection is made, no voltage exists.

Bonding Versus Grounding

Bonding is the permanent joining of metallic parts to form a continuous, conductive path. Since the earth is generally not a good conductor, bonding is used to provide a low-impedance metallic path between all metallic parts. This, in essence, bypasses the earth and overcomes its relatively high impedance. A good grounding system is a combination of solid connections between metallic parts and the earth as well as between all metallic parts.

Voltage Hazards

Figure 6.3 illustrates the four standard voltage hazards which are associated with and relieved by proper system grounding. If a system is ungrounded and the nonenergized metallic parts become energized, the metallic parts will have a measurable voltage between themselves and ground. If the system is grounded by driving ground electrodes into the earth, current will flow from the rods into the earth. At each ground electrode, the voltage will rise relative to the remote reference point. The voltage will drop off away from the electrodes and peak at each electrode. This situation creates the four types of voltage hazards as follows:

- *Step voltage.* As a worker steps across the ground, the front foot will be at a different potential than the rear foot. This effect is caused by the voltage gradient created by the ground electrodes (Fig. 6.3). Step voltage can easily reach lethal levels. It can be mitigated by increasing the number of grounding electrodes, increasing bonding between the metal parts, and employing a grounding grid.

- *Touch voltage.* Because of the voltage gradient, the voltage of the earth only a short distance from the grounded metallic equipment will be different than the equipment. Thus, if a worker touches the grounded equipment, his or her feet will be at a different potential than his or her hands. This voltage can be lethal. Touch voltage is mitigated by increasing the number of grounding electrodes, increasing bonding between metal parts, and employing a grounding grid.

- *Mesh voltage.* Mesh voltage is the worst case of touch voltage. Cause, effect, and mitigation methods are identical to those described previously under Touch Voltage.

- *Transferred voltage.* Because metal parts have a much lower impedance than the earth, the voltage drop between remote locations is lower on the metallic connections than the earth. This means that the earth may be at a significantly different voltage than the metallic connections. Transferred voltages are particularly noticeable on neutral wires which are grounded at the service point and nowhere else. Transferred potential can be mitigated by providing the entire area with a ground grid; however, this solution is infeasible in any but the smallest systems. Transferred voltage must be mitigated by avoiding contact with conductors from remote locations and/or using rubber insulating gloves.

FIGURE 6.3 Four voltage hazards related to system grounding. (*Courtesy Institute of Electrical and Electronic Engineers.*)

System Grounds

What Is a System Ground?   A *system ground* is the connection of one of the conductors to the earth. Such a connection is accomplished by connecting an electric wire to the selected system conductor and the grounding electrode.

Why Are Systems Grounded?   Power systems have conductors grounded for a variety of safety and operational reasons including

- Grounded systems provide sufficient short-circuit current for efficient operation of protective equipment.
- Grounded systems are less prone to transient overvoltages which can cause insulation failures.
- Grounded systems are generally more easily protected from lightning.
- Solidly grounded systems are less prone to resonant conditions which can cause equipment and insulation failures.

What Systems Must Be Grounded?   The NEC requires that both ac and dc systems be grounded. Table 6.5 summarizes low-voltage dc grounding requirements, and Table 6.6 summarizes low-voltage ac grounding requirements.

How Are Systems Grounded?   Electrical systems are grounded by connecting one of the electric conductors to earth. The conductor chosen and the location of the ground are determined as part of the engineering design for the system. Figures 6.4 through 6.7 illustrate four different low-voltage circuits and how they are grounded. Note that in some cases, the point of ground is determined by regulatory requirements such as the NEC.

The wire(s) that must be grounded depend on the voltage level and the system application. For dc systems, one of the conductors or the neutral wire is to be grounded depending on the type of system (Table 6.5). For ac systems, the NEC specifies five different locations for the selection of the grounding point for ac systems. Table 6.7 identifies each of the five locations.

Systems with voltages between 480 and 1000 V phase to phase may be grounded through an impedance to limit the amount of fault current. In the circuit shown in Fig. 6.8, the resistor will oppose current flow between the earth and the phase wires.

FIGURE 6.4   Grounding a 120-V single-phase circuit.

FIGURE 6.5   Grounding a 240/120-V single-phase, three-wire circuit.

TABLE 6.5 DC Circuits which Require Grounding

Type of circuit	Circuits to be grounded	Exceptions/comments
Two-wire dc	All	Systems less than 50 V or greater than 300 V between conductors need not be grounded
		Limited-area industrial systems with ground detectors need not be grounded
		Certain rectifier-derived dc systems do not need to be grounded
		DC fire protective signaling circuits with no more than 0.030 A may not need to be grounded
Three-wire dc	All	The neutral wire is grounded

Note: See the current edition of the National Electrical Code for details.

TABLE 6.6 AC Circuits which Require Grounding

Type of circuit	Circuits to be grounded	Exceptions/comments
AC systems 50 to 1000 V	If maximum voltage to ground is less than 50 V Three-phase, 4-wire wye, if neutral is a circuit conductor Three-phase, 4-wire delta with midpoint grounded on one leg In some cases when grounded service conductor is uninsulated	The National Electrical Code has many exceptions to these grounding requirements

Note: See the current edition of the National Electrical Code for details.

TABLE 6.7 Typical Grounding Requirements for Low-Voltage Systems

Type of premises wiring circuit	Location of ground
One-phase, 2-wire	Either conductor (Fig. 6.4) ·
One-phase, 3-wire	The neutral conductor (Fig. 6.5)
Multiphase with one wire common to all phases	The common conductor (not illustrated)
Multiphase systems required on grounded phase	One of the phase conductors (not illustrated)
Three-phase, 4-wire circuits	The neutral conductor (Fig. 6.6)
240/120, 3-phase, 4-wire	The center point of the grounded leg (Fig. 6.7)

FIGURE 6.6   Grounding a 208/120-V three-phase, four-wire system.

FIGURE 6.7   Grounding a 240/120-V, three-phase, four-wire system.

For example, assume that the phase A wire falls to the earth. The circuit that is formed will be composed of the power system's phase-to-neutral voltage (277 V) impressed across the series combination of the power system's impedances plus the grounding resistor. If the grounding resistor is properly sized, it will limit the fault current to any maximum value that is chosen during the design.

By limiting the amount of fault current, resistance-grounded systems provide a somewhat higher level of safety. However, the engineer making the design decision to ground through a resistor must take into consideration more variables than just safety. Protective systems, ground fault current, voltage transients, and many other such concerns must be considered before the engineer decides to use a resistance-grounded system.

Equipment Grounds

What Is an Equipment Ground?   An *equipment ground* is an electrically conductive connection between the metallic parts of equipment and the earth. For example, transformer cases and cores are connected to the earth—this connection is called an

FIGURE 6.8 High resistance grounded 480/277-V, three-phase, four-wire system.

equipment ground. Note that the metallic parts of equipment are grounded and bonded together. This bonding serves to reduce the voltage potential between all metallic parts and the earth.

Why Is Equipment Grounded? The equipment ground is one of the most important aspects of grounding as far as safety is concerned. Workers are constantly in contact with transformer shells, raceways, conduits, switchgear frames, and all the other conductive, non–current-carrying parts. Proper equipment grounding and bonding ensures that the voltage to which workers will be subjected is kept to a minimum. Proper bonding and grounding mitigates touch and step voltages.

How Is Equipment Grounded? The NEC requires that the path to ground from circuits, equipment, and metal enclosures must meet the conditions listed in Table 6.8. The NEC does not allow the earth to be the sole equipment grounding conductor. Simply setting metal equipment on the earth is not sufficient. Equipment must be connected to the earth via metal electrodes and conductors.

Equipment used in grounded systems is grounded by bonding the equipment grounding conductor to the grounded service conductor and the grounding electrode conductor. That is, the equipment ground is connected to the system ground. Equipment used in ungrounded systems is grounded by bonding the equipment grounding conductor to the grounding electrode conductor.

What Equipment Must Be Grounded? Tables 6.9 through 6.12 list the types of equipment that must be grounded according to the NEC. Always refer to the current edition of the NEC for up-to-date information.

TABLE 6.8 Equipment Grounding Requirements

- Must be permanent and continuous
- Must have the capacity to conduct any fault current likely to be imposed on it
- Must have sufficiently low impedance to limit the voltage to ground and to facilitate the operation of the circuit protective devices

TABLE 6.9 Grounding Requirements for Equipment Fastened in Place or Connected by Permanent Wiring

Must ground	Exceptions
• Equipment within 8 ft (2.44 m) horizontally or 5 ft (1.52 m) vertically of ground or grounded metal objects subject to human contact • Equipment located in wet or damp locations • Equipment in electrical contact with other metallic objects • Equipment located in classified hazardous locations • Equipment which is supplied by metal-clad, metal-sheathed, metal-raceway, or other wiring method which provides an equipment ground • Equipment which operates with any terminal in excess of 150 V to ground	• Enclosures for switches or circuit breakers used for other than service equipment and accessible to qualified persons only • Metal frames of electrically heated appliances; exempted by special permission, in which case the frames shall be permanently and effectively insulated from ground • Distribution apparatus, such as transformer and capacitor cases, mounted on wooded poles, at a height exceeding 8 ft (2.44 m) above ground or grade level • Listed equipment protected by a system of double insulation, or its equivalent, shall not be required to be grounded. Such equipment must be distinctively marked

TABLE 6.10 Grounding Requirements for Equipment Fastened in Place or Connected by Permanent Wiring

Must ground	Exceptions
Switchboard frames and structures	Frames of 2-wire dc switchboards where effectively insulated
Pipe organs (generator and motor frames)	Where the generator is effectively insulated from ground and from the motor driving it
Motor frames	
Enclosures for motor controllers	Enclosures attached to ungrounded portable equipment Lined covers of snap switches
Elevators and cranes	
Garages, theaters, and motion picture studios	Pendant lamp-holders supplied by circuits less than 150 V to ground
Electric signs	
Motion picture projection equipment	
Remote-control, signaling, and fire protective signaling circuits	
Lighting fixtures	
Motor-operated water pumps	

TABLE 6.11   Nonelectric Equipment
Grounding Requirements

Must ground
Cranes
Elevator cars
Electric elevators
Metal partitions
Mobile homes and recreational vehicles

TABLE 6.12   Grounding Requirements for Equipment Connected by Cord and Plug

Must ground	Exceptions
In classified hazardous locations	
In systems which are operated in excess of 150 V to ground	Motors, where guarded
	Metal frames of electrically heated appliances, exempted by special permission, in which case the frames shall be permanently and effectively insulated from ground
	Listed equipment protected by a system of double insulation, or its equivalent, shall not be required to be grounded. Where such a system is employed, the equipment shall be distinctively marked
In residential occupancies • Refrigerators, freezers, and air conditioners • Clothes washing/drying machines, sump pumps, aquariums • Hand-held motor-operated tools including snow blowers, hedge clippers, etc. • Portable hand lamps	Listed equipment protected by a system of double insulation, or its equivalent, shall not be required to be grounded. Where such a system is employed, the equipment shall be distinctively marked
In other than residential occupancies • Refrigerators, freezers, air conditioners • Clothes washing/drying machines, electronic computers/data-processing equipment, sump pumps, aquariums • Hand-held, motor-operated tools including hedge clippers, lawn mowers, snow blowers, etc. • Cord- and plug-connected appliances used in damp or wet locations • Tools likely to be used in wet or conductive locations • Portable hand lamps	Tools and hand lamps in wet locations when supplied though an isolating transformer with an ungrounded secondary of not over 50 V Listed equipment protected by a system of double insulation, or its equivalent, shall not be required to be grounded. Where such a system is employed, the equipment shall be distinctively marked

SAFETY EQUIPMENT

Overview

Because of the delusion that "low voltage can't hurt you," many workers do not use safety equipment when working on or near energized, low-voltage conductors. As described previously in this chapter, the amount of available energy in the system determines its lethal effects, not the voltage. Low-voltage systems are extremely hazardous and should be treated with the respect they deserve. The following sections describe the types of safety equipment that should be worn when working on or near energized, low-voltage conductors. The recommendations given are minimum recommendations. If additional or more stringent protection is desired or required, it should be worn.

Hard Hats

Protective headgear for persons working on or near energized, low-voltage circuits should provide both mechanical and electrical protection. Since the ANSI class C helmet provides no electrical protection, class C helmets should not be worn. Workers should be supplied with and should wear either ANSI class A or class B helmets. If workers are never required to work around high-voltage circuits, the ANSI class A helmet may be used. If, however, workers are required to work around both high- and low-voltage circuits, they should be supplied with and should wear ANSI class B helmets. Table 6.13 summarizes the characteristics of the three ANSI classes.

Eye Protection

Even low-voltage systems are capable of producing extremely powerful and hazardous electric arcs and blast. This is especially true of 480-V and 575-V systems. Because of this, eye protection for electrical workers should provide protection against heat and optical radiation. ANSI standard Z87.1-1989 provides a selection

TABLE 6.13 Summary of the Characteristics for ANSI Classes A, B, and C

Class	Description	Comments
A	Reduce the impact of falling objects and reduce danger of contact with exposed, low-voltage conductors. Representative sample shells are proof-tested at 2200 V phase to ground	Recommended to be worn by personnel working around only low-voltage circuits
B	Reduce the impact of falling objects and reduce danger of contact with exposed high-voltage conductors. Representative sample shells are proof-tested at 20,000 V phase to ground	Recommended to be worn by personnel working around high- and low-voltage circuits
C	Intended to reduce the force of impact of falling objects. This class offers no electrical protection	Should not be worn by personnel working on or around energized conductors of any voltage

chart as well as a chart which illustrates the various protection options that are available. The selection chart is reproduced in this handbook as Table 6.14 and eye protection options are shown in Fig. 6.9.

Electrical workers should consider using eye protection that combines both heat and optical radiation protection. Table 6.14 and Fig. 6.9 show several different types of equipment that will provide such protection including types B, C, D, E, and F. If arcing and molten splashing is possible, as with open-door switching or racking of circuit breakers, the type N eye protection should be employed.

Arc Protection

Low-voltage systems can create and sustain significant electric arcs accompanied by electric blast. Employees performing work in 575-V, 480-V, or 208-V phase-to-phase systems should wear the type of clothing listed in Table 6.15.

A. Spectacle, No Sideshield
B. Spectacle, Half Sideshield
C. Spectacle, Full Sideshield
D. Spectacle, Detachable Sideshield
E. Spectacle, Non-Removable Lens
F. Spectacle, Lift Front
G. Cover Goggle, No Ventilation
H. Cover Goggle, Indirect Ventilation
I. Cover Goggle, Direct Ventilation
J. Cup Goggle, Direct Ventilation
K. Cup Goggle, Indirect Ventilation
L. Spectacle, Headband Temple
M. Cover Welding Goggle, Indirect Ventilation
N. Faceshield
O. Welding Helmet, Hand Held
P. Welding Helmet, Stationary Window
Q. Welding Helmet, Lift Front

*The illustrations shown are only representative of protective devices commonly available at the time of the writing of this standard. Protective devices do not need to take the forms shown, but must meet the requirements of the standard.

NOTES:
(1) Care shall be taken to recognize the possibility of multiple and simultaneous exposure to a variety of hazards. Adequate protection against the highest level of each of the hazards must be provided.
(2) Operations involving heat may also involve optical radiation. Protection from both hazards shall be provided.
(3) Faceshields shall only be worn over primary eye protection.
(4) Filter lenses shall meet the requirements for shade designations in Table 1.
(5) Persons whose vision requires the use of prescription (Rx) lenses shall wear either protective devices fitted with prescription (Rx) lenses or protective devices designed to be worn over regular prescription (Rx) eyewear.

(6) Wearers of contact lenses shall also be required to wear appropriate covering eye and face protection devices in a hazardous environment. It should be recognized that dusty and/or chemical environments may represent an additional hazard to contact lens wearers.
(7) Caution should be exercised in the use of metal frame protective devices in electrical hazard areas.
(8) Refer to Section 6.5, Special Purpose Lenses.
(9) Welding helmets or handshields shall be used only over primary eye protection.
(10) Non-sideshield spectacles are available for frontal protection only.

FIGURE 6.9 Eye protection devices. (Refer to Table 6.14 for selection criteria.) (*Courtesy American National Standards Institute.*)

TABLE 6.14 Eye Protection Selection Chart

	Assessment SEE NOTE (1)	Protector type[1]	Protectors	Limitations	Not recommended
IMPACT	Chipping, grinding, machining, masonry work, riveting, and sanding	Flying fragments, objects, large chips, particles, sand, dirt, etc.	B, C, D, E, F, G, H, I, J, K, L, N	Spectacles, goggles, face shields SEE NOTES (1) (3) (5) (6) (10) For severe exposure add N	Protective devices do not provide unlimited protection SEE NOTE (7)	Protectors that do not provide protection from side exposure Filter or tinted lenses that restrict light transmittance, unless it is determined that a glare hazard exists. Refer to Optical Radiation
HEAT	Furnace operations, pouring, casting, hot dipping, gas cutting, and welding	Hot sparks	B, C, D, E, F, G, H, I, J, K, L, *N	Face shields, goggles, spectacles *For severe exposure add N SEE NOTE (2) (3)	Spectacles, cup and cover type goggles do not provide unlimited facial protection SEE NOTE (2)	Protectors that do not provide protection from side exposure
		Splash from molten metals	*N	*Face shields worn over goggles H, K SEE NOTE (2) (3)		
		High temperature exposure	N	Screen face shields, reflective face shields SEE NOTE (2) (3)	SEE NOTE (3)	
CHEMICAL	Acid and chemicals handling, degreasing, plating	Splash	G, H, K *N	Goggles, eyecup and cover types *For severe exposure, add N	Ventilation should be adequate but well protected from splash entry	Spectacles, welding helmets, hand shields
		Irritating mists	G	Special-purpose goggles	SEE NOTE (3)	
DUST	Woodworking, buffing, general dusty conditions	Nuisance dust	G, H, K	Goggles, eyecup and cover types	Atmospheric conditions and the restricted ventilation of the protector can cause lenses to fog. Frequent cleaning may	

OPTICAL RADIATION

		typical filter lens shade SEE NOTE (9)	Protectors		Protectors that do not provide protection from optical radiation SEE NOTE (4)
Welding:					
Electric Arc	O, P, Q	10-14	Welding helmets or Welding shields	Protection from optical radiation is directly related to filter lens density. SEE NOTE (4). Select the darkest shade that allows adequate task performance	
Welding:		SEE NOTE (9)			
Gas	J, K, L, M, N, O, P, Q	4-8	Welding goggles or welding face shield		
Cutting		3-6			
Torch brazing		3-4		SEE NOTE (3)	
Torch soldering	B, C, D, E, F, N	1.5-3	Spectacles or welding face shield		
Glare	A, B	Spectacle SEE NOTE (9) (10)		Shaded or special-purpose lenses, as suitable SEE NOTE (8)	

[1] Refer to Fig. 6.9 for protector types.
Source: Courtesy of American National Standards Institute.

6.17

TABLE 6.15 Recommended Arc Protection and Clothing for Persons Working on or near Energized Low-Voltage Conductors

Description of work	Type of clothing
Routine work on or close to energized conductors (circuits above 50 V to ground)	Flame retardant work clothing ($4\frac{1}{2}$ oz/yd or more)—or equivalent
Open box switching and/or fuse removal (circuits 208-V phase to phase and higher)	Flame retardant work clothing and/or flash suits (6 oz/yd or more)—or equivalent
Installation or removal of low-voltage circuit breakers and/or motor starters with energized bus (circuits 208 V phase to phase or higher)	Flame retardant work clothing and/or flash suits (6 oz/yd or more)—or equivalent

Note: Head, eye, and insulating protection should also be worn. See Chap. 2 for additional information on the use of various types of protective clothing.

Rubber Insulating Equipment

The introduction of the so-called low-voltage rubber glove has made the use of insulating protection much more convenient than in the past. Personnel working on or near energized low-voltage conductors should wear low-voltage rubber gloves with appropriate leather protectors. Such gloves will have red ANSI labels and are rated for use in circuits of up to and including 1000 V rms.

Voltage-Testing Devices

Proximity or contact testers intended for use in low-voltage circuits should be used to test circuits and to verify that they are de-energized and safe to work on. Voltage-testing devices are described in Chap. 2. Examples of low-voltage–measuring instruments are shown in Figs. 6.10 through 6.12. Workers should use receptacle and GFCI testers such as that shown in Fig. 6.13. These testers are especially important for the verification of the ground path in an operation duplex receptacle.

(a) (b)

FIGURE 6.10 Volt-stick proximity voltage sensor for use on circuits up to 600 V. (*Courtesy Santronics, Inc.*)

FIGURE 6.11 Safety voltage/continuity tester for circuits of 600 V ac or dc and less. (*Courtesy Ideal Industries, Inc.*)

SAFETY PROCEDURES

General

The general procedures described in Chap. 3 should be used on all circuits in excess of 50 V to ground. The following sections describe key procedures which apply to low-voltage circuits.

FIGURE 6.12 Digital readout contact type safety voltmeter for circuits of 1000 V ac and dc or less. (*Courtesy Tegam, Inc.*)

Approach Distances

The OSHA Safety-Related Work Practices Rule (CFR Title 29, Part 1910, Subpart S, Paragraphs 331 through 335) defines minimum approach distances to energized overhead lines for qualified and unqualified employees. Table 6.16 lists these approach distances for low-voltage circuits for qualified employees. Unqualified employees are instructed not to approach overhead energized circuits any closer than 10 ft (3 m). Although these approach distances are clearly defined as being for overhead lines, they may be used as guidelines for any exposure to energized electric circuits. If employees need to work near any energized circuits closer than the values given in Table 6.16, they should use rubber insulating equipment to protect themselves.

Voltage Measurement

The voltage-measurement techniques defined in Chap. 3 should be employed on circuits of all voltages, including 1000 V and below. Note that although the OSHA stan-

TABLE 6.16 Approach Distances for Qualified Employees

Voltage range (phase to phase)	Minimum approach distance
300 V and less	Avoid contact
Over 300 V, not over 750 V	1 ft 0 in (30.5 cm)

FIGURE 6.13 Receptacle and GFCI tester. (*Courtesy Direct Safety Company, Phoenix, Arizona.*)

dards do not require the three-step measurement process for circuits of below 600 V, common practice in the industry does, in fact, call for instrument checks both before and after the actual circuit measurement.

Locking and Tagging

Lockout-tagout and energy control procedures apply to circuits of all voltage levels. Refer to Chap. 3 for detailed discussions of lockout-tagout procedures.

Closing Protective Devices After Operation

Workers should never reclose any protective device after it has operated, until it has been determined that it is safe to do so. Several criteria may be used to determine whether or not it is safe to reclose the protective device (Table 6.17). Other conditions may or may not indicate a safe reclosing situation.

TABLE 6.17 Typical Situations which May Allow Reclosing of a Protective Device which has Operated

---

- The faulted section of the system is found and repaired
- The nature of the protective device makes it clear that no hazard is present. For example if the device which operated is an overload type of device, it may be safe to reclose
- The reclosing operation can be made in such a way that the workers are not exposed to additional hazard. For example, if the reclosing operation can be made by remote control, and if all personnel are kept away from all parts of the circuit, it may be reclosed

---

CHAPTER 7
MEDIUM- AND HIGH-VOLTAGE SAFETY SYNOPSIS

INTRODUCTION

High-voltage systems* have three uniquely hazardous characteristics. First, high-voltage systems are very high energy systems. This means that they easily establish and maintain hazardous arc and blast conditions. Second, most workers do not have much experience working on or around such systems. Personnel ignorance can lead to very serious accidents and injuries. And finally, high voltages can puncture through the keratin skin layer, virtually eliminating the only significant skin resistance. Lack of knowledge can be corrected by personnel training. Chapter 9 covers the topic of personnel training in great detail.

The energy content and skin-puncturing characteristics of high-voltage systems are inherent to their nature. Safety precautions must be strictly observed to reduce the possibility of accidents, and safety equipment must be worn to reduce the severity of accidents.

This chapter highlights some of the key or critical safety concepts related to high-voltage systems. Many of the types of safety precautions used in high-voltage systems are identical to those used in low-voltage systems. Such precautions have been repeated in this chapter.

HIGH-VOLTAGE EQUIPMENT

Current Transformers

Note: The material in this section applies to current transformers used in low-, medium-, and high-voltage circuits.

---

* ANSI/IEEE standard 141-1986 defines low-voltage systems as those which are less than 1000 V, medium-voltage systems as those equal to or greater than 1000 v and less than 100,000 v, and high-voltage systems as those equal to or greater than 100,000 v. To simplify notation, this chapter will refer to all systems of 1000 v or higher as *high-voltage* systems.

FIGURE 7.1 Typical current transformers. (*Courtesy AVO Multi-Amp Institute.*)

Current transformers (CTs) (Fig. 7.1), are used to reduce primary current levels to lower values which are usable by instruments such as meters and protective relays. In doing this the primary winding of the current transformer is connected in series with the system load current and the secondary winding is connected to the instruments (Fig. 7.2).

If the secondary of an energized transformer is open-circuited, an extremely high voltage appears at the secondary (Fig. 7.3). Depending on the type of transformer and the conditions at the time of the open circuit, this high voltage can create arc and blast hazards. Current transformers can explode violently when their secondary

FIGURE 7.2 Schematic diagram of a current transformer connection.

FIGURE 7.3 Open circuit on secondary of current transformer.

circuits are opened. *Caution: Never open-circuit the secondary of an energized current transformer. A CT secondary circuit should always be terminated with rated load or a short circuit.*

When working on or near CT circuits, personnel should always be aware of the hazard and should wear rubber gloves, arc protective clothing, and face shields if working on the wiring for the circuit. The primary circuit should be de-energized before the secondary wiring is opened.

GROUNDING SYSTEMS OF OVER 1000 V

The subject of electrical grounding is a complex one. The following sections focus on the grounding concepts and requirements of high-voltage systems as they relate to safety. For more complete coverage of electrical grounding refer to the various ANSI/IEEE standards including IEEE Guide for Safety in AC Substation Grounding—ANSI/IEEE standard 80 and IEEE Recommended Practice for Grounding of Industrial and Commercial Power Systems—ANSI/IEEE standard 142

What Is a Ground?

A ground is an electrically conducting connection between equipment or an electric circuit and the earth, or to some conducting body that serves in place of the earth. If properly made, the earth or conducting body and the circuit or system will all maintain the same relative voltage.

Figure 7.4*a* shows an electrical system that is not grounded. In such a situation, a voltage will exist between the ground and some of the metallic components of the power system. In Fig. 7.4*b*, the earth connection has been made. When the system is grounded, the voltage is reduced to zero between the previously energized sections of the system.

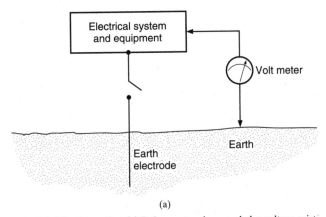

(a)

FIGURE 7.4   Grounding. (*a*) Before system is grounded, a voltage exists between the system and the earth.

(b)

FIGURE 7.4   Grounding. (*b*) When ground connection is made, no voltage exists.

Bonding Versus Grounding

Bonding is the permanent joining of metallic parts to form a continuous, conductive path. Since the earth is generally not a good conductor, bonding is used to provide a low-impedance metallic path between all metallic parts. This, in essence, bypasses the earth and overcomes its relatively high impedance. A good grounding system is a combination of solid connections between metallic parts and the earth as well as between all metallic parts.

Voltage Hazards

Figure 7.5 illustrates the four standard voltage hazards which are associated with and relieved by proper system grounding. If a system is ungrounded and the nonenergized metallic parts become energized, the metallic parts will have a measurable voltage between themselves and ground. If the system is grounded by driving ground electrodes into the earth, current will flow from the rods into the earth. At each ground electrode the voltage will rise relative to the remote reference point. The voltage will drop off away from the electrodes and peak at each electrode. This situation creates the four types of voltage hazards as follows:

- *Step voltage.*   As a worker steps across the ground, the front foot will be at a different potential than the rear foot. This effect is caused by the voltage gradient created by the ground electrodes (Fig. 7.5). Step voltage can easily reach lethal levels. Step voltage can be mitigated by increasing the number of grounding electrodes, increasing bonding between the metal parts, and employing a grounding grid.

- *Touch voltage.*   Because of the voltage gradient, the voltage of the earth, only a short distance from the grounded metallic equipment, will be different than the equipment. Thus if a worker touches the grounded equipment, his or her feet will be at a different potential than his or her hands. This voltage can be lethal. Touch voltage is mitigated by increasing the number of grounding electrodes, increasing bonding between metal parts, and employing a grounding grid.

FIGURE 7.5 Four voltage hazards related to system grounding. (*Courtesy Institute of Electrical and Electronic Engineers.*)

- *Mesh voltage.* Mesh voltage is the worst case of touch voltage. Cause, effect, and mitigation methods are identical to those described previously under Touch Voltage.

- *Transferred voltage.* Because metal parts have a much lower impedance than the earth, the voltage drop between remote locations is lower on the metallic connections than the earth. This means that the earth may be at a significantly different voltage than the metallic connections. Transferred voltages are particularly noticeable on neutral wires which are grounded at the service point and nowhere else. Transferred potential can be mitigated by providing the entire area with a ground grid; however, this solution is infeasible in any but the smallest systems. Transferred voltage must be mitigated by avoiding contact with conductors from remote locations and/or using rubber insulating gloves.

System Grounds

What Is a System Ground? A *system ground* is the connection of one of the conductors to the earth. Such a connection is accomplished by connecting an electric wire to the selected system conductor and the grounding electrode.

Why Are Systems Grounded? Power systems have conductors grounded for a variety of safety and operational reasons including

- Grounded systems provide sufficient short-circuit current for efficient operation of protective equipment.

- Grounded systems are less prone to transient overvoltages which can cause insulation failures.

- Grounded systems are generally more easily protected from lightning.

- Solidly grounded systems are less prone to resonant conditions which can cause equipment and insulation failures.

What Systems Must Be Grounded?   The NEC allows the grounding of permanently installed electrical utilization systems and requires the grounding of mobile electrical supply systems. If the mobile supply system is supplied by a high-voltage delta system, the NEC requires that a ground be derived using a grounding transformer. The National Electrical Safety Code requires that electric utility supply systems be grounded.

How Are Systems Grounded?   Electrical systems are grounded by connecting one of the electrical conductors to earth. The conductor chosen and the location of the ground are determined as part of the engineering design for the system. With systems that have delta transformer or generator windings, the neutral, and therefore the ground point, can be derived by using a grounding transformer. Figure 7.6 shows a grounded wye-delta transformer used to derive a system neutral and ground. Figure 7.7 shows a zigzag transformer used for the same purpose.

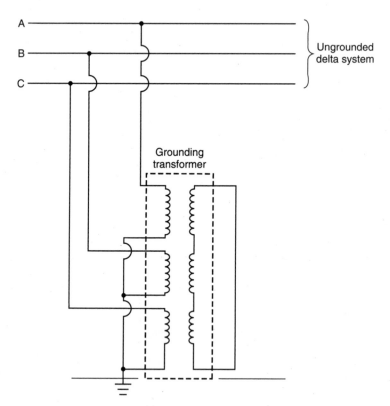

FIGURE 7.6   Grounded wye-delta transformer used to derive a system ground.

The zigzag transformer (Fig. 7.7) is the most commonly used method for deriving grounds on high-voltage systems. The windings consist of six equal parts, each designed for one-third of the line-to-line voltage; two of these parts are placed on each leg and connected as shown in Fig. 7.7. In the case of a ground fault on any line, the ground current flows equally in the three legs of the autotransformer, and

FIGURE 7.7 Grounding autotransformer with interconnected Y or zigzag windings.

the interconnection offers the minimum impedance to the flow of the single-phase fault current.

Equipment Grounds

What Is an Equipment Ground? An *equipment ground* is an electrically conductive connection between the metallic parts of equipment and the earth. For example, transformer cases and cores are connected to the earth—this connection is called an equipment ground. Note that the metallic parts of equipment are grounded and bonded together. This bonding serves to reduce the voltage potential between all metallic parts and the earth.

Why Is Equipment Grounded? The equipment ground is one of the most important aspects of grounding as far as safety is concerned. Workers are constantly in contact with transformer shells, raceways, conduits, switchgear frames, and all the other conductive, non–current-carrying parts. Proper equipment grounding and bonding ensures that the voltage to which workers will be subjected is kept to a minimum. Proper bonding and grounding mitigates touch and step voltages.

How Is Equipment Grounded? The NEC requires that the path to ground from circuits, equipment and metal enclosures must meet the conditions listed in Table 7.1. Equipment used in grounded systems is grounded by bonding the equipment grounding conductor to the grounded service conductor and the grounding electrode conductor. That is, the equipment ground is connected to the system ground. Equipment used in ungrounded systems is grounded by bonding the equipment grounding conductor to the grounding electrode conductor.

TABLE 7.1 Equipment Grounding Requirements

- Must be permanent and continuous
- Must have the capacity to conduct any fault current likely to be imposed on it
- Must have sufficiently low impedance to limit the voltage to ground and to facilitate the operation of the circuit protective devices

---

What Equipment Must Be Grounded? All non–current-carrying metal parts of fixed, portable, and mobile high-voltage equipment and associated fences, housings, enclosures, and supporting structures shall be grounded.

The NEC does allow two exceptions to this rule: High-voltage equipment does not have to be grounded if

1. It is isolated from ground and located so as to prevent any person who can make contact with ground from contacting the metal parts when the equipment is energized

2. It is certain pole-mounted distribution equipment that is exempted

Refer to the current edition of the NEC for detailed information.

SAFETY EQUIPMENT

Overview

Since the amount of available energy in the system determines its lethal effects, and since high-voltage systems are generally very high energy systems, high-voltage systems are extremely hazardous and should be treated with the utmost respect.

The following sections describe the types of safety equipment that should be worn by persons working on or near energized, high-voltage conductors. The recommendations given are minimum recommendations. If additional or more stringent protection is desired or required, it should be worn.

Hard Hats

Protective headgear for persons working on or near energized, low-voltage circuits should provide both mechanical and electrical protection. Personnel working on or near energized high-voltage circuits should be supplied with and should wear ANSI class B helmets. ANSI class A and class C helmets are not acceptable. The ANSI class A helmet is not rated or tested for use in high-voltage circuits and the ANSI class C helmet provides no electrical insulation at all. Table 7.2 summarizes the characteristics of the three ANSI classes.

Eye Protection

High-voltage systems are capable of producing extremely powerful and hazardous electric arcs and blast; therefore, eye protection for electrical workers should provide protection against heat and optical radiation. ANSI standard Z87.1-1989 provides a selection chart as well as a chart which illustrates the various protection options that are available. The selection chart is reproduced in this handbook as Table 7.3 and eye protection options are shown in Fig. 7.8.

Electrical workers should consider using eye protection that combines both heat and optical radiation protection. Table 7.3 and Fig. 7.8 show several different types of protection that will provide such protection including types B, C, D, E, and F. If arcing and molten splashing is possible, as with open-door switching or racking of circuit breakers, the type N eye protection should be employed.

TABLE 7.2 Summary of the Characteristics for ANSI Classes A, B, and C

Class	Description	Comments
A	Reduce the impact of falling objects and reduce danger of contact with exposed, low-voltage conductors. Representative sample shells are proof-tested at 2200 V phase to ground	Recommended to be worn by personnel working around only low-voltage circuits
B	Reduce the impact of falling objects and reduce danger of contact with exposed high-voltage conductors. Representative sample shells are proof-tested at 20,000 V phase to ground	Recommended to be worn by personnel working around high- and low-voltage circuits
C	Intended to reduce the force of impact of falling objects. This class offers no electrical protection	Should not be worn by personnel working on or around energized conductors of any voltage

Arc Protection

High-voltage systems create and sustain significant electric arcs accompanied by electric blast. Workers performing routine work on or around energized, high-voltage conductors should wear flame retardant work clothing or its equivalent with a rating of $4\frac{1}{2}$ oz/yd or more. Workers operating open-air switches or performing open-door switching procedures should wear flame retardant flash suits or their equivalent with a rating of 10 oz/yd or more.

FIGURE 7.8 Eye protection devices. Refer to Table 7.3 for selection criteria.

TABLE 7.3 Eye Protection Selection Chart

	Assessment SEE NOTE (1)	Protector type[1]	Protectors	Limitations	Not recommended
IMPACT	Chipping, grinding, machining, masonry work, riveting, and sanding	B, C, D, E, F, G, H, I, J, K, L, N	Spectacles, goggles, face shields SEE NOTES (1) (3) (5) (6) (10) For severe exposure add N	Protective devices do not provide unlimited protection SEE NOTE (7)	Protectors that do not provide protection from side exposure Filter or tinted lenses that restrict light transmittance, unless it is determined that a glare hazard exists. Refer to Optical Radiation
HEAT	Furnace operations, pouring, casting, hot dipping, gas cutting, and welding	B, C, D, E, F, G, H, I, J, K, L, *N	Face shields, goggles, spectacles *For severe exposure add N SEE NOTE (2) (3)	Spectacles, cup and cover type goggles do not provide unlimited facial protection SEE NOTE (2)	Protectors that do not provide protection from side exposure
	Splash from molten metals	*N	*Face shields worn over goggles H, K SEE NOTE (2) (3)		
	High temperature exposure	N	Screen face shields, reflective face shields SEE NOTE (2) (3)	SEE NOTE (3)	
CHEMICAL	Acid and chemicals handling, degreasing, plating	G, H, K *N	Goggles, eyecup and cover types *For severe exposure, add N	Ventilation should be adequate but well protected from splash entry	Spectacles, welding helmets, hand shields
	Irritating mists	G	Special-purpose goggles	SEE NOTE (3)	
DUST	Woodworking, buffing, general dusty conditions	G, H, K	Goggles, eyecup and cover types	Atmospheric conditions and the restricted ventilation of the protector can cause lenses to fog. Frequent cleaning may	
	Nuisance dust				

Operation		Typical filter lens shade	Protectors		
Welding:			SEE NOTE (9)		
Electric Arc	O, P, Q	10-14	Welding helmets or Welding shields	Protection from optical radiation is directly related to filter lens density. SEE NOTE (4). Select the darkest shade that allows adequate task performance	Protectors that do not provide protection from optical radiation SEE NOTE (4)
Welding:		SEE NOTE (9)			
Gas	J, K, L, M, N, O, P, Q	4-8	Welding goggles or welding face shield		
Cutting		3-6			
Torch brazing		3-4		SEE NOTE (3)	
Torch soldering	B, C, D, E, F, N	1.5-3	Spectacles or welding face shield		
Glare	A, B	Spectacle SEE NOTE (9) (10)		Shaded or special-purpose lenses, as suitable SEE NOTE (8)	

[1] Refer to Fig. 6.9 for protector types.
Source: Courtesy of American National Standards Institute.

Rubber Insulating Equipment

Rubber insulating equipment and appropriate leather protectors should be used by personnel who are working on or around energized, high-voltage conductors. Rubber gloves, rubber sleeves, rubber blankets, line hose, and other such protective devices should be employed anytime workers must approach such conductors. Rubber insulating equipment used around high-voltage systems must have a rating sufficient for the voltage of the system. ANSI class 1, 2, 3, or 4 rubber insulating goods should be employed as required.

Voltage-Testing Devices

Proximity or contact testers intended for use in high-voltage circuits should be used to test circuits and to verify that they are de-energized and safe to work on. Voltage-testing devices are described in Chap. 2. An example of a high-voltage—measuring instrument is shown in Fig. 7.9.

FIGURE 7.9 "TIC" tracer proximity voltage sensor for use on circuits up to 35,000 V. (*Courtesy TIF Electronics.*)

SAFETY PROCEDURES

General

The general procedures described in Chap. 3 should be used on all high-voltage circuits. The following sections describe key procedures which apply to high-voltage circuits.

Approach Distances

The OSHA Safety Related Work Practices Rule (CFR Title 29, Part 1910, Subpart S, Paragraphs 331 through 335) defines minimum approach distances to energized overhead lines for qualified and unqualified employees. Table 7.4 lists these approach distances for high-voltage circuits for qualified employees. Unqualified employees are instructed not to approach overhead energized circuits any closer than 10 ft (3 m). Although these approach distances are clearly defined as being for overhead lines, they may be used as guidelines for any exposure to energized electric circuits. If employees need to work near any energized circuits closer than the values given in Table 7.4, they should use rubber insulating equipment to protect themselves.

TABLE 7.4   Approach Distances for Qualified Employees

Voltage range (phase to phase)	Minimum approach distance
Over 750 V, not over 4 kV	1 ft 6 in (46 cm)
Over 2 kV, not over 15 kV	2 ft 0 in (61 cm)
Over 15 kV, not over 37 kV	3 ft 0 in (91 cm)
Over 37 kV, not over 87.5 kV	3 ft 6 in (107 cm)
Over 87.5 kV, not over 121 kV	4 ft 0 in (122 cm)
Over 121 kV, not over 140 kV	4 ft 6 in (137 cm)

Voltage Measurement

The voltage-measurement techniques defined in Chap. 3 should be employed on circuits of all voltages.

Locking and Tagging

Lockout-tagout and energy control procedures apply to circuits of all voltage levels. Refer to Chap. 3 for detailed discussions of lockout-tagout procedures.

Closing Protective Devices After Operation

Workers should never reclose any protective device after it has operated, until it has been determined that it is safe to do so. Several criteria may be used to determine whether or not it is safe to reclose the protective device (Table 7.5).

Other conditions may or may not indicate a safe reclosing situation. ANSI/IEEE standard 141-1986 defines low-voltage systems as those which are less than 1000 V, medium-voltage systems as those equal to or greater than 1000 V and less than 100,000 V, and high-voltage systems as those equal to or greater than 100,000 V. To simplify this notation, this chapter will refer to all systems of 1000 V or higher as *high-voltage* systems.

TABLE 7.5   Typical Situations Which May Allow Reclosing of a Protective Device Which Has Operated

---

* The faulted section of the system is found and repaired
* The nature of the protective device makes it clear that no hazard is present. For example, if the device which operated is an overload type of device, it may be safe to reclose
* The reclosing operation can be made in such a way that the workers are not exposed to additional hazard. For example, if the reclosing operation can be made by remote control, and if all personnel are kept away from all parts of the circuit, it may be reclosed

---

CHAPTER 8
SAFETY MANAGEMENT AND ORGANIZATIONAL STRUCTURE

INTRODUCTION

An electrical safety program will only be effective if management puts a strong commitment behind it. This chapter will develop some of the key management concepts and procedures that must be present for a safety program to work. Of course, electrical safety is only part of an overall safety program; consequently, much of the material in this chapter is applicable to the entire safety effort.

The procedures introduced in this chapter should be applicable to all types of electrical installations. However, the effectiveness of any specific program must be determined by ongoing evaluations.

Safety organizations should be responsible to the very highest management levels and generally should not report to operations. Safety-related decisions should not be made by personnel with direct, bottom-line responsibility.

ELECTRICAL SAFETY PROGRAM DEVELOPMENT

An electrical safety program is composed of a variety of procedures, techniques, rules, and methods. Each of these individual items must be developed independently; the sum of them then adds up to the overall safety program. The development of an entire program becomes the accumulation of all the individual procedures.

This does not mean that the development of a safety program is a hodgepodge effort. On the contrary, the whole procedure should be viewed as an engineering design problem. The program should be put together by a committee composed of management, safety, and technical personnel.

Company Safety Policy

All safety programs should be underwritten by a company and/or departmental safety policy. Although specific policy statements must vary from industry to industry, all policies should contain the following key statements:

1. The company is committed to safe work practices.
2. Safety is the premier consideration in performing work.
3. Employees will be required to follow all company safety procedures.
4. If a job cannot be safely done, it need not be done.
5. Each individual employee is uniquely responsible for his or her own personal safety.
6. The cooperation of all personnel will be required to sustain the safety program.

Assessing the Need

The development or revision of an electrical safety program should begin with an evaluation of any existing programs. This initial survey should closely examine and catalog the number and types of electrical accidents. Investigators should also be creative in their analysis. That is, they should identify potential hazards as well as demonstrated ones.

One of the most effective ways to catalog safety hazards is to perform a safety audit. Safety audits are discussed later in this chapter.

Problems and Solutions

Based on the results of the survey, accidents and potential problem areas should be cataloged into *cause* categories. The specific categories selected should be chosen to fit the industry. Good starting points are the seven categories used by the Occupational Safety and Health Administration in the development of the Safety-Related Work Practices Rule. These categories, illustrated in Table 8.1, can be used for most electrical accidents. The specific installation should develop additional categories or subcategories as required so that very few accidents fall into category 7.

TABLE 8.1   Categories to Classify Accidents or Potential Accidents

1. Use of equipment or material too close to exposed energized lines
   a. Vehicles (e.g., cranes and dumptrucks)
   b. Other mechanical equipment (e.g., augers and derricks)
   c. Tools and materials (e.g., ladders and tree limbs)
2. Failure to use electrical protective equipment
3. Assuming an unsafe position
4. Failure to deenergize (and lockout/tagout) equipment
5. Use of visibly defective electric equipment
6. Blind reaching, drilling, digging, etc.
7. No unsafe work practice or not enough information to classify

Identification of the safety problems will inevitably lead to solution concepts. These solutions should take the form of specific plans and programs which can be implemented to the new or existing electrical safety program.

Program Implementation

After the analysis phase, the solutions can be integrated into the facility's safety program. The method used here will depend upon the facility; however, a reasonable starting point would be the development of an energy control program similar to that described in Chap. 3.

Examples

The following two examples will illustrate the steps just outlined. Notice that the first example is a real problem since actual injuries were documented. The second problem is a potential for injury since although no one has yet been injured, a strong potential exists for such injury.

Electric Shock While Replacing Low-Voltage Fuses. Assume that your electrical safety audit has identified several instances where employees were shocked during the removal and/or installation of 120-V fuses. Table 8.2 shows the problem, solution, and implementation required to provide a safer work environment.

TABLE 8.2   Example of Fuse Removal Safety Procedure Development

Need Assessment	In the last 5 years, 15 employees have been shocked while removing and/or replacing low voltage cartridge fuses. Five of the injuries were extremely serious. No deaths have occurred
Problem(s)	Review of the problems indicate that employees must, from time to time work on such circuits when they are energized. Further investigation shows that employees are using channel lock type pliers to remove the fuses. Employees are not using rubber insulating gloves during such "hot" work
Solutions	To resolve this problem, employees will be supplied with insulated tools which are specifically designed for the removal and replacement of fuses. Employees are already supplied with rubber insulating gloves
Implementation	A procedure is added to the employee safety procedures manual which specifies the following:
	When removing or replacing fuses, the bus which feeds them shall first be de-energized unless doing so introduces additional hazard or unless de-energizing requires a major plant outage. Removing energized fuses is classified as hot work. Only qualified, trained personnel shall be allowed to remove and replace energized fuses
	Low voltage cartridge type fuses shall be removed using only approved, insulated fuse pullers
	Employees shall wear at least the minimum required safety equipment when removing or replacing energized low voltage, cartridge type fuses. Minimum safety equipment shall include hard hats, safety glasses or goggles, and electrical insulating rubber gloves approved for the voltage level encountered
	The new procedure should be introduced at an employee safety training meeting. The complete procedure should be demonstrated and employees should be checked to make certain that they understand it

Protection for Arc Injury During Switching Operations.   Not all safety procedures are developed based on local facility experience. In this example we assume that the local safety personnel have reviewed other industrial safety programs with respect to flash protection. They have discovered that other companies have experienced severe injuries during routine switching and racking operations. Furthermore, they discover that other companies have implemented successful programs which involve the use of flash suits. The number of flash-related injuries has dropped at these other companies. Table 8.3 was developed based on this analysis.

Results Assessment

Few, if any, procedures will endure forever without modification. Personnel replacements, equipment changes, enhanced operating experience, and new safety innovations will require that any safety program be periodically reviewed and updated. The following criteria should be used to evaluate the need to revise an existing safety procedure:

1. Accidents
2. Employee suggestions
3. Employee safety committee recommendations (see next section)

TABLE 8.3   Example of Flash Suit Safety Procedure Development

Need Assessment	Companies of similar size and business, with comparably sized electrical systems have had problems with severe flash injuries. These same companies have implemented flash suit use during certain phases of their operations, and have exhibited a marked decrease in the number of injuries
Problem(s)	Employees must, from time to time, perform open door circuit breaker switching, remove motor starters from cubicles, and operate open air disconnect switches. This exposes them to more than a normal electrical arc hazard
Solutions	To resolve this problem, the company will supply and require the use of flame retardant flash suits
Implementation	A procedure is added to the employee safety procedures manual which specifies that employees shall be required to wear flame retardant flash suits when performing open door switching, motor starter removal or installation, or open air switch operation. This requirement applies to all medium voltage circuits and all low voltage circuits with ampacities in excess of 100 amperes. This requirement is in addition to other safety equipment including hardhats, eye protection, and rubber gloves with protective leather covers
	The new procedure should be introduced at an employee safety training meeting. The complete procedure should be demonstrated and employees should be checked to make certain that they understand it

EMPLOYEE PARTICIPATION

Reason

Electrical safety programs that are developed and/or administered without employee input will be ineffective. Employees know their jobs better than anyone. They understand those procedures with which they are comfortable and those which seem wrong. An electrical safety program which is developed without complete employee involvement has very little chance of success.

Method

Employee safety committees provide the best method for ensuring employee participation in a safety program. Such committees should be composed of a minimum of three employees chosen by their peers. The committee should have regularly scheduled meetings on a monthly basis—more often if required by accidents or emergency conditions. The meetings should be held on company time.

Employee safety committees should be intimately involved with the entire safety program from initial design to ongoing results evaluations. They should be officially sanctioned by management and should have direct access to executive management. A limited, but useful, travel budget should be made available to the committee to allow them to attend seminars and visit other facilities to study other safety programs. Although the specific responsibilities of such a committee may vary from one company to another, the following may be used as guidelines.

Safety Program Development. Because of their familiarity with their jobs, employees are in a unique position to evaluate safety needs. What appears to be a perfectly safe procedure to a layperson may be obviously unsafe to a skilled, qualified worker. Furthermore, employees will often talk to their peers more freely than to supervisors or management.

An employee safety committee will be able to identify problems and solutions that outsiders might miss. Because of this, the safety committee should be directly involved with the safety program development and/or modification described earlier in this chapter.

Safety Meetings. Employees should control all or at least part of their safety meetings. Legislative or regulatory requirements should be scheduled by management and safety personnel; however, other safety-related presentations should be generated by employees and administrated through the employee safety committee.

Accident Investigation. The committee should be involved in the investigation of accidents. The best way to ensure this involvement is to have the employee safety committee appoint a member to serve on the accident investigation team. Accident investigation is a very demanding science and should not be performed by those unfamiliar with the information presented in Chap. 3.

Employee Training. The safety committee should be allowed to review and recommend employee safety-related training. Employees who have been to outside safety training courses should be interviewed by the safety committee. The committee should then issue an annual recommendation for additional or modified training.

This report should be considered a primary source of information when training budgets and schedules are produced.

SAFETY MEETINGS

The venerable safety meeting is one of the most universal of all safety vehicles. This one brief period combines training, program review, new concept presentation, and hazard notification all in one. The specific design and implementation of a safety meeting is necessarily dependent on the organization arrangement of the company. The following items highlight some of the key imperatives in the structure of a safety meeting.

Who Attends

Safety meetings should be attended by all personnel who are affected by the safety topics which will be discussed. Those who should attend electrical safety meetings include the electricians, electrical technicians, electrical supervisors, electrical department management, safety personnel with electrical responsibility, and anyone else who may be exposed to any of the electrical hazards.

Safety meetings should be chaired by employees, preferably members of the employee safety committee. Remember that the company's attitude toward proper safety can make an enormous difference in employee attitudes.

What Material Should Be Covered

The safety meeting should have a standard, but flexible, schedule. Table 8.4 shows the type of schedule that should be included. Flexibility is the key word. One of the most frequent complaints about safety meetings is that they always contain the same old messages, are presented the same old way, and use the same old films. The program should be flexible and new. Employees should be consulted as to topics which they feel may be relevant.

TABLE 8.4 Typical Safety Meeting Schedule

- Welcome and Review of Topics to be covered
- Accident Report
    Summary of Accidents
    Analysis and Lessons Learned
    Procedure/Policy Modifications if Any
- Training Schedules and/or Safety Awards
- Meeting Topic Presentation
- Employee Safety Suggestions
- Questions/Answers
- Announcement of Next Meeting and Adjournment

Avoid using the safety meeting time for non–safety-related information. General company announcements should be made at general employee meetings, not at safety meetings.

Also remember that employees who are injured at home cannot report to work. Safety meetings should also address home safety issues. Topics such as safe use of appliances, house wiring safety, home lightning protection, and first aid can be useful to employees both on and off the job.

When Meetings Should Be Held

To accommodate work schedules, many companies hold their safety meetings at the beginning of the work day. Others may wait until the end of the day. Try moving the time of the meetings around. When the results of the meeting are evaluated, as described later, the most appropriate time will be that in which the greatest amount of information is imparted.

For real variety, some companies have found that continually moving the meeting times is effective. Some companies even hold meetings at night and invite spouses to attend. This approach allows the whole family to become involved in safety and allows the employer to present home safety topics more effectively.

Safety meetings should only be canceled when absolutely no other option is available. Major operational emergencies such as fires and major outages are the only acceptable reasons for canceling a safety meeting.

Where Meetings Should Be Held

Variety should also be exploited when choosing meeting locations. Most meetings will be held at the work site for economic reasons; however, some meeting topics might call for different locations. For example, a demonstration of the proper use of hot sticks might best be held at a substation area, while tool safety training might be most effective if presented in the shop. *Remember that when demonstrations are given, even more extreme safety precautions should be taken.*

Evening safety meetings can be held at private banquet rooms or restaurants with meeting facilities. The meeting can be integrated with a social occasion which will allow management personnel, safety personnel, employees, and families to discuss problems and share solutions on a more informal basis. When such meetings are held, they should remain serious, with safety as the premier topic.

How Long Meetings Should Be

Meetings held at the workplace should be kept to a maximum of 1 h unless some special topic or presentation requires more time. Remember that a safety meeting is a training presentation. Adult training sessions are best kept to short segments. Thus, if a meeting requires more than the 1-h time period, be certain that breaks are given every 45 min or so. Evening meetings may be somewhat longer if a dinner or other social event is integrated with the meeting.

Evaluation of Safety Meetings

Like all parts of a safety program, meetings should be constantly evaluated. Employee questionnaires and quizzes should be used to evaluate the quality of the meetings and the amount of information retained. These evaluations can be done on an anonymous basis so that employees feel free to share negative as well as positive comments. When tests or questionnaires identify problem areas, the meeting structure should be modified to correct the problem.

Follow-through.   The safety program will not work if the company is not truly committed. When safety suggestions are made, the company should follow through and report back to the employee in writing. The employee safety committee should monitor suggestions and intervene if the company is not following through properly.

OUTAGE REPORTS

Safety hazards and electrical outages are frequently related to each other. Knowledge of the details which surround an electrical outage can be invaluable in pinpointing safety hazards. Outage reports can be used to

1. Target potential or existing safety hazards
2. Justify maintenance or additions to a power system to increase reliability
3. Help to gather data for designing better power systems or additions to other plants or facilities
4. Outage reports should include

   - Time and length of outage
   - Cause of outage if known
   - Results of outage (costs, injuries, etc.)

SAFETY AUDITS

Description

Depending on the intended extent, audits vary from short, simple inspections of specific problems or areas to large, companywide reviews which explore every facet of a safety program. Whatever their size or complexity, a safety audit is performed to review and assess the ongoing safety elements of a business. Audits are designed to identify the weaknesses and strengths of a safety program.

Process.   A comprehensive audit starts with a review of upper-management safety awareness and attitudes and continues through the entire organization. During the procedure, every facet of the safety program is reviewed, cataloged, critiqued, and— if necessary—modified.

Attitudes.   The attitudes of company personnel can make or break the effectiveness of a safety audit. Many employees tend to take safety audits very personally. A properly run safety audit should not be performed as an inquisition. Honest errors should be noted and corrected without hostile indictments or defensive recriminations. All personnel should be aware that a safety audit is only one tool used to make the workplace safer for everyone.

Audits Versus Inspections.   Some references differentiate between an audit and an inspection. In such references, audits are portrayed as major, comprehensive efforts which include all facets of the safety program. Inspections, on the other hand, are smaller, more concise efforts which may assess only one small area or procedure.

While there may be some psychological advantage in separating the two terms, remember that both are intended to identify, and subsequently eliminate, existing or potential safety hazards.

Purposes

The single most important purpose of a safety audit is to identify and eliminate safety hazards. There are, however, additional side benefits and purposes which are realized including

1. Employee morale is improved as safety problems are eliminated.
2. Audits provide a dynamic record of safety performance.
3. A positive cycle of safety improvement is created. That is, departments which get good scores tend to work harder to maintain their high scores. Departments which do not do as well tend to work harder to improve for the next audit.
4. Managers at all levels are made aware of many safety problems and procedures which they might not otherwise discover. For example, an audit which includes analysis of OSHA compliance may make managers aware of OSHA rules which were previously unknown.
5. When performed as a "family" procedure, a safety audit can actually enhance employer-employee relations. Employees respect management teams who truly put employee safety first.

Procedure

The safety audit should review and evaluate each element of the safety procedure. Site-inspection trips, personnel interviews, task observation, and documentation review are among the methods that may be used. Each portion of the company that is reviewed will have its own specific concerns. Note that the items presented in the following sections are intended for example only. Specific facilities may require more or different audit criteria.

Facilities.   Checkpoints for the electrical physical plant include the following:

1. Is the electric equipment kept clean?
2. Are safety exits clearly marked and unblocked by wire reels, ladders, and other such equipment?
3. Are relay flags and other such indicators kept reset?
4. Is explosion-proof equipment properly maintained and sealed?
5. Are all electrical grounds in place and secure?

Employees.   Properly trained, alert employees are at the heart of any safety program. An individual employee is always the person most responsible for his or her own personal safety. The following points are typical of the types of checks that should be made to audit the safety awareness of individual employees.

1. Are employees adequately trained?
2. Are employees familiar with their safety handbook?
3. Do employees know where all electrical safety equipment is located?
4. Can employees successfully perform safety-related procedures such as safety grounding and voltage measurement?
5. Are personnel familiar with the electrical safety one-line diagram?
6. Are employees familiar with the safety techniques that are unique to the various voltage levels to which they will be exposed?

Management.   Good safety practice starts at the top. If management includes itself in the audit process, employees will accept that they too must be reviewed. Management involvement is more than just window dressing, however. Other management audit points include the following:

1. Does the facility have a formal, written safety policy?
2. Are safety rules enforced uniformly?
3. Is there an employee safety committee to which management defers when technical and day-to-day decisions must be made?
4. Does management promote both on-the-job and off-the-job safety?
5. Does management provide, at company expense, CPR and other such training?

Safety Equipment.   Various rules and regulations require the use of approved electrical safety equipment. The following points are typical of safety equipment checks during an audit.

1. Is safety equipment readily available for all personnel?
2. Have all rubber goods been tested within the required period?
3. Are meters and instruments mechanically sound and electrically operable?
4. Are test equipment fuses properly sized?
5. Are safety interlocks operational and not bypassed?
6. Are safety signs, tags, warning tapes, and other such warning devices readily available to all employees?

Safety Procedures.   Energy control and other such safety procedures must be properly developed and implemented. A few of the key points for procedures include

1. Are written switching orders required for planned outages?
2. Is a written copy of the lockout-tagout procedure available to all personnel?
3. Are all employees trained in electrical safety grounding?
4. Are safety procedures followed for each and every operation or are they bypassed in the interest of production?

Documentation.   Safety electrical one line diagrams and other such documents are too frequently ignored and allowed to fall behind or remain inaccurate. The following key points should be checked for safety related documentation:

1. Are the electrical portions of the company safety handbook up to date and consistent with currently accepted safety practice?

2. Are copies of all safety standards and practices readily available to all personnel?

3. Is the safety electrical one-line diagram up to date, accurate, and legible?

4. Are accident reporting forms, test sheets, procedures, and other such operational aids readily available?

The Audit Team

Audit teams should be composed of safety personnel, management personnel, and employees. Because of their familiarity with safety auditing techniques, safety personnel should, generally, be the *team leaders*. The audit and assessment tasks should be shared equally by all team members.

The number of team members will, of course, depend upon the size of the facility or facilities being audited. A minimum of three members is recommended even for very small facilities. This will allow representations for safety, management, and employees.

Some companies use the employee safety committee to spearhead safety audits. The safety committee assigns audit personnel, reviews audit results, and continues to follow-up on changes.

Audit Tools

The principle tool of the safety audit is the checklist (Table 8.5). A checklist of this type should be developed for every area involved in the audit. In addition to such checklists, audit team members should be supplied with copies of safety procedures, standards, and other such documents. Team members can thus evaluate whether the procedures and standards are being followed or not.

Follow-up

Emergency or life-threatening problems should be corrected immediately. Problems that are left uncorrected continue to put employees and equipment at risk. More-

TABLE 8.5 Typical Check List Items for Facilities Audit

Check Item	Y/N	Comments
Electrical Equipment Clean?		
Access to energized areas controlled?		
Exits from areas free of obstruction?		
Explosion proof equipment properly maintained?		
Explosion proof equipment only in controlled areas?		
Cubicle doors properly latched?		
Electrical room equipment properly stored?		

over, major audits which do not result in problem correction send very negative signals to employees.

Follow-up to correct a problem should occur within a very short time after the results of the audit. Major safety problems should be corrected immediately. Action on less serious problems should begin within 1 month of the audit.

When audit results call for additional employee training, major system modification, or other such long-term expenditures, management should develop the plan within 1 month. No one expects major expenditures to be performed on a short-term basis; however, safety considerations must be met in a timely and effective manner.

The audit report should be written as soon as the audit is complete. The timetable for the correction of observed problems should be based on three criteria as follows:

1. How serious is the problem? If an accident caused by this problem would result in very severe injuries or high levels of damage, the problem should be corrected immediately. This criteria is the most important of the three, and it should outweigh any other considerations.

2. What is the likelihood that an accident will occur as a result of the problem noted in the audit? If there is little possibility of an accident, correction of the problem may be relegated to a lower status.

3. How much will it cost to fix the problem?

Internal Versus External Audits

Although companies usually employ their own personnel in the performance of a safety audit, sometimes an external firm may be used. Each approach has its own advantages and disadvantages. Three principle reasons may call for the use of an external consultant in the performance of a safety audit:

1. Consultants perform such audits on a routine basis and, therefore, tend to be more efficient than inexperienced employees.

2. Consultants tend to be dispassionate and therefore more objective in their analysis.

3. In-house personnel may not be available because of work schedules.

Of course, the use of consultants has some disadvantages as well, such as the following:

1. Consultants lack familiarity with their clients in-house systems and conditions.

2. Employees may not speak as freely with an outsider as they do with their own coworkers.

CHAPTER 9

SAFETY TRAINING METHODS AND SYSTEMS

INTRODUCTION

"Here's your rubber gloves. Go follow Joe." Until just a few years ago, this was the ultimate safety training method for many facilities. Fortunately, safety training professionals have managed to get two critical messages across:

1. Bad training is worse than no training at all.
2. Good training is both an art and a science.

This chapter defines "good" training and shows how it can augment a safety program. The information can be used by both employers and consultants alike. Consultants can use the information to help set up training programs for their clients. Employers can use the information to evaluate training consultants and/or take preliminary steps to set up their own training programs. *Note:* This information is applicable to all types of technical training.

Safety Training Definitions

For the purposes in this chapter, *training* is defined as a formal process used to generate a positive change in the behavior of an individual or group of individuals. Notice the use of the word "formal." Training must be "on purpose." Never allow training to just happen. Organize it, develop objectives, and administer.

Training is not the same thing as education, although training may well include education. Education is used to add to the cognitive skills and abilities of an individual or individuals. In other words, education teaches you how to think, while training modifies your behavior.

Behavioral modification is the core of training; however, there are many different types of behavioral modification. Three examples follow.

1. Many training companies offer training courses wherein they attempt to teach general electrical safety procedures. While these courses are generally excellent, they do not directly address the specific procedures of each student's company. Rather, the courses emphasize the importance of good safety and show clients what should be done. The behavioral change that occurs is an increase in the safety effort.

Such an increase will lead to many benefits; however, the student will need additional safety training in his or her own specific job requirements.

2. Many in-house training programs teach the safety aspects of the maintenance or operation of a range of specific types of equipment. For example, a 4-day program which teaches the maintenance of low-voltage power circuit breakers will spend great amounts of time discussing and showing the safety aspects of the particular equipment. This type of behavior modification is relatively specific in that it teaches detailed procedures for a class of equipment—low-voltage power circuit breakers. The desired behavior is the use of proper safety techniques to ensure that students will safely maintain their breakers.

3. A manufacturer's training program on a specific piece of equipment is a third example. When the manufacturer of an uninterruptible power supply (UPS) offers a course on the operation and maintenance of their UPS system, very specific safety procedures are taught. In this instance, the manufacturer knows that good maintenance and operation will result in fewer problems. However, the manufacturer also knows that trained personnel must perform the maintenance safely. Here, the desired modification is reduced to a relatively few, very specific procedures.

In each of the examples given above, the training programs should be prefaced with educational objectives. An *educational objective* is a specific, measurable behavioral change required of the student. For example, in a lockout-tagout course, an objective might be as follows: "The student is expected to determine that a given system has been de-energized by correctly performing the three-step voltage-measurement process." A complete list of objectives should precede every module in a training program. The use of objectives allows the trainer and the trainee to be measured accurately and objectively. All the training discussed in this chapter will be objective-based training.

Training Myths

The electrical safety industry has at least two major training myths. These myths hurt or in some cases eliminate the implementation of good training programs.

Myth #1: My People Can Learn by Just "Doing Their Job." This is the ultimate in "go follow Joe" thinking. The fact is that today's electrical systems are too complex to permit self-training unless it is very well organized and documented. The best result from such an approach will be slow, very expensive learning curves. The more likely result will be employees who learn improperly and make potentially grave errors.

Misconceptions are among the biggest problems for professional trainers. Adult learners have substantially more trouble unlearning a concept than they do learning one. While experience is definitely the best teacher, experience should be prefaced with a properly organized and presented training experience.

Of course, well-designed self-training programs are an excellent source of training. The key word here, however, is *designed*. Simply turning an employee loose with an instruction book is not effective.

Myth #2: My Supervisors Can Train My People. Training is a part of every supervisor's job, but it should not be allowed to become the only part for three basic reasons. First, in today's highly regulated workplace, a supervisor has his or her hands full with the day-to-day requirements of supervising. They simply do not have the time to put in the detailed effort required for good training. Second, good technical or supervision skills do not necessarily include good training skills. The ability to train well is an art. The third consideration here is the "person with a briefcase" syndrome. Employees tend to listen closely and learn from a trainer from outside the company. The feeling is that this person brings a fresh viewpoint to the job. Frankly, this belief has some merit. The outside viewpoint can often instill skills and ideas that are not available from inside.

Conclusion

1. Insurance companies are increasing safety requirements for their insured companies.
2. The technology of power systems continues to spiral upward.
3. Systems grow at an ever increasing rate.
4. Regulatory requirements continue to spiral.

All these facts demand that employees be trained. Good training is available from a variety of sources.

ELEMENTS OF A GOOD TRAINING PROGRAM

If you do not know what it is made of, it is hard to build. Because of this fact, many companies, even with strong training commitment, have poor training programs. From a safety training standpoint three types of training can be defined—classroom, on-the-job, and self-training. A complete adult training package must include all three of these methods assembled in a formal, planned program. Each method has certain critical elements, some of them shared.

Classroom Training

Classrooms.   When most of us think of classrooms, we think of the rooms where we went to grade school ... the small, cramped desks with books underneath the seat, chalk dust, and the spinsterly schoolmarm. Adult classrooms need to be designed for adults.

- The classroom should be spacious but not huge. The students should not be cramped together and should have sufficient table or desk space to spread out their texts and other materials.
- The classroom should be well lit and quiet. Dim lighting is more conducive to sleeping than learning, and noise from a nearby production facility can completely destroy the learning process.
- The classroom should be as far from the students' work area as possible. This serves two purposes.
  1. A remote location tends to focus the student on learning.
  2. Interruptions by well-meaning supervisors are minimized.

- All required audiovisual equipment should be readily available. Screens should be positioned for easy viewing and controls should be readily accessible to the instructor. Avoid using a white board for a screen due to the glare.

Laboratories.   The adult learner must learn by doing. For safety training, learning by doing means laboratory sessions and/or on-the-job training. Many of the design features mentioned for classrooms also apply to laboratories. However, there are a few special considerations.

1. Avoid using the same room for both laboratory and classroom. A room large enough for both is usually too large for effective classroom presentation. Too small a room, on the other hand, crowds the students during lecture and laboratory. Equipment needed to train students in procedures should be placed in positions where it does not interfere with the lecture presentation.
2. Initial training on safety procedures should be done on de-energized equipment.
3. Students should work in groups to help support each other.

Materials.   Student materials can easily make or break a training program. Although a complete material design treatise is beyond the scope of this book, a few critical considerations follow:

1. All student text chapters should be prefaced by concise, measurable training objectives.
2. Illustrations should be legible and clear. Avoid photocopies when possible. Also, put illustrations on separate pages which may be folded out and reviewed while the student reads the text. Nothing detracts more than flipping back and forth from text to illustration.
3. Students should have copies of all visual aids used by the instructor.
4. Laboratories should have lab booklets which clearly define the lab objectives and have all required information at the students' fingertips.
5. Avoid using manufacturer's instruction literature for texts. While these types of documents make excellent reference books, they are not designed for training purposes.

Instructors.   No one has really defined what makes the difference between a good instructor and a mediocre one. Some of the most technically qualified individuals make poor instructors while others are excellent. Some excellent public speakers are very poor instructors, while others are quite good. A few points are common to all good instructors.

1. Good instructors *earn* the respect of their students by being honest with them. No student expects an instructor to know everything there is to know about a subject. An instructor who admits that he or she does not know has taken a giant step toward earning respect.
2. Instructors must have *field* experience in the area that they are teaching. Learning a subject from a textbook or an instruction manual does not provide sufficient depth. (Unless, of course, the material is theoretical.)
3. Instructors must be given adequate time to prepare for a presentation. Telling an instructor on Friday that a course needs to be taught on the following Monday will lead to poor training. Even a course an instructor has taught many times before should be thoroughly reviewed before each session.

4. Avoid using a student's supervisor for the instructor. A supervisor will often expect the student to learn *because* he or she is the supervisor. In addition, the student may feel uncomfortable asking questions.

Frequency of Training.   How often to train is an extremely complex problem. Management must balance the often conflicting requirements of production schedules, budgetary constraints, insurance regulations, union contracts, and common sense with the needs of the individual employee to know what he or she is doing.

Overshadowing all this, however, is one basic fact—the employee who is not learning is moving backward. Technology and regulations are changing constantly; therefore, employees must be trained constantly. In general, the following three points can be made:

1. Employees in technical positions should be constantly engaged in a training program. Two or even three short courses per year are not unreasonable or unwarranted. The courses should be intensive, and related directly to the job requirements of the employee.

2. Employee training should be scheduled strategically to occur before job requirements. In other words, an employee charged with cable testing during an outage should go to a cable testing school a few weeks prior to the outage. Few of us can remember a complex technical procedure for 2 or 3 years.

3. Training should be provided at least as often as required by regulatory requirements. Remember that standards and regulations only call out minimum requirements.

On-the-Job Training (OJT)

On-the-job training will be discussed in great detail in a later section. As far as the elements of laboratories, instructors, materials, and frequency of training are concerned, virtually all the previous discussion applies with the following additions:

1. The laboratory for OJT is the whole plant or facility. The student learns while actually on the job.

2. In OJT, the supervisor is often the most logical choice for an instructor. In this role, however, the instructor does not usually get involved in a direct one-on-one training session. Rather the instructor gives the student the objectives for each OJT session and then evaluates progress.

3. Good training is done on purpose. A complete training program will have OJT materials which include objectives, reading materials, and examples of what is to be done. In addition the student should have a record card (called a *qual* card in the military) which identifies each area of responsibility. When the student has performed satisfactorily, the instructor checks off on the card to indicate successful completion.

4. Since employees are on the job every day, they are (theoretically) learning every day. This is not, however, true OJT. Remember that all good training is done on purpose. Typically a student should be given one specific OJT assignment every week. An instructor (supervisor) should observe the successful completion of the assignment, and the employee should be given credit for the job.

Self-training

Most well-intentioned self-training fails simply because it is not organized. An adult must know what is expected before he or she can perform. In this sense then, self-training has much in common with OJT, and virtually all the comments which apply to OJT also apply to self-training.

The most important element of self-training is materials. The material for self-training must be written very carefully. Small, self-supporting modules which are prefaced with clear objectives should serve as the core for self-training materials. Each module should be ended with self-progress quizzes. After the student completes each module or related group of modules, an examination should be administered by the instructor.

Conclusion

When confronted with requirements for training, such as those previously outlined, many companies are staggered by what appears to be a very expensive investment. The investment made in training is returned many times over in improved safety, morale, and productivity. Furthermore, a training program that does not have the proper elements will probably not be good training, and poor training is worse than no training at all.

ON-THE-JOB TRAINING

The major difference between 25 years of experience and 1 year of experience repeated 25 times is OJT. Good, well-planned, on-purpose OJT is the heart and soul of an adult learning program. Adults must learn by doing, and the workplace is the best laboratory. The three major segments of OJT include setup, implementation, and evaluation.

You must involve the employees in the development of this program. Their input and feedback will be critical every step of the way. The employee safety committee can also be used as a training committee and should oversee every aspect of the training program development and presentation.

Note that safety topics are especially suitable for presentation in an OJT format. The best way to memorize critical safety procedures is while actually performing them under field conditions. Note also, however, that special supervision must be made when personnel are learning safety procedures with energized equipment.

Setup

As noted previously, all training must be properly planned. Good training implies that it is being done on purpose. The setup portion is the most critical of all and must be properly executed because it serves as the foundation.

Step 1.   Define the employees' job functions. This step (often called a job analysis) is critical to all training but especially to OJT. Since OJT takes place while actually on the job, you must know what your employees do before you can train them. This is a simple concept, but it is surprising how many organizations miss this step. The performance of the job analysis can be as simple as asking your employees to make a list of what they do. The analysis of time sheets is another good approach. A final source of information is to ask your supervisors to list job functions for employees.

Notice that interviewing supervisors is the last of the three approaches. Unfortunately, company management and supervision are not always as closely in tune with day-to-day employee activities as they should be. This is not always true, but too often it is.

At the conclusion of this step, you should have a complete listing of the major jobs performed by your employees; for example, one major job is to remove motor starters from motor control centers with energized buses.

To simplify this step, concentrate on major job functions. Detail can be added as the OJT program develops over the years.

Step 2. Isolate the job functions that are practical and measurable. For example, you may have one task such as troubleshooting the south plant UPS system. While troubleshooting is a trainable skill, it is very difficult to measure troubleshooting ability in an OJT environment. The example given in the previous step (e.g., removal of starters from motor control centers) is measurable and practical. Initially only the practical and measurable skills should be included in the OJT program. As your program's sophistication increases, you may wish to add more cognitive skills.

As each job function is determined, it should be identified with a simple numbering system. For example, the starter removal might be job function number 1; cable testing, job function number 2; and so on. This makes it possible to keep records of which job functions employees have received training in.

Step 3. Break each job function into tasks, subtasks, and detailed procedures. Using our relay testing as an example, we might develop several tasks including the de-energizing of the cubicle, proper use of safety equipment, mechanically removing the starter, and so forth. The safety clothing subtasks would include the proper voltage measurement, inspection of rubber gloves, application of safety grounds, and so on. The detailed procedures can be developed either in-house or from manufacturer's literature.

Step 4. Develop training objectives for the tasks and subtasks. The objectives should have the measurement criteria contained within them. The following examples use the motor starter removal as its subject.

Task

1.0 The employee shall independently remove a low-voltage motor starter from its cubicle. The job shall be performed using all applicable company safety standards.

Subtasks

1.1   The employee shall perform a safety inspection for a set of low-voltage rubber gloves.

1.2   The employee shall wear a flash suit, previously inspected rubber gloves, hard hat, and face shield.

1.3   The employee shall stop the motor and de-energize the starter module. He or she shall demonstrate proper procedure and stand in a safe work location while performing these steps.

Here we have shown only one of the objectives; there would be several more, one for each safety task and one for the mechanical procedures.

Step 5. Develop the written materials necessary to support the program. The following should be developed as a minimum:

1. Complete set of written objectives.
2. Written, detailed description of each task. To accomplish this portion, manufacturer's literature may augment in-house–developed materials.
3. Diagrams, illustrations, or examples.
4. Employee record cards. The cards should have space for the employee's name, classification, and other demographic data. The majority of the card should contain space for completed job functions (by identification code), time of completion, and supervisor's initials indicating successful completion.

Implementation

The implementation phase of an OJT program should be a simple extension of the setup phase.

Step 1. Select several of the job functions to be used as trial runs of the OJT program. At the same time, select an experienced group of employees to receive the initial training. Develop the record cards for each employee.

Step 2. Thoroughly indoctrinate each of the test employees in the program and give them advance knowledge of what is expected. Of course, if you have been properly including the employees in the development phase, this step will be unnecessary.

Step 3. Introduce the training one job function at a time. Scheduling should be made by working the program into the normal work schedule. That is, when plant scheduling requires relay testing, use the opportunity to provide the OJT.

Step 4. Have the employee's supervisor go over the task with the employee and make certain the employee thoroughly understands what is required of him or her. Remember, this is training and the supervisor is the instructor in this case. The employee should perform the work, with the instructor giving guidance. The supervisor should watch the employee in the task and make certain all tasks are performed to within measurement criteria.

Step 5. After each training session is completed, thoroughly evaluate the results. See the next section for a more detailed description of evaluation.

Step 6. Gradually involve each existing and new employee in the OJT program. Anytime an employee is called upon to perform a new job function or task, the OJT program should be implemented and the employee's record card should be updated accordingly.

Evaluation

Step 1. The results each employee obtains should be measured against the criteria established during the setup phase. Do not make any assumptions based on just one or two employees. Poor performance by several employees could mean the program is bad, or it could mean that more classroom training is required.

Step 2. Interview the employees in a confidential manner. Give them a chance to critique the entire training program. All aspects—materials, implementation, objectives—should be reviewed.

Step 3. Interview the supervisor to get his or her feedback.

Step 4. Based on the first three steps, modify the program as required.

Step 5. Every 2 years review the program from top to bottom.

Conclusion

One major misstep taken by many organizations when they enter the world of OJT is to forget the key word—*training*. On-the-job training is not an on-the-job test. Rather it is on-the-job *training*. Remember that and do not forget to provide the necessary field instruction as the program progresses.

In general, OJT will not stand alone. It must be accompanied by good classroom instruction and/or self-training properly implemented and monitored. As stated in the previous section, OJT can be the most cost-effective of all the parts of a training program.

TRAINING CONSULTANTS AND VENDORS

Only very large companies can justify having their own, completely self-supporting, in-house training organizations. Even when in-house organizations exist, they frequently use outside vendors for support and special programs. In other words, you should use training consultants and vendors for the same reasons you use any consultant or vendor—when time, personnel, expertise, or economics make it impossible to perform the task yourself.

Training consultants fall roughly into three categories—those who provide canned programs, those who develop and present tailored programs, and those who provide training analysis. Of course, some companies fit into more than one of the categories.

Canned Programs and Materials

Programs. Companies which provide the short 1-week, manufacturer's type of seminars have proliferated since the early 1960s. Training programs are available in electrical safety, circuit breaker maintenance, relay testing, uninterruptible power supplies, programmable logic controllers, and a host of other such topics. Usually these courses are from 3 days to 2 weeks in duration. They are normally presented either in a training center or at a hotel with adequate meeting facilities. Some of them are equipment-specific, while others are generic in nature. Pricing varies, but these seminars generally offer a very economical approach when you have only one or two employees to train.

Learning by mail programs, called correspondence schools, also fall into this general category. Some companies have been providing programmed mail-order instruction for decades. The correspondence schools are especially useful for vocational-type training at a more generic level.

The vocational technical schools (votechs), both private and public, fill yet another need in this arena. Many companies are requiring 2-year associate's degrees or the equivalent for employment in certain technical areas. The votech schools provide such programs. Most of the votechs have evening courses, thus allowing students to attend in their free time.

Each of these three types of programs has its own advantages. The 1-week seminar is very intensive and provides training in very specialized areas in a hurry. The correspondence schools are very effective for students who have schedules that make attending classes difficult. The votech types of programs are excellent for those students who wish to start at the beginning and learn the entire discipline.

Materials. As a subcategory, some organizations will sell training materials such as programmed courses, videotapes, and/or interactive video programs. The principle difference between these materials and the correspondence school is that the materials may be used to present training to many people in one organization. These packages may also cover very specific equipment maintenance and/or operations.

Tailored Programs

When a company is truly committed to highly cost-effective training, they should opt for the tailored program. Often surprisingly affordable, tailoring may be as simple as taking a canned 1-week course and teaching only about the equipment which is in use at the particular plant or company. Most of the large vendors are glad to do this sort of tailoring. Other vendors will develop entire tailored presentations to a client's specification.

This type of service is usually most useful when your organization has a large number of people to train in a given area or areas. For example, immediately prior to a major maintenance shutdown, you may wish to have five or ten of your maintenance personnel trained in cable testing and maintenance. Such training is usually much more affordable than sending individual employees to single presentations.

Some training consultants will develop completely tailored programs based on existing industry standard texts, for example, safety programs based on NFPA 70E or substation maintenance based on an electric equipment text. Such programs are extremely effective and are generally no more costly than those described above.

Training Analysis

Sometimes, a company may have no idea what its training needs are. This is less common than in years past, but it does still happen. Training consultants can be retained to provide an entire training systems analysis. The major areas in such a development include needs analysis, job and task analysis, and curriculum development.

Needs Analysis. Also called a front-end analysis, the needs analysis is the starting point for any training program. The overall method is too complex to consider in this book; however, the general principle is quite simple. Desired performance is compared to actual performance for the workers under consideration. If the desired performance is below nominal, training is indicated.

Job and Task Analysis.   This portion is usually a part of the needs or front-end analysis. The procedure involves defining each employee's job functions in measurable objective terms; breaking each job function into tasks and subtasks; and finally writing these job functions, tasks, and subtasks as measurable learning objectives. These learning objectives are then used as the basis for the training programs.

Curriculum Development.   The actual curriculum is written and/or selected to fulfill the learning objectives developed during the job and task analysis. However, how this is accomplished may be quite flexible. For example, if a given group of employees has the responsibility to perform routine maintenance on the uninterruptible power supply, the learning objectives may be met by sending the group to one of the canned courses discussed above.

Evaluating Training Vendors and Consultants

Evaluation of any training must be based on the learning objectives. In order to know how well we are doing we must know what we intended to do. Training must be objective-based and done on purpose. Proper evaluation demands that such an approach be used. With this in mind, the evaluation of vendor training can be made by using four simple criteria.

Does the Vendor Provide Properly Documented, Objective-Based Training?   If the answer to this is no, do not use that vendor. Of course, this does not apply directly to some of the situations described in this book. However, even training analysis consultants can be checked for competency in and knowledge of objective-based learning.

Does the Vendor Listen Closely to Your Desires and Counsel You if He or She Believes that You Are Wrong?   One of the most difficult things for any consultant to do is to argue with his or her client. Remember, the client pays the bills. Therefore, if your consultant listens, and then counsels (or argues) with you when he or she believes you are wrong, that consultant has your best interests at heart.

Does the Vendor Provide Only Qualified and Competent Personnel?   Consultants are only as good as the people they employ. Take the time to quiz the individuals that your consultant provides. Ask for resumes and, where applicable, interview the individuals. Even qualified people will not be effective if they have a personality conflict with you.

Did the Program Meet the Objectives That Were Set Out at the Beginning?   Do not depend on course critiques and/or personal evaluations of attendees. Give quizzes where applicable. Sit down with employees and have them review the material that they learned. Develop your own short quiz based on the course materials and administer it to your employees. The quiz can be administered orally, in written form, or as a field-type performance quiz. (For example, one task might be to "test this relay like they taught you at school.")

As a corollary to this last question, always insist that a vendor administer performance quizzes as part of a training program. Quizzes do three things:

1. They measure the student's performance.
2. They measure the trainer's performance.
3. They measure the course's success.

In some cases union contracts may make quizzing difficult or impossible; however, since the quizzes also measure the quality of the training that occurs, many unions are eager for their members to be tested. In this way, they know their members are receiving proper and adequate training treatment.

Conclusion

The use of training consultants is really no different in concept than the use of any other consultant or contractor. You should first determine what you need, monitor what you are getting, and, finally, evaluate what you got.

TRAINING PROGRAM SETUP—A STEP-BY-STEP METHOD

If it is organized, good training does not have to be prohibitively expensive. A well-organized training program may be developed with a four-step approach:

1. Setup
2. Implementation
3. Evaluation
4. Modification

As you read the following description of the four steps, remember that you may need help with some of them. Like any specialized skill or discipline, a sophisticated training program may call for the assistance of consultants. The more comprehensive the training effort, the more likely the need for some help.

Setup

Needs Analysis. Not all organizations are in need of a comprehensive training effort. Some, for example, may need only special skills training in a few isolated areas. A needs analysis is performed to determine what, if any, training is needed in the organization. You should consult three sources to assess your needs—employees, supervisors and managers, and company performance.

1. *Employees.* Formally poll your employees for training requirements. Usually they know their shortcomings better than anyone. The poll should be concise and sincere. Be prepared for a revelation because experience has shown that, more often than not, employers and employees have very different views about the state of their training.

2. *Supervisors and managers.*   Extend the training poll to your management and supervision. Give them a chance to tell you where training deficiencies are causing problems. Their input should be solicited for their employees and their own training needs. Do not forget to include yourself in this analysis. Employees at all levels may need training.

3. *Company performance.*   An honest evaluation of company performance can be one of the best sources of training needs assessment. The most obvious example of this element is in the area of safety. Do some departments have a consistent record of safety problems? Such a department is an obvious target for safety training. Remember to involve your employees and supervisors in the review and analysis of the material. The people who are going to receive the training should be involved at all stages.

Job and Task Analysis.   After the needs analysis is complete, you should have a well-defined set of training needs. The next step is the performance of a job and task analysis (JTA) for each of the areas which require training. This critical step defines the actual composition of a given job. The JTA involves the following three steps.

1. *Employee interviews.*   Each employee is interviewed, and a listing is made of the jobs and tasks that he or she performs. The listing should be very detailed to allow for the development of performance objectives.

2. *Supervisor and manager interviews.*   The department supervisors are interviewed to obtain their input to the jobs and tasks performed by their employees. This listing is compared to the one developed by the employee interviews, and modifications are made as required. Many training problems disappear when this step is performed since supervisors and employees develop a common understanding of the task at hand.

3. *Job performance observation.*   Employees are observed in the performance of their jobs. The job and task listings developed during the interviews are reviewed and refined to be consistent with actual performance. Remember that the actual performance of the given job is under question, so do not modify a JTA based on performance observation unless you are certain that the job is being performed correctly.

Performance Objective Development.   Based upon the results of the JTA, a set of measurable performance objectives is developed. You may wish to develop training objectives in two tiers—terminal objectives and enabling objectives. *Terminal objectives* are broad-based objectives that represent the actual required behavior. *Enabling objectives* are "sub" objectives that define skills required to meet a given terminal objective. The following give examples.

- Terminal objectives. The employee will be able to test a Westinghouse induction disk overcurrent relay. The tests will be performed using the manufacturer's instruction leaflet, a transformer-loaded overcurrent relay test set and associated instructions, and the company-supplied test sheet. Test results shall be as defined in the relay instruction leaflet.

- Enabling objectives

  1. The employee will be able to describe the purpose and use of each of the controls on the transformer-loaded test set.
  2. The employee will be able to describe the pickup and timing adjustments on the Westinghouse induction disk overcurrent relay. (Add other objectives as defined from the JTA.)

Structure Development. The information generated during the needs analysis, JTA, and performance objectives development is reviewed, and an overall structure for the training effort is defined. Of course, not all companies are going to need a large, expensive training center with a staff of trainers.

- *In-house training.* If you define an extensive training need with many ongoing course requirements, you may need to consider the development and use of an in-house training system. The materials for such training can include both specifically developed and/or vendor-supplied materials. On-the-job training is usually a very important part of in-house training.
- *Vendor-supplied training.* Specific skills such as cable testing, relay testing, breaker testing, and instrument repair may best be supplied by training companies that specialize in these areas. In fact, in some cases an entire program may be implemented through commercially purchased training.
- *Self-study.* Many skills can be learned effectively through one of the many self-study programs that are commercially available. Even if a program of this type is not purchased, employees should be encouraged (monetarily if necessary) to put in some study time on their own.

Infrastructure Development

1. Training department organization
   a. The training department should report to the executive level of management. This is especially important for technical training departments.
   b. Training department supervisors should be technically qualified personnel. Furthermore, training supervisors should maintain a teaching schedule.
   c. Salaries for training department personnel should be equal to or exceed the salaries of equivalent level personnel in other departments.
2. Training facilities. The selection of a training facility will depend upon the quantity and nature of the training that you wish to conduct. If you plan to use a lot of outside vendors, you may be able to use their facilities. Conference rooms, local meeting centers, and hotel facilities may also be viable alternatives. Specialized laboratory needs may require the construction of facilities. As an alternative to this, you may consider using your company work areas for laboratories; however, this is not recommended as a general practice.

Implementation

The implementation step does not need to wait until the program is completely set up. Vendor courses may (and probably should) be implemented as soon as they are defined. This shows employees that you are serious about training and allows for training needs to be addressed immediately.

Course Development. Courses must be developed or purchased to fulfill the objectives defined during the Setup step.

1. *Purchased materials.* Both self-study and classroom materials are available for purchase from a variety of training vendors. Make certain that the purchased materials meet the objectives defined during the Setup step.
2. *Developed materials.* Although somewhat more expensive, developing company-specific course materials has some distinct advantages. In the first place, your

employees will tend to identify with materials that are obviously site-specific; moreover, presentation time is optimized since all material is company-specific. Note that these materials may be developed either by in-house personnel or by consultants.

Program Presentation. The actual presentation of the training program will depend upon the extent and type of training being implemented. Some courses may be presented on an ongoing basis. For example, skills updates such as cable testing, motor and generator maintenance, and the like may be repeated immediately before maintenance intervals that will require those skills. Safety training should be repeated frequently, especially in areas such as life saving and CPR.

Training in areas such as basic electricity, mathematics, and other such topics is usually performed only once per employee. Large companies may need to schedule such training on a regular basis to allow for turnover. Smaller companies, however, may opt to use self-training or correspondence courses for such topics.

Evaluation

Although evaluation is identified as a separate step, it should be an ongoing effort employed at every level of the training program. Five basic elements of the training program may be used to analyze its effectiveness—test review, course critiques, employee interviews, course content, and needs analysis.

Test Review. Examinations evaluate the student, the instructor, and the course. They should be administered for every training course. Tests should be reviewed for a variety of problems such as

- *Commonly missed questions.* If one question or group of questions is consistently missed by all students, you have a problem with the instructor and/or the course.
- *Consistently high or low grades.* If the average grades on a test are consistently high or low, the course is probably too easy or difficult, respectively. Another possible cause of such a problem is that the course material does not fulfill the course objectives.

Course Critiques. Carefully review the course critiques for trouble spots. Consistently high or low evaluations may be an indication of a problem. Take the occasional "sour grapes" critique with a grain of salt.

Employee Interviews. Periodically interview employees to keep your finger on their pulse. Make certain that the employees are learning and that the training program is accomplishing what you intended.

Course Content. Electrical technology is changing rapidly. Although basic electrical principles remain the same, testing technology changes rapidly. Periodically you must have your course materials reviewed for technical accuracy and relevance. Nothing frustrates students more than learning yesterday's technology.

Needs Analysis. Periodically update the performance of the needs analysis. Make certain that the desired behavioral objectives are being met. Ask the following questions:

1. Has company performance improved as desired?
2. Is employee and supervisor morale at the levels you wished to achieve?
3. Is your company safety record acceptable?

Whatever criteria was used to establish the original need for the training program must be evaluated. If the desired changes have occurred, then the program is meeting its goals.

Modification

Update and modify your training program based on your evaluation. Although this may seem obvious, a surprising number of companies evaluate their programs and then make no changes. An evaluation is useless if no changes are implemented.

INDEX

Index note: The *f.* after a page number refers to a figure; the *t.* to a table.

ABOUT THE AUTHOR

A registered professional engineer, John Cadick has specialized for over two decades in electrical engineering, training, and management. In 1986, he created Cadick Professional Services, a consulting firm in Garland, Texas. His firm specializes in electrical engineering and training, working extensively in the area of safety and regulatory compliance. Prior to the creation of Cadick Professional Services, John Cadick held the office of Vice President and General Manager of Southwest Engineers of Louisiana, an independent electrical testing and consulting firm. Mr. Cadick is a widely published author of numerous articles and technical papers in industry periodicals. His expertise in electrical engineering and testing coupled with his extensive experience in application of personal computers to electrical power systems makes Mr. Cadick a highly respected and sought after consultant in the industry.